MLI Made Easy

MLI Made Easy

Kuldeep Sharma

Wolters Kluwer

Published by:
Kluwer Law International B.V.
PO Box 316
2400 AH Alphen aan den Rijn
The Netherlands
E-mail: international-sales@wolterskluwer.com
Website: lrus.wolterskluwer.com

Sold and distributed by:
Wolters Kluwer Legal & Regulatory U.S.
7201 McKinney Circle
Frederick, MD 21704
United States of America
Email: customer.service@wolterskluwer.com

ISBN 978-94-035-3260-8

e-Book: ISBN 978-94-035-3261-5
web-PDF: ISBN 978-94-035-3262-2

About the Author

Kuldeep Sharma, an erstwhile officer of the Indian Revenue Service, has worked for over thirty years in the Income Tax Department, wherein he has had the opportunity to work at multiple levels in Direct Taxes, i.e. in field dispensations, as well as, tax policy department under the aegis of Central Board of Direct Taxes (CBDT) and has garnered wide experience in taxation of corporates and non-corporates (including individuals).

The last ten years of his service have been completely dedicated to the field of International Taxation and Transfer Pricing (IT&TP), wherein he has accredited himself in a variety of roles, involving Transfer Pricing (TP) audits, processing of Advance Pricing Agreements or Advance Pricing Arrangements (APAs). For four years, he has worked in the Foreign Tax and Tax Research Division of CBDT, wherein, apart from handling policy issues related to non-residents, Country-by-Country Reporting, Tax Treaty Negotiations and Complex APA, Mutual Agreement Procedure (MAP) cases, he has been actively engaged in matters involving Base Erosion and Profit Shifting (BEPS) and the Multilateral Convention to Implement Tax Treaty Related Measures to Prevent Base Erosion and Profit Shifting (MLI).

Kuldeep Sharma holds BSc (Physics) Hons. as well as an MBA (Finance). His years of practical experiences in Direct Taxes have enabled him to successfully achieve the status of ADIT Graduate accredited by the Chartered Institute of Taxation, UK.

For any clarification, he may be contacted at cooldip.sharma@gmail.com

Table of Contents

Preface

My induction into the field of Multilateral Convention to Implement Tax Treaty Related Measures to Prevent Base Erosion and Profit Shifting ('MLI' or 'Convention' or 'Instrument') came at a time when I had already spent a considerable number of years doing TP audits and processing of APAs for the Income Tax Department, CBDT, India. Despite MLI being quite different from the TP related work that I had been engaged in for many years, I was able to quickly adapt to the change on account of having had sufficient experience in the past in handling of Double Taxation Avoidance Agreement (DTAA) and international tax-related matters. At the same time, I must also admit that the MLI, initially, gave me some sleepless nights owing to its unique characteristics. Things settled down soon enough, and in the process, I became a voracious reader of various articles, publications on MLI, both domestic and international, which provided me deeper insights into the subject. All this while, it made me realise that there were some lingering misconceptions over its provisions among various stakeholders. This realisation led to the germination of an idea to write this book so as to address such misconceptions to the best of my understanding of the subject. Another motivating factor to author this book was to bring all necessary material to understand the MLI under one roof in a manner which is simple and easy to understand.

The MLI happens to be the first successfully concluded multilateral tax treaty and has the distinction of universal participation. This factor required that the book be presented in a way that it finds acceptance across the globe. Hence, while drafting the book, extra effort has been made to include figures and tables so that MLI's provisions are easier to understand by all the stakeholders involved, viz. tax officers, tax professionals/advisors, taxpayers, academicians and others (such as law students) in any part of the world. Where tax treaties do not already have provisions to prevent BEPS, MLI introduces such provisions therein, specifically designed to counter BEPS. The MLI Articles containing substantive provisions have been analysed in detail in the book from the perspective of worldwide DTAAs (referred to as Covered Tax Agreements (CTAs) under the MLI) on taking into account the 'MLI positions' taken by jurisdictions across the world under various notification clauses. In my view, MLI's substantive and procedural provisions explained in this book will immensely facilitate the understanding of each and every reader across all jurisdictions.

As far as the structure of the book itself is concerned, it is divided into six chapters. *Chapter 1* is dedicated to BEPS Project, Action Reports thereof and detailed discussions of BEPS Action Reports which are covered under the MLI. *Chapter 2* provides an introduction to the MLI, its background, preamble, benefits and distinguished features. *Chapter 3* is the nucleus of the book, providing insights into the structure of the MLI, the way MLI operates, with in-depth discussions on Compatibility Clauses, Notification Clauses, Opting-in Mechanisms, Alternative Provisions and Opting-Out Mechanisms (Reservations). Chapter 3 also carries detailed discussions on all the substantive articles of the MLI in a very structured manner, *inter alia*, providing an introduction to the article at a glance, status in the pre-BEPS Project era having gaps in tax treaties leading to BEPS and how such gaps are being addressed through the MLI. In addition, under each substantive provision of the MLI, positions taken under the MLI by Denmark, India, the Netherlands and other jurisdictions have been provided with the purpose to illustratively explain the impact of opt-in provisions, alternative provisions, reservations, notifications on the respective CTAs. It is expected that these illustrations will further enhance the understanding of all readers as to how MLI modifies the CTAs. *Chapter 4* covers the procedural provisions of the MLI wherein each article is discussed in detail and explains the relevance of such provisions in implementation of the MLI. *Chapter 5* discusses the statistical data on the MLI and its impact on the tax treaty network. It also covers the experiences had in the course of implementation of the MLI, as well as, role of synthesised texts in helping various stakeholders to understand MLI's effects on CTAs it covers and modifies. *Chapter 6* provides concluding remarks, including a table titled 'MLI at a Glance' encapsulating the procedural provisions of the MLI for the benefit of readers to enable an expeditious understanding of MLI's distinguished features and its application on CTAs.

Readers will find that few topics like reservations, notifications, etc. have been dealt with at more than one place in the book. The same has been done intentionally so as to, initially, provide an introduction of a particular provision to succinctly explain as to how that provision works under the MLI and depending on its importance, that particular provision is discussed in more detail under the relevant Part/Article of MLI.

The statistics discussed in the book are as at 31 December 2020 and include notifications made by Parties, as well as, Signatories. Since MLI is a dynamic instrument, statistics reflected in this book may undergo a change in future; as more jurisdictions may sign the MLI going forward, a change in MLI position may be effected by the Signatories while submitting their respective instrument of ratification to the Depositary and/or revised notifications may be made by jurisdictions in future, as permissible under the MLI.

List of Abbreviations

AE	Associated Enterprise
APA	Advance Pricing Agreement or Advance Pricing Arrangement
ATO	Australian Taxation Office
BEPS	Base Erosion and Profit Shifting
CA	Competent Authority
CARICOM	Agreement Among the Governments of the Member States of the Caribbean Community
CbCR	Country-by-Country Reporting
CBDT	Central Board of Direct Taxes
CFA	Committee on Fiscal Affairs, OECD
CFC	Controlled Foreign Company
CoP	Conference of the Parties
CTA	Covered Tax Agreement
CTPA	Centre for Tax Policy and Administration, OECD
DAPE	Dependent Agent Permanent Establishment
DEMPE	Development, Enhancement, Maintenance, Protection and Exploitation
DTAA	Double Taxation Avoidance Agreement
DTAC	Double Taxation Avoidance Convention
EBITDA	Earnings Before Interest, Taxes, Depreciation and Amortisation
EIE	Entry into Effect
EIF	Entry into Force
FAQ	Frequently Asked Questions
FDI	Foreign Direct Investment
FHTP	Forum on Harmful Tax Practices
FTA	Forum on Tax Administration on MAP, OECD
G20	Group of Twenty

GAAR	General Anti-avoidance Rule
GDP	Gross Domestic Product
IBFD	International Bureau of Fiscal Documentation
ICT	Information and Communication Technology
IF	Inclusive Framework, OECD
ILC	International Law Commission
IT&TP	International Taxation and Transfer Pricing
LOB	Limitation on Benefits
MAP	Mutual Agreement Procedure
MLI	Multilateral Convention to Implement Tax Treaty Related Measures to Prevent Base Erosion and Profit Shifting
MNE	Multinational Enterprise
MTC	Model Tax Convention, OECD
OECD	Organisation for Economic Co-operation and Development
PE	Permanent Establishment
POEM	Place of Effective Management
PPT	Principal Purpose Test
PSLA	Law Administration Practice Statement
SAAR	Specific Anti-avoidance Rules
SDG	Sustainable Development Goal
S-LoB	Simplified Limitation on Benefits
TDS	Tax Deducted at Source
TIEA	Tax Information Exchange Agreement
TP	Transfer Pricing
UN	United Nations
VCLT	Vienna Convention on the Law of Treaties
WHT	Withholding Tax

List of Figures

List of Tables

Acknowledgements

My sincere gratitude to my colleagues and friends in the Organisation for Economic Co-operation and Development (OECD), Paris and across various tax jurisdictions around the world, particularly the Tax Administration in India, for their constant encouragement and guidance imparted to me in the areas of International Taxation, TP, APA and last, but not the least, in the field of Multilateral Convention to Implement Tax Treaty Related Measures to Prevent Base Erosion and Profit Shifting ('MLI' or 'Convention' or 'Instrument').

In regard to the MLI, I was fortunate to have had the opportunity to interact with tax experts from the OECD during plenary meetings of the ad hoc Group held at the OECD, Paris, as well as, the MLI workshops/seminars held in Poland, Mexico, UAE which helped me immensely in shaping my thoughts and understanding of the Convention. Lengthy discussions with them have helped me tremendously in developing a deep insight and understanding of the instrument. This treatise is, therefore, a sharing of my understanding of the subject.

I would like to extend my profound gratitude to my family which has been my constant pillar of support and has gladly permitted me to devote time meant for them to my academic pursuits. Also, especially, I would like to acknowledge that my elder daughter Ms Raunicka Sharma, a BBA-LLB student from Symbiosis Law School, Noida, India, extended all her help in providing incisive insights into the contours of the book, data collection and research, including its final proofreading, whereas, my younger daughter, Ms Paavnieka Sharma (student of Class X), designed the tables and figures of the book.

Despite *MLI Made Easy* being my maiden venture, I felt part of Wolters Kluwer team right from the very inception of my interactions with them. This book may not have been possible without the confidence and faith Wolters Kluwer had in me.

Executive Summary

1. The Multilateral Convention to Implement Tax Treaty Related Measures to Prevent Base Erosion and Profit Shifting ('MLI' or 'Convention' or 'Instrument') is one of the outcomes of the OECD/G20 Project to tackle Base Erosion and Profit Shifting (the 'BEPS Project'), i.e. tax planning strategies that exploit gaps and mismatches in tax rules to artificially shift profits to low or no-tax locations where there is little or no economic activity, resulting in little or no overall corporate tax being paid.[1]

2. The BEPS Action Plan was developed by the OECD Committee on Fiscal Affairs (CFA) and endorsed by the G20 Leaders in September 2013. After two years of work, the CFA, including all OECD and G20 countries working on an equal footing, produced the Final BEPS Package, which was endorsed by the OECD Council and the G20 Leaders in November 2015. The BEPS Project identified 15 actions to address BEPS in a comprehensive manner providing countries and economies the tools they need to ensure that profits are taxed where economic activities generating the profits are performed, while at the same time, giving businesses greater certainty by reducing disputes over the application of international tax rules and standardising compliance requirements. It was agreed that out of 15 actions, 4 actions are minimum standards, meaning that countries have agreed that the standard must be implemented.[2] Out of the 4 minimum standards agreed under the BEPS Action Reports, i.e. Actions 5, 6, 13 and 14, the MLI implements minimum standards contained in Actions 6 and 14 only. The other tax treaty-related BEPS Action Reports being implemented through the MLI are Actions 2 and 7, respectively. An introduction to all BEPS Action Reports has been provided in Chapter 1 of the book (refer paragraphs 7, 8), whereas BEPS Action Reports covered under the MLI are discussed at length in paragraphs 9, 10 of Chapter 1 of the book.

3. The Convention operates to modify tax treaties between two or more Parties to the Convention. It will not function in the same way as an Amending Protocol to a single existing treaty, which would directly amend the text of the CTA; instead, it will be

1. Refer Explanatory Statement to the MLI, para. 1.
2. *Id.*, para. 3.

applied alongside existing tax treaties, modifying their application in order to implement the BEPS measures.[3] The purpose and objective of the Convention is to swiftly implement the tax treaty-related BEPS measures[4] (refer paragraph 12 in Chapter 2).

4. The Action 15 Report, titled, 'Developing a Multilateral Instrument to Modify Bilateral Tax Treaties', concluded that a multilateral instrument, providing an innovative approach to enable countries to swiftly modify their bilateral tax treaties to implement measures developed in the course of the work on BEPS, is desirable and feasible, which was developed with the assistance of a group of experts in public international law and international tax law (refer paragraph 13 in Chapter 2).

5. The MLI has entered into force on 1 July 2018 and it started producing effect from 1 January 2019. As at 31 December 2020, the MLI has been signed by 95 jurisdictions and ratified by 60 of them. The MLI was first ratified by Austria (on 22 September 2017), followed by the Isle of Man (on 25 October 2017), Jersey (on 15 December 2017), Poland (on 23 January 2018) and Slovenia (on 22 March 2018) being the fifth jurisdiction to ratify the MLI. For all these five jurisdictions, MLI has entered into force on 1 July 2018 and they became Parties to the MLI. Thereafter, Serbia, Sweden, New Zealand, UK ratified MLI in June 2018 following which the MLI entered into force for these countries on 1 October 2018. The next lot of ratifications happened in the month of September 2018 when Lithuania, Israel, the Slovak Republic, Australia, France, Japan ratified; hence, the MLI entered into force for these countries on 1 January 2019. The process of ratification of the MLI by various jurisdictions has moved forward sedately since then. In September 2020, another round of substantial ratifications happened when Bosnia and Herzegovina, Albania, Costa Rica, Jordan, Egypt ratified the MLI (refer paragraph 14 in Chapter 2).

6. An instrument as multilateral as the MLI could have been feasible only if it had some unique features and benefits for the contracting jurisdictions. These are discussed at length in Chapter 2 in paragraphs 15-23. At the same time, it was necessary for the MLI to be drafted in a structured manner (refer paragraphs 24-26 in Chapter 3) and its way of operation had to be streamlined and consistent to enable seamless modification of the CTAs (refer paragraphs 27-35 in Chapter 3). This became possible with an efficacious use of compatibility clauses (refer paragraphs 38-48 in Chapter 3), notification clauses (refer paragraphs 49-53 in Chapter 3), opting-in mechanisms (refer paragraphs 54-59 in Chapter 3), alternative provisions (refer paragraphs 60-62 in Chapter 3) and reservations (refer paragraphs 63-70 in Chapter 3). The MLI provisions have been so designed that the treaty provisions they apply alongside take effect symmetrically, except for certain instances which were deemed necessary and appropriate by the ad hoc Group (refer paragraph 71 in Chapter 3).

7. Part I of the MLI comprising its scope and interpretation of terms used therein is discussed in paragraphs 72-88 in Chapter 3. The substantive provisions of the MLI are provided in Articles 3-26 (Parts II-VI). A plain reading of all these articles demonstrates

3. *Id.*, para. 13.
4. *Id.*, para. 14.

that the design of Part VI of the MLI (containing Articles 18-26) is different as it provides rules relevant for different steps of the mandatory binding arbitration procedure, which require more details, as well as, more tailor-made exceptions than the tax treaty-related BEPS measures established in the other substantive provisions of the MLI. The substantive provisions of the MLI comprising Articles 3-17 are discussed at length in paragraphs 92-451 in Chapter 3. The impact of provisions of the Vienna Convention on the substantive provisions of the MLI has been discussed at appropriate places in the book. In line with the Vienna Convention, the provisions contained in Articles 3 through 17 of the MLI are to be interpreted in accordance with the ordinary principle of treaty interpretation, which is that a treaty shall be interpreted in good faith in accordance with the ordinary meaning to be given to the terms of the treaty in their context and in light of its object and purpose. Each substantive provision of the MLI has been discussed in a very harmonious manner, as explained hereunder, so as to provide clarity to the nuances embedded in each article:

- An introduction to the article at a glance, *inter alia*, providing information on the relevant BEPS Action Report, resulting provisions incorporated in OECD Model Tax Convention 2017, substantive (BEPS) provisions incorporated in the particular article of the MLI, along with initial information on opt-in provisions, alternative provisions, compatibility clause, reservations and notifications present in that MLI article.
- Status in the pre-BEPS Project era having gaps in tax treaties leading to BEPS and how such gaps are being addressed through that MLI article have been discussed in detail in each MLI article.
- Detailed discussions have been made in respect of compatibility clause, reservations and notifications to be made by various jurisdictions depending upon their respective MLI positions.
- Positions taken by countries under the MLI have also been provided with the purpose to illustratively explain the impact of opt-in provisions, alternative provisions, reservations, notifications and compatibility clause on the respective CTAs. It is expected that these illustrations will further enhance the understanding of all readers as to how MLI modifies the CTAs.

8. Among various substantive provisions of the MLI as contained in Articles 3 through 17, maximum anxiety among the Tax Practitioners has been caused by the Principal Purpose Test (PPT) provisions, being introduced through Article 7 of the MLI as a minimum standard. To provide clarity, elaborate discussions have been done in the book to explain the interaction between PPT and Simplified Limitation on Benefits (refer paragraphs 217-221), as well as, characteristics embedded in the PPT provisions (refer paragraphs 222-229).

9. Part VI of the MLI establishes the mandatory binding arbitration procedure as an optional set of provisions. The Subgroup on Arbitration developed provisions for the mandatory binding arbitration of mutual agreement procedure cases when the competent authorities are unable to reach agreement within a fixed period of time.

Although the BEPS Action 14 Report recommended the implementation of the mandatory binding arbitration procedure in tax treaties, it did not recommend the substantive measures. That is why the Subgroup on Arbitration produced all the provisions reflected in Part VI of the MLI, comprising nine articles (Articles 18 through 26 under the MLI), that address both the substance of those provisions and its technical application to CTAs. Part VI is intended to operate as a single cohesive arbitration provision and is discussed in paragraphs 452-470 in Chapter 3. A number of jurisdictions, namely Albania, Argentina, Armenia, Bahrain, Belize, Bosnia and Herzegovina, Bulgaria, Burkina Faso, Cameroon, Chile, China, Colombia, Costa Rica, Côte d'Ivoire, Croatia, Cyprus, the Czech Republic, Egypt, Estonia, Gabon, Georgia, Guernsey, Hong Kong, Hungary, Iceland, India, Indonesia, the Isle of Man, Israel, Jamaica, Jersey, Jordan, Kazakhstan, Kenya, Korea, Kuwait, Latvia, Lithuania, Malaysia, Mexico, Monaco, Morocco, Nigeria, North Macedonia, Norway, Oman, Pakistan, Panama, Peru, Poland, Qatar, Romania, Russia, San Marino, Saudi Arabia, Senegal, Serbia, Seychelles, the Slovak Republic, South Africa, Tunisia, Turkey, Ukraine, the United Arab Emirates, Uruguay, have not opted for Part VI (Arbitration) provisions contained in Articles 18-26 of the MLI, whereas, as of now, there are 30 jurisdictions which have made notification under Article 18 and have chosen to apply Part VI, namely Andorra, Australia, Austria, Barbados, Belgium, Canada, Curaçao, Denmark, Fiji, Finland, France, Germany, Greece, Ireland, Italy, Japan, Liechtenstein, Luxembourg, Malta, Mauritius, the Netherlands, New Zealand, Papua New Guinea, Portugal, Singapore, Slovenia, Spain, Sweden, Switzerland, UK (refer paragraph 455).

10. The Final Provisions (Articles 27-39) as contained in Part VII of the MLI (refer paragraphs 471-550 in Chapter 4) deal with the procedural provisions of the MLI. These provisions are relevant for the implementation of the MLI by the Parties and the Depositary and carry significant influence to impact the substance of tax treaties. The impact of provisions of the Vienna Convention on the procedural provisions of the MLI has been discussed at appropriate places in the book.

11. Among the procedural provisions of the MLI as contained in Part VII of the MLI, there are certain misconceived interpretations in regard to entry into effect provisions of Article 35. An attempt has been made to put such notions to rest by making elaborate discussions on the meaning of the phrase 'on or after' used in Article 35 of the MLI (refer paragraphs 528-532), meaning of the term 'other taxes' used in Article 35 of the MLI (refer paragraph 533) and various interpretational issues on entry into effect provisions under the MLI (refer paragraphs 534, 535).

12. In order to appreciate the impact made by the MLI on the tax treaty network across the world, an analysis in respect of 95 MLI Signatories has been carried out (refer paragraphs 552, 553 in Chapter 5) on the following lines:

- number of CTAs notified by each of the 95 Signatories;
- number of matching CTAs (where a jurisdiction has notified a particular CTA and its treaty partner (Signatory) has done likewise);

- number of One-Way CTAs (where a jurisdiction has notified a CTA but its treaty partner (Signatory) has not notified the same); and
- number of Waiting CTAs (where a jurisdiction has notified a CTA but its treaty partner has not signed the MLI till date).

The data set reveals that the pack of countries which have notified maximum number of CTAs is led by UK (121 CTAs notified), followed by France (initially, at the time of ratification 91 CTAs were notified, and this number has since increased to 120 when France made a notification under Article 29(5) of the MLI by notifying more CTAs under the MLI), UAE (114 CTAs notified), China (101 CTAs notified), Belgium (99 CTAs notified), India (93 CTAs notified), Romania (91 CTAs notified). The impact of MLI will increase with more countries signing the MLI, and simultaneously, with a reduction in the number of One-Way and Waiting CTAs going forward. Out of 95 Signatories to the MLI, all are members of the Inclusive Framework (IF), except Cyprus, Fiji and Kuwait. Signing of MLI by non-members of the IF is a positive signal conveying importance attached to the MLI and faith reposed in its ability to introduce anti-BEPS measures in a swift manner.

13. MLI preserves the tax sovereignty of its Parties and has been successful in overcoming the main barrier to the conclusion of a worldwide multilateral tax treaty until now. The MLI happens to be the first successfully concluded multilateral tax treaty and has the distinction of universal participation, with as much as 95 jurisdictions having signed the MLI as on 31 December 2020, out of which 60 jurisdictions have ratified it. MLI has opened doors for signing of more such multilateral tax treaties in future, which is why, experts are positing that for implementation of proposals on tax consequences of the digitalised economy under preparation by the OECD, an instrument exactly like the MLI can be used.

14. In line with the title of the book *MLI Made Easy*, for the benefit of readers, the procedural provisions of the MLI have been encapsulated in a ready reckoner, to enable a quick understanding. Accordingly, a checklist titled 'MLI at a Glance' has been devised on MLI's features and its application on CTAs (refer paragraph 570 in Chapter 6). A brief introduction of various Parts and Articles of the MLI is provided in Figure 1.

Figure 1 Parts and Articles of the MLI

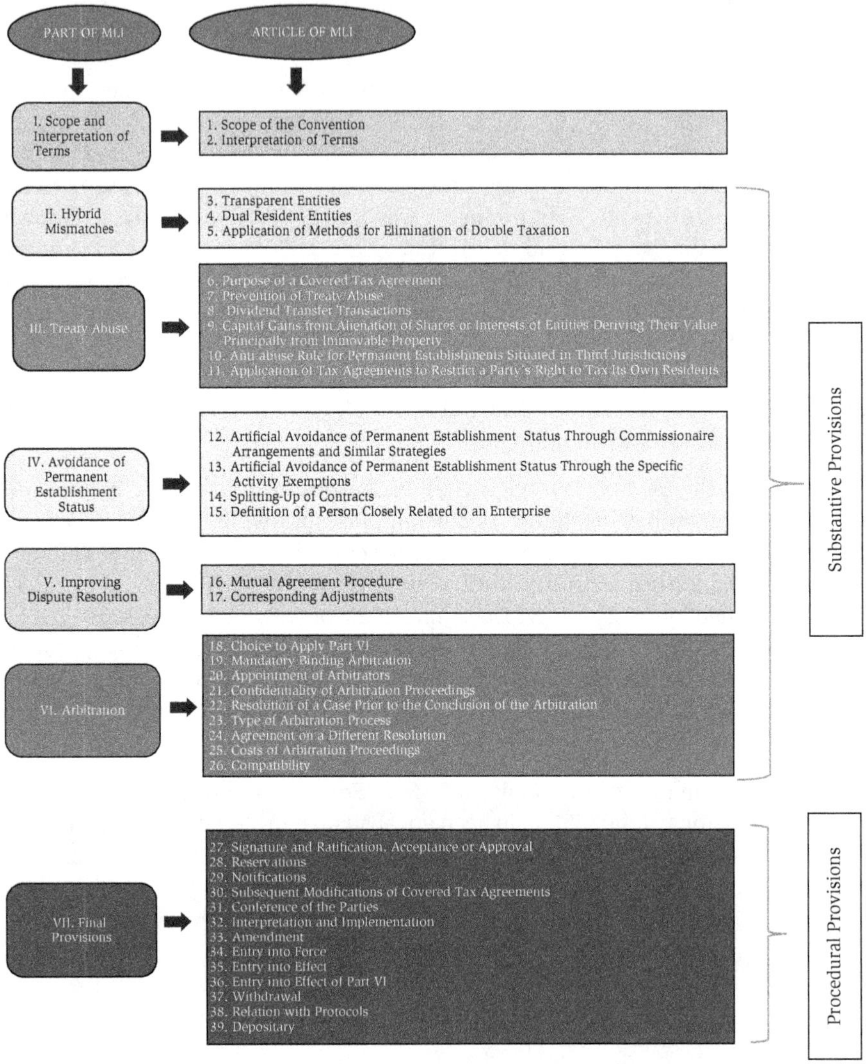

CHAPTER 1
Introduction

The Multilateral Convention to Implement Tax Treaty Related Measures to Prevent Base Erosion and Profit Shifting (MLI) is an outcome of the Base Erosion and Profit Shifting (BEPS) Action Plan developed by the Organisation for Economic Co-operation and Development (OECD) Committee on Fiscal Affairs (CFA) and endorsed by the Group of Twenty (G20) Leaders. The BEPS Project identified 15 actions to address BEPS in a comprehensive manner, wherein out of the 4 minimum standards agreed under the BEPS Action Reports, i.e. Actions 5, 6, 13 and 14, the MLI implements minimum standards contained in Actions 6 and 14. The other tax treaty-related BEPS Action Reports being implemented through the MLI are Actions 2 and 7, respectively.

1. A primary role of governments across the world is to promote social welfare in the fields of health, education, old age care, employment generation, infrastructure development, etc. To make this objective sustainable, all-round economic development is important, which in turn gets accelerated with copious revenue generation. Revenue generated, *inter alia*, in the form of Direct Taxes (income tax, corporate tax), therefore, plays a pivotal role and facilitates roll out of various welfare schemes, infrastructure projects, etc. The average overall rate of taxation among the Group of Twenty and other advanced economies was around 23% of Gross Domestic Product (GDP) in 2018, compared with 18% among the developing and emerging market economies. Assessing an appropriate level of 'tax burden' (revenue in the form of taxes) is a critical element of fiscal policy with implications for economic growth.[5]

2. Enhanced international cooperation is also needed to ensure that sufficient means of implementation exist to provide countries the opportunity to achieve the Sustainable Development Goals (SDGs). In today's fast-paced digitalised world, economic prosperity is inherently dependent upon technology and capital. The developing countries, for their economic growth, need support of the developed countries in the form of

5. Refer UN Economic and Social Council, Report of Secretary General (para. 38, under the heading '*Finance*') https://undocs.org/E/2019/68 accessed on 1 July 2020.

investment of capital, seamless flow of technology and rapid scaling up of the business opportunities. This has led to a substantial increase in cross-border transactions over the years and instances of double taxation where a taxpayer is a resident of one nation, but earns income in another. Intragroup trade accounts for approximately 50% of global transactions.[6] Out of these global transactions, the developing countries are likely to have a significant proportion of cross-border transactions within the Multinational Enterprise (MNE) groups and, hence, these transactions shall be subjected to transfer pricing (TP) regulations and assessment procedures in the host country. The resultant double taxation is either of the following two forms:

(1) Juridical double taxation – same income taxed twice in the hands of the same taxpayer in two different jurisdictions for identical periods.
(2) Economic double taxation – same income taxed in the hands of two separate taxpayers, which are Associated Enterprises (AEs), in two different jurisdictions.

3. In order to provide relief from double taxation arising on account of cross-border transactions so as to facilitate investment of capital, seamless flow of technology and overall business environment, countries, therefore, enter into Double Taxation Avoidance Agreements (DTAAs) under public international law and are governed by the principles laid down under the Vienna Convention on the Law of Treaties[7] (hereinafter 'Vienna Convention' or 'VCLT').

4. With the passage of time, taking advantage of the lack of coordination of the international tax rules, many MNEs and other taxpayers exploited arbitrages in tax treaties and domestic laws to reduce their worldwide tax obligations and have indulged in treaty abuse, which can be categorised into the following two types:

(1) The taxpayer circumvents limitations of the treaty itself, generally known as treaty shopping. Treaty shopping involves strategies through which a person who is not a resident of a country that is part of a specific tax treaty tries to take advantage of the benefits of that treaty that is available only for residents of treaty partners. In treaty shopping, the transaction is not illegal per se; rather, the objective of the transaction is created artificially. To uphold instances of treaty shopping, it is necessary to prove that the transaction entered into by the taxpayer is artificial, hence not acceptable.
(2) Instances where the taxpayer circumvents domestic laws by using treaty provisions. This can be tackled by coordinating between domestic anti-abuse provisions and treaty anti-abuse provisions.

6. Refer OECD Work on Taxation (2018-19) (p. 15) http://www.oecd.org/tax/centre-for-tax-policy-and-administration-brochure.pdf accessed on 1 July 2020.
7. Refer Vienna Convention on the Law of Treaties https://treaties.un.org/doc/publication/unts/volume%201155/volume-1155-i-18232-english.pdf.

5. Shoring up pertinent policy measures against tax base erosion, in particular in developing countries, and ensuring a fair allocation of tax revenues would be vital for financing sustainable development and effectively pursuing the SDGs.[8] Eliminating opportunities for cross-border tax avoidance, evasion and the effective/efficient prevention of double taxation are critical to building an international tax system that supports economic growth and a resilient global economy. Globalisation has exacerbated the impact of gaps and frictions among different countries' tax systems. As a result, some features of the current bilateral tax treaty system facilitated Base Erosion and Profit Shifting (BEPS) which needed to be addressed.

1.1 BASE EROSION AND PROFIT SHIFTING

6. BEPS[9] refers to tax planning strategies used by MNEs that exploit gaps and mismatches in tax rules to avoid paying tax. Developing countries' higher reliance on corporate income tax means they suffer from BEPS disproportionately. BEPS practices cost countries USD 100-USD 240 billion in lost revenue annually. On 12 February 2013, the Group of Twenty (G20) and the Organisation for Economic Co-operation and Development (OECD) released their report on BEPS. Afterwards, on 19 July 2013, an action plan with 15 Action Points was published. Working together within OECD/G20 Inclusive Framework (IF) on BEPS, 137[10] countries and jurisdictions are collaborating on the implementation of 15 measures to tackle tax avoidance, improve the coherence of international tax rules and ensure a more transparent tax environment.

1.2 BEPS ACTION REPORTS

7. OECD and G20 countries adopted a 15-Point Action Plan to address BEPS in September 2013. These reports set the stage for policy recommendations to eliminate the flaws detected in the international and domestic tax systems. The Action Plan identified 15 actions along three key pillars:

(1) introducing coherence in the domestic rules that affect cross-border activities;
(2) reinforcing substance requirements in the existing international standards;
(3) improving transparency as well as certainty.

8. Refer Sustainable Development Goals https://www.un.org/sustainabledevelopment/sustainable-development-goals/ accessed on 1 July 2020.
9. Refer OECD – What Is BEPS? http://www.oecd.org/tax/beps/about/ accessed on 1 July 2020.
10. Refer Members of the OECD/G20 Inclusive Framework on BEPS https://www.oecd.org/tax/beps/inclusive-framework-on-beps-composition.pdf accessed on 1 July 2020.

8. The 15 actions[11] set out below, in brief, equip governments with domestic and international rules and instruments to address tax avoidance, ensuring that profits are taxed where economic activities generating the profits are performed:

(1) *Action 1 Report*[12] *– Addressing the Tax Challenges of the Digital Economy*
The digital economy is the result of a transformative process brought by information and communication technology (ICT), which has made technologies cheaper, more powerful, and widely standardised, improving business processes and bolstering innovation across all sectors of the economy. Some of the key features of the digital economy and its business models exacerbate BEPS risks. To address broader tax challenges raised by the digital economy, the following options were analysed:
   (i) a new nexus in the form of a significant economic presence;
   (ii) a withholding tax (WHT) on certain types of digital transactions; and
   (iii) an equalisation levy.
Countries were given the option to introduce any of the above three options in their domestic laws as additional safeguards against BEPS, provided they respect existing treaty obligations, or in their bilateral tax treaties.

(2) *Action 2 Report*[13] *– Neutralising the Effects of Hybrid Mismatch Arrangements*
Hybrid mismatch arrangements exploit differences in the tax treatment of an entity or instrument under the laws of two or more tax jurisdictions to achieve double non-taxation, including long-term deferral. These types of arrangements are widespread and result in a substantial erosion of the taxable bases of the countries concerned. They have an overall negative impact on competition, efficiency, transparency and fairness. This Report sets out recommendations for changes to domestic law and changes to the OECD Model Tax Convention (MTC). Once translated into domestic and treaty law, these recommendations will neutralise hybrid mismatches, by putting an end to multiple deductions for a single expense, deductions without corresponding taxation or the generation of multiple foreign tax credits for one amount of foreign tax paid. By neutralising the mismatch in tax outcomes, the rules will prevent these arrangements from being used as a tool for BEPS without adversely impacting cross-border trade and investment.

(3) *Action 3 Report*[14] *– Designing Effective Controlled Foreign Company Rules*

11. Refer OECD – BEPS Actions http://www.oecd.org/tax/beps/beps-actions/ accessed on 1 July 2020.
12. Action 1: BEPS 2015 Final Report, OECD/G20 Base Erosion and Profit Shifting Project http://www.oecd.org/tax/beps-2015-final-reports.htm.
13. Action 2: BEPS 2015 Final Report, OECD/G20 Base Erosion and Profit Shifting Project http://www.oecd.org/tax/beps-2015-final-reports.htm.
14. Action 3: BEPS 2015 Final Report, OECD/G20 Base Erosion and Profit Shifting Project http://www.oecd.org/tax/beps-2015-final-reports.htm.

Controlled foreign company (CFC) rules respond to the risk that taxpayers with a controlling interest in a foreign subsidiary can strip the base of their country of residence and, in some cases, other countries by shifting income into a CFC. Without such rules, CFCs provide opportunities for profit shifting and long-term deferral of taxation. The Report sets out recommendations in the form of building blocks. These recommendations are not minimum standards, but they are designed to ensure that jurisdictions that choose to implement them will have rules that effectively prevent taxpayers from shifting income into foreign subsidiaries.

(4) *Action 4 Report*[15] *– Limiting Base Erosion Involving Interest Deductions and Other Financial Payments*
Multinational groups achieve favourable tax results by adjusting the amount of debt in a group entity. BEPS risks in this area may arise in three basic scenarios:
  (i) Groups placing higher levels of third-party debt in high-tax countries.
  (ii) Groups using intragroup loans to generate interest deductions in excess of the group's actual third-party interest expense.
  (iii) Groups using third-party or intragroup financing to fund the generation of tax-exempt income.
To address these risks, the recommended approach is based on a fixed ratio rule which limits an entity's net deductions for interest and payments economically equivalent to interest to a percentage of its earnings before interest, taxes, depreciation and amortisation (EBITDA). To ensure that countries apply a fixed ratio that is low enough to tackle BEPS, while recognising that not all countries are in the same position, the recommended approach includes a corridor of possible ratios between 10% and 30%.

(5) *Action 5 Report*[16] *– Countering Harmful Tax Practices More Effectively, Taking into Account Transparency and Substance*
Current concerns are primarily about preferential regimes that risk being used for artificial profit shifting and about a lack of transparency in connection with certain rulings. Countries have agreed that the substantial activity requirement used to assess preferential regimes should be strengthened in order to realign taxation of profits with the substantial activities that generate them. Several approaches were considered and consensus was reached on the 'nexus approach'. This same principle can also be applied to other preferential regimes so that such regimes would be found to require substantial activities where they grant benefits to a taxpayer to the extent that the taxpayer undertook the core income-generating activities required to produce the type of income covered by the preferential

15. Action 4: BEPS 2015 Final Report, OECD/G20 Base Erosion and Profit Shifting Project http://www.oecd.org/tax/beps-2015-final-reports.htm.
16. Action 5: BEPS 2015 Final Report, OECD/G20 Base Erosion and Profit Shifting Project http://www.oecd.org/tax/beps-2015-final-reports.htm.

regime. In the area of transparency, a framework covering all rulings that could give rise to BEPS concerns, in the absence of their compulsory spontaneous exchange, has been agreed. The framework covers six categories of rulings:

(i) rulings related to preferential regimes;
(ii) cross-border unilateral advance pricing arrangements or Advance Pricing Agreements (APAs) or other unilateral TP rulings;
(iii) rulings giving a downward adjustment to profits;
(iv) permanent establishment (PE) rulings;
(v) conduit rulings; and
(vi) any other type of ruling where the Forum on Harmful Tax Practices (FHTP) agrees in the future that the absence of exchange would give rise to BEPS concerns.

The Action 5 Report is one of the four BEPS minimum standards.[17] Each of the four BEPS minimum standards is subject to peer review in order to ensure timely and accurate implementation and thus safeguard the level playing field. All members of the IF on BEPS commit to implementing the Action 5 minimum standard, and commit to participating in the peer review.

(6) *Action 6 Report*[18] *– Preventing the Granting of Treaty Benefits in Inappropriate Circumstances*

This project identifies treaty abuse, and in particular treaty shopping, as one of the most important sources of BEPS concerns. Taxpayers engaged in treaty shopping and other treaty abuse strategies undermine tax sovereignty by claiming treaty benefits in situations where these benefits were not intended to be granted, thereby depriving countries of tax revenues. Countries have therefore agreed to include anti-abuse provisions in their tax treaties, including a minimum standard to counter treaty shopping. The Report includes new treaty anti-abuse rules that provide safeguards against the abuse of treaty provisions and offer a certain degree of flexibility regarding how to do so, *inter alia*, by adopting the following approach:

(i) A clear statement (preamble) will be included in tax treaties providing that the States that enter into a tax treaty intend to avoid creating opportunities for non-taxation or reduced taxation through tax evasion or avoidance, including through treaty shopping arrangements.
(ii) A specific anti-abuse rule, the limitation on benefits (LOB) rule, which limits the availability of treaty benefits to entities that meet certain conditions, will be included in the OECD MTC. These conditions, which are based on the legal nature of the entity, ownership of

17. Refer OECD – BEPS Action 5, Harmful Tax Practices – Minimum Standard http://www.oecd.org/tax/beps/beps-actions/action5/ accessed on 1 July 2020.
18. Action 6: BEPS 2015 Final Report, OECD/G20 Base Erosion and Profit Shifting Project http://www.oecd.org/tax/beps-2015-final-reports.htm.

the entity, and general activities of the entity, seek to ensure that there is a sufficient link between the entity and its State of residence.

(iii) In order to address other forms of treaty abuse, including treaty shopping situations that would not be covered by the LOB rule described above, a more general anti-abuse rule based on the principal purposes of transactions or arrangements (the Principal Purpose Test or 'PPT' rule) will be included in the OECD MTC. Under that rule, if one of the principal purposes of transactions or arrangements is to obtain treaty benefits, these benefits would be denied unless it is established that granting these benefits would be in accordance with the object and purpose of the provisions of the treaty.

BEPS Action 6[19] addresses treaty shopping through new treaty provisions whose adoption forms part of a minimum standard that members of the BEPS IF have agreed to implement. It also includes specific rules and recommendations to address other forms of treaty abuse. Action 6 identifies tax policy considerations jurisdictions should address before deciding to enter into a tax agreement.

(7) *Action 7 Report*[20] *– Preventing the Artificial Avoidance of Permanent Establishment Status*

Tax treaties generally provide that the business profits of a foreign enterprise are taxable in a State (of source) only to the extent that the enterprise has in that State (of source) a PE to which the profits are attributable. The definition of PE included in tax treaties is, therefore, crucial in determining whether a non-resident enterprise must pay income tax in another State. This Report proposes a review of PE definition to prevent the use of certain common tax avoidance strategies that are currently used to circumvent the existing PE definition, such as arrangements through which taxpayers replace subsidiaries that traditionally acted as distributors by commissionaire arrangements, with a resulting shift of profits out of the country where the sales took place without a substantive change in the functions performed in that country. Changes to the PE definition are also necessary to prevent the exploitation of the specific exceptions to the PE definition currently provided for by Article 5(4) of the OECD MTC (2014). BEPS concerns related to Article 5(4) also arise from what is typically referred to as the 'fragmentation of activities', which shall be addressed by the anti-fragmentation rule proposed by this Report. Also, the exception in Article 5(3) of the OECD MTC (2014), which applies to construction sites, has given rise to abuses through the practice of splitting-up contracts between closely related enterprises, will get addressed through recommendations of this Report.

19. Refer OECD – BEPS Action 6, Prevention of tax treaty abuse – Minimum Standard http://www.oecd.org/tax/beps/beps-actions/action6/ accessed on 1 July 2020.
20. Action 7: BEPS 2015 Final Report, OECD/G20 Base Erosion and Profit Shifting Project http://www.oecd.org/tax/beps-2015-final-reports.htm.

(8) *Action 8-10 Report*[21] – *Aligning Transfer Pricing Outcomes with Value Creation*

These reports deal with TP rules and have focused on three key areas to ensure that the TP rules secure outcomes that see operational profits allocated to the economic activities which generate them. Work under Action 8 looked at TP issues relating to transactions involving intangibles, since misallocation of the profits generated by valuable intangibles has contributed to BEPS. Members of the MNE group are to be compensated based on the value they create through functions performed, assets used and risks assumed in the development, enhancement, maintenance, protection and exploitation (DEMPE) of intangibles. Work under Action 9 addressed the level of returns to funding provided by a capital-rich MNE group member, where those returns do not correspond to the level of activity undertaken by the funding company. Work under Action 10 focused on other high-risk areas, including the scope for addressing profit allocations resulting from transactions which are not commercially rational for the individual enterprises concerned (re-characterisation), the scope for targeting the use of TP methods in a way which results in diverting profits from the most economically important activities of the MNE group, and neutralising the use of certain types of payments between members of the MNE group (such as management fees and head office expenses) to erode the tax base in the absence of alignment with value creation.

The Report determines that risks contractually assumed by a Party that cannot in fact exercise meaningful and specifically defined control over the risks, or does not have the financial capacity to assume the risks, will be allocated to the Party that does exercise such control and does have the financial capacity to assume the risks.

For intangibles, the Guidance clarifies that legal ownership alone does not necessarily generate a right to all (or indeed any) of the return that is generated by the exploitation of the intangible. The group companies performing important functions, controlling economically significant risks and contributing assets, as determined through the accurate delineation of the actual transaction, will be entitled to an appropriate return reflecting the value of their contributions.

(9) *Action 11 Report*[22] – *Measuring and Monitoring BEPS*

Indicators of BEPS activity highlight BEPS behaviours using different sources of data, employing different metrics, and examining different BEPS channels. When combined and presented as a dashboard of indicators, they confirm the existence of BEPS, and its continued increase in scale in

21. Actions 8-10: BEPS 2015 Final Report, OECD/G20 Base Erosion and Profit Shifting Project http://www.oecd.org/tax/beps-2015-final-reports.htm.
22. Action 11: BEPS 2015 Final Report, OECD/G20 Base Erosion and Profit Shifting Project http://www.oecd.org/tax/beps-2015-final-reports.htm.

recent years. These BEPS indicators confirm that profit shifting is occurring, is significant in scale and likely to be increasing, and creates adverse economic distortions. The BEPS indicators identified under this Report are *inter alia* as below:

(i) the profit rates of MNE affiliates located in lower-tax countries are higher than their group's average worldwide profit rate;
(ii) the effective tax rates paid by large MNE entities are estimated to be 4-8½ percentage points lower than similar enterprises with domestic-only operations;
(iii) foreign direct investment (FDI) is increasingly concentrated;
(iv) the separation of taxable profits from the location of the value-creating activity is particularly clear with respect to intangible assets, and the phenomenon has grown rapidly;
(v) debt from both related and third parties are more concentrated in MNE affiliates in higher statutory tax-rate countries.

(10) *Action 12 Report*[23] *– Mandatory Disclosure Rules*
This Report provides a modular framework that enables countries without mandatory disclosure rules to design a regime that fits their need to obtain early information on potentially aggressive or abusive tax planning schemes and their users. The recommendations in this Report do not represent a minimum standard and countries are free to choose whether or not to introduce mandatory disclosure regimes. Where a country wishes to adopt mandatory disclosure rules, the recommendations provide the necessary flexibility to balance a country's need for better and timelier information with the compliance burdens for taxpayers. The Report also sets out specific recommendations for rules targeting international tax schemes as well as for the development and implementation of more effective information exchange and cooperation between tax administrations. The main objective of mandatory disclosure regimes is to increase transparency by providing the tax administration with early information regarding potentially aggressive or abusive tax planning schemes and to identify the promoters and users of those schemes. Another objective of mandatory disclosure regimes is deterrence: taxpayers may think twice about entering into a scheme if it has to be disclosed. In order to successfully design an effective mandatory disclosure regime, certain features need to be considered: who reports, what information to report, when the information has to be reported, and the consequences of non-reporting.

(11) *Action 13 Report*[24] *– Transfer Pricing Documentation and Country-by-Country Reporting (CbCR)*

23. Action 12: BEPS 2015 Final Report, OECD/G20 Base Erosion and Profit Shifting Project http://www.oecd.org/tax/beps-2015-final-reports.htm.
24. Action 13: BEPS 2015 Final Report, OECD/G20 Base Erosion and Profit Shifting Project http://www.oecd.org/tax/beps-2015-final-reports.htm.

This Report contains revised standards for TP documentation and a template for CbCR of income, taxes paid and certain measures of economic activity. A three-tiered standardised approach to TP documentation has been developed as a minimum standard:

(i) first, the Guidance on TP documentation requires MNEs to provide tax administrations with high-level information regarding their global business operations and TP policies in a 'master file' that is to be available to all relevant tax administrations;

(ii) second, it requires that detailed transactional TP documentation be provided in a 'local file' specific to each country, identifying material-related party transactions, the amounts involved in those transactions, and the company's analysis of the TP determinations they have made with regard to those transactions;

(iii) third, large MNEs are required to file a Country-by-Country Report that will provide annually and for each tax jurisdiction in which they do business the amount of revenue, profit before income tax and income tax paid and accrued. It also requires MNEs to report their number of employees, stated capital, retained earnings and tangible assets in each tax jurisdiction. Finally, it requires MNEs to identify each entity within the group doing business in a particular tax jurisdiction and to provide an indication of the business activities each entity engages in.

This information should make it easier for tax administrations to identify whether companies have engaged in TP and other practices that have the effect of artificially shifting substantial amounts of income into tax-advantaged environments. The master file and the local file are to be delivered by MNEs directly to local tax administrations. Country-by-Country Reports should be filed in the jurisdiction of tax residence of the ultimate parent entity and shared between jurisdictions through automatic exchange of information, pursuant to government-to-government mechanisms such as the Multilateral Convention on Mutual Administrative Assistance in Tax Matters, bilateral tax treaties or tax information exchange agreements (TIEAs). In limited circumstances, secondary mechanisms, including local filing, can be used as a backup. These CbCR requirements have been implemented for fiscal years beginning on or after 1 January 2016 and apply to MNEs with annual consolidated group revenue equal to or exceeding EUR 750 million.

(12) *Action 14 Report*[25] – *Making Dispute Resolution Mechanisms More Effective*
The measures developed under Action 14 of the BEPS Action Plan aim to strengthen the effectiveness and efficiency of the mutual agreement procedure (MAP) process. They aim to minimise the risks of uncertainty and

25. Action 14: BEPS 2015 Final Report, OECD/G20 Base Erosion and Profit Shifting Project http://www.oecd.org/tax/beps-2015-final-reports.htm.

unintended double taxation by ensuring the consistent and proper implementation of tax treaties, including the effective and timely resolution of disputes regarding their interpretation or application through the MAP. Through the adoption of this Report, countries have agreed to important changes in their approach to dispute resolution, in particular by having developed a minimum standard with respect to the resolution of treaty-related disputes, committed to its rapid implementation and agreed to ensure its effective implementation through the establishment of a robust peer-based monitoring mechanism.

(13) *Action 15 Report*[26] *– Developing a Multilateral Instrument to Modify Bilateral Tax Treaties*

The goal of Action 15 is to streamline the implementation of the tax treaty-related BEPS measures. This is an innovative approach with no exact precedent in the tax world. This Action Plan provides for an analysis of the tax and public international law issues related to the development of a multilateral instrument to enable countries that wish to do so to implement measures developed in the course of the work on BEPS and amend bilateral tax treaties. On the basis of this analysis, it was decided that the interested countries will develop a multilateral instrument designed to provide an innovative approach to international tax matters, reflecting the rapidly evolving nature of the global economy and the need to adapt quickly to this evolution. Accordingly, a mandate for the formation of an ad hoc Group to develop a multilateral instrument on tax treaty measures to tackle BEPS was approved by the OECD Committee on Fiscal Affairs (CFA) and endorsed by the G20 Finance Ministers and Central Bank Governors in February 2015. The objective of the ad hoc Group was to develop a multilateral instrument to modify existing bilateral tax treaties solely in order to swiftly implement the tax treaty measures developed in the course of the OECD-G20 BEPS Project. The ad hoc Group was made open to participation from all interested countries on an equal footing and it was decided that it be served by the OECD Secretariat. The ad hoc Group began its work with the aim to open the multilateral instrument for signature by 31 December 2016. Participation in the development of the multilateral instrument was decided to be voluntary.

1.3 BEPS ACTION REPORTS COVERED UNDER THE MLI

9. The Multilateral Convention to Implement Tax Treaty Related Measures to Prevent Base Erosion and Profit Shifting (MLI) is an outcome of BEPS Action 15 Report, with an objective to modify existing bilateral tax treaties solely in order to swiftly implement

26. Action 15: BEPS 2015 Final Report, OECD/G20 Base Erosion and Profit Shifting Project http://www.oecd.org/tax/beps-2015-final-reports.htm.

the tax treaty measures developed in the course of the OECD-G20 BEPS Project. The purpose[27] of BEPS Action 15 is summarised in the following text:

> Analyse the tax and public international law issues related to the development of a Multilateral Instrument to enable jurisdictions that wish to do so to implement measures developed in the course of the work on BEPS and amend bilateral tax treaties. On the basis of this analysis, interested Parties will develop a Multilateral Instrument designed to provide an innovative approach to international tax matters, reflecting the rapidly evolving nature of the global economy and the need to adapt quickly to this evolution.

10. The MLI covers four BEPS Action Reports, i.e. Actions 2, 6, 7 and 14, out of which Action Reports 6 and 14 contain the minimum standards. The remaining two minimum standards under Action Reports 5 and 13 are not being implemented through the MLI as it was felt that their implementation requires substantial customisation to a particular jurisdiction, which would be challenging in the context of a multilateral instrument. A brief introduction to Actions 2, 6, 7 and 14 Reports is given above. These reports are discussed in some more detail hereunder along with an initial introduction of the articles of the MLI which are implementing these reports:

(1) *Action 2 Report*[28] *– Neutralising the Effects of Hybrid Mismatch Arrangements*
The Report *inter alia* deals with the application of tax treaties to hybrid entities, i.e. entities that are not treated as taxpayers by either or both States that have entered into a tax treaty (such as partnerships in many countries). The Report has proposed to include in the OECD MTC (OECD, 2010) a new provision and detailed Commentary that will ensure not only that benefits of tax treaties are granted in appropriate cases to the income of these entities but also that these benefits are not granted where neither State treats, under its domestic law, the income of such an entity as the income of one of its residents. These provisions are being implemented through Article 3 of the MLI.
The Report also describes three alternative ways in which countries may address problems arising from the inclusion of the exemption method in treaties with respect to items of income that are not taxed in the State of source. These provisions are being implemented through Article 5 of the MLI.

(2) *Action 6 Report*[29] *– Preventing the Granting of Treaty Benefits in Inappropriate Circumstances*
Countries can implement the minimum standard enshrined under Action 6 Report by including a Preamble Statement (through Article 6 of MLI) as well as the following in their treaties (through Article 7 of MLI):

27. Action 15: BEPS 2015 Final Report, OECD/G20 Base Erosion and Profit Shifting Project (p. 9) http://www.oecd.org/tax/beps-2015-final-reports.htm.
28. Action 2: BEPS 2015 Final Report, OECD/G20 Base Erosion and Profit Shifting Project.
29. Action 6: BEPS 2015 Final Report, OECD/G20 Base Erosion and Profit Shifting Project.

(i) the combined approach of a Simplified LOB and PPT rule; or
(ii) the PPT rule alone (default option).

The detailed LOB[30] rule supplemented by a mechanism that would deal with conduit financing arrangements not already dealt with in tax treaties (one of the recommendations of the BEPS Action 6 Report) is not being implemented through the MLI, given that the detailed LOB provision requires substantial bilateral customisation, which would be challenging in the context of a multilateral instrument; hence, the MLI does not include a detailed LOB provision.

Other recommendations of the BEPS Action 6 Report include new rules to be included in tax treaties in order to address other forms of treaty abuse. These targeted rules address the following:

(i) situations where an entity is resident of two Contracting States (Article 4 of MLI);
(ii) certain dividend transfer transactions that are intended to lower artificially WHTs payable on dividends (Article 8 of MLI);
(iii) transactions that circumvent the application of the treaty rule that allows source taxation of shares of companies that derive their value primarily from immovable property (Article 9 of MLI); and
(iv) situations where the State of residence exempts the income of PEs situated in third States and where shares, debt-claims, rights or property are transferred to PEs set up in countries that do not tax such income or offer preferential treatment to that income (Article 10 of MLI).

The Report also addresses specific issues related to the interaction between treaties and domestic anti-abuse rules so as to prevent application of tax treaties to restrict a Contracting State's right to tax its own residents, through Article 11 of the MLI, that codifies the principle that treaties do not restrict a State's right to tax its own residents (subject to certain exceptions).

(3) *Action 7 Report*[31] *– Preventing the Artificial Avoidance of PE Status*

This Report includes the changes that will be made to the definition of PE in Article 5 of the OECD MTC so as to restore taxation in a number of cases where cross-border income would otherwise go untaxed or would be taxed at very low rates.

A commissionaire arrangement is frequently used by MNEs to escape from invocation of PE provisions in the source State. It may be loosely defined as an arrangement through which a person sells products in a State in its own name but on behalf of a foreign enterprise that is the owner of these products. Through such an arrangement, a foreign enterprise is able to sell its products in a State without technically having a PE to which such sales may be attributed for tax purposes and without, therefore, being taxable in

30. Refer Explanatory Statement to the MLI, para. 90.
31. Action 7: BEPS 2015 Final Report, OECD/G20 Base Erosion and Profit Shifting Project.

that State on the profits derived from such sales. Since the person that concludes the sales does not own the products that it sells, that person cannot be taxed on the profits derived from such sales and may only be taxed on the remuneration that it receives for its services (usually a commission). A foreign enterprise that uses a commissionaire arrangement does not have a PE because it is able to avoid the application of Article 5(5) of the OECD MTC, to the extent that the contracts concluded by the person acting as a commissionaire are not binding on the foreign enterprise. Since Article 5(5) relies on the formal conclusion of contracts in the name of the foreign enterprise, it is possible to avoid the application of that rule by changing the terms of contracts without material changes in the functions performed in the source State. Similar strategies that seek to avoid the application of Article 5(5) involve situations where contracts which are substantially negotiated in a State are not formally concluded in that State because they are finalised or authorised abroad, or where the person that habitually exercises an authority to conclude contracts constitutes an 'independent agent' to which the exception of Article 5(6) applies even though it is closely related to the foreign enterprise on behalf of which it is acting. These concerns are being addressed through Article 12 read with Article 15 of the MLI.

Artificial avoidance of PE status through the specific exceptions, generally considered to be of a preparatory or auxiliary nature, in Article 5(4) of the OECD MTC have been on the rise due to dramatic changes in the way business is conducted. Depending on the circumstances, activities previously considered to be merely preparatory or auxiliary in nature may nowadays correspond to core business activities. In order to ensure that profits derived from core activities performed in a country can be taxed in that country, Article 5(4) is modified to ensure that each of the exceptions included therein is restricted to activities that are otherwise of a 'preparatory or auxiliary' character. BEPS concerns related to Article 5(4) also arise from what is typically referred to as the 'fragmentation of activities'. Given the ease with which MNEs may alter their structures to obtain tax advantages, it is important to clarify that it is not possible to avoid PE status by fragmenting a cohesive operating business into several small operations in order to argue that each part is merely engaged in preparatory or auxiliary activities that benefit from the exceptions of Article 5(4). These BEPS concerns are being addressed through the provisions of Article 13 read with Article 15 of the MLI.

The exception in Article 5(3) of the OECD MTC, which applies to construction sites, has given rise to abuses through the practice of splitting-up contracts by an enterprise or between closely related enterprises. These concerns are being addressed through the provisions of Article 14 read with Article 15 of the MLI.

(4) *Action 14 Report*[32] – *Making Dispute Resolution Mechanisms More Effective*
The minimum standard agreed by all countries adhering to the outcomes of the BEPS Project under this Report shall ensure:
(i) that treaty obligations related to the MAP are fully implemented in good faith and that MAP cases are resolved in a timely manner;
(ii) the implementation of administrative processes that promote the prevention and timely resolution of treaty-related disputes; and
(iii) that taxpayers can access the MAP when eligible.

The minimum standards under Action 14 Report are being implemented through Article 16 of the MLI. The Elements of Minimum Standard mandated by the Action 14 Report are *inter alia* stated as below:

(i) *Element 1.1* – Countries should include paragraphs 1 through 3 of Article 25 of the OECD MTC in their tax treaties, as interpreted in the Commentary and subject to the variations in these paragraphs provided for under Elements 3.1 and 3.3 of the minimum standard; they should provide access to MAP in TP cases and should implement the resulting mutual agreements (e.g., by making appropriate adjustments to the tax assessed). Paragraphs 1 through 3 of Article 25 provide a mechanism, independent from the ordinary legal remedies available under domestic law, through which the competent authorities (CAs) of the Contracting States may resolve differences or difficulties regarding the interpretation or application of the Convention on a mutually agreed basis.
(ii) *Element 1.2* – Countries should provide MAP access in cases in which there is a disagreement between the taxpayer and the tax authorities making the adjustment as to whether the conditions for the application of a treaty anti-abuse provision have been met or as to whether the application of a domestic law anti-abuse provision is in conflict with the provisions of a treaty.
The commitment under 1.2 of the minimum standard deals only with access to MAP, which is distinct from any obligation to endeavour to resolve the case pursuant to paragraph 2 of Article 25. If a country would seek to limit or deny MAP access in all or certain of these cases, it should specifically and expressly agree on such limitations with its treaty partners, which should include a requirement to notify treaty partner CAs about such cases and the facts and circumstances involved.
(iii) *Element 1.3* – Countries should commit to a timely resolution of MAP cases: countries commit to seek to resolve MAP cases within an average time frame of 24 months.
(iv) *Element 1.4* – Countries should enhance their CA relationships and work collectively to improve the effectiveness of the MAP by becoming members of the Forum on Tax Administration on MAP (FTA MAP Forum).

32. Action 14: BEPS 2015 Final Report, OECD/G20 Base Erosion and Profit Shifting Project.

(v) *Element 1.5* – Countries should provide timely and complete reporting of MAP statistics, pursuant to an agreed reporting framework to be developed in coordination with the FTA MAP Forum.

(vi) *Element 1.6* – Countries should commit to have their compliance with the minimum standard reviewed by their peers in the context of the FTA MAP Forum.

(vii) *Element 1.7* – Countries should provide transparency with respect to their positions on MAP arbitration.

(viii) *Element 2.1* – Countries should publish rules, guidelines and procedures to access and use the MAP and take appropriate measures to make such information available to taxpayers. Countries should ensure that their MAP guidance is clear and easily accessible to the public.

(ix) *Element 2.2* – Countries should publish their country MAP profiles on a shared public platform.

(x) *Element 2.3* – Countries should ensure that the staff in charge of MAP processes have the authority to resolve MAP cases in accordance with the terms of the applicable tax treaty, in particular without being dependent on the approval or the direction of the tax administration personnel who made the adjustments at issue or being influenced by considerations of the policy that the country would like to see reflected in future amendments to the treaty.

(xi) *Element 2.4* – Countries should not use performance indicators for their CA functions and staff in charge of MAP processes based on the amount of sustained audit adjustments or maintaining tax revenue.

(xii) *Element 2.5* – Countries should ensure that adequate resources are provided to the MAP function.

(xiii) *Element 2.6* – Countries should clarify in their MAP guidance that audit settlements between tax authorities and taxpayers do not preclude access to MAP. If countries have an administrative or statutory dispute settlement/resolution process independent from the audit and examination functions and that can only be accessed through a request by the taxpayer, countries may limit access to the MAP with respect to the matters resolved through that process. Countries should notify their treaty partners of such administrative or statutory processes and should expressly address the effects of those processes with respect to the MAP in their public guidance on such processes and in their public MAP programme guidance.

(xiv) *Element 2.7* – Countries with bilateral APA programmes should provide for the rollback of APAs in appropriate cases, subject to the applicable time limits.

(xv) *Element 3.1* – Both CAs should be made aware of MAP requests being submitted and should be able to give their views on whether the request is accepted or rejected. In order to achieve this, countries should either:
- amend paragraph 1 of Article 25 to permit a request for MAP assistance to be made to the CA of either Contracting State; or
- where a treaty does not permit a MAP request to be made to either Contracting State, implement a bilateral notification or consultation process for cases in which the CA to which the MAP case was presented

does not consider the taxpayer's objection to be justified (such consultation shall not be interpreted as consultation as to how to resolve the case).

(xvi) *Element 3.2* – Countries' published MAP guidance should identify the specific information and documentation that a taxpayer is required to submit with a request for MAP assistance. Countries should not limit access to MAP based on the argument that insufficient information was provided if the taxpayer has provided the required information.

(xvii) *Element 3.3* – Countries should include in their tax treaties the second sentence of paragraph 2 of Article 25 ('Any agreement reached shall be implemented notwithstanding any time limits in the domestic law of the Contracting States'). Countries that cannot include the second sentence of paragraph 2 of Article 25 in their tax treaties should be willing to accept alternative treaty provisions that limit the time during which a Contracting State may make an adjustment pursuant to Article 9(1) or Article 7(2), in order to avoid late adjustments with respect to which MAP relief will not be available.

The minimum standard is complemented by a set of Best Practices. The Best Practices agreed under Action 14 Report are *inter alia* stated as below:

(a) *Best Practice 1*: Countries should include paragraph 2 of Article 9 of the OECD MTC in their tax treaties. This best practice is being implemented through Article 17 of MLI.

(b) *Best Practice 2*: Countries should have appropriate procedures in place to publish agreements reached pursuant to the authority provided by the first sentence of paragraph 3 of Article 25 'to resolve by mutual agreement any difficulties or doubts arising as to the interpretation or application of the Convention' that affect the application of a treaty to all taxpayers or to a category of taxpayers (rather than to a specific taxpayer's MAP case) where such agreements provide guidance that would be useful to prevent future disputes and where the CAs agree that such publication is consistent with principles of sound tax administration.

(c) *Best Practice 3*: Countries should develop the 'global awareness' of the audit/examination functions involved in international matters through the delivery of FTA's 'Global Awareness Training Module' to appropriate personnel.

(d) *Best Practice 4*: Countries should implement bilateral APA programmes.

(e) *Best Practice 5*: Countries should implement appropriate procedures to permit, in certain cases and after an initial tax assessment, taxpayer requests for the multiyear resolution through the MAP of recurring issues with respect to filed tax years, where the relevant facts and circumstances are the same and subject to the verification of such facts and circumstances on audit. Such procedures would remain subject to the requirements of paragraph 1 of Article 25: a request to resolve an issue with respect to a particular taxable year would only be allowed where the case has been presented within three years of the first notification of the action resulting in taxation not in accordance with the Convention with respect to that taxable year.

(f) *Best Practice 6*: Countries should take appropriate measures to provide for a suspension of collection procedures during the period a MAP case is pending. Such a suspension of collections should be available, at a minimum, under the same conditions as applicable to a person pursuing a domestic administrative or judicial remedy.

(g) *Best Practice 7*: Countries should implement appropriate administrative measures to facilitate recourse to the MAP to resolve treaty-related disputes, recognising the general principle that the choice of remedies should remain with the taxpayer.

(h) *Best Practice 8*: Countries should include in their published MAP guidance an explanation of the relationship between the MAP and domestic law administrative and judicial remedies. Such public guidance should address, in particular, whether the CA considers itself to be legally bound to follow a domestic court decision in the MAP or whether the CA will not deviate from a domestic court decision as a matter of administrative policy or practice.

(i) *Best Practice 9*: Countries' published MAP guidance should provide that taxpayers will be allowed access to the MAP so that the CAs may resolve through consultation the double taxation that can arise in the case of bona fide taxpayer-initiated foreign adjustments – i.e., taxpayer-initiated adjustments permitted under the domestic laws of a treaty partner which allow a taxpayer under appropriate circumstances to amend a previously filed tax return to adjust: (i) the price for a transaction between AEs or (ii) the profits attributable to a PE, with a view to reporting a result that is, in the view of the taxpayer, in accordance with the arm's-length principle.

For such purposes, a taxpayer-initiated foreign adjustment should be considered bona fide where it reflects the good faith effort of the taxpayer to report correctly the taxable income from a controlled transaction or the profits attributable to a PE and where the taxpayer has otherwise timely and properly fulfilled all of its obligations related to such taxable income or profits under the tax laws of the two Contracting States.

(j) *Best Practice 10*: Countries' published MAP guidance should provide guidance on the consideration of interest and penalties in the MAP.

(k) *Best Practice 11*: Countries' published MAP guidance should provide guidance on multilateral MAPs and APAs.

In addition to the commitment to implement the minimum standard by all countries adhering to the outcomes of the BEPS Project, certain countries have declared their commitment to provide for mandatory binding MAP arbitration in their bilateral tax treaties as a mechanism to guarantee that treaty-related disputes will be resolved within a specified time frame. The mandatory binding MAP arbitration provision was decided to be developed as part of the negotiation of the multilateral instrument envisaged by Action 15 of the BEPS Action Plan and is contained in Part VI (Articles 18-26) of the MLI.

For the benefit of readers, a synopsis of BEPS Action Reports and their implementation through the MLI is provided in Figure 2.

Figure 2 BEPS Action Reports

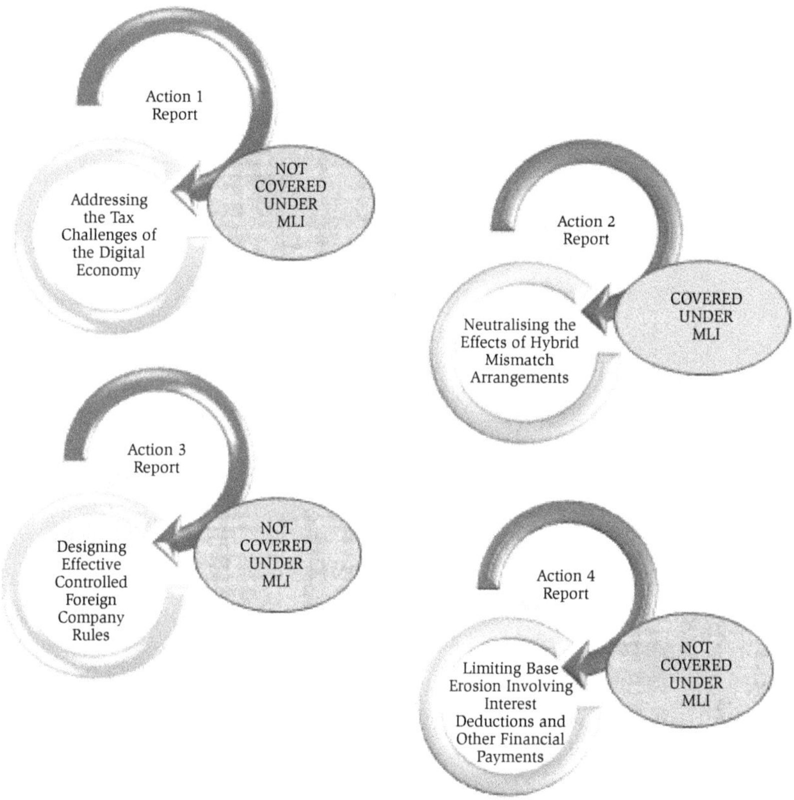

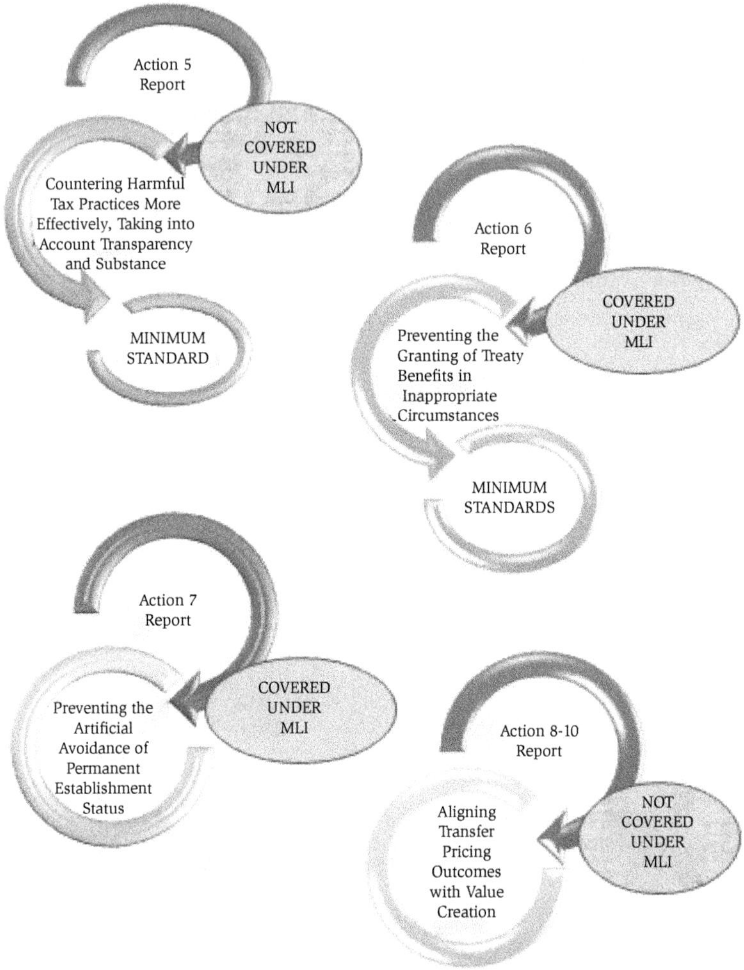
Action 5
Report
NOT
COVERED
UNDER
MLI
Countering Harmful
Tax Practices More
Effectively, Taking into
Account Transparency
and Substance
MINIMUM
STANDARD
Action 6
Report
COVERED
UNDER
MLI
Preventing the
Granting of Treaty
Benefits in
Inappropriate
Circumstances
MINIMUM
STANDARDS
Action 7
Report
COVERED
UNDER
MLI
Preventing the
Artificial
Avoidance of
Permanent
Establishment
Status
Action 8-10
Report
NOT
COVERED
UNDER
MLI
Aligning
Transfer
Pricing
Outcomes
with Value
Creation

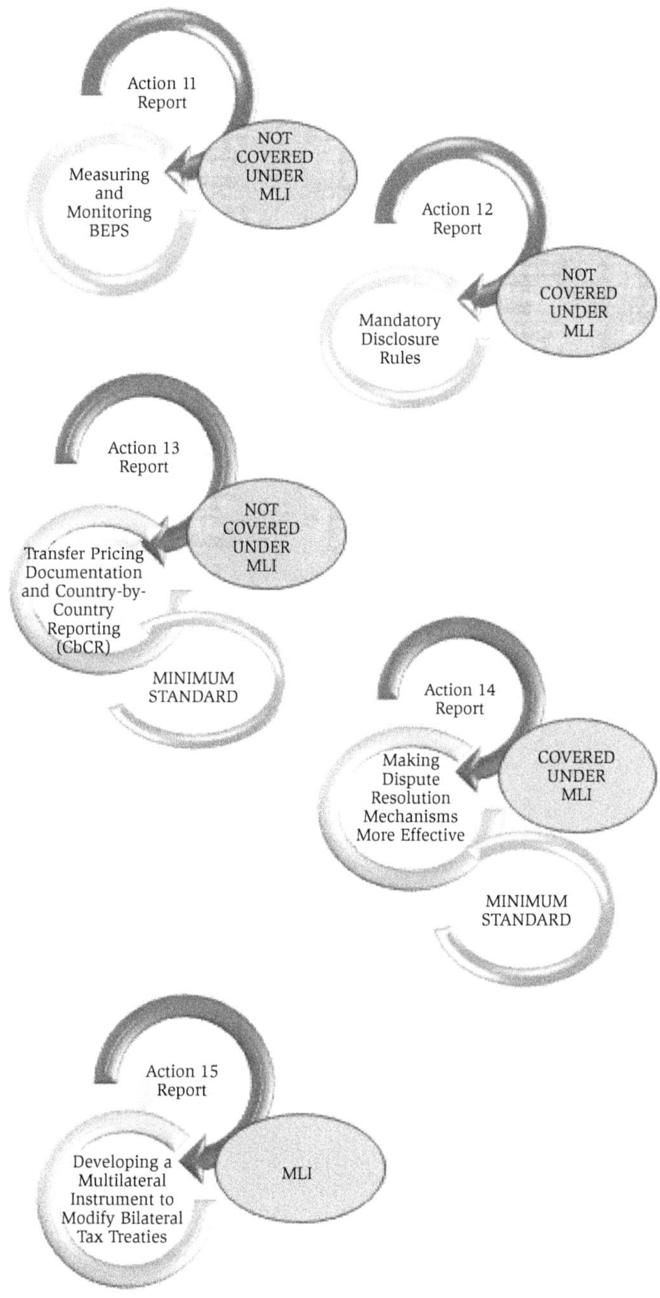
Action 11
Report
Measuring
and
Monitoring
BEPS
NOT
COVERED
UNDER
MLI
Action 12
Report
Mandatory
Disclosure
Rules
NOT
COVERED
UNDER
MLI
Action 13
Report
Transfer Pricing
Documentation
and Country-by-
Country
Reporting
(CbCR)
NOT
COVERED
UNDER
MLI
MINIMUM
STANDARD
Action 14
Report
Making
Dispute
Resolution
Mechanisms
More Effective
COVERED
UNDER
MLI
MINIMUM
STANDARD
Action 15
Report
Developing a
Multilateral
Instrument to
Modify Bilateral
Tax Treaties
MLI

CHAPTER 2
MLI: Introduction

The purpose and objective of the MLI is to swiftly implement the tax treaty-related BEPS measures. The MLI operates to modify tax treaties between two or more Parties to the Convention and does not function in the same way as an Amending Protocol to a single existing treaty, which would directly amend the text of the Covered Tax Agreement (CTA); instead, it will be applied alongside existing tax treaties, modifying their application in order to implement the BEPS measures. The MLI has entered into force on 1 July 2018 and it started producing effect from 1 January 2019. As at 31 December 2020, the MLI has been signed by 95 jurisdictions and ratified by 60 of them.

2.1 BACKGROUND OF THE MLI

11. The BEPS Action Plan was developed by the OECD CFA and endorsed by the G20 Leaders in September 2013. It identified 15 actions to address BEPS in a comprehensive manner, and set out deadlines to implement those actions. Action 15 of the BEPS Action Plan provided for an analysis of the possible development of a multilateral instrument to implement tax treaty-related BEPS measures 'to enable jurisdictions that wish to do so to implement measures developed in the course of the work on BEPS and amend bilateral tax treaties'. Thus, the MLI[33] is one of the outcomes of the OECD/G20 Project to tackle Base Erosion and Profit Shifting (the 'BEPS Project'), i.e. tax planning strategies that exploit gaps and mismatches in tax rules to artificially shift profits to low or no-tax locations where there is little or no economic activity, resulting in little or no overall corporate tax being paid.

12. *Preamble and Objective of MLI:*[34] The preamble recognises that MLI is an outcome of a mandate by the G20 nations to the OECD which culminated in the OECD-G20 BEPS Project Reports. The countries participating in the OECD-G20 BEPS Project agreed to

33. Refer Explanatory Statement to the MLI, paras 1 and 2.
34. Action 15: BEPS 2015 Final Report, OECD/G20 Base Erosion and Profit Shifting Project.

establish an ad hoc Group. The ad hoc Group developed the MLI to modify existing bilateral tax treaties solely in order to swiftly implement the tax treaty measures developed in the course of the OECD-G20 BEPS Project in a coordinated and consistent manner across the network of existing tax treaties without the need to bilaterally renegotiate each such treaty.[35] The preamble of the MLI *inter alia* includes the provisions of Article 6(1) of the MLI also to make it abundantly clear at the very outset that the Parties to the MLI recognised the need to ensure that existing agreements for the avoidance of double taxation on income are interpreted to eliminate double taxation with respect to the taxes covered by those agreements without creating opportunities for non-taxation or reduced taxation through tax evasion or avoidance (including through treaty shopping arrangements aimed at obtaining reliefs provided in those agreements for the indirect benefit of residents of third jurisdictions). This statement included in the preamble itself is intended to clarify the strong will of the Parties to the MLI to ensure that, henceforth, Covered Tax Agreements (CTAs) must be interpreted in line with their preamble language which is to be modified through the minimum standard contained in Article 6(1) of the MLI.

13. The MLI was developed by an ad hoc Group, which started its substantive work in November 2015, comprising the following participants:

(a) Membership of the ad hoc Group was thrown open to all interested States/jurisdictions. All members of the ad hoc Group participated on an equal footing.
(b) Non-State jurisdictions participated in the ad hoc Group as Observers upon a specific invitation by the ad hoc Group.
(c) Relevant international and regional intergovernmental organisations were invited by the ad hoc Group to participate as Observers.

14. The MLI was adopted/concluded on 24 November 2016, and on 7 June 2017, the first signing ceremony was held at the OECD, Paris, when ministers and high-level officials from 76 States and non-State jurisdictions signed or formally expressed their intention to sign the MLI.[36] As at 31 December 2020, the MLI has been signed by 95 jurisdictions and ratified by 60 of them. Following the ratification of the MLI and notification of their final position by five jurisdictions, the MLI has entered into force on 1 July 2018 and it started producing effect from 1 January 2019. In this process, the MLI was first ratified by Austria (on 22 September 2017), followed by the Isle of Man (on 25 October 2017), Jersey (on 15 December 2017), Poland (on 23 January 2018) and Slovenia (on 22 March 2018) being the fifth jurisdiction to ratify the MLI. For all these five jurisdictions, MLI has entered into force on 1 July 2018 and they became Parties to the MLI. Thereafter, Serbia, Sweden, New Zealand, UK ratified the MLI in June 2018

35. Refer Explanatory Statement to the MLI, para. 21.
36. Refer OECD – Ground-Breaking Multilateral BEPS Convention Signed at OECD Will Close Loopholes in Thousands of Tax Treaties Worldwide http://www.oecd.org/tax/ground-breaking-multilateral-beps-convention-will-close-tax-treaty-loopholes.htm accessed on 4 July 2020.

following which the MLI entered into force for these countries on 1 October 2018. The next lot of ratifications happened in the month of September 2018 when Lithuania, Israel, the Slovak Republic, Australia, France, Japan ratified; hence, the MLI entered into force for these countries on 1 January 2019. The process of ratification of the MLI by various jurisdictions has moved forward sedately since then. In September 2020, another round of substantial ratifications happened when Bosnia and Herzegovina, Albania, Costa Rica, Jordan, Egypt ratified the MLI.

2.2 BENEFITS OF THE MLI[37]

15. Swift modification of bilateral tax treaties – Implementation of the Final BEPS Package shall require changes to model tax conventions as well as to the bilateral tax treaties based on those model conventions. The sheer number of bilateral treaties (more than three thousand) would make bilateral updates to the treaty network burdensome and time-consuming, limiting the effectiveness of multilateral efforts. The Action 15 Report,[38] 'Developing a Multilateral Instrument to Modify Bilateral Tax Treaties', concluded that a multilateral instrument (MLI) shall provide an innovative approach to enable countries to swiftly modify their bilateral tax treaties to implement measures developed in the course of the work on BEPS.

16. Sovereignty of States remains protected – MLI addresses treaty-based BEPS issues while respecting sovereign autonomy in tax matters. The concept of sovereign autonomy is a basic principle underpinning the international order and providing the foundation for the negotiation of international treaties. Governments have historically used domestic legislation and bilateral treaties to reach the appropriate balance between national sovereignty and international cooperation in this area. As BEPS results from the interactions of multiple countries' laws and treaties, governments need to collaborate more intensively through a multilateral instrument both to prevent the tax treaty network from facilitating BEPS and to protect their tax sovereignty.

17. Prevention of unilateral and uncoordinated measures by jurisdictions – MLI responds to the political imperatives driving the BEPS Project. It allows BEPS abuses to be curtailed and governments to swiftly achieve their international tax policy goals without creating the risk of violating existing bilateral treaties that would arise from the use of unilateral and uncoordinated measures.

18. Allows developing countries to reap the benefits of multilateral efforts to tackle BEPS – The MLI provides developing countries with the opportunity to fully benefit from the BEPS Project. For developing countries, the practical problems that are encountered in trying to address BEPS from within the bilateral tax treaty system alone are even more relevant than for developed countries. Developing countries find it more difficult than other countries both to conclude double tax treaties and to interest other countries in tax treaty (re)negotiation, and their tax treaty negotiation expertise is often

37. Action 15: BEPS 2015 Final Report, OECD/G20 Base Erosion and Profit Shifting Project.
38. Refer Explanatory Statement to the MLI, paras 4 and 5.

more limited than in the governments of developed economies. MLI, therefore, has offered the best opportunity to ensure that developing countries reap the benefits of multilateral efforts to tackle BEPS.

19. Encourages certainty and reduces unpredictable tax environment for businesses - MLI has increased the consistency and helped ensure the continued reliability of the international tax treaty network, providing additional certainty for business. In contrast to amendments to thousands of bilateral tax treaties, MLI has been able to address BEPS and produce consistent results. The multilateral nature of the instrument has focussed the attention of a large number of highly qualified treaty negotiators on a single document that could incorporate the language deemed most appropriate by all concerned countries. In addition, having a single text, instead of thousands of similar but slightly varying texts, would be more likely to produce consistent interpretation across jurisdictional boundaries. As a result, a common international understanding has developed about the meaning of the text of the provisions of the multilateral instrument.

20. An instrument which is highly flexible - Flexibility, respect for bilateral relations, and a targeted scope are key features of the MLI. The benefits of swift implementation, improved consistency, certainty, and efficiency have been achieved as bilateral specificities and tax sovereignty have been fully respected under the MLI. On the other hand, in order to feel comfortable moving ahead in tackling BEPS, countries got an assurance that other countries are tackling BEPS simultaneously. Parties have, therefore, committed to a core set of provisions as part of MLI, but then have the possibility to opt out, opt in or choose between alternative - and clearly delineated - provisions with respect to other issues covered by the instrument.

21. Drafted by jurisdictions on an equal footing - A level playing field has ensured broader participation, as more than hundred countries participated on an equal footing, as part of the ad hoc Group, in drafting the MLI text and its Explanatory Statement.

22. An instrument which coexists with the existing bilateral tax treaty network - The MLI would coexist with the existing bilateral tax treaty network. Like existing tax treaties, this instrument would be governed by international law and would be legally binding on the Parties. MLI modifies a limited number of provisions common to most existing bilateral treaties, and for those treaties that do not already have such provisions, add new provisions specifically designed to counter BEPS. It also clarifies the compatibility with tax treaties of other anti-BEPS measures developed in the course of the BEPS Project. The MLI is accompanied by an Explanatory Statement to facilitate the implementation of the provisions contained therein.

2.3 FEATURES OF THE MLI

23. The MLI is the first worldwide multilateral tax treaty which is expected to modify the worldwide tax treaty network so as to eliminate BEPS. The innovative techniques used by the ad hoc Group mandated with the task of drafting the MLI text and its Explanatory Statement have enabled modification of expectedly more than three thousand[39] bilateral tax treaties. Given the novel approach, the MLI is bestowed with some strikingly differentiating features, stated hereunder, which has made this possible:

(a) The MLI modifies[40] numerous tax treaties without replacing them and is applied alongside existing bilateral treaties.
(b) The MLI was concluded on a multilateral basis but has bilateral effects.
(c) The MLI enables countries to go through only one ratification procedure in their Parliament in order to modify their whole treaty network rather than seeking separate ratification of amendments to each bilateral treaty.
(d) It provides Signatories/Parties to the MLI with a high level of flexibility, allowing them to opt for CTAs and MLI provisions based on their individual aspirations/requirements.
(e) The compatibility clauses, notification clauses, opting-in mechanisms, alternative provisions and reservations (opting-out mechanisms) have provided immense flexibility to the instrument. A jurisdiction's list of CTAs, reservations and notifications is submitted in the form of a completed template to the Depositary and constitutes the jurisdiction's 'MLI Position'.[41]
(f) The instrument is dynamic and retains the possibility for the Signatories/Parties to subsequently modify their MLI position (in specific cases and circumstances), based on respective envisioned requirements.
(g) The MLI provisions allow subsequent modifications of the DTAA (referred to as CTA under the MLI) as may be agreed by the CAs of the DTAA involved.
(h) If the CAs are unable to resolve any question in regard to the interpretation or implementation of the MLI, the same may be referred to the Conference of the Parties (CoP) to be served by the Depositary (Secretary General of the OECD).
(i) The MLI contains provisions to enable the instrument itself getting modified and amended by convening a CoP.
(j) Any Party may, at any time, withdraw from the MLI by means of a notification to the Depositary (Secretary General of the OECD).
(k) The MLI may be supplemented by one or more Protocols.

39. Refer Note by the OECD Directorate for Legal Affairs, para. 12 http://www.oecd.org/tax/treaties/legal-note-on-the-functioning-of-the-MLI-under-public-international-law.pdf accessed on 23 July 2020.
40. *Id.*, para. 15.
41. *Id.*, para. 21.

CHAPTER 3

MLI: Structure and Substantive Provisions

The MLI has some unique features and benefits for the contracting jurisdictions. The MLI has been constructed in a structured manner and its way of operation is streamlined and consistent to enable seamless modification of the CTAs. This became possible with an efficacious use of compatibility clauses, notification clauses, opting-in mechanisms, alternative provisions and reservations. The MLI provisions have been so designed that the treaty provisions they apply alongside take effect symmetrically, except for certain instances of asymmetry which were deemed necessary and appropriate by the ad hoc Group. The substantive provisions of the MLI are provided in Articles 3-26 (Parts II-VI). Part VI of the MLI establishes the mandatory binding arbitration procedure as an optional set of provisions. A plain reading of all these articles demonstrates that the design of Part VI of the MLI (containing Articles 18-26) is different as it provides rules relevant for different steps of the mandatory binding arbitration procedure, which require more details as well as more tailor-made exceptions than the tax treaty-related BEPS measures established in the other substantive provisions of the MLI. To provide enhanced clarity, elaborate discussions have been made to explain the interaction between PPT and Simplified Limitation on Benefits (S-LoB) as well as characteristics embedded in the PPT provisions.

3.1 STRUCTURE OF THE MLI

24. The MLI[42] has its own preamble, and the MLI text is divided into seven parts containing 39 articles in all. In order to explain the MLI provisions to all the stakeholders concerned and facilitate uniform application of the MLI, the OECD has also released an Explanatory Statement[43] to the MLI, which was prepared and adopted by the ad hoc Group on 24 November 2016 along with the MLI text. The substantive

42. Refer MLI Text http://www.oecd.org/tax/treaties/multilateral-convention-to-implement-tax-treaty-related-measures-to-prevent-BEPS.pdf.
43. Refer Explanatory Statement to the MLI http://www.oecd.org/tax/treaties/explanatory-statement-multilateral-convention-to-implement-tax-treaty-related-measures-to-prevent-BEPS.pdf.

provisions of the MLI are contained in Parts II-VI (Articles 3-26 of the MLI), whereas the procedural provisions of the MLI are contained in Part VII (Articles 27-39 of the MLI). A bird's-eye view of various Parts and Articles of the MLI is provided in Table 1.

Table 1 Parts and Articles of the MLI

S.N	*Part of MLI*	*Title*	*Article of MLI*	*Title of Article*
1	I	Scope and Interpretation of Terms	1	Scope of the Convention
			2	Interpretation of Terms
2	II	Hybrid Mismatches	3	Transparent Entities
			4	Dual Resident Entities
			5	Application of Methods for Elimination of Double Taxation
3	III	Treaty Abuse	6	Purpose of a Covered Tax Agreement
			7	Prevention of Treaty Abuse
			8	Dividend Transfer Transactions
			9	Capital Gains from Alienation of Shares or Interests of Entities Deriving Their Value Principally from Immovable Property
			10	Anti-abuse Rule for Permanent Establishments Situated in Third Jurisdictions
			11	Application of Tax Agreements to Restrict a Party's Right to Tax Its Own Residents
4	IV	Avoidance of Permanent Establishment Status	12	Artificial Avoidance of Permanent Establishment Status Through Commissionaire Arrangements and Similar Strategies
			13	Artificial Avoidance of Permanent Establishment Status Through the Specific Activity Exemptions
			14	Splitting-Up of Contracts
			15	Definition of a Person Closely Related to an Enterprise
5	V	Improving Dispute Resolution	16	Mutual Agreement Procedure
			17	Corresponding Adjustments

S.N	*Part of MLI*	*Title*	*Article of MLI*	*Title of Article*
6	VI	Arbitration	18	Choice to Apply Part VI
			19	Mandatory Binding Arbitration
			20	Appointment of Arbitrators
			21	Confidentiality of Arbitration Proceedings
			22	Resolution of a Case Prior to the Conclusion of the Arbitration
			23	Type of Arbitration Process
			24	Agreement on a Different Resolution
			25	Costs of Arbitration Proceedings
			26	Compatibility
7	VII	Final Provisions	27	Signature and Ratification, Acceptance or Approval
			28	Reservations
			29	Notifications
			30	Subsequent Modifications of Covered Tax Agreements
			31	Conference of the Parties
			32	Interpretation and Implementation
			33	Amendment
			34	Entry into Force
			35	Entry into Effect
			36	Entry into Effect of Part VI
			37	Withdrawal
			38	Relation with Protocols
			39	Depositary

25. The structure[44] of each substantive provision of the MLI (with the exception of the provisions of Part VI), i.e. Articles 3-17, is as follows:

(a) Agreed BEPS measures that form the basis of the provision of the MLI are at the vanguard of Articles 3 through 17. These paragraphs generally duplicate the language of the provisions that were developed during the course of the BEPS Project, with certain modifications.
(b) Compatibility clauses which define the relationship between the provisions of the MLI and CTAs in objective terms.
(c) Reservation clauses that define the reservation(s) permitted with respect to each provision (in line with the agreement reached on the relevant BEPS measure).

44. Refer Explanatory Statement to the MLI, para. 15.

(d) Notification clause(s) reflecting choices of optional (opt-ins) and alternative provisions.
(e) Notification clause(s) to ensure clarity about existing provisions in the CTAs that are within the scope of compatibility clauses, so that the provision of MLI supersedes or modifies the existing (and notified) provisions of a CTA.

26. Part VI of the Convention (Articles 18 through 26) reflects the result of the work of the Subgroup on Arbitration to develop provisions for the mandatory binding arbitration of MAP cases in which the CAs are unable to reach agreement within a fixed period of time. The structure[45] of the articles of Part VI differs from the structure of the other substantive articles of the MLI. These differences reflect the fact that Part VI is intended to operate as a single cohesive arbitration provision. Thus, rather than including a compatibility clause in each Article of Part VI, rules for compatibility with existing provisions are consolidated in Article 26. In addition, while Part VI includes some defined reservations, Parties that choose to apply Part VI are also permitted to formulate their own reservations with respect to the scope of cases that will be eligible for arbitration (subject to acceptance by the other Parties).

3.2 WAY MLI OPERATES

27. MLI applies to the CTAs. In accordance with Article 2(1)(a) of the MLI, a CTA is a treaty or DTAA in force between two or more Parties to the MLI, as long as each of the Parties has notified it as a treaty covered by the MLI, i.e. the positive list approach,[46] thereby, preventing modification of a tax treaty through the MLI without the consent of other contracting jurisdictions. Thus, if one of the Parties notifies a tax treaty as a CTA and the other does not, then the MLI does not modify that tax treaty.

28. Since MLI provisions are to be read side by side with the CTA provisions, compatibility clauses determining the relationship between the MLI provisions and the CTA provisions have been incorporated in all[47] substantive articles of the MLI. Hence, MLI does not function[48] as an Amending Protocol to the CTA. MLI constitutes a new agreement[49] that coexists with and applies alongside the CTAs, as envisaged in Articles 30, 39, 40 of the Vienna Convention.

29. A jurisdiction is required to sign the MLI and provide its provisional MLI position including the list of CTAs to the Depositary. The MLI provides for the following three

45. *Id.*, para. 20.
46. Refer Nathalie Bravo's 'A Multilateral Instrument for Updating the Tax Treaty Network' IBFD Doctoral Series 52, p. 67.
47. There are two exceptions to this rule: (1) Art. 15 of the MLI applies together with Arts 12, 13 and 14 of the MLI to be read with CTA provisions, and (2) Compatibility Clause dealing with Part VI, which is established in Art. 26 but refers to the whole Part VI of the MLI.
48. Refer Explanatory Statement to the MLI, para. 13.
49. Refer Nathalie Bravo's 'A Multilateral Instrument for Updating the Tax Treaty Network' IBFD Doctoral Series 52, pp. 60 and 64.

options with regard to the list of reservations and notifications to be submitted at the time of signature and ratification:

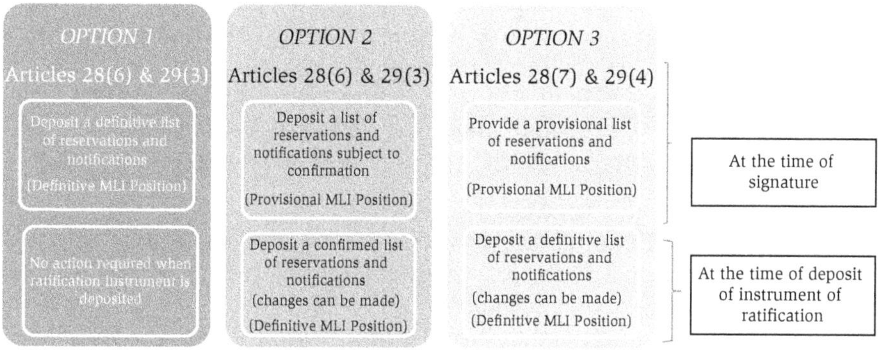

30. In respect of jurisdictions,[50] namely, Albania, Australia, Barbados, Bosnia and Herzegovina, Burkina Faso, Canada, Costa Rica, Cyprus, the Czech Republic, Finland, Georgia, Germany, Guernsey, India, Indonesia, Ireland, the Isle of Man, Japan, Jersey, Jordan, Kazakhstan, Korea, Latvia, Liechtenstein, Lithuania, Mauritius, New Zealand, Norway, Panama, Portugal, Russia, San Marino, Saudi Arabia, Singapore, Slovenia, Ukraine, the United Arab Emirates, UK, at the time of MLI signing, a provisional list of expected reservations and notifications was made pursuant to Articles 28(7) and 29(4) of the MLI. At the time of ratification, these countries submitted their final list of reservations and notifications in pursuance to Articles 28(5) and 29(1) of the MLI. On the other hand, at the time of MLI signing, jurisdictions, namely, Austria, Belgium, Chile, Iceland, Israel, Luxembourg, Malta, Monaco, Poland, Qatar, Serbia, the Slovak Republic, Sweden, Switzerland, submitted their list of reservations and notifications pursuant to Articles 28(6) and 29(3) of the MLI, which were subsequently confirmed upon at the time of deposit of the instrument of ratification. In the case of Denmark, Pakistan, at the time of MLI signing, a provisional list of expected reservations and notifications was made pursuant to Articles 28(6) and 29(3) of the MLI, whereas, at the time of ratification, they submitted their final list of reservations and notifications in pursuance to Articles 28(5) and 29(1) of the MLI. In the case of Egypt, France, Uruguay, Oman, at the time of MLI signing, a provisional list of expected reservations and notifications was made pursuant to Articles 28(7) and 29(4) of the MLI, whereas, at the time of ratification, Egypt, France, Uruguay, Oman submitted their respective final list of reservations and notifications in pursuance to Articles 28(6) and 29(3) of the MLI. In the case of Curaçao, at the time of MLI signing, a provisional list of expected reservations and notifications was made pursuant to Articles 28(4) and 29(2) of the MLI (submitted by the Netherlands in respect of Curaçao), whereas, at the time of ratification (referred to as acceptance in the Netherlands), Curaçao submitted its final

50. Refer OECD – Signatories and Parties to the MLI http://www.oecd.org/tax/treaties/beps-mli-signatories-and-parties.pdf accessed on 31 December 2020.

list of reservations and notifications in pursuance to Articles 28(4), 28(5), 29(1) and 29(2) of the MLI (submitted by the Netherlands in respect of Curaçao). In the case of the Netherlands, at the time of MLI signing, a provisional list of expected reservations and notifications was made pursuant to Articles 28(7) and 29(4) of the MLI, whereas, at the time of ratification (referred to as acceptance in the Netherlands), the Netherlands submitted its final list of reservations and notifications in pursuance to Articles 28(4), 28(5), 29(1) and 29(2) of the MLI. Signing of the MLI is the first step to demonstrate a jurisdiction's intent to implement anti-BEPS measures, whereas provisions of the MLI take effect only when MLI is ratified and enters into force for that jurisdiction.

31. Since the MLI and CTAs must be applied and interpreted side by side, in cases in which their provisions conflict, the provisions of MLI supersede or prevail over those of the CTAs to the extent of their incompatibility.

32. *Flexible nature of MLI*: The objective of the treaty makers was to provide a high level of flexibility in the MLI, so that, despite their different tax policies and economic interests, all States and non-State jurisdictions interested in fighting BEPS could join the instrument to swiftly implement the tax treaty-related BEPS measures into their tax treaty network. As a result, the MLI, to a great extent, favours the sovereignty of States and envisages universal participation to eliminate BEPS practices. The flexible[51] nature of MLI is demonstrated by the following:

(a) The Parties to the MLI are at liberty to specify the tax treaties to which the Convention applies.
(b) The Parties to the MLI may at any time expand the scope[52] of application of the MLI by notifying additional tax treaties as CTAs, as MLI does not have any time limits for producing new notifications.
(c) A jurisdiction may not notify all its tax treaties as CTAs to enable separate negotiation on bilateral basis or such treaties already incorporate and implement BEPS measures.[53]
(d) MLI allows its Parties to conclude subsequent modifications to the CTAs, even if those modifications relate to provisions already modified through the MLI. This flexibility in the MLI is provided as jurisdictions would always like to retain their sovereignty and never give up their liberty to conclude international agreements modifying existing ones.
(e) Parties to the MLI can also notify tax treaties not[54] yet in force as CTAs under the MLI.
(f) The following mechanisms embedded in the MLI accord flexibility to it:
    - Opting-in mechanisms offering Parties the possibility to take on additional commitments.

51. Refer Explanatory Statement to the MLI, para. 14.
52. *Id.*, para. 303.
53. *Id.*, para. 26.
54. *Id.*, para. 32.

- A choice among alternative provisions.
- Exclusionary or opting-out mechanisms (reservations) allowing for the exclusion of legal effects of certain provisions, including flexibility with respect to opting-out provisions that relate to minimum standards only in limited circumstances, such as where a Party's CTAs already meet that minimum standard. Where a minimum standard can be satisfied in multiple alternative ways, the MLI does not give preference to a particular way of meeting the minimum standard.

(g) Parties having taken reservations at the time of ratification of MLI may subsequently withdraw the same.

(h) The MLI contains provisions to enable the instrument itself getting modified and amended by convening a CoP.

(i) Any Party may, at any time, withdraw from the MLI by means of a notification to the Depositary (Secretary General of the OECD).

33. A Party, while notifying a tax treaty as a CTA, must also notify all the Amending Protocols or accompanying instruments thereto, so as to avoid any confusion regarding the scope and content of the CTA modified through the MLI.[55]

34. Treaty-by-treaty opt-ins, alternative provisions and reservations are, in general, not permitted under the MLI. However, to avoid that provisions of CTAs that already counter BEPS practices are modified through the MLI, the ad hoc Group created categories of reservations based on objectively defined characteristics.[56] The effects of reservations based on objectively defined characteristics are subject to the notifications provided for in Article 28(8) of the MLI, which lays down that reservations enumerated therein will apply only to the provisions of the CTAs duly notified by the reserving Party. Such reservations would not apply to any CTA which is not included in the lists required by Article 28(8) of the MLI.[57]

35. The application of MLI does not extend over the following aspects:

(a) MLI does not change the objective scope of the CTAs. All CTAs, modified by the MLI provisions, will continue to apply to the taxes defined therein. That is why tax treaties can be notified as CTAs even if they cover other taxes in addition to income tax, i.e. capital taxes, taxes on capital gains, inheritance taxes and gift taxes.

(b) MLI does not change the territorial or geographical[58] scope of the CTAs.

55. *Id.*, para. 33.
56. Refer Nathalie Bravo's 'A Multilateral Instrument for Updating the Tax Treaty Network' IBFD Doctoral Series 52, p. 227.
57. Refer Explanatory Statement to the MLI, para. 281.
58. *Id.*, para. 31.

36. *Role of Explanatory Statement to the MLI*: In order to explain the MLI provisions to all concerned stakeholders, OECD has also released an Explanatory Statement[59] to the MLI, which was prepared and adopted by the ad hoc Group (including the Subgroup on Arbitration) on 24 November 2016 along with the MLI text. The Explanatory Statement can also be viewed as a tool facilitating uniform and harmonised interpretation of the provisions of the MLI. It, therefore, reflects the agreed understanding of the negotiators with respect to the MLI. It includes descriptions of the types of treaty provisions which are intended to be covered and the ways in which they are intended to be modified. While this Explanatory Statement is intended to clarify the operation of the MLI to modify CTAs, it is not intended to address the interpretation[60] of the underlying BEPS measures (except with respect to the mandatory binding arbitration provision contained in Articles 18 through 26). The Explanatory Statement and the BEPS Action Reports may be classified as interpretation material under Article 31(4) or Article 32 of the Vienna Convention. Neither has a legally binding character; however, both merit immense significance when engaging in interpretation of the MLI.

37. The effect of each of the provisions of the MLI on the CTA is established through compatibility clauses, notification clauses, options and reservations which are explained in the following paragraphs.

3.2.1 Compatibility Clauses

38. The main object and purpose of the MLI is to modify the CTAs in an effort to eliminate BEPS opportunities; it is logical that its compatibility clauses claim prevalence of the MLI. That is why, in order to implement BEPS measures, the MLI provides for compatibility clauses, which define the relationship of the provisions of the MLI and the provisions of the CTAs. The ad hoc Group of the MLI included a compatibility clause in each of the substantive provisions of the MLI. There are two exceptions to this rule:

(1) Article 15 of the MLI (Definition of a Person Closely Related to an Enterprise) applies together with the relevant provisions of the MLI, i.e. Articles 12, 13 and 14 of the MLI to be read with CTA provisions.
(2) Compatibility clause dealing with mandatory binding arbitration procedure, which is established in Article 26 but refers to the whole Part VI of the MLI, as Part VI of the MLI operates as a single cohesive provision.[61]

39. The compatibility clauses of the MLI are formed by two main elements:

(i) First, the compatibility clauses describe the provisions of the CTAs that are subject to modification. This was done due to the following reasons:

59. *Id.*, para. 11.
60. *Id.*, para. 12.
61. *Id.*, para. 20.

(a) References to article number of a CTA may have created confusion as in many treaties enumeration styles, wording and scopes vary for similar provisions. This is because the MLI modifies not only those CTAs that follow OECD MTC but also those CTAs that follow the United Nations (UN) Model or CTAs that do not follow either of these two models.
(b) It allows for the exclusion of certain provisions of the CTAs that might deal with a similar or related matter in a different way than the MLI that treaty makers agreed not to modify.
(c) It provides certainty to stakeholders who are able to clearly identify which specific provisions of the CTAs are being modified by the MLI.

(ii) Second, the compatibility clauses prescribe the effects of the provisions they relate to over the provisions of the CTAs. In all the cases set out below, the existing agreement between the contracting jurisdictions as set out in the bilateral tax treaty is modified by the MLI. Accordingly, there is no difference in the legal[62] functioning of the MLI provisions described below:
(a) Wording used in the compatibility clause 'in place of' implies that a provision of the MLI replaces the provisions of the CTA.
(b) Wording used in the compatibility clause 'applies to' or 'modifies' implies that a provision of the MLI changes the application of the provisions of the CTA without replacing them.
(c) Wording used in the compatibility clause 'in the absence of' implies that a provision of the MLI supplements the provisions of the CTAs that do not contain a similar provision.
(d) Wording used in the compatibility clause 'in place of or in the absence of' implies that a provision of the MLI replaces, supersedes or supplements the provisions of the CTA, depending upon certain conditions.

3.2.1.1 Role of Compatibility Clauses in Detail

40. Although compatibility clauses have been discussed above, it is important to delve deeper into their nature, role and application, as they constitute a very important connection between the provisions of MLI vis-à-vis the CTAs and prescribe the effects of the provisions they relate to over the provisions of the CTAs. The compatibility clauses, in many ways, are the cornerstones to enable seamless reading of provisions of the CTAs modified by the MLI.

41. On simultaneously applying the provisions of two international treaties to at least one of the Parties in the same circumstances, such provisions may accumulate (align) or conflict (incompatible) with each other. Accumulation (alignment) happens if both treaties can be applied without generating contradictions, either because one of the

62. Refer Note by the OECD Directorate for Legal Affairs http://www.oecd.org/tax/treaties/legal-note-on-the-functioning-of-the-MLI-under-public-international-law.pdf (paras 19, 20) accessed on 23 July 2020.

treaties complements the rights or obligations set out in the other or because it confirms them. Conflict (incompatibility) between the two treaties happens when the fulfilment of the obligations or exercise of the rights under one treaty, potentially, results in infringement of the other treaty.[63]

42. Rules on application of successive treaties relating to the same subject matter are governed by the provisions of Article 30 of the Vienna Convention. Since MLI provisions are to be read side by side with the CTA provisions, a reader should be able to achieve a harmonious reading of the provisions of the two treaties, which has been made possible by the 'compatibility clauses' enshrined in the MLI. Provisions that claim that a treaty is subject to or prevails over others are known as 'compatibility clauses'. The International Law Commission (ILC) defines a compatibility clause[64] as 'a clause intended to regulate the relation between the provisions of the treaty and those of another treaty or of any other treaty relating to the matters with which the treaty deals'.

43. *Lex Posterior Principle*: If a treaty neither terminates an earlier treaty in its entirety nor defines its relationship with other treaties through compatibility clauses, the *lex posterior*[65] principle established in Article 30(3), (4) of the Vienna Convention applies. According to the residual rule of the *lex posterior* principle, if the provisions of both treaties cannot be implemented at the same time, the effects and consequences under the latter treaty must be implemented, giving them preference over the effects and consequences of the earlier treaty.

44. *Lex Specialis Principle*: As a result of the application of the *lex specialis*[66] principle (a recognised general principle of public international law), the more specific rule prevails over the more general rule, despite the fact that the more special rule is the earlier of the rules. The rationale behind the *lex specialis* principle as a tool to resolve a conflict of treaties lies in the belief that the 'special norm reflects most closely, precisely and/or strongly the consent or expression of will of the states in question'. Thus, as the special rule is the most specific one and approaches the subject at hand the closest, it should be given preference. However, the MLI and its Explanatory Statement do not[67] refer to the *lex specialis* principle, as the provisions of the MLI and CTA have the same degree of generality.

45. Since MLI provisions are to be read side by side with the CTA provisions, provisions of these two instruments may accumulate or conflict or do so partially[68] as explained hereunder:

---

63. Refer Nathalie Bravo's 'A Multilateral Instrument for Updating the Tax Treaty Network' IBFD Doctoral Series 52, p. 102.
64. *Id.*, p. 107.
65. *Id.*, p. 110.
66. *Id.*, p. 114.
67. *Id.*, pp. 149-150.
68. *Id.*, p. 116.

(1) A provision of the MLI may accumulate with a provision of the CTA in the following two situations:
   (i) when MLI confirms the provision already contained in the CTA; and
   (ii) when MLI adds or complements the provision of the CTA.
(2) On the other hand, a provision of the MLI may conflict with a provision of a CTA when the solutions offered by them provide different results.

46. Under the MLI, the compatibility clauses[69] prescribe the effects[70] of the provisions they relate to over the provisions of the CTAs. These are discussed in detail in Table 2.

Table 2 Description of Operation of Compatibility Clauses

S.N.	*Compatibility Clause*	*Description of Operation*
1	Compatibility clauses that provide that the MLI applies 'in place of' an existing provision of a CTA	- Where a provision of the MLI applies only 'in place of' an existing provision of a CTA, the provision is intended to replace an existing provision if one exists, and is not intended to apply if a provision does not exist in the CTA - Even though, theoretically, in certain cases, the provision of the CTA could accumulate with the provision of the MLI, the compatibility clauses of this type avoid accumulation by prescribing that the provision of the MLI replaces[71] the provision of the CTA
2	Compatibility clauses that provide that the MLI 'applies to' or 'modifies' an existing provision of a CTA	- Where a provision of the MLI 'applies to' or 'modifies' an existing provision of the CTA, the provision of the MLI is intended to change the application of an existing provision without replacing it, and therefore can only apply if there is an existing provision - Accordingly, these MLI provisions can only apply if there is an existing provision in the CTA, as described in the compatibility clause - The provisions of the MLI containing the compatibility clauses that prescribe that they apply to/modify provisions of the CTAs do not deal with exactly the same subject matter as per

69. Refer Explanatory Statement to the MLI, para. 15.
70. Refer Note by the OECD Directorate for Legal Affairs http://www.oecd.org/tax/treaties/legal-note-on-the-functioning-of-the-MLI-under-public-international-law.pdf (para. 22) accessed on 23 July 2020.
71. Refer Nathalie Bravo's 'A Multilateral Instrument for Updating the Tax Treaty Network' IBFD Doctoral Series 52, pp. 129-130.

S.N.	*Compatibility Clause*	*Description of Operation*
		provisions of the CTAs described therein; they only deal with a related matter. Thus, the provision of the MLI can only change the scope[72] of application of the provisions of the CTA
3	Compatibility clauses that provide that the MLI applies 'in the absence of' an existing provision of a CTA	– Where a provision of the MLI applies only 'in the absence of' an existing provision, the provision of the MLI will apply only in cases where all Contracting Jurisdictions notify the absence of an existing provision of the CTA – MLI provisions are intended to apply only when the CTAs do not contain the provisions described in the compatibility clauses
4	Compatibility clauses that provide that the MLI applies 'in place of or in the absence of' an existing provision of a CTA	– Where a provision of the MLI applies 'in place of or in the absence of' an existing provision of the CTA, the provision of the MLI will apply in all cases – If all Contracting Jurisdictions notify the existence of an existing provision, that provision will be replaced by the provision of the MLI (to the extent described in the relevant compatibility clause) – Where the Contracting Jurisdictions do not notify the existence of a provision, the provision of the MLI will still apply. If there is in fact a relevant existing provision which has not been notified by all Contracting Jurisdictions, the provision of the MLI will prevail over that existing provision of the CTA, superseding it to the extent that it is incompatible with the relevant provision of the MLI – If there is no existing provision, the provision of the MLI will, in effect, be added to the CTA

47. Meaning in MLI of 'replace' and 'supersede' – Though the literal meaning of these terms appears to be the same, there is a very thin line dividing these two terms:

(1) MLI to replace – If the provisions of MLI contain a compatibility clause that prescribes that it applies 'in place of' a provision of a CTA, the provision of MLI replaces that provision of the CTA; i.e., it impedes the application of the whole provision of the CTA that deals with the same subject matter.
(2) MLI to supersede – If the provision of the MLI contains a compatibility clause that prescribes that it applies 'in place of or in the absence of' a provision of a CTA and not all the Parties notify that a similar provision

72. *Id.*, pp. 130-131.

exists or does not exist in the CTA, it does not impede the application of the provision of the CTA. Therefore, in these cases, the provisions of the MLI and the CTA will apply, to the extent that they are compatible and the provision of MLI does not replace that of the CTA. In these cases, apparently, the compatibility clause does not resolve the potential conflict of treaties, and to achieve this objective, recourse[73] needs to be taken to the *lex posterior*[74] principle enshrined in Article 30(3) of the Vienna Convention. The exact result of resolving a conflict of treaties under the *lex posterior* principle would depend on the scope and meaning of the provision of the CTA, as explained hereunder:

- In some cases, the provision of the MLI and the provision of the CTA may totally conflict, and as a result of the *lex posterior* principle, only the provision of the MLI would be applicable.
- In some other cases, the provision of the MLI and the provision of the CTA may partially conflict; consequently, the provision of the CTA would be partially applicable, depending on the extent of its compatibility with the provision of the MLI.
- In the remaining cases, if the CTA does not contain a similar provision, as a result of the *lex posterior* principle, the provision of the MLI would be added.

However, the term 'supersede' cannot be equated[75] with the application of the *lex posterior* principle. If the term 'supersede' was to be equated with the application of the *lex posterior* principle, the MLI will, in some cases, fail to produce its effects and thus will fail to achieve its object and purpose of modifying CTAs, as would happen when a CTA is notified (as an additional notification) post entry into force (EIF) of the MLI itself. Thus, in this case, for applying the compatibility clause 'in place of or in the absence of' a provision of a CTA, when not all the Parties notify that a similar provision exists or does not exist in the CTA, the term 'supersede' must then be understood as claiming that the MLI prevails over the CTA regardless of whether the *lex posterior* principle can be applied to resolve the potential conflict of treaty provisions or not. Hence, in this case, even if the CTA is a later treaty in force vis-à-vis the MLI, the object and purpose of the MLI of modifying the CTAs to implement BEPS measures must prevail over the *lex posterior* principle.

48. A bird's-eye view of the types of compatibility clauses incorporated in various articles of the MLI is provided in Table 3.

73. Refer Explanatory Statement to the MLI, para. 16.
74. Refer Note by the OECD Directorate for Legal Affairs http://www.oecd.org/tax/treaties/legal-note-on-the-functioning-of-the-MLI-under-public-international-law.pdf (para. 16) accessed on 23 July 2020.
75. Refer Nathalie Bravo's 'A Multilateral Instrument for Updating the Tax Treaty Network' IBFD Doctoral Series 52, pp. 140-141.

Table 3 Article-Wise Incorporation of Compatibility Clauses

S.N.	*Article*	*Title of Article*	*Para Defining Compatibility Clause*	*Provision in the MLI Article to Which the Compatibility Clause Applies*	*Compatibility Clause Applicable*			
					'in place of'	*'applies to' or 'modifies'*	*'in the absence of'*	*'in place of or in the absence of'*
1	3	Transparent Entities	4	– Applies to paragraph 1 (as modified by paragraph 3) of Article 3				√
2	4	Dual Resident Entities	2	– Applies to paragraph 1 of Article 4				√
3	5	Application of Methods for Elimination of Double Taxation	3	– Applies to Option A		√		
			5	– Applies to Option B		√		
			7	– Applies to Option C	√			
4	6	Purpose of a CTA	2	– Applies to paragraph 1 of Article 6				√
5	7	Prevention of Treaty Abuse	2	– Applies to paragraph 1 of Article 7 which is the PPT rule				√

S.N.	Article	Title of Article	Para Defining Compatibility Clause	Provision in the MLI Article to Which the Compatibility Clause Applies	*Compatibility Clause Applicable*			
					'in place of'	*'applies to' or 'modifies'*	*'in the absence of'*	*'in place of or in the absence of'*
			5	– Applies to paragraph 4 of Article 7 which pertains to establishing discretionary relief as an additional paragraph to the PPT rule		√		
			14	– Applies to paragraphs 8-13 of Article 7 which is the S-LoB				√
6	8	Dividend Transfer Transactions	2	– Applies only to minimum holding period in paragraph 1 of Article 8				√
7	9	Capital Gains from Alienation of Shares Deriving Their Value Principally from Immovable Property	2	– Applies to paragraph 1 of Article 9				√
			5	– Applies to paragraph 4 of Article 9				√
8	10	Anti-abuse Rule for PEs Situated in Third Jurisdictions	4	– Applies to paragraphs 1 through 3 of Article 10				√

S.N.	Article	Title of Article	Para Defining Compatibility Clause	Provision in the MLI Article to Which the Compatibility Clause Applies	*Compatibility Clause Applicable*			
					'in place of'	'applies to' or 'modifies'	'in the absence of'	'in place of or in the absence of'
9	11	Application of Tax Agreements to Restrict a Party's Right to Tax Its Own Residents	2	– Saving Clause – Applies to paragraph 1 of Article 11				√
10	12	Artificial Avoidance of PE Status Through Commissionaire Arrangements & Similar Strategies	3(a)	– Applies to paragraph 1 (DAPE)	√			
			3(b)	– Applies to paragraph 2 (Agent of an Independent Status)	√			
11	13	Artificial Avoidance of PE Status Through Specific Activity Exemptions	5(a)	– Applies to Option A or B	√			
			5(b)	– Applies to paragraph 4 providing anti-fragmentation Rule (applies by default)		√		
12	14	Splitting-Up of Contracts	2	– Applies to paragraph 1 of Article 14				√
13	15	Definition of a Person Closely Related to an Enterprise	– Applies in cases where Articles 12, 13 and 14 of MLI apply					

S.N.	*Article*	*Title of Article*	*Para Defining Compatibility Clause*	*Provision in the MLI Article to Which the Compatibility Clause Applies*	*Compatibility Clause Applicable*			
					'in place of'	*'applies to' or 'modifies'*	*'in the absence of'*	*'in place of or in the absence of'*
14	16	Mutual Agreement Procedure	4(a)(i)	– Applies to 1st sentence of paragraph 1 of Article 16				√
			4(a)(ii) – 1st limb*	– Applies to 2nd sentence of paragraph 1 of Article 16 (where the time period is less than three years)	√			
			4(a)(ii) – 2nd limb*	– Applies to 2nd sentence of paragraph 1 of Article 16 (where there is no mention of time period)			√	
			4(b)(i)	– Applies to 1st sentence of paragraph 2 of Article 16			√	
			4(b)(ii)	– Applies to 2nd sentence of paragraph 2 of Article 16			√	

S.N.	Article	Title of Article	Para Defining Compatibility Clause	Provision in the MLI Article to Which the Compatibility Clause Applies	*Compatibility Clause Applicable*			
					'in place of'	*'applies to' or 'modifies'*	*'in the absence of'*	*'in place of or in the absence of'*
			4(c)(i)	– Applies to 1st sentence of paragraph 3 of Article 16			√	
			4(c)(ii)	– Applies to 2nd sentence of paragraph 3 of Article 16			√	
15	17	Corresponding Adjustments	2	– Applies to paragraph 1 of Article 17				√
16	26	Arbitration – Compatibility	1	– Applies to Part VI				√

* Article 16(4)(a)(ii) pertains to the compatibility clause in respect of the second sentence of paragraph 1 of Article 16 of the MLI on MAP. This compatibility clause is unique in itself, as it contains two different compatibility clauses, i.e. 'in place of' or 'in the absence of' which apply separately depending on the CTA provisions which will get modified. To elaborate, 'in place of' shall apply where the treaty provisions equivalent to the second sentence of paragraph 1 of Article 16 contain time period shorter than three years, whereas, 'in the absence of' shall apply where the treaty provisions equivalent to the second sentence of paragraph 1 of Article 16 contain no time period and hence, time period of three years shall get introduced. The provisions contained in Article 16(4)(a)(ii) of the MLI are as below:

ii) The second sentence of paragraph 1 shall apply *in place of* provisions of a Covered Tax Agreement that provide that a case referred to in the first sentence of paragraph 1 must be presented within a specific time period that is shorter than three years from the first notification of the action resulting in taxation not in accordance with the provisions of the Covered Tax Agreement, or *in the absence of* a provision of a Covered Tax Agreement describing the time period within which such a case must be presented.

3.2.2 Notification Clauses

49. The MLI provides different types of notifications that the Parties must send to the Depositary, who, in turn, is required to communicate them to the rest of the Parties/Signatories. Thus, the notifications allow dissemination of commitments adopted by the Parties/Signatories under the MLI among themselves, through the Depositary.

50. The notification clauses under various articles of the MLI require that each Party to the MLI identifies the article and paragraph of the CTA that are within the scope of a compatibility clause. These notifications ensure that Parties agree on which provisions of their CTA are or are not subject to modification by the MLI. These notifications also enable various other stakeholders to identify the provisions of the CTA being modified by the MLI. An inadvertent omission of notification of existing provisions can be addressed by making an additional notification pursuant to Article 29(6)[76] of the MLI.

51. Notification clauses were introduced in the MLI to ensure clarity and transparency about existing provisions of CTAs that are within the scope of the compatibility clauses. When an MLI provision modifies specific types of existing provisions described in compatibility clauses, Parties are generally required to make a notification to identify which existing provisions of CTAs are within the scope of compatibility clauses. Exception to this rule, for example, can be found in Article 6(3) of MLI, where Parties are required to notify under paragraph 6 a list of CTAs that does not contain a provision described in paragraph 3 of Article 6 of MLI.

52. The notification clauses ensure clarity and transparency about the existing or absent provisions in CTAs that are modified by the MLI. While the notifications sometimes trigger the application of the MLI, the extent to which the MLI modifies existing provisions of CTAs is always as provided in the compatibility clauses. This means that the compatibility clauses in the MLI interact with the notification clauses also, included in each substantive provision of the MLI. As an illustration, notifications made under Article 12(5) by a pair of Contracting Jurisdictions only trigger the application of the MLI. The extent to which the MLI would modify the existing provision notified (i.e., provisions based on Article 5(5) of the OECD MTC or on Article 5(5)(a) UN Model Convention) would be limited by the compatibility clause in Article 12(3)(a). In this case, the MLI would only operate on an existing provision as set out in Article 12(3)(a) of the MLI. For existing provisions based on the UN Model Convention, Article 5(5)(b) would not be modified by the MLI, even if a pair of Contracting Jurisdictions would notify Article 5(5) in its entirety.[77]

53. Relationship between compatibility-notification clauses and the result they produce is depicted in Table 4.

76. Refer Explanatory Statement to the MLI, para. 18.
77. *Id.*, para. 163.

Table 4 Relationship Between Compatibility–Notification Clauses & Impact

Compatibility Clause	*Notification Clause*	*Impact*
'in place of'	Matching notification required for provision to apply	- MLI provision to apply if provision in CTA exists - MLI provision not to apply if no provision in CTA exists
'applies to' or 'modifies'	Matching notification required for provision to apply	- MLI provision changes application of relevant CTA provision without replacing it
'in the absence of'	Matching notification required for provision to apply	- MLI to add a provision in the absence/omission of the same in a CTA
'in place of or in the absence of'	Matching notification	- MLI provision will replace (effect same as 'in place of' compatibility clause) the CTA provision or supplement (effect same as 'in the absence of' compatibility clause) the CTA provision
	Mismatch in notification	- Supersession of MLI provisions to the extent of incompatibility with the CTA provisions. In essence, supersession effectively leads to application of the new MLI provisions - Thus, MLI provision will apply in all cases of this compatibility clause

3.2.3 Opting-In Mechanisms

54. The BEPS Action 15 Report[78] has recommended using opting-in mechanisms under the MLI. Opt-in (or contracting-in) mechanisms are defined 'as provisions stipulating that the Parties to a treaty may accept obligations which, in the absence of explicit acceptance, would not be automatically applicable to them'. The goal of such mechanisms is to allow Parties which are ready to do so to commit to further action in pursuit of the objectives of the treaty and have the purpose of enlarging or increasing the obligations of the declaring State in comparison to what is generally expected from the Parties to a multilateral treaty.

55. The reason for providing optional treaty provisions in the MLI is that in some cases, the work on BEPS resulted in a main provision that could be supplemented with an additional provision.[79]

78. Action 15: BEPS 2015 Final Report, OECD/G20 Base Erosion and Profit Shifting Project, pp. 46 and 47.
79. Refer Explanatory Statement to the MLI, para. 14.

56. Under the MLI, the following opt-in provisions have been incorporated, providing multiple alternative ways to address a particular BEPS issue:

(a) Notification of CTAs – The ‘positive list’ approach adopted by the ad hoc Group has characteristics similar to an opting-in mechanism. Only if all the Contracting States of a tax treaty send a notification listing the tax treaty as being a CTA, will it get notified. In addition, Article 29(5) allows the Parties to extend the list of tax treaties, as being covered as CTAs.
(b) Article 6(3) of the MLI – The language provided in Article 6(3) of the MLI can be added to the new preamble language provided in Article 6(1) of the MLI. Although both Article 6(1) and 6(3) are outputs of the BEPS Action 6 Report, the additional language contained in Article 6(3) of the MLI is not part of the minimum standard set out in BEPS Action 6 Report.
(c) Article 7(3)-(5) of the MLI – According to Article 7(3) of the MLI, Parties may choose to apply the discretionary relief provision to their tax treaties, as the optional provision is not part of the minimum standard set out in the BEPS Action 6 Report; hence, the Parties to the MLI are not obliged to opt in to it. For the said optional provision to apply to a CTA, all Parties are required to opt in to its application by making a notification under Article 7(17)(b) of MLI.
(d) Article 7(6)-(13) of the MLI – Article 7 of the MLI allows the Parties to opt in for the Simplified Limitation on Benefits (S-LoB) rule in addition to the PPT rule to deny treaty benefits in inappropriate circumstances. The general rule contained in Article 7(6) of the MLI is that the S-LoB will apply only when all the Parties to a CTA have opted in for the said provision. In addition, Parties have also been provided the option to make a statement in paragraph (17)(a) under Article 7 that while such Parties accept the application of paragraph 1 alone as an interim measure, it intends where possible to adopt a LOB provision, in addition to or in replacement of paragraph 1, through bilateral negotiation.
(e) Article 9(3)-(5) of the MLI – This provision was established to modify CTAs that do not contain a treaty provision similar or equivalent to Article 13(4) of the OECD MTC (2014) dealing with gains derived by a resident of a Contracting State from the alienation of shares or other rights of participation in an entity situated in the other Contracting State when such shares or rights derived a certain part of their value from immovable property. The said complementary provision modifies CTAs only when the corresponding Parties have opted in to the provision.

57. In addition, under the MLI, the following opt-in provisions have also been incorporated following the work resulting in a main provision that could be supplemented with an additional provision:

(a) Mandatory binding arbitration procedure under the MLI – It is established in Part VI of the MLI, i.e. Articles 18-26. As set out in Article 18 of the MLI, Part VI applies only when all Parties to a CTA have opted in to it. The adoption of the opting-in approach allowed that a subgroup of the members of the ad hoc Group could be established with the purpose of only discussing the mandatory binding provision. The Subgroup on Arbitration discussed in detail the form and substance that the provisions dealing with the mandatory binding arbitration procedure should have.

(b) Within the rules provided in the MLI concerning the mandatory binding arbitration procedure, two other optional provisions can be found as below:

   (i) Article 23(4), (5) of the MLI – As per these provisions, if opted in, the CAs of the Parties involved in a mandatory binding arbitration procedure must ensure that the person that presented the case and their legal advisers agree not to disclose any information received from the CAs or the arbitral panel during the procedure. If the person that presented the case or their legal advisers disclose information after the request for arbitration has been filed, the procedure shall get terminated. As per provisions contained in Article 23(4), this optional provision applies to a CTA even if only one of its Parties has notified its willingness to opt in. This is a solitary case of unilateral opt-in provision. Raison d'etre of the same lies in importance of confidentiality attached to the mandatory binding arbitration procedure.

   (ii) Article 24(1), (2) of the MLI – In case, Parties opt in to Article 24(1), (2), a decision of the arbitral panel will not be binding and, thus, may not be implemented if the CAs agree on a different resolution within three calendar months after the arbitral decision has been issued. This optional provision, in contrast to the preceding one, applies only if all the Parties to a CTA have notified their willingness to opt in.

58. The notifications of the opt-in provisions are expressly covered/included in Article 29(1)(e), (f), (h), (p), (q) and (r). In addition, Article 28(2)(a) expressly refers to the case in which a Party to the MLI decides to adopt the optional Part VI establishing the mandatory binding arbitration procedure after it has ratified the MLI. Further, Article 29(6) of the MLI enables Parties to make additional notifications pursuant to Article 29(1)(b) through (s) by means of a notification to the Depositary. Thus, Parties to the MLI may, at any time, i.e. even after deposit of instrument of ratification, notify in written form to the Depositary, their decision to opt in to any of the optional provisions contained in the MLI.

59. Article 28(2)(a) of the MLI shows that the ad hoc Group had the intention of allowing Parties to undertake additional commitments by opting in to the optional provisions after the instrument entered into force. This conclusion applies not only to Part VI establishing the mandatory binding arbitration procedure but also to all other optional provisions provided for in the MLI, as all of them are covered by Article 29(6), which allows Parties to make additional notifications[80] after the time of signature or after the time of depositing the instrument of ratification. In this sense, a Party to the MLI that may initially be apprehensive about the application of a certain optional provision may decide to opt in to that provision in the future if, after evaluation of practical operation of that provision, it considers that the same may be suitable for its tax treaty relations. The ad hoc Group had kept this window open as this will enlarge the treaty obligations of such Parties to avoid BEPS, which in effect is the main object and purpose of the MLI.

3.2.4 Alternative Provisions

60. The BEPS Action 15 Report[81] has also suggested the use of alternative provisions in the MLI. The use of alternative provisions in treaties is already provided in Article 17(2) of the Vienna Convention, which states as below:

> The consent of a State to be bound by a treaty which permits a choice between differing provisions is effective only if it is made clear to which of the provisions the consent relates.

61. The MLI incorporates the following two types of alternative provisions:

(1) Article 5(1), (2), (4) and (6) of the MLI – These provisions provide the Parties with three alternatives to avoid cases of double non-taxation for States that have adopted the exemption method for eliminating double taxation, because, as anticipated by the ad hoc Group, some of the treaty-related BEPS measures have resulted in multiple alternative ways to address a particular BEPS issue.

(2) Article 13(1)-(3) of the MLI – These provisions provide two different alternatives to the Parties to deal with the artificial avoidance of PE status through the specific activity exemptions. In this case, the reason for providing alternative provisions does not relate to multiple alternative ways to counter BEPS practices, but to the interpretation that Parties give to the auxiliary or preparatory requirement that the activities listed in treaty provisions similar or equivalent to Article 5(4) of the OECD MTC (2014) must fulfil to be considered as exceptions to the PE status.

62. The ad hoc Group did not expressly indicate in the MLI whether Parties can choose alternative provisions after ratification (it does not mean that Parties can 'change' the application of alternative provisions if they have already exercised their prerogative at the time of ratification when they submitted their final position to the Depositary).

---

80. Refer Nathalie Bravo's 'A Multilateral Instrument for Updating the Tax Treaty Network' IBFD Doctoral Series 52, pp. 187-188.
81. Action 15: BEPS 2015 Final Report, OECD/G20 Base Erosion and Profit Shifting Project, pp. 45 and 46.

However, based on the fact that Article 29(6) of the MLI allows Parties to make additional notifications after ratification and the fact that the notifications regarding the alternative provisions are listed among the allowed additional notifications in Article 29(1)(d), (l), it appears that Parties can notify[82] their choice of alternative options after the EIF of the MLI.

3.2.5 Opting-Out Mechanisms (Reservations)

63. In accordance with Article 2(1)(d) of the Vienna Convention, the term 'reservation' means as below:

> (d) 'reservation' means a unilateral statement, however phrased or named, made by a State, when signing, ratifying, accepting, approving or acceding to a treaty, whereby it purports to exclude or to modify the legal effect of certain provisions of the treaty in their application to that State.

64. Even though MLI provides for detailed rules on reservations, they are largely inspired by Articles 19-23 of the Vienna Convention. Although reservations are unilateral acts, they produce their legal effects only after they have been accepted, expressly or implicitly by another Party to the treaty. The reserving Party need not explain the reasons behind a reservation, as it is its sovereign right; hence, reservations create flexibility and enable States to conclude multilateral treaties, like the MLI, that they otherwise would have been reluctant or unable to sign.

65. The BEPS Action 15 Report has allowed jurisdictions to make only those reservations that are listed in the substantive provisions, to help them tailor their commitment[83] with regard to other Parties based on their tax policies.

66. Once a reservation has been established, it excludes or modifies the application of the treaty provisions for the reserving jurisdiction and the accepting jurisdiction. As a result of reservation made in accordance with Article 28(1) of the MLI, the provision of the MLI to which the reservation relates does not apply to all CTAs of the reserving Party or of a subset of them. The effects of reservations under Article 28(1) of the MLI are generally reciprocal and symmetrical[84] unless provided otherwise.

67. The coordinating effect of the MLI gets accentuated if it is taken into account that the reservations apply to all CTAs of a reserving jurisdiction. Reservations have the purpose of excluding or modifying the legal effects of treaty provisions. Therefore, reservations reduce rather than increase treaty obligations.

---

82. Refer Nathalie Bravo's 'A Multilateral Instrument for Updating the Tax Treaty Network' IBFD Doctoral Series 52, p. 197.
83. Action 15: BEPS 2015 Final Report, OECD/G20 Base Erosion and Profit Shifting Project, pp. 19 and 22.
84. Refer Explanatory Statement to the MLI, para. 270.

68. The reservations listed in various substantive provisions of the MLI are the only authorised opt-outs.[85] Some provisions were considered by the treaty makers as a core set of rules, i.e. the provisions that set the minimum standards, with permitted reservations being more limited than the rest of the provisions of the MLI. Parties to the MLI can only opt out of the core set of rules if their CTAs already contain a provision that satisfies the minimum standards or if they intend to adopt a provision or a practice that will satisfy the minimum standards.

69. *Withdrawal of reservations*: The rules of the MLI dealing with withdrawal and replacement of reservations are, by and large, inspired by Article 22 of the Vienna Convention. Since reservations are unilateral acts, they may be withdrawn without the consent of other Parties to the treaty. Under Article 28(9) of the MLI, Parties which have made reservations may withdraw it or replace it with a more limited reservation by means of a notification to the Depositary. A replacement of the reservation is possible if the Party limits or restricts the scope of original reservation. Withdrawal or replacement of reservations can be done at any time, with the aim that it allows Parties to further modify the CTAs through the MLI, which in turn has the larger aim to expand a Party's commitment to avoiding or countering BEPS. Hence, Parties having made a reservation for the entirety of an article not to be applied for all its CTAs may withdraw that reservation entirely, or replace it with a reservation solely with respect to certain CTAs, as permissible in that particular article. However, a reverse of this action is not permissible; i.e., a Party initially having made a reservation with respect to certain CTAs cannot replace it with an all-encompassing (full) reservation for the entirety of that article not to be applied to all its CTAs.[86] For a withdrawal or replacement of a reservation to produce its full effects, it is necessary that in the CTAs notified by the Party withdrawing reservation, other Parties have not made similar reservation. Hence, it is important to remember that under the matching reservation mechanism being followed in MLI, treaty provisions are automatically excluded or modified to the extent of reservation for both the reserving jurisdiction and the non-reserving jurisdiction, as if an identical reservation had been made by both these jurisdictions. Thus, if the other Party to a CTA has also made a reservation that excludes or modifies the application of the provision of the MLI to which the withdrawal or replacement of the reservation relates, the withdrawal or replacement of the reservation by the first Party will not produce its effects for that particular CTA.

70. Further, Post-ratification of MLI, a Party is not permitted to make new reservations, so as to maintain integrity and consistent application of the MLI, except under few circumstances mentioned as below:

(i) opting for a new CTA under Article 29(5) of MLI; or
(ii) a Party subsequently opts in for Part VI of MLI and is then allowed to make reservations pertaining to Part VI only.

85. Refer Nathalie Bravo's 'A Multilateral Instrument for Updating the Tax Treaty Network' IBFD Doctoral Series 52, p. 172.
86. Refer Explanatory Statement to the MLI, para. 282.

3.2.6 Instances of Asymmetrical Application of MLI Provisions

71. The MLI provisions have been so designed that the treaty provisions they apply alongside take effect symmetrically, except for the following instances having specific purposes:

(a) Article 5 of MLI provides for the asymmetrical application of the alternative options established therein. This means that if a Party decides one of the options of Article 5 to apply to its own residents, such an option will apply independently of whether the rest of the Parties to a CTA have chosen to apply the same, a different or none of the options. The ad hoc Group decided to accept the asymmetrical application of the alternative provisions based on the general practice commonplace in international tax law that in tax treaties, Contracting States choose[87] the method for the avoidance of double taxation that best suits their domestic tax policy.

(b) Article 7(7)(b) of MLI, wherein a Party is allowed to apply the S-LoB rule within a tax treaty relation even if not all of the other Parties to a CTA chose to apply it. The avenue for this asymmetrical application lies in BEPS Action 6 Report, which provides that the minimum standard can be met through three different mechanisms:
   (1) PPT rule alone;
   (2) PPT rule plus S-LoB rule; and
   (3) detailed LoB rule together with anti-conduit measures (not implemented through the MLI).

   Sub-paragraph (b) of Article 7(7)[88] allows Parties that choose to apply the PPT alone to permit the S-LoB Provision to be applied asymmetrically with respect to a CTA. Under sub-paragraph (b), a Contracting Jurisdiction to a CTA that chooses to apply the S-LoB Provision would apply the PPT and the S-LoB Provision in determining whether to grant the benefits of the CTA, while the other Contracting Jurisdiction that does not choose to apply the S-LoB Provision would apply the PPT alone in determining whether to grant treaty benefits. For this to happen, it is necessary that the Parties that do not opt in to the application of the S-LoB rule express, through a notification to the Depositary, that they accept the application of the S-LoB rule by the rest of the Parties to the CTA. In other words, the asymmetrical application of the S-LoB rule is only possible when all the Parties to the CTA reach a unanimous consent on the asymmetrical application of this rule.

(c) In Article 35(2) of MLI, use of the word 'solely' at the beginning of paragraph 2 is intended to make clear that this choice would apply asymmetrically and would apply only with respect to the application of paragraphs 1(a) and 5(a) of Article 35 by the Contracting Jurisdiction that opted for it.

---

87. *Id.*, para. 60.
88. *Id.*, para. 102.

(d) In Article 35(3) of MLI, in the same manner as Article 35(2), the word 'solely' is intended to make clear that this option may lead to asymmetrical entry into effect (EIE) of MLI's provisions between Contracting Jurisdictions.

3.3 PART I OF MLI: SCOPE AND INTERPRETATION OF TERMS

3.3.1 Article 1 of MLI: Scope of the Convention

72. Article 1 defines the scope of application of the MLI. The MLI modifies all DTAAs, referred to as CTAs, as defined in Article 2(1)(a) of the instrument. The Parties to the MLI may at any time expand the scope of application of the MLI by notifying[89] additional tax treaties.

73. In order to illustrate, Australia[90] has notified 42 DTAAs as CTAs under the MLI, including Australia-Austria DTAA, whereas Austria[91] has notified 38 DTAAs as CTAs under the MLI, but DTAA with Australia has not been notified therein. Hence, the Australia-Austria DTAA is outside the scope of the MLI. On the other hand, both Australia and the Netherlands[92] have notified their DTAA as CTA under the MLI; hence, Australia-Netherlands DTAA shall be within the scope of the MLI.

74. India[93] has notified 93 DTAAs as CTAs under the MLI; hence, for India, MLI will modify these 93 notified CTAs (subject to signing/ratification of MLI by the treaty partners and inclusion of India as a CTA by the respective treaty partners). India's DTAA with China[94] (in the MLI position submitted by China at the time of MLI signing, it has notified 101 DTAAs as CTAs) has not been notified under the MLI by both the Parties; hence, the India-China DTAA is outside the scope of MLI (as in the Amending Protocol signed by the two countries, notified on 17-07-2019,[95] anti-BEPS provisions have been duly incorporated in the India-China DTAA).

89. *Id.*, para. 303.
90. Refer Australia's Position under the MLI http://www.oecd.org/tax/treaties/beps-mli-position-australia-instrument-deposit.pdf.
91. Refer Austria's Position under the MLI http://www.oecd.org/tax/treaties/beps-mli-position-austria-instrument-deposit.pdf.
92. Refer The Netherlands' Position under the MLI http://www.oecd.org/tax/treaties/beps-mli-position-netherlands-instrument-deposit.pdf.
93. Refer India's Position under the MLI http://www.oecd.org/tax/treaties/beps-mli-position-india-instrument-deposit.pdf.
94. Refer China's Position under the MLI http://www.oecd.org/tax/treaties/beps-mli-position-china.pdf.
95. Refer Amending Protocol of India-China DTAA notified on 17 July 2019 https://www.incometaxindia.gov.in/Pages/international-taxation/dtaa.aspx accessed on 26 July 2020.

3.3.2 Article 2 of MLI: Interpretation of Terms

75. Article 2 defines certain terms like CTA, Party, Contracting Jurisdiction and Signatory. In addition, there are certain definitions provided in Article 7 (concerning S-LoB) and Article 15 (definition of 'a person closely related to an enterprise'). The placement of these definitions assumes its own importance as definitions provided in Article 2 pertain to the whole instrument, including its procedural rules; whereas, definitions in Articles 7 and 15 apply to the substantive provisions of the MLI. Terms defined by the MLI do not need any further interpretation. Any definition of a term given to it by the MLI overrides any other definition the term may have while applying the provisions of a CTA as modified by the MLI. Like any other international treaty, the MLI should be interpreted in accordance with Articles 31 and 32 of the Vienna Convention.

Article 2(1)(a)

76. A covered CTA under Article 2(1)(a) of the MLI is the one that both Parties have notified as an agreement that they want the MLI to modify. The definition of CTA contains the following two conditions, both of which must be satisfied:

(1) the treaty must be concluded with the intention to avoiding double taxation with respect to taxes on income and it must be in force between two or more Parties; and
(2) all Parties must have sent a notification to the Depositary listing the treaty for the avoidance of double taxation, and any amending or accompanying instruments thereto, as a CTA.

77. It is possible for a Party to include in the list of agreements provided under Article 2(1)(a)(ii) an agreement which has been signed but has not[96] yet entered into force. In such cases, the Party should notify the Depositary in due course of the date of EIF of that agreement since that is the date on which it can become a CTA. In such cases, two possible scenarios may arise:

(1) If the date of EIF of such a tax treaty is before the MLI came into force for that Party, it will be considered as a CTA and the MLI will modify it.
(2) However, where the date of EIF of such a tax treaty is after the date when the MLI has entered into force for that Party pursuant to Article 34(2), such a notification will be considered an extension of the list of agreements pursuant to Article 29(5); i.e., such an agreement shall be considered as a new CTA and consequently, the provisions of EIE shall apply thereto accordingly under Article 35(5) of the MLI.

78. There are two ways in which the MLI may cover CTAs concluded by non-State jurisdictions or territories: (i) jurisdictions may become Parties to the MLI by being

96. Refer Explanatory Statement to the MLI, para. 32.

listed by name in the text of Article 27(1)(b) at the time of adoption of the text of the MLI or by being subsequently authorised to sign and ratify the MLI by a decision by consensus of the Parties and Signatories pursuant to Article 27(1)(c); or (ii) pursuant to Article 2(1)(a)(i)(B), a State Party may include in its list of CTAs tax agreements concluded by a jurisdiction or territory for whose international relations it is responsible.[97]

79. The MLI is intended to modify both bilateral and multilateral tax treaties. In this light, the definition of CTA states that the tax treaty in force may be between two or more Parties. Hence, regional multilateral tax treaties can also be notified as CTAs and be modified through the MLI. For example, the agreement among the Governments of the Member States of the Caribbean Community (CARICOM agreement signed on 06-07-1994 and entered into force on 30-11-1994 between Antigua and Barbuda, Barbados, Belize, Dominica, Grenada, Guyana, Jamaica, St. Kitts and Nevis, Saint Lucia, St. Vincent and the Grenadines, Trinidad and Tobago) has been notified as a CTA by Belize[98] and Jamaica[99] until now. At the time of signing of the MLI, Barbados[100] notified the said agreement, whereas, in its final position submitted at the time of ratification, the same has not been notified. If all the Member States of the CARICOM agreement join the MLI and going forward decide to notify the said agreement as a CTA, it could potentially have the distinction of being the first regional multilateral tax treaty to be modified through the MLI.

80. The Explanatory Statement[101] states that a tax treaty can be notified as a CTA, even if it does not exclusively cover income taxes. Some common taxes in addition to income taxes covered by tax treaties are capital taxes, taxes on capital gains, inheritance taxes and gift taxes. Tax treaties covering capital taxes, or taxes on capital gains,[102] inheritance taxes and gift taxes, in addition to income taxes can also be notified as CTAs. A sample is as below:

(a) Convention Between the Government of the French Republic and the Government of the State of Kuwait for the Avoidance of Double Taxation

97. *Id.*, para. 28.
98. Refer Belize's Position under the MLI https://research.ibfd.org/#/doc?url=/linkresolver/static/tt_bz_02_eng_2019_tt__td1_a2#tt_bz_02_eng_2019_tt__td1_a2 accessed on 26 July 2020 and http://www.oecd.org/tax/treaties/beps-mli-position-belize.pdf.
99. Refer Jamaica's Position under the MLI https://research.ibfd.org/#/doc?url=/linkresolver/static/tt_jm_02_eng_2018_tt__td1_a2#tt_jm_02_eng_2018_tt__td1_a2 accessed on 26 July 2020 and http://www.oecd.org/tax/treaties/beps-mli-position-jamaica.pdf.
100. Refer Barbados' Position under the MLI http://www.oecd.org/tax/treaties/beps-mli-position-barbados.pdf and http://www.oecd.org/tax/treaties/beps-mli-position-barbados-instrument-deposit.pdf.
101. Note: para. 78 of the Explanatory Statement *inter alia* provides that despite the insertion of the phrase 'taxes on income and on capital' in the text of preamble through recommendation of Action 6 Report, the ad hoc Group inserted the phrase 'taxes covered by this agreement' in the preamble language as contained in para. 1 of Art. 6 of the MLI so as to address (modify) even those CTAs under the MLI that cover additional taxes or use different phrasing for the taxes covered.
102. Refer Explanatory Statement to the MLI, para. 25.

with Respect to Taxes on Income, Capital and Inheritances[103] (both France and Kuwait have included this DTAA as a CTA in their respective MLI position).

(b) Convention Between the Federal Republic of Germany and the Kingdom of Denmark for the Avoidance of Double Taxation with Respect to Taxes on Income and on Capital and with Respect to Taxes on Estates and Inheritances and on Gifts and Concerning Assistance in Tax Matters[104] (Denmark did not notify the said DTAA as a CTA in its MLI position, whereas Germany notified the said DTAA as a CTA in its provisional MLI position and excluded the same in its final list of CTAs submitted at the time of ratification).

81. Agreements[105] applying only to shipping and air transport or to social security are not intended to be modified by the MLI.

82. There are instances, when notifying the CTAs in their MLI positions, Parties to an agreement (Amending Protocol) have notified different dates of EIF and disagree on a single date. In Ireland's[106] case, its DTAA with India has notification mismatch in the date of EIF. On taking India's[107] case, there are agreements with Armenia, Croatia, Ireland, New Zealand, Portugal, Thailand, Turkey and UK having such notification mismatches in dates of EIF of the DTAA/Amending Protocol. It has been clarified by the OECD through its frequently asked questions (FAQs)[108] on MLI that in the case where each Contracting Jurisdiction has clearly identified the same agreement, such agreement could be a CTA even though there is a disagreement on the date of EIF and there would not be any problem from a legal perspective.

83. Despite the fact that the MLI is a separate treaty, its existence hinges on the CTAs. The MLI applies between its Parties only when such Parties have notified their treaty as a CTA. If no such CTA exists, the MLI does not create new rights or obligations between its Parties for the purpose of avoidance of double taxation. Accordingly, the termination of CTA itself would have inevitable consequences for applying the MLI; i.e., if a CTA is terminated, the MLI could no longer apply to it.

103. Refer Convention Between France and Kuwait https://research.ibfd.org/#/compare/side-by-side?url=tt_fr-kw_04_eng_1982_tt__ad4,tt_fr-kw_04_eng_1982_tt__td3.
104. Refer Convention Between Germany and Denmark https://research.ibfd.org/#/compare/side-by-side?url=tt_dk-de_06_eng_1995_tt__ad2,tt_dk-de_06_eng_1995_tt__td1.
105. Refer Explanatory Statement to the MLI, para. 25.
106. Refer Ireland's Position under the MLI http://www.oecd.org/tax/treaties/beps-mli-position-ireland-instrument-deposit.pdf.
107. Refer India's Position under the MLI http://www.oecd.org/tax/treaties/beps-mli-position-india-instrument-deposit.pdf.
108. Refer OECD's FAQs on MLI https://community.oecd.org/docs/DOC-113848 accessed on 26 July 2020.

Article 2(1)(b)

84. Article 2(1)(b) defines the term 'Party' as used throughout the Convention to refer to States, as well as jurisdictions which have signed the Convention pursuant to Article 27(1)(b) or (c) of the MLI, for which the Convention is in force pursuant to Article 34 of the MLI.

Article 2(1)(c)

85. Under Article 2(1)(c) of the MLI, the term 'Contracting Jurisdiction' refers to the States, jurisdictions or territories that are Parties to a CTA. Even non-State jurisdictions[109] can be Parties to the MLI, like Guernsey, the Isle of Man, Jersey.

Article 2(1)(d)

86. Under Article 2(1)(d) of the MLI, the term 'Signatory' refers to States and jurisdictions that have signed the MLI pursuant to Article 27(1) but, for which, the MLI is not yet in force.

Article 2(2)

87. Article 2(2) of the MLI establishes a rule for the interpretation of terms not defined under the MLI, providing that, unless the context otherwise requires, the undefined terms should have the same meaning they have under the relevant CTA at the time the instrument is applied;[110] i.e., the recourse is to be made dynamically. The term 'context'[111] must be interpreted taking into account, *inter alia*, the object and purpose of the MLI, as stated in its preamble (which is to ensure swift, coordinated and consistent implementation of the treaty-related BEPS measures in a multilateral context), as well as all interpretation materials set out in Articles 31 and 32 of the Vienna Convention. The term 'context' should be understood broadly and falling back to the relevant CTAs should be an exception when interpreting the MLI.

88. Article 2(2) of the MLI establishes the following path for the interpretation of terms used in the MLI. First, it must be decided whether a term is defined in the MLI. The second step, if the answer to the first question is 'no', is to determine whether the term in question be interpreted out of the context of the MLI. Third, it is necessary to ascertain the term's meaning in the relevant CTA. If it is so defined, that definition will also apply for purposes of applying the MLI. Fourth, if the CTA does not contain a definition, but the term is nevertheless used in the CTA as an undefined term, the correct meaning should – by virtue of Article 3(2) of the OECD Model – be derived from the relevant definition in domestic law, unless the context requires otherwise. Fifth, if the term in question is not even used in the CTA, no reference can be made to domestic law by virtue of Article 3(2) of the OECD Model. In that case, the meaning is to be

109. Refer Explanatory Statement to the MLI, para. 35.
110. *Id.*, para. 37.
111. *Id.*, para. 38.

determined by reference to the general rules of interpretation in the Vienna Convention.[112]

The notifications made by treaty partners under Article 2 of the MLI and impact/outcome thereof are provided in Figure 3.

Figure 3 Article 2(1)(a): Definition of CTA – Flowchart on Notifications & Their Impact

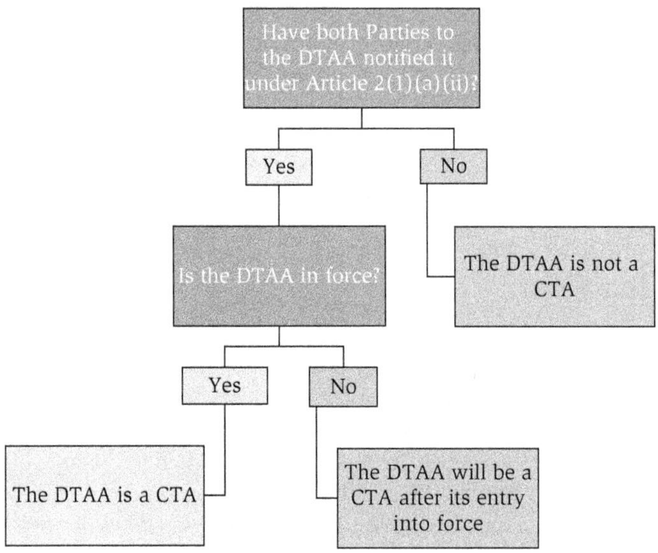

3.4 SUBSTANTIVE PROVISIONS OF THE MLI

89. The substantive provisions of the MLI are provided in Articles 3-26. A plain reading of all these articles demonstrates that the design of Part VI of the MLI (containing Articles 18-26) is different as it provides rules relevant for different steps of the mandatory binding arbitration procedure, which require more details, as well as more tailor-made exceptions than the tax treaty-related BEPS measures established in the other substantive provisions of the MLI.

90. The substantive provisions of the MLI in respect of Articles 3-17 always include the agreed treaty-related BEPS measures, as proposed in the BEPS Final Reports 2, 6, 7 and 14. The BEPS provisions have been adapted to address the challenges arising from applying them on a multilateral basis as well as to the specific terminology[113] used in the MLI. Similarly, the MLI has replaced the cross-references to articles and paragraphs

112. Refer Article by Werner C. Haslehner Titled 'A Multilateral Interpretation of the Multilateral Instrument (and Covered Tax Agreements)' https://research.ibfd.org/#/doc?url=/collections/bit/html/bit_2020_04_o2_2.html (s. 3.1) accessed on 2 September 2020.

113. Refer Explanatory Statement to the MLI, para. 15.

of the OECD MTC that were contained in the treaty-related BEPS measures. Also, in order to address differences in underlying provisions, i.e. deviations from the OECD MTC, the substantive provisions of the MLI include terms that are not found in the OECD MTC but are common in tax treaties.

91. The structure of the substantive provisions of the MLI in respect of Articles 3-17 *inter alia* includes the following:

- Agreed treaty-related BEPS measures, as proposed in the BEPS Final Reports 2, 6, 7 and 14.
- Compatibility clauses which define the relationship between each provision of the MLI and the relevant provision of the CTAs.
- Reservation clauses which include the possibility of opting out of the whole or certain parts of an article of MLI.
- Notification clauses which work together with the compatibility clauses and ensure clarity about the existing provisions of the CTAs that are within the scope of the compatibility clauses.
- Additional notifications to allow Parties to opt in for optional provisions or alternative provisions.

3.5 PART II OF MLI: HYBRID MISMATCHES

3.5.1 Article 3 of MLI: Transparent Entities

92. The interplay between Article 3 of MLI, corresponding BEPS Report(s) and the resulting provisions incorporated in OECD MTC 2017 is represented in a table as below:

MLI		*BEPS Final Report*		*OECD MTC 2017*	
Article	*Title of Article*	*BEPS Action Plan*	*Title of BEPS Action Plan*	*Article*	*Title of Article*
3	Transparent Entities	Action 2	Neutralising the Effects of Hybrid Mismatch Arrangements	1(2)	Persons Covered
		Action 6	Preventing the Granting of Treaty Benefits in Inappropriate Circumstances	23A, 23B	Methods for Elimination of Double Taxation

93. The article at a glance is as below:

Substantive (BEPS) Provisions under Para(s)	*Opt-In Provisions under Para*	*Alternative Provisions under Para*	*Compatibility Clause*		*Reservations under Para*	*Notifications under Para*
			Para	*Type*		
1-3	None	None	4	'in place of or in the absence of'	5	5, 6

Status in Pre-BEPS Project Era

94. The OECD MTC in the past did not contain adequate provisions to ensure that hybrid instruments and entities (as well as dual resident entities) are not unduly used to obtain the benefits of treaties. Similarly, the MTC did not address taxation issues arising from transactions undertaken by transparent entities. The 1999 OECD report on the Application of the OECD MTC to Partnerships[114] (the Partnership Report, OECD, 1999) contains an extensive analysis of the application of treaty provisions to partnerships, including in situations where there is a mismatch in the tax treatment of the partnership. The main conclusions of the Partnership Report, which have been included in the Commentary of the OECD MTC 2014, seek to ensure that the provisions of tax treaties produce appropriate results when applied to partnerships, in particular in the case of a partnership that constitutes a hybrid entity. The said Report suggested that where a partnership is not treated as a resident (being transparent) and the partner in whose hands income of partnership is taxed is resident of that State, benefit of tax treaty shall be provided to the extent the income is taxed in the hands of resident partner.

95. The Partnership Report (OECD, 1999), however, did not expressly address the application of tax treaties to entities other than partnerships. In order to address that issue, as well as the fact that some countries have found it difficult to apply the conclusions of the Partnership Report, it was decided in the course of BEPS Action 2 to include in the OECD MTC 2014 new provision and Commentary, which will ensure that income of transparent entities is treated, for the purposes of the Convention, in accordance with the principles of the Partnership Report. This will ensure not only that the benefits of tax treaties are granted in appropriate cases but also that these benefits are not granted where neither Contracting State treats, under its domestic law, the income of an entity as the income of one of its residents. The envisaged outcome of BEPS Action 2 is the increased coherence of the international tax system and the removal of the incentive for the taxpayer to exploit gaps. This should lead to a

114. Refer OECD (1999), The Application of the OECD Model Tax Convention to Partnerships, Issues in International Taxation, No. 6, OECD Publishing, Paris.

reduction in tax administration costs, which may result from the expected disappearance of these arrangements after the implementation of the BEPS Action 2. In short, BEPS Action 2 may have more of a deterrent rather than a revenue-raising effect.[115]

96. In order to provide relief of double taxation in view of situations mentioned above, it was agreed in the course of BEPS Action 6 that, as a matter of principle, Articles 23A and 23B of the OECD Model only required a Contracting State to relieve double taxation when income was taxable in the other State under treaty provisions allowing that other State to tax the relevant income as the State of source or as a State where there is a PE to which that income is attributable. The BEPS Action 6 proposed changes to Articles 23A and 23B in order to confirm that principle.

Article 3(1)

97. The concept of 'fiscally transparent' used in the paragraph refers to situations where, under the domestic law of a Contracting State, the income (or part thereof) of the entity or arrangement is not taxed at the level of the entity or the arrangement but at the level of the persons who have an interest in that entity or arrangement. For example, in India, there is no concept of fiscally transparent entities, whereas provisions related to fiscally transparent entities are present in various countries such as China, Denmark, Norway, Sweden, the Netherlands, UK, US and others. In France,[116] under Article 8 and Article 218 bis of the Code général des impôts (CGI), French partnerships are 'translucent' and not transparent for tax purpose. This means that a French partnership has a fiscal personality, fills a tax return even if the tax is effectively paid by their partners. According to the French domestic legislation, French partnerships are always tax resident in France. In Argentina,[117] a partnership is generally treated as fiscally transparent for Argentine income tax purposes. Partnerships are required to file annual information returns. The resident partners, rather than the partnership itself, are subject to income tax under the Income Tax Act. However, partnerships have the option to file and pay income tax instead of their partners.

98. This Article addresses concerns posed by hybrid mismatches and income derived by entities or arrangements treated as wholly or partly fiscally transparent. Under the provisions of Article 3(1) of the MLI, income derived by an entity treated as fiscally transparent under tax law of a Contracting State shall be considered to be income of the resident of that State (who will thus be considered as a person covered by a tax treaty) but only to the extent such income is treated for the purpose of taxation, as its resident's income. This will ensure not only that the benefits of tax treaties are granted

115. Refer Moritz Scherleitner's 'Addressing Tax Arbitrage with Hybrid Financial Instruments – A Multidisciplinary Study and Proposal for Developed and Developing Countries' IBFD Doctoral Series 54, p. 199.
116. Refer France – Information on Residency for Tax Purposes, s. II(2) https://www.oecd.org/tax/automatic-exchange/crs-implementation-and-assistance/tax-residency/France-Tax-Residency.pdf accessed on 25 December 2020.
117. Refer Global Tax Guide to Doing Business in Argentina https://www.dentons.com/en/issues-and-opportunities/global-tax-guide-to-doing-business-in/argentina accessed on 25 December 2020.

in appropriate cases but also that these benefits are not granted where neither Contracting State treats, under its domestic law, the income of an entity as the income of one of its resident. Hence, this Article tackles double non-taxation of income derived by or through transparent entities or arrangements that are treated as fiscally transparent under the tax law of one of the Contracting States. Also, jurisdictions should not be expected to grant treaty benefits in cases where they are unable to ascertain whether a person is truly entitled to such benefits. The solution[118] offered in Article 3 links the tax treatment of the transparent entity or arrangement in one Contracting State to the treatment given by the other Contracting State.

99. The following Example illustrates the application of this paragraph:

> State A and State B have concluded a treaty identical to the Model Tax Convention. State A considers that an entity established in State B is a company and taxes that entity on interest that it receives from a debtor resident in State A. Under the domestic law of State B, however, the entity is treated as a partnership and the two members in that entity, who share equally all its income, are each taxed on half of the interest. One of the members is a resident of State B and the other one is a resident of a country with which States A and B do not have a treaty. The paragraph provides that in such case, only half of the interest shall be considered, for the purposes of Article 11, to be income of a resident of State B for the purposes of grant of treaty benefits under the treaty between A and B.

100. Paragraph 1 only applies for the purposes of the MLI and does not, therefore, require a Contracting State to change the way in which it attributes income or characterises entities for the purposes of its domestic law. In the example above, while paragraph 1 provides that half of the interest shall be considered, for the purposes of Article 11, to be income of a resident of State B, this will only affect the maximum amount of tax that State A will be able to collect on the interest and will not change the fact that State A's tax will be payable by the entity. Thus, assuming that the domestic law of State A provides for a 30% WHT on the interest, the effect of paragraph 1 will simply be to reduce the amount of tax that State A will collect on the interest (so that half of the interest would be taxed at 30% and half at 10% under the treaty between States A and B) and will not change the fact that the entity is the relevant taxpayer for the purposes of State A's domestic law.

Article 3(2)

101. On applying paragraph 1, a situation may arise where the two States involved tax income as income of its resident, and if both States provide relief of tax levied in the other country, this may, inadvertently, create a situation of double non-taxation. In order to address this issue, Article 3(2) expressly recognises the accepted principle that Articles 23A and 23B of the OECD MTC does not require the resident jurisdiction to relieve double taxation when the provisions of a CTA allow taxation by the other jurisdiction solely on the basis that the relevant income is also income derived by a

118. Refer Nathalie Bravo's 'A Multilateral Instrument for Updating the Tax Treaty Network' IBFD Doctoral Series 52, p. 88.

resident of that other jurisdiction. Hence, paragraph 2 of Article 3 provides that State taxing as a resident State is obliged to provide relief only to the extent the other State has taxed as per provisions of the treaty. Accordingly, where the other State has taxed solely in the capacity of residence, the first State is not obliged to provide relief.

102. To elaborate further, in some cases, the same income may be taxed by each Contracting State as income of one of its residents. This may happen where, for example, one of the Contracting States taxes the worldwide income of an entity that is a resident of that State whereas the other State views that entity as fiscally transparent and taxes the members of that entity who are residents of that other State on their respective share of the income. The phrase '*shall not apply to the extent that such provisions allow taxation by that other Contracting Jurisdiction solely because the income is also income derived by a resident of that other Contracting Jurisdiction*' clarifies that in such cases, both States are not reciprocally obliged to provide relief for each other's tax levied exclusively on the basis of the residence of the taxpayer and that each State is therefore only obliged to provide relief of double taxation to the extent that taxation by the other State is in accordance with provisions of the CTA that allow taxation of the relevant income as the State of source or as a State where there is a PE to which that income is attributable, thereby excluding taxation that would solely be the result of the residence of a person in that other State. While this result would logically follow from the wording of Articles 23A and 23B, even in the absence of that phrase, the addition of the phrase removes any doubt in this respect.[119]

Article 3(3)

103. Paragraph 1 of the article provides that income derived by or through an entity or arrangement will be considered to be income of a resident of a Contracting Jurisdiction (and will thus be considered as a person covered by a tax treaty) if the income is treated by that Contracting Jurisdiction as the income of a resident of that Contracting Jurisdiction. Where either Contracting Jurisdiction of the relevant CTA opts out of Article 11 (under paragraph 3(a)) of the MLI, a saving clause that relates solely to paragraph 1 of Article 3 will be added at the end of the said paragraph 1 to ensure that its application will not interfere with the taxation by a Contracting Jurisdiction of its residents.

Compatibility Clause

104. Paragraph 4 is the compatibility clause under Article 3 of MLI, which addresses the relationship between Article 3(1) (as it may be modified by Article 3(3)) and existing provisions of the same type. It is intended to address all of the above types of provision, by indicating that Article 3(1) (as it may be modified by Article 3(3)) would replace provisions of a CTA to the extent that they address whether income derived through entities or arrangements that are treated as fiscally transparent under the tax

119. Refer s. A, p. 89 of Action 6: BEPS 2015 Final Report, OECD/G20 Base Erosion and Profit Shifting Project and Refer OECD MTC 2017, para. 11.1 of the Commentary on Arts 23A and 23B.

law of a Contracting Jurisdiction will be treated as income of a resident of a Contracting Jurisdiction, or would be added where such provisions do not exist. Where an existing provision addresses both the treatment of fiscally transparent entities and arrangements and the treatment of tax-exempt entities that are not fiscally transparent, such a provision would be superseded only with respect to the treatment of fiscally transparent entities.[120]

Reservations under Paragraph 5

105. Various possible reservations which jurisdictions may make based on their respective positions are as below:

(i) Under sub-paragraph (a), jurisdictions may opt out of Article 3 entirely with respect to all CTAs, as the same is not a minimum standard.
(ii) Under sub-paragraph (b), jurisdictions may opt out of Article 3(1) with respect to CTAs that already contain a provision described in compatibility clause present in Article 3(4).
(iii) Under sub-paragraph (c), jurisdictions may opt out of Article 3(1) with respect to CTAs that already contain a provision described in Article 3(4) which denies treaty benefits in the case of income derived by or through an entity or arrangement established in a third jurisdiction.
(iv) Under sub-paragraph (d), jurisdictions may opt out of Article 3(1) with respect to CTAs that already contain a provision described in Article 3(4) which identifies in detail the treatment of specific fact patterns and types of entities or arrangements.
(v) Under sub-paragraph (e), jurisdictions may opt out of Article 3(1) with respect to CTAs that already contain a provision described in Article 3(4) which identifies in detail the treatment of specific fact patterns and types of entities or arrangements and deny treaty benefits in the case of income derived by or through an entity or arrangement established in a third jurisdiction.
(vi) Under sub-paragraph (f), jurisdictions may opt out of Article 3(2) with respect to all CTAs.
(vii) Under sub-paragraph (g), jurisdictions may only apply Article 3(1) to CTAs that already contain a provision described in Article 3(4) which identifies in detail the treatment of specific fact patterns and types of entities or arrangements.

Notifications

106. Depending upon the position taken by various jurisdictions, the following notifications are required to be made under Article 3 of the MLI:

(i) Jurisdictions intending to make reservations under paragraph 5 are required to make notifications under sub-paragraphs (a)-(g), as the case may be.

120. Refer Explanatory Statement to the MLI, para. 44.

(ii) Under paragraph 6, jurisdictions which have not made the reservations described in various sub-paragraphs of paragraph 5 shall make notifications of their CTAs depending upon the particular fact pattern existing in such CTAs. Where a Party has made the reservation described in paragraph 5(g), the notification would include only the provisions of the CTAs that are subject to that reservation. Such a provision would be replaced by paragraph 1 (as it may be modified by paragraph 3) to the extent provided in paragraph 4 where all Parties to the CTA have made such a notification. In all other cases, paragraph 1 (as it may be modified by paragraph 3) will apply to the CTA, but the existing provisions of the CTA would be superseded only to the extent that those provisions are incompatible with paragraph 1 (as it may be modified by paragraph 3).

Denmark's Position[121] under the MLI

107. Denmark recognises the concept of fiscally transparent entities, e.g. partnerships, whereby taxation does not happen at entity level. Denmark's Position under Article 3 of the MLI is illustratively explained by citing the corresponding MLI position of some of its treaty partners as below:

(a) Denmark has made a notification under Article 3(6) of the MLI in respect of CTA with US and has notified Article 4(1)(d) of Denmark-US DTAA.[122] On the other hand, US is not a Signatory to the MLI as of now; with the result, provisions of Article 3 of the MLI shall not apply to the Denmark-US DTAA.
(b) Denmark has not made any reservation under Article 3 of the MLI, whereas one of the CTAs notified by it, i.e. Australia, has made reservation under Article 3(5)(d) in respect of CTAs with France, Japan only. Further, both Denmark and Australia[123] have not made any reservation under Article 11(3)(a) of the MLI; with the result, paragraphs 1 and 2 of Article 3 of MLI shall apply to Denmark-Australia DTAA.
(c) Denmark and one of the CTAs notified by it, i.e. Poland,[124] have not made any reservation under Article 3 and Article 11(3)(a) of the MLI; with the result, paragraphs 1 and 2 of Article 3 of MLI shall apply to Denmark-Poland DTAA.[125]

121. Refer Denmark's Position under the MLI http://www.oecd.org/tax/treaties/beps-mli-position-denmark-instrument-deposit.pdf.
122. Refer Denmark-US DTAA https://research.ibfd.org/#/doc?url=/data/treaty/docs/html/tt_dk-us_01_eng_1999_tt__td2.html accessed on 27 July 2020.
123. Refer Australia's Position under the MLI http://www.oecd.org/tax/treaties/beps-mli-position-australia-instrument-deposit.pdf.
124. Refer Poland's Position under the MLI http://www.oecd.org/tax/treaties/beps-mli-position-poland-instrument-deposit.pdf.
125. Refer Denmark-Poland Synthesised Text https://research.ibfd.org/#/doc?url=/data/treaty/docs/html/tt_dk-pl_02_eng_2001_tt__td3.html accessed on 27 July 2020.

India's Position[126] under the MLI

108. In accordance with India's Income Tax Act, 1961, there is no concept of transparent entities and all such entities, viz., partnership firms, trusts, etc., are taxed. India has taken a reservation for the entirety of the article not to apply. A probable factor stimulating this decision could have been that the provisions of Article 3(1) cover even the fiscally transparent entities situated in third-country jurisdictions with which India may not be having a treaty; hence, there may not be any visibility to the tax treatment given in such third-country jurisdictions. This view gets clarified on reading India's Position in the OECD MTC 2017, wherein India has reserved the right not to include paragraph 2 of Article 1 in its tax treaties. Further, India does not agree with the view expressed in paragraph 7 of the Commentary on Article 1 that the term 'income derived by or through an entity or arrangement' includes income derived by or through an entity that may not be a resident of either of the Contracting States. India considers that this term includes only such income that is derived by or through entities that are resident of one or both Contracting States. This position taken by India in OECD MTC 2017 is duly reflected in Article 1(2) of India-China DTAA[127] introduced by the Amending Protocol notified on 17-07-2019, wherein provisions similar to Article 3(1) of the MLI have been inserted, by restricting that the fiscally transparent entity is established in 'either Contracting State' for this provision to apply. Another change introduced in the DTAA was that the entity is treated as 'wholly fiscally transparent', as against Article 3(1) of MLI providing that the entity is treated as 'wholly or partly fiscally transparent'. With these changes, Article 3(1) of the MLI was modified and is reflected in Article 1(2) of India-China DTAA as below:

> For the purposes of this Agreement, income derived by or through an entity or arrangement that is *established in either Contracting State* and that is treated as *wholly fiscally transparent* under the tax law of either Contracting State shall be considered to be income of a resident of a Contracting State only to the extent that the income is treated, for the purposes of taxation by that State, as the income of a resident of that State.

The Netherlands' Position[128] under the MLI

109. In the Netherlands, partnership, closed limited partnership, closed fund for mutual account are considered as fiscally transparent entities,[129] whereby taxation does not happen at entity level. The Netherlands has made a couple of notifications under Article 3 of the MLI. Its position under Article 3 of the MLI is illustratively

126. Refer India's Position under the MLI http://www.oecd.org/tax/treaties/beps-mli-position-india-instrument-deposit.pdf.
127. Refer India-China DTAA https://www.incometaxindia.gov.in/Pages/international-taxation/dtaa.aspx accessed on 27 July 2020.
128. Refer The Netherland's Position under the MLI http://www.oecd.org/tax/treaties/beps-mli-position-netherlands-instrument-deposit.pdf.
129. Refer The Netherlands – Information on Residency for Tax Purposes https://www.oecd.org/tax/automatic-exchange/crs-implementation-and-assistance/tax-residency/Netherlands-Tax-Residency.pdf accessed on 28 July 2020.

explained by citing the corresponding MLI position of some of its treaty partners as below:

(a) Under Article 3(5)(d) of the MLI, the Netherlands has reserved the right for paragraph 1 not to apply to its CTAs with Japan, UK and US as these CTAs already contain a provision described in Article 3(4) of the MLI which identifies in detail the treatment of specific fact patterns and types of entities or arrangements. On taking the Netherlands-Japan CTA as an illustration, it is seen that in its notifications, Japan[130] has *inter alia* made a reservation under Article 3(5)(f) for paragraph 2 of Article 3 of MLI not to apply to all its CTAs. Hence, the impact of MLI provisions on the Netherlands-Japan CTA[131] is found to be as below:
   - Since the Netherlands has notified Japan under Article 3(5)(d) of the MLI, paragraph 1 of Article 3 of MLI shall not apply.
   - Since Japan has made a reservation under Article 3(5)(f), paragraph 2 of Article 3 of MLI shall not apply.

(b) Further, pursuant to Article 3(6) of the MLI, the Netherlands has notified a number of CTAs, including its CTA with Norway, which contain a provision described in Article 3(4) that is not subject to a reservation under Article 3(5)(c) through (e) of the MLI. On the other hand, pursuant to Article 3(5)(b) of the MLI, Norway[132] reserves the right for paragraph 1 not to apply to its CTA with India only as it already contains a provision described in Article 3(4). Hence, the impact of MLI provisions on the Netherlands-Norway CTA is found to be as below:
   - Article 3(1), as modified by Article 3(3) of MLI, would apply as the Netherlands has also made a reservation under Article 11(3)(a) of the MLI.
   - Article 3(2) shall apply.

Few Snapshots of Positions[133] Taken by Other Countries under the MLI

110. Jurisdictions that have made reservations under Article 3(5)(a) for the entirety of the article not to apply to their CTAs are, namely, Albania, Austria, Bahrain, Barbados, Belize, Bosnia and Herzegovina, Bulgaria, Burkina Faso, Cameroon, Canada, China, Colombia, Costa Rica, Côte d'Ivoire, Curaçao, Cyprus, the Czech Republic, Egypt, Estonia, Finland, France, Gabon, Georgia, Germany, Greece, Guernsey, Hong Kong, Hungary, Iceland, India, Indonesia, the Isle of Man, Italy, Jamaica, Jersey, Jordan,

130. Refer Japan's Position under the MLI http://www.oecd.org/tax/treaties/beps-mli-position-japan-instrument-deposit.pdf.
131. Refer The Netherlands-Japan Synthesised Text https://research.ibfd.org/#/doc?url=/data/treaty/docs/html/tt_jp-nl_01_eng_2010_tt__td3.html accessed on 28 July 2020.
132. Refer Norway's Position under the MLI http://www.oecd.org/tax/treaties/beps-mli-position-norway-instrument-deposit.pdf.
133. Refer OECD – Signatories and Parties to the MLI http://www.oecd.org/tax/treaties/beps-mli-signatories-and-parties.pdf.

Kazakhstan, Korea, Kuwait, Latvia, Liechtenstein, Lithuania, Malta, Mauritius, Mexico, Monaco, Morocco, North Macedonia, Oman, Pakistan, Panama, Peru, Portugal, Qatar, San Marino, Saudi Arabia, Senegal, Serbia, Seychelles, Singapore, Slovenia, Sweden, Switzerland, Tunisia, Ukraine, the United Arab Emirates.

111. Jurisdictions that have made reservations under Article 3(5)(b) of the MLI are, namely, Chile, Ireland, Norway and Spain.

112. Until now, no jurisdiction has made any reservation under Article 3(5)(c), (e), (g) of the MLI.

113. Jurisdictions that have made reservations under Article 3(5)(d) of the MLI are, namely, Australia and the Netherlands.

114. Jurisdictions that have made reservations under Article 3(5)(f) of the MLI are, namely, Ireland, Japan, Luxembourg, Malaysia and UK.

115. Australia and New Zealand have made a notification under Article 3(6) of MLI, wherein both countries have notified Article 1(2) of Australia-New Zealand Double Taxation Avoidance Convention (DTAC); with the result, Article 3(1) of MLI shall replace[134] Article 1(2) of Australia-New Zealand DTAC. Further, both countries have not made any reservation under Article 3(5)(f) of the MLI; with the result, Article 3(2) of MLI applies[135] and supersedes the provisions of Article 23 of the said DTAC in respect of elimination of double taxation.

116. In respect of Japan and New Zealand notifications under the MLI, it is seen that Japan has made a reservation under Article 11(3)(a) of the MLI ('Saving Clause'). Pursuant to Article 3(5)(f) of the MLI, Japan has made a reservation for Article 3(2) of the MLI not to apply to its CTAs. Further, both Japan and New Zealand have made a notification under Article 3(6) of MLI, wherein both countries have notified Article 4(5) of Japan-New Zealand DTAC; with the result, Article 4(5) of the DTAC is replaced[136] by paragraph 1 (as modified by paragraph 3) of Article 3 of the MLI.

117. In addition to the above, some more notifications made by various jurisdictions and the impact on their respective CTAs are *inter alia* tabulated as below:

134. Refer Australia-New Zealand Synthesised Text https://research.ibfd.org/#/doc?url=/data/treaty/docs/html/tt_au-nz_01_eng_2009_tt__td2.html accessed on 28 July 2020.

135. *Id.*

136. Refer Japan-New Zealand Synthesised Text https://research.ibfd.org/#/doc?url=/data/treaty/docs/html/tt_jp-nz_01_eng_2012_tt__td2.html accessed on 28 July 2020.

Jurisdiction	*Position Taken*	*Treaty Partner*	*Position Taken*	*Outcome under the MLI*
Australia	- Reservation under Article 3(5)(d) in respect of CTAs with France, Japan - Notification under Article 3(6) in respect of CTAs with Mexico, New Zealand, US	India	- Reservation under Article 3(5)(a)	Article 3 would not apply
Australia	-do-	France	- Reservation under Article 3(5)(a)	Article 3 would not apply
Australia	-do-	Japan	- Reservation under Article 3(5)(f) - Notification under Article 3(6) in respect of CTAs with Australia, France, Germany, Netherland, New Zealand, Portugal, UK - Reservation under Article 11(3)(a)	Article 3(1), (2) would not apply
Ireland	- Reservation under Article 3(5)(b) in respect of CTA with US - Reservation under Article 3(5)(f) - Reservation under Article 11(3)(a)	Japan	-do-	- Article 3(1) (as modified by Article 3(3)) would apply and supersede the provisions of the agreement to the extent of incompatibility - Article 3(2) would not apply

Jurisdiction	*Position Taken*	*Treaty Partner*	*Position Taken*	*Outcome under the MLI*
Ireland	-do-	Spain	- Reservation under Article 3(5)(b) in respect of CTA with Finland, US, UK - Reservation under Article 11(3)(a)	- Article 3(1) (as modified by Article 3(3)) would apply and supersede the provisions of the agreement to the extent of incompatibility - Article 3(2) would not apply
Spain	- Reservation under Article 3(5)(b) in respect of CTA with Finland, US, UK - Reservation under Article 11(3)(a)	UK	- Reservation under Article 3(5)(f) - Notification under Article 3(6) in respect of CTAs with Spain, etc.	Article 3(1), (2) would not apply

The various notifications made by treaty partners under Article 3 of the MLI and impact/outcome thereof on the respective CTAs are provided in Figure 4.

Figure 4 Article 3: Transparent Entities – Flowchart on Notifications & Their Impact

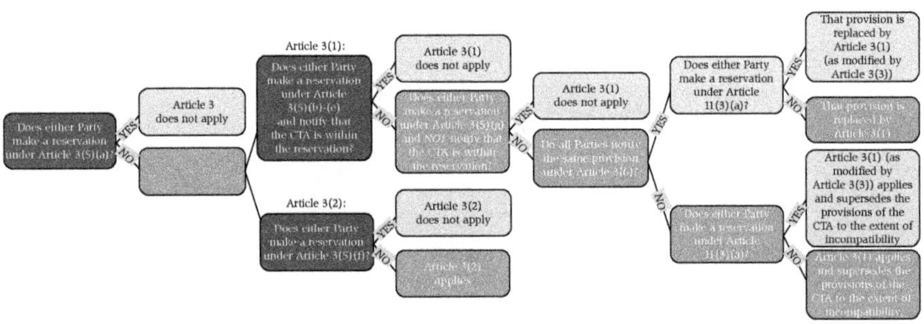

Source: OECD – Toolkit for Application of the Multilateral Instrument for BEPS Tax Treaty Related Measures https://www.oecd.org/tax/treaties/application-toolkit-multilateral-instrument-for-beps-tax-treaty-measures.htm.

3.5.2 Article 4 of MLI: Dual Resident Entities

118. The interplay between Article 4 of MLI, corresponding BEPS Report and the resulting provisions incorporated in OECD MTC 2017 is represented in a table as below:

MLI		*BEPS Final Report*		*OECD MTC 2017*	
Article	*Title of Article*	*BEPS Action Plan*	*Title of BEPS Action Plan*	*Article*	*Title of Article*
4	Dual Resident Entities	Action 6	Preventing the Granting of Treaty Benefits in Inappropriate Circumstances	4(3)	Resident

119. The article at a glance is as below:

Substantive (BEPS) Provisions under Para(s)	*Opt-In Provisions under Para*	*Alternative Provisions under Para*	*Compatibility Clause*		*Reservations under Para*	*Notifications under Para*
			Para	*Type*		
1	None	None	2	'in place of or in the absence of'	3	3, 4

Status in Pre-BEPS Project Era

120. Article 4 of the OECD MTC defines the term 'Resident of a Contracting State' and provides for rules to resolve cases of double residence. In the OECD MTC (2014), Article 4(3) provided that in respect of persons other than an individual who is resident of both Contracting States, it shall be deemed, by default, to be a resident of the State in which its place of effective management (POEM) is situated.

121. 'Dual residence' refers to a situation where a person other than an individual desiring to avail treaty benefit is considered resident of both the Contracting States involved. Accordingly, it is not possible to allocate taxing rights between the State of residence and source and both countries tax the global income considering such person as a resident of their respective State. Dual residence arises as on applying paragraph 1 of Article 4 of the treaty, resort is made to the domestic tax laws of both the Contracting States involved. Different States provide different rules for determining residential status, due to which there is no global consistency in this respect. In some States, POEM is considered as test of residence, while in some States, place of incorporation, conduct of active business, etc. are considered as a test of residence.

122. Thus, instead of considering POEM as a tie-breaker rule, BEPS Action Plan 6 provides for adopting MAP to deal with the situation of dual residence. In other words, in case a person other than an individual is considered as resident of both the Contracting States, Article 4 of MLI provides that CAs shall endeavour to determine the residence through MAP (rather than POEM as the tie-breaker rule as in Article 4(3) of the OECD MTC 2014).

Article 4(1)

123. Article 4 of MLI modifies the tie-breaker rule applicable to persons other than individuals that are residents of more than one Contracting Jurisdiction. On application of Article 4 of MLI, the contracting jurisdictions will need to engage in a MAP to determine the State in which such person must be deemed to be a resident. If the contracting jurisdictions cannot reach an agreement, the person will not be entitled to any relief or exemption from tax provided in the relevant CTA, except as agreed upon by the CAs.

124. There had been a number of tax avoidance cases involving dual resident companies, which needed to be addressed on a case-by-case basis. As a result, paragraph 1 of the article provides that the CAs of the contracting jurisdictions shall endeavour to resolve by mutual agreement cases of dual residence of a person other than an individual. For this purpose, CAs would be expected to take account of various factors, such as where the meetings of the person's board of directors or equivalent body are usually held, where the chief executive officer and other senior executives usually carry on their activities, where the senior day-to-day management of the person is carried on, where the person's headquarters are located, which country's laws govern the legal status of the person, where its accounting records are kept, etc.

125. As paragraph 1 explicitly denies the benefits of the CTA in the absence of an agreement between the CAs of the Contracting Jurisdictions, the failure to grant such benefits cannot be viewed as taxation that is not in accordance with the provisions of the CTA. As an illustration, this would mean that cases in which benefits are denied due to a failure of the CAs of the Contracting Jurisdictions to reach agreement would not be eligible for arbitration under a CTA that provides for arbitration of cases of taxation that is not in accordance with the provisions of the CTA.

Compatibility Clause

126. In accordance with paragraph 2, Article 4 of the MLI applies in place of or in the absence of all types of tie-breaker rules to determine the residence of persons other than individuals, by incorporating provisions providing that the CAs of the contracting jurisdictions shall endeavour to determine by mutual agreement the jurisdiction of which the dual resident person is a resident for the purposes of a CTA, having regard to its POEM, the place where it is incorporated or otherwise constituted and any other relevant factors, and that, in the absence of such agreement, such person shall not be entitled to any relief or exemption from tax provided by the CTA except to the extent and in such manner as may be agreed upon by the CAs of the contracting jurisdictions.

127. Existing 'tie-breaker' provisions addressing the residence of persons other than individuals take a variety of forms. For example, some (such as Article 4(3) of the UN MTC, and of the OECD MTC prior to the BEPS Project) break the tie in favour of the POEM, some focus on the place of organisation, and others call for determination by mutual agreement but do not explicitly deny benefits in the absence of such a determination. Existing tie-breaker provisions also include provisions addressing such cases by denying treaty benefits without requiring the CAs to endeavour to reach mutual agreement on a single Contracting Jurisdiction of residence. The provisions of Article 4 would replace all such types of tie-breaker rules with respect to the residence of persons other than individuals. Where a single provision of a CTA provides for a tie-breaker rule applicable to both individuals and persons other than individuals, paragraph 1 would apply in place of that provision only to the extent that it relates to a person other than an individual.[137]

128. Paragraph 1 of Article 4 of MLI shall not apply in cases of dual-listed company arrangements. A dual-listed company arrangement generally refers to an arrangement, adopted by certain publicly listed companies, that reflects a commonality of management, operations, shareholders' rights, purpose and mission through an agreement or a series of agreements between two parent companies, each with its own stock exchange listing, together with special provisions in their respective articles of association including in some cases, for example, the creation of special voting shares. Under these types of structures, while the participating companies retain their separate entity legal status, the position of the parent company shareholders is, as far as possible, the same as if they held shares in a single company, with the same dividend entitlement and same rights to participate in the assets of the dual-listed companies in the event of a winding up. Arrangements of this type occur in relatively few jurisdictions, and treaty provisions addressing them are typically customised in detail to the circumstances of those jurisdictions in order to ensure the determination of a single Contracting Jurisdiction of residence for each participating company.[138]

Reservations under Paragraph 3

129. Various possible reservations which jurisdictions may make based on their respective positions are as below:

(i) Under sub-paragraph (a), jurisdictions may opt out of Article 4 entirely with respect to all CTAs, as the same is not a minimum standard.
(ii) Under sub-paragraph (b), jurisdictions may opt out of Article 4 entirely with respect to all CTAs that already contain provisions which require the CAs of the Contracting Jurisdictions to endeavour to reach mutual agreement on a single Contracting Jurisdiction of residence.
(iii) Under sub-paragraph (c), jurisdictions may opt out of Article 4 entirely with respect to all CTAs that already contain provisions which deny treaty benefits without requiring the CAs of the Contracting Jurisdictions to endeavour to reach mutual agreement on a single Contracting Jurisdiction of residence.
(iv) Under sub-paragraph (d), jurisdictions may opt out of Article 4 entirely with respect to all CTAs that already contain provisions which require the CAs of the Contracting Jurisdictions to endeavour to reach mutual agreement on a

137. Refer Explanatory Statement to the MLI, para. 52.
138. *Id.*, para. 53.

single Contracting Jurisdiction of residence, and that set out the treatment of that person under the CTA where such an agreement cannot be reached.

(v) Under sub-paragraph (e), jurisdictions may replace the last sentence of Article 4(1), i.e., 'In the absence of such agreement, such person shall not be entitled to any relief or exemption from tax provided by the Covered Tax Agreement except to the extent and in such manner as may be agreed upon by the competent authorities of the Contracting Jurisdictions' by 'In the absence of such agreement, such person shall not be entitled to any relief or exemption from tax provided by the Covered Tax Agreement.'

This provision could be construed as an amendment of Article 4(1) of MLI itself, instead of a reservation, as it aims to modify the text of the article and not to modify or limit its legal effect. Although the purpose of Article 4(3)(e) does not seem to be in conformity with the definition of reservations as provided for in the Vienna Convention, the ad hoc Group has labelled it as such.

(vi) Under sub-paragraph (f), jurisdictions may opt out of Article 4 entirely with respect to CTAs concluded with Parties that have replaced the last sentence of Article 4(1) under Article 4(3)(e).

Notifications

130. Depending upon the position taken by various jurisdictions, the following notifications are required to be made under Article 4 of the MLI:

(i) Jurisdictions intending to make reservations under paragraph 3 are required to make notifications under sub-paragraphs (a)-(f), as the case may be.

(ii) Under paragraph 4, jurisdictions which have not made the reservations described in various sub-paragraphs of paragraph 3 shall make notifications of their CTAs depending upon the particular fact pattern existing in such CTAs. Accordingly, they shall notify the Depositary of whether each of their CTAs contains an existing provision that is not subject to a reservation under paragraph 3(b) through (d). Such a provision would be replaced by the provisions of paragraph 1 (as it may be modified by the reservation under paragraph 3(e)) where all Parties to the CTA have made such a notification. In all other cases, paragraph 1 (as it may be modified by the reservation under paragraph 3(e)) would apply to the CTA, but would supersede the existing provisions of the CTA only to the extent that those provisions are incompatible with paragraph 1 (as it may be modified by the reservation under paragraph 3(e)).

Denmark's Position[139] under the MLI

131. Denmark has not made any reservation under this Article. Accordingly, under Article 4(4) of the MLI, Denmark has notified all its 64 CTAs to the Depositary. The

139. Refer Denmark's Position under the MLI http://www.oecd.org/tax/treaties/beps-mli-position-denmark-instrument-deposit.pdf.

impact of provisions of Article 4 of the MLI on some of Denmark's DTAAs is reflected as below:

Denmark's CTA in MLI	*Position Taken by Treaty Partner*	*Outcome*
Belgium, Bulgaria, Chile, Croatia, Cyprus, the Czech Republic, Estonia, Greece, Hungary, Italy, Korea, Kuwait, Latvia, Lithuania, Luxembourg, Malaysia, Malta, Mexico*, Morocco, North Macedonia, Portugal, Singapore, Tunisia, Turkey, Ukraine	Reservation under Article 4(3)(a) of MLI	Article 4 of MLI would not apply
Argentina, Canada, China, Egypt, India, Ireland, Israel, Jamaica, Kenya, New Zealand, Pakistan, Poland, Romania, Russia, Serbia, the Slovak Republic, Slovenia, South Africa, United Kingdom	Similar notification as Denmark's	Relevant provision of CTA would be replaced by Article 4(1) of MLI
Australia, Indonesia	Reservation under Article 4(3)(e) of MLI	Relevant provision of CTA would be replaced by Article 4(1) of MLI & last sentence of Article 4(1) of MLI would be replaced with the text described in Article 4(3)(e) of MLI, implying that in the absence of any agreement between the CAs, no relief may be granted under the CTA

*Mexico has *inter alia* made reservation under Article 4(3)(d) of the MLI in respect of its CTA with Denmark.

India's Position[140] under the MLI

132. India has not made any reservation under this Article. Under India's present tax treaties (pre-MLI position), tie-breaker rule in respect of dual residence cases of persons other than individuals is based on the principle of POEM. The formulation as per paragraph 1 of MLI denying treaty benefits altogether or to the extent determined by CAs is not available in India's treaties. As dual residence cases of persons other than individuals often involve tax avoidance arrangements, this may have been a probable factor stimulating India's decision of not opting out of this Article. Accordingly, under

140. Refer India's Position under the MLI http://www.oecd.org/tax/treaties/beps-mli-position-india-instrument-deposit.pdf.

Article 4(4) of the MLI, India has notified all its CTAs, other than CTA with Greece, to the Depositary containing similar provisions. The impact of provisions of Article 4 of MLI on some of India's DTAAs is reflected as below:

India's CTA in MLI	*Position Taken by Treaty Partner*	*Outcome*
Albania, Austria, Belgium, Bulgaria, Croatia, Cyprus, the Czech Republic, Estonia, Finland, France, Georgia, Hungary, Iceland, Italy, Jordan, Korea, Kuwait, Latvia, Lithuania, Luxembourg, Malaysia, Malta, Morocco, North Macedonia, Portugal, Qatar, Saudi Arabia, Singapore, Spain, Sweden, Turkey, Ukraine, the United Arab Emirates	Reservation under Article 4(3)(a) of MLI	Article 4 of MLI would not apply
Armenia, Canada, Colombia, Denmark, Egypt, Ireland, Israel, Kazakhstan, Kenya, Mexico, the Netherlands, New Zealand, Norway, Poland, Romania, Russia, Serbia, the Slovak Republic, Slovenia, South Africa, United Kingdom, Uruguay	Similar notification as India's	Relevant provision of CTA would be replaced by Article 4(1) of MLI
Australia, Fiji, Indonesia, Japan	Reservation under Article 4(3)(e) of MLI	Relevant provision of CTA would be replaced by Article 4(1) of MLI & last sentence of Article 4(1) of MLI would be replaced with the text described in Article 4(3)(e) of MLI, implying that in the absence of any agreement between the CAs, no relief may be granted under the CTA

The Netherlands' Position[141] under the MLI

133. The Netherlands has not made any reservation under this Article. Accordingly, under Article 4(4) of the MLI, the Netherlands has notified all its 81 CTAs to the Depositary. The impact of provisions of Article 4 of the MLI on some of the Netherlands' DTAAs is reflected as below:

141. Refer The Netherlands' Position under the MLI http://www.oecd.org/tax/treaties/beps-mli-position-netherlands-instrument-deposit.pdf.

The Netherlands' CTA in MLI	*Position Taken by Treaty Partner*	*Outcome*
Albania, Austria, Bahrain, Barbados, Bosnia & Herzegovina, Croatia, the Czech Republic, Estonia, Finland, France, Georgia, Greece, Hong Kong, Hungary, Iceland, Italy, Jordan, Korea, Kuwait, Latvia, Lithuania, Luxembourg, Malaysia, Malta, Mexico*, Morocco, North Macedonia, Panama, Portugal, Qatar, Saudi Arabia, Singapore, Sweden, Tunisia, Turkey, the United Arab Emirates	Reservation under Article 4(3)(a) of MLI	Article 4 of MLI would not apply
Argentina, Armenia, Canada, China, Egypt, India, Israel, Jamaica, Kazakhstan, Kenya, New Zealand, Nigeria, Norway, Oman, Pakistan, Romania, Russia, Serbia, the Slovak Republic, Slovenia, South Africa, United Kingdom	Similar notification as the Netherlands'	Relevant provision of CTA would be replaced by Article 4(1) of MLI
Australia, Indonesia, Japan	Reservation under Article 4(3)(e) of MLI	Relevant provision of CTA would be replaced by Article 4(1) of MLI & last sentence of Article 4(1) of MLI would be replaced with the text described in Article 4(3)(e) of MLI, implying that in the absence of any agreement between the CAs, no relief may be granted under the CTA

*Mexico has made reservation under Article 4(3)(d) of the MLI *inter alia* in respect of its CTA with the Netherlands.

Few Snapshots of Positions[142] Taken by Other Countries under the MLI

134. Jurisdictions that have made reservations under Article 4(3)(a) for the entirety of the article not to apply to their CTAs are, namely, Albania, Andorra, Austria, Bahrain, Barbados, Belgium, Belize, Bosnia and Herzegovina, Bulgaria, Burkina Faso, Cameroon, Chile, Cote d'Ivoire, Croatia, Curaçao, Cyprus, the Czech Republic, Estonia,

142. Refer OECD – Signatories and Parties to the MLI http://www.oecd.org/tax/treaties/beps-mli-signatories-and-parties.pdf.

Finland, France, Gabon, Georgia, Germany, Greece, Guernsey, Hong Kong, Hungary, Iceland, the Isle of Man, Italy, Jersey, Jordan, Korea, Kuwait, Latvia, Liechtenstein, Lithuania, Luxembourg, Malaysia, Malta, Mauritius, Monaco, Morocco, North Macedonia, Panama, Portugal, Qatar, San Marino, Saudi Arabia, Seychelles, Singapore, Spain, Sweden, Switzerland, Tunisia, Turkey, Ukraine, the United Arab Emirates.

135. Jurisdictions that have made reservations under Article 4(3)(b) of the MLI are, namely, Ireland, Oman and Russia.

136. Jurisdictions that have made reservations under Article 4(3)(c) of the MLI are, namely, Indonesia and Mexico.

137. Jurisdictions that have made reservations under Article 4(3)(d) of the MLI are, namely, Mexico, Norway, Peru and Romania.

138. Jurisdictions that have made reservations under Article 4(3)(e) of the MLI are, namely, Australia, Costa Rica, Fiji, Indonesia, Japan, Papua New Guinea and Peru.

139. Only Ireland has made a reservation under Article 4(3)(f) of the MLI.

140. Under the MLI, Australia has made a reservation under Article 4(3)(e), while Ireland has made a reservation under Article 4(3)(f); with the result, Article 4 of MLI shall not apply to Australia-Ireland CTA.

141. Under the MLI, in respect of Russia[143] it is seen that:

- Russia has made reservation under Article 4(3)(b) in respect of its treaties with Argentina, Armenia, Belarus, Chile, Cyprus, Ecuador, Egypt, Finland, Iceland, Indonesia, Israel, Kazakhstan, Korea, Latvia, Lithuania, Luxemburg, Malta, Mexico, Norway, Singapore, Sri Lanka, US; with the result, Article 4 of the MLI shall not apply to these CTAs.
- On taking Australia as the corresponding treaty partner, which has made reservation under Article 4(3)(e), it is seen that both Russia and Australia have made similar notifications under Article 4(4) of MLI (as provisions similar to Article 4(3)(b) of MLI do not exist in Russia-Australia CTA); with the result, relevant provision of Russia-Australia CTA would be replaced by Article 4(1) of MLI and last sentence of Article 4(1) of MLI would be replaced with the text described in Article 4(3)(e) of MLI, implying that in the absence of any agreement between the CAs, no relief may be granted under the CTA.

142. Under the MLI, in respect of Norway[144] it is seen that:

143. Refer Russia's Position under the MLI http://www.oecd.org/tax/treaties/beps-mli-position-russian-federation-instrument-deposit.pdf.
144. Refer Norway's Position under the MLI http://www.oecd.org/tax/treaties/beps-mli-position-norway-instrument-deposit.pdf.

- Norway has made reservation under Article 4(3)(d) in respect of its treaties with Bulgaria, Chile, Cyprus, Estonia, Latvia, Lithuania, Romania, Serbia, UK; with the result, Article 4 of MLI shall not apply to these CTAs.
- On taking Japan as the corresponding treaty partner, which has made reservation under Article 4(3)(e) of the MLI, it is seen that both Norway and Japan have made similar notifications under Article 4(4) of MLI (as provisions similar to Article 4(3)(d) of MLI do not exist in Norway-Japan CTA); with the result, relevant provision of Norway-Japan CTA would be replaced by Article 4(1) of MLI and last sentence of Article 4(1) of MLI would be replaced with the text described in Article 4(3)(e) of MLI, implying that in the absence of any agreement between the CAs, no relief may be granted under the CTA.

143. Since Indonesia and Mexico have made similar reservations under Article 4(3)(c) of the MLI, Article 4 of the MLI would not apply to Indonesia-Mexico CTA.

The various notifications made by treaty partners under Article 4 of the MLI and impact/outcome thereof on the respective CTAs are provided in Figure 5.

Figure 5 Article 4: Dual Resident Entities – Flowchart on Notifications & Their Impact

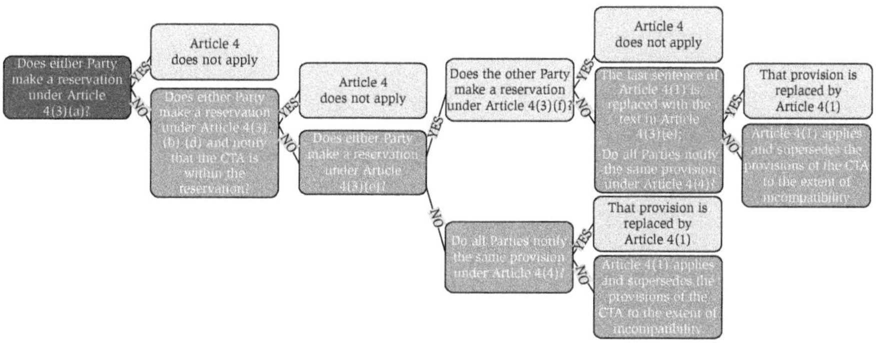

Source: OECD – Toolkit for Application of the Multilateral Instrument for BEPS Tax Treaty Related Measures https://www.oecd.org/tax/treaties/application-toolkit-multilateral-instrument-for-beps-tax-treaty-measures.htm.

3.5.3 Article 5 of MLI: Application of Methods for Elimination of Double Taxation

144. The interplay between Article 5 of MLI, corresponding BEPS Report and the resulting provisions incorporated in OECD MTC 2017 is represented in a table as below:

MLI		*BEPS Final Report*		*OECD MTC 2017*	
Article	*Title of Article*	*BEPS Action Plan*	*Title of BEPS Action Plan*	*Article*	*Title of Article*
5	Application of Methods for Elimination of Double Taxation	Action 2	Neutralising the Effects of Hybrid Mismatch Arrangements	23A(4), 23B	Methods for Elimination of Double Taxation

145. The article at a glance is as below:

Substantive (BEPS) Provisions under Para(s)	*Opt-In Provisions under Para*	*Alternative Provisions under Para*	*Compatibility Clause*		*Reservations under Para*	*Notifications under Para*
			Para	*Type*		
1, 2, 4, 6	None	2, 4, 6	3, 5, 7	'applies to' and 'in place of'	8, 9	8, 9, 10

Status in Pre-BEPS Project Era

146. In tax treaties where State of residence followed exemption method for elimination of double taxation, problems were noticed with respect to certain items of income (like dividend, interest income) which were not being taxed in the State of source also, leading to double non-taxation. As regards Article 23A (Exemption Method), paragraph 2 of that Article provides that in the case of items of income covered by Articles 10, 11 of the OECD MTC 2014, it is the credit method, and not the exemption method, that is applicable. However, a number of bilateral tax treaties depart from these provisions of Article 23A and provide for the application of exemption method with respect to dividends received from foreign companies in which a resident company has a substantial shareholding. While paragraph 4 of Article 23A may address some situations of hybrid mismatch arrangements where income is otherwise exempted from tax in State of source (so that paragraph 1 of Article 23A does not apply and no exemption from tax is therefore granted to such income in the State of residence), many tax treaties do not include that provision as well. BEPS Action 2 Plan addresses such potential double non-taxation issues that may arise in tax treaties.

Article 5(1)

147. In view of the double non-taxation arising on following exemption method under Article 23A in the State of residence in respect of certain items of income (which are treated as exempt in the State of source also), States that enter into tax treaties providing for the application of the exemption method with respect to such incomes, therefore, should consider the inclusion of paragraph 4 of Article 23A in their tax treaties, although these States should also recognise that the provision will only provide a partial solution to the problem. A more complete solution that should be considered by these States would be to include in their treaties such rules that would expressly allow them to apply the credit method, as opposed to the exemption method, with respect to such incomes that are deductible in the Payer State. In addition, these States (of residence) may also wish to consider a more general solution to the problems of non-taxation resulting from potential abuses of the exemption method, which would be for States not to include the exemption method in their treaties. Under that approach, the credit method would be provided for in tax treaties, thereby ensuring the relief of juridical double taxation.

148. Article 5 of the MLI allows asymmetrical application of MLI provisions permitting each Party to apply its chosen option to its own residents. These provisions address problems arising from the inclusion of the exemption method in tax treaties with respect to items of income that are not taxed in the State of source. The provisions modify the methods for eliminating double taxation in order to avoid cases of double non-taxation for States that have adopted the exemption method under Article 23A of the OECD MTC 2014. Article 5 of the MLI provides the following three options to the Parties, or, to apply none of these three options:

(1) Option A (in paragraph 2 of Article 5).
(2) Option B (in paragraph 4 of Article 5).
(3) Option C (in paragraph 6 of Article 5).

Option A under Article 5(2)

149. Option A (in paragraph 2 of Article 5) is akin to Article 23A(4) of the OECD MTC 2014 and addresses potential abuses of the exemption method that may result in the non-taxation of certain items of income or capital. Option A provides a partial solution to these potential abuses of the exemption method by providing that provisions of a CTA that would otherwise exempt income or capital derived by a resident of a Contracting Jurisdiction shall not apply where the other Contracting Jurisdiction (the source jurisdiction) applies the provisions of that CTA to exempt such income or capital from tax or to limit the rate at which such income or capital may be taxed.

150. The paragraph applies where, on the one hand, the State of source interprets the provisions of the treaty in such a way that an item of income or capital falls under a provision of the treaty that eliminates its right to tax that item or limits the tax (reduced rate of tax) that it can impose while, on the other hand, the State of residence adopts a different interpretation of the provisions of the treaty and thus considers that the item may be taxed in the State of source. Option A contains a switch-over clause that tackles cases of such double non-taxation due to different interpretation of tax treaty provisions by State of source and State of residence, respectively. Under Option A, in order to apply method for elimination of double taxation, State of residence 'switches' from exemption method to credit method in case the particular item of income or capital is taxed in the State of source at reduced rate or is treated as exempt from taxation. Hence, the State of residence shall allow as a deduction from tax on such income or capital of its resident of an amount equal to the tax paid in the State of source.

Option B under Article 5(4)

151. Option B (in paragraph 4 of Article 5) reflects new drafting to expressly allow a Contracting Jurisdiction to apply the credit method rather than the exemption method with respect to dividends that are deductible in the Contracting Jurisdiction of the payer. The approach taken in Option B offers a more complete solution than Option A to problems arising from the inclusion of the exemption method in tax treaties with respect to items of income that are not taxed in the jurisdiction of source.

152. Option B also contains a switch-over clause that applies in State of residence in cases where State of residence treats such income as dividend which is deductible in the State of source. On applying Option B, the State of residence shall allow as a deduction from the tax on the income of that resident an amount equal to the income tax paid in the other State of source.

Option C under Article 5(6)

153. Option C (in paragraph 6 of Article 5) is based on Article 23B of the OECD MTC and allows a Contracting Jurisdiction to adopt the credit method for the relief of juridical double taxation in place of the exemption method. Option C provides a more general solution than Options A and B to the problem of non-taxation resulting from potential abuses of the exemption method.

154. Option C provides for credit method for Parties which instead of implementing a switch-over clause might prefer to replace the exemption method in their CTA with the credit method – equivalent to Article 23B of the OECD Model.

Compatibility Clauses

155. Paragraph 3 is the compatibility clause of Option A, which describes the interaction between Option A and the provisions of CTAs. The compatibility clause indicates that Option A would apply to CTAs that would otherwise require a Contracting Jurisdiction to exempt income that the other Contracting Jurisdiction subjects to a reduced rate of tax or exempts based on its application of the CTA. This would apply, for example, to provisions of the type found in Article 23A of the OECD and UN Model Tax Conventions, as well as provisions of CTAs implementing the exemption method for the elimination of double taxation.[145] Option A may not apply to provisions of CTA that grant exclusive taxing rights to the jurisdiction of residence with respect to specific types of income, such as provisions that exempt dividends from source taxation[146]

145. Refer Explanatory Statement to the MLI, para. 64.
146. *Id.*, para. 65.

where no tax is actually payable on such income under the provisions of the domestic laws of the State of source.[147]

156. Paragraph 5 is the compatibility clause of Option B, which describes the interaction between Option B and the provisions of CTAs. The compatibility clause indicates that Option B would apply to CTAs that would otherwise require a Contracting Jurisdiction to exempt income derived by its residents from dividends that are deductible in the Contracting Jurisdiction of the payer.[148]

157. Paragraph 7 is the compatibility clause of Option C, which describes the interaction between Option C and the provisions of CTAs. The compatibility clause indicates that Option C would apply in place of provisions of a CTA that, for the purposes of eliminating double taxation, require a Contracting Jurisdiction to exempt from tax in that Contracting Jurisdiction income derived or capital owned by a resident of that Contracting Jurisdiction which, in accordance with the provisions of the CTA, may be taxed in the other Contracting Jurisdiction.[149] Option C may not replace existing provisions intended to clarify that dividends that would be exempt from tax under the domestic law of the Contracting Jurisdiction of residence would be exempt under the CTA as well.[150]

Reservations under Paragraphs 8, 9

158. The possible reservations which jurisdictions may make based on their respective positions are as below:

(i) Under paragraph 8, jurisdictions may opt out of Article 5 entirely with respect to identified CTAs or all CTAs if none of the Options is chosen under Article 5(1), as the same is not a minimum standard. Paragraph 8 provides that a State that does not choose to apply one of the options of Article 5 may reserve the right not to apply the entire article to one or more identified CTAs, given the concern that accepting asymmetrical application across the board could disrupt the balance of certain bilateral tax treaties. As provided in Article 28(3) of MLI, unless explicitly provided otherwise, a reservation applies symmetrically. Accordingly, when a Contracting Jurisdiction to an agreement makes a reservation under Article 5(8) of MLI with respect to the agreement, the entirety of Article 5 does not apply for not only that Contracting Jurisdiction but also the other Contracting Jurisdiction. Such effect of the reservation enables a Party to prevent the other Contracting Jurisdiction of its CTA from applying Article 5 asymmetrically.

(ii) Under paragraph 9, jurisdictions not opting for Option C may not permit the other Contracting Jurisdiction(s) to apply Option C with respect to identified CTAs or all CTAs. Jurisdictions making a reservation under paragraph 9,

147. Refer OECD MTC 2017, para. 56.2 of the Commentary on para. 4 of Art. 23A.
148. Refer Explanatory Statement to the MLI, para. 67.
149. *Id.*, para. 70.
150. *Id.*, para. 71.

however, may opt for Options A or B, as the case may be. For example, Liechtenstein has made a reservation under Article 5(9), but has opted for Option A in its notification under Article 5(10) of the MLI.

159. The purpose of the provisions established in Article 5(8), (9) is to exclude the legal effect of the entirety of Article 5 or Option C, respectively, not only for the reserving Party - which, in any case, has not opted in to any option (Option C in particular) - but also for other Parties to the MLI with which it has a CTA. Such provisions, although applicable asymmetrically, pursue to rebalance the rights and obligations established in the CTAs, which could be distorted due to the unilateral decisions of one of the Parties to opt in to one of the alternative provisions of Article 5 of MLI, as Article 5 of MLI provides for the asymmetrical application of the alternative options established therein. Thus, in a way, the provisions contained in Article 5(8), (9) do not create inequalities, but counterbalance them. The rationale[151] behind both reservations is to avoid that tax incentives granted by the State of source (normally, developing countries) to encourage foreign investment in their jurisdiction may be nullified due to the unilateral decision of the State of residence to apply a switch-over clause or to replace the exemption method with the credit method. If a jurisdiction opts in to the application of one of the switch-over clauses or the credit method, that jurisdiction would have the right to tax the amounts foregone by the State of source due to the implementation of tax incentives to enhance cross-border investments. Moreover, taxpayers would have no major incentives to invest in the State of source, since the taxes foregone by the State of source would be paid in the State of residence instead. In this respect, the ad hoc Group has not followed the position taken by the OECD in its report titled 'Tax Sparing: A Reconsideration'.[152]

Notifications

160. Depending upon the position taken by various jurisdictions, the following notifications are required to be made under Article 5 of the MLI:

(i) Jurisdictions intending to make reservations under paragraphs 8, 9 are required to make notifications as the case may be.
(ii) Under paragraph 10, jurisdictions which have not made the reservations described in various sub-paragraphs of paragraphs 8, 9 shall make notifications requiring each Party that has chosen to apply an Option under paragraph 1 to notify the Depositary of:
   - its choice of Option;
   - each CTA containing a provision within the scope of the compatibility clause for that Option; and
   - the article and paragraph number of each such provision in the CTA.

151. Refer Nathalie Bravo's 'A Multilateral Instrument for Updating the Tax Treaty Network' IBFD Doctoral Series 52, p. 224.
152. Refer OECD - Tax Sparing - A Reconsideration https://read.oecd-ilibrary.org/taxation/tax-sparing_9789264162433-en#page1 accessed on 29 July 2020.

To ensure clarity, an Option will only apply with respect to a provision of a CTA if the Party that chose to apply the Option makes such a notification with respect to that provision.

Denmark's Position[153] under the MLI

161. Denmark has chosen Option C under Article 5(1) of the MLI and has notified its treaties with Brazil, Poland and the Slovak Republic pursuant to Article 5(10)(c) of the MLI. Depending on the position taken by the respective treaty partner, the modification of CTA provisions by the MLI provisions is stated as below:

Treaty Partner	*Position Taken by Treaty Partner*	*Outcome under the MLI*
Brazil	Not a Signatory to the MLI	MLI not applicable to Denmark-Brazil DTAC
Poland[154]	Choice of Option C	Option C would apply to Article 22(1)(a) of the Denmark-Poland CTA[155]
The Slovak Republic[156]	Choice of Option C	Option C would apply to Article 23(2) of the Denmark-Slovak Republic CTA

India's Position[157] under the MLI

162. India has not made any reservation under this Article. In most of India's treaties, India already has the credit method for elimination of double taxation, except for its treaties with Bulgaria, Egypt, Greece and the Slovak Republic. Hence, India has chosen Option C under Article 5(1) of MLI with the intent to replace 'exemption method' with 'credit method' in these four treaties through the MLI. Depending on the position taken by the respective treaty partner, the modification of CTA provisions by the MLI provisions is stated as below:

153. Refer Denmark's Position under the MLI http://www.oecd.org/tax/treaties/beps-mli-position-denmark-instrument-deposit.pdf.
154. Refer Poland's Position under the MLI http://www.oecd.org/tax/treaties/beps-mli-position-poland-instrument-deposit.pdf.
155. Refer Denmark-Poland Synthesised Text https://research.ibfd.org/#/doc?url=/data/treaty/docs/html/tt_dk-pl_02_eng_2001_tt__td3.html#tt_dk-pl_02_eng_2001_tt__td3_a22 accessed on 30 July 2020.
156. Refer Slovak Republic's Position under the MLI http://www.oecd.org/tax/treaties/beps-mli-position-slovak-republic-instrument-deposit.pdf.
157. Refer India's Position under the MLI http://www.oecd.org/tax/treaties/beps-mli-position-india-instrument-deposit.pdf.

Treaty Partner	*Position Taken by Treaty Partner*	*Outcome under the MLI*
Bulgaria[158]	Reservation under Article 5(8) of MLI with respect to all of its CTAs	Article 5 would not apply
Egypt[159]	No notification	Option C chosen by India would apply
Greece[160]	Reservation under Article 5(8) of MLI with respect to its CTAs incl. India	Article 5 would not apply
The Slovak Republic[161]	Choice of Option C	Option C chosen by India and the Slovak Republic would apply

The Netherlands' Position[162] under the MLI

163. The Netherlands has chosen Option A under Article 5(1) of the MLI and has notified a number of treaties, including its CTAs with Serbia, the Slovak Republic, Slovenia and others, pursuant to Article 5(10) of the MLI. As an illustration and depending on the position taken by some of its treaty partners, the modification of CTA provisions by the MLI provisions is stated as below:

Treaty Partner	*Position Taken by Treaty Partner*	*Outcome under the MLI*
Serbia[163]	Reservation under Article 5(8) of MLI with respect to all of its CTAs	Article 5 would not apply[164]
The Slovak Republic	Choice of Option C	Option A chosen by the Netherlands and Option C chosen by the Slovak Republic would apply to relevant provisions of the Netherlands-Slovak Republic CTA

158. Refer Bulgaria's Position under the MLI http://www.oecd.org/tax/treaties/beps-mli-position-bulgaria.pdf.
159. Refer Egypt's Position under the MLI http://www.oecd.org/tax/treaties/beps-mli-position-egypt-instrument-deposit.pdf.
160. Refer Greece's Position under the MLI http://www.oecd.org/tax/treaties/beps-mli-position-greece.pdf.
161. Refer Slovak Republic's Position under the MLI http://www.oecd.org/tax/treaties/beps-mli-position-slovak-republic-instrument-deposit.pdf.
162. Refer The Netherlands' Position under the MLI http://www.oecd.org/tax/treaties/beps-mli-position-netherlands-instrument-deposit.pdf.
163. Refer Serbia's Position under the MLI http://www.oecd.org/tax/treaties/beps-mli-position-serbia-instrument-deposit.pdf.
164. Refer The Netherlands-Serbia Synthesised Text https://research.ibfd.org/#/doc?url=/data/treaty/docs/html/tt_nl-rs_02_eng_1982_tt__td2.html#tt_nl-rs_02_eng_1982_tt__td2_a23 accessed on 30 July 2020.

Treaty Partner	*Position Taken by Treaty Partner*	*Outcome under the MLI*
Slovenia[165]	No notification under Article 5	Option A chosen by the Netherlands would apply to relevant provisions of Netherlands-Slovenia CTA[166]

Few Snapshots of Positions[167] Taken by Other Countries under the MLI

164. Jurisdictions that have made reservation under Article 5(8) of the MLI are, namely, Albania, Bahrain, Bosnia and Herzegovina, Bulgaria, Canada, Costa Rica, Croatia, Cyprus, the Czech Republic, France, Greece, Guernsey, Hong Kong, Hungary, Iceland, Indonesia, the Isle of Man, Jamaica, Jersey, Kazakhstan, Kenya, Korea, Latvia, Malaysia, Malta, Mauritius, Morocco, North Macedonia, Oman, Panama, Qatar, Russia, San Marino, Saudi Arabia, Serbia, Seychelles, Singapore, South Africa, Sweden, Ukraine.

165. Jurisdictions that have made reservations under Article 5(9) of the MLI are, namely, Estonia, Liechtenstein, Luxembourg and Switzerland.

166. Jurisdictions that have notified Option A under Article 5(10) of the MLI include Austria, Côte d'Ivoire, Curaçao, Estonia, Liechtenstein, Luxembourg, the Netherlands and Switzerland. As of now, no jurisdiction has notified Option B under Article 5(10) of the MLI. Jurisdictions that have notified Option C under Article 5(10) of the MLI include Argentina, Cameroon, Denmark, Gabon, India, Norway, Pakistan, Poland, Portugal, Romania, Senegal, the Slovak Republic, Spain, Turkey, Uruguay.

167. For more illustrations, based on the positions taken by certain jurisdictions under Article 5 of the MLI, the modification of CTA provisions by the MLI provisions is stated as below:

Jurisdiction	*Position Taken*	*Treaty Partner*	*Position Taken*	*Outcome under the MLI*
Austria	Option A	Belgium	No notification	Option A chosen by Austria would apply
Austria	Option A	Singapore	Reservation under Article 5(8) of MLI with respect to all of its CTAs	Article 5 would not apply

165. Refer Slovenia's Position under the MLI http://www.oecd.org/tax/treaties/beps-mli-position-slovenia-instrument-deposit.pdf.
166. Refer The Netherlands-Slovenia Synthesised Text https://research.ibfd.org/#/doc?url=/data/treaty/docs/html/tt_nl-si_01_eng_2004_tt__td2.html#tt_nl-si_01_eng_2004_tt__td2_a22 accessed on 30 July 2020.
167. Refer OECD – Signatories and Parties to the MLI http://www.oecd.org/tax/treaties/beps-mli-signatories-and-parties.pdf.

Jurisdiction	*Position Taken*	*Treaty Partner*	*Position Taken*	*Outcome under the MLI*
Austria	Option A	India	Option C	Option A chosen by Austria only would apply (in its notification under Article 5(10), India had not notified CTA with Austria as India already has credit method)
Austria	Option A	The Netherlands	Option A	Option A chosen by Austria and the Netherlands would apply in respect of relevant CTA provisions notified by each of them
Liechtenstein	- Reservation under Article 5(9) with respect to all CTAs - Notification of Option A under Article 5(10) & CTA with Georgia notified	Georgia	No notification	Option A would apply for Liechtenstein (no impact of Article 5 of MLI for Georgia)

The various notifications made by treaty partners under Article 5 of the MLI and impact/outcome thereof on the respective CTAs are provided in Figure 6.

Figure 6 Article 5: Application of Methods for Elimination of Double Taxation – Flowchart on Notifications & Their Impact

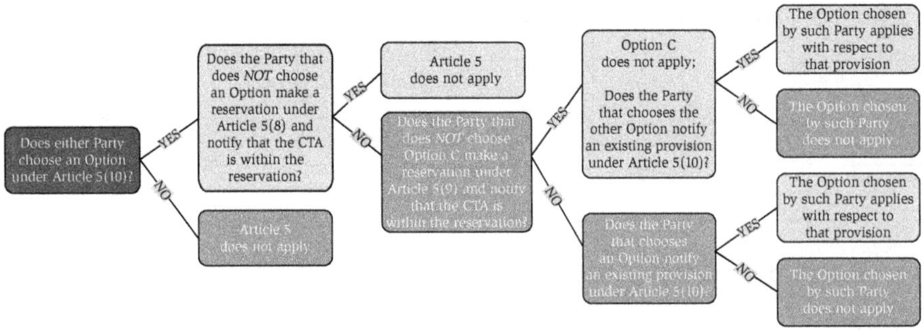

Source: OECD – Toolkit for Application of the Multilateral Instrument for BEPS Tax Treaty Related Measures https://www.oecd.org/tax/treaties/application-toolkit-multilateral-instrument-for-beps-tax-treaty-measures.htm.

3.6 PART III OF MLI: TREATY ABUSE

3.6.1 Article 6 of MLI: Purpose of a Covered Tax Agreement

168. The interplay between Article 6 of MLI, corresponding BEPS Report and the resulting provisions incorporated in OECD MTC 2017 is represented in a table as below:

MLI		*BEPS Final Report*		*OECD MTC 2017*	
Article	*Title of Article*	*BEPS Action Plan*	*Title of BEPS Action Plan*	*Article*	*Title of Article*
6	Purpose of a Covered Tax Agreement	Action 6	Preventing the Granting of Treaty Benefits in Inappropriate Circumstances	Preamble	

169. The article at a glance is as below:

Substantive (BEPS) Provisions under Para(s)	*Opt-In Provisions under Para*	*Alternative Provisions under Para*	*Compatibility Clause*		*Reservations under Para*	*Notifications under Para*
			Para	*Type*		
1, 3	3	None	2	'in place of or in the absence of'	4	4, 5, 6

Status in Pre-BEPS Project Era

170. Earlier, provisions of tax treaties were developed with the prime objective of preventing double taxation. This was reflected in the title proposed in both the 1963 Draft Double Taxation Convention on Income and Capital and the 1977 Model Double Taxation Convention on Income and Capital, which was:

> Convention between (State A) and (State B) for the avoidance of double taxation with respect to taxes on income and on capital.

Subsequently, the Commentary on Article 1 was modified to provide expressly that tax treaties were not intended to encourage tax avoidance or evasion and later that paragraph was amended to clarify that the prevention of tax avoidance was also a purpose of tax treaties. However, intention to prevent tax evasion and tax avoidance was not expressly mentioned in the Preamble of OECD MTC.

BEPS Action 6 Report

171. In view of the recommendations of the BEPS Action 6 Report, it was decided to state clearly, in the title recommended by the OECD MTC, that the prevention of tax evasion and avoidance is a purpose of tax treaties. It was also decided that the OECD MTC should recommend a preamble that provides expressly that States that enter into a tax treaty intend to eliminate double taxation without creating opportunities for tax evasion and avoidance (including through treaty shopping arrangements aimed at obtaining reliefs provided in this Convention for the indirect benefit of residents of third States). The clear statement of the intention of the Signatories to a tax treaty that appears in the preamble will be relevant to the interpretation and application of the provisions of that treaty. According to the basic rule of interpretation of treaties in Article 31(1) of the Vienna Convention, '*[a] treaty shall be interpreted in good faith in accordance with the ordinary meaning to be given to the terms of the treaty* in their context *and in the light of* its object and purpose' [emphasis added]. Article 31(2) of Vienna Convention confirms that, for the purpose of this basic rule, the context of the treaty includes its preamble.[168]

Article 6 of MLI

172. With the modification of the preamble of a CTA by Article 6 of the MLI, the objectives being achieved are to make sure the object and purpose of tax treaties includes preventing tax treaty abuse (tax evasion or avoidance, including through treaty shopping arrangements), is in line with the Action 6 minimum standards agreed in the context of the BEPS Project, by inserting in the preamble of tax treaties a statement on the intention to eliminate double taxation without creating opportunities for non-taxation or reduced taxation.

173. Article 6 of the MLI sets out the new language of the preamble, which includes:

- Under paragraph 1 – Statement comprising minimum standard which refers to the intention of the Contracting States to eliminate double taxation without creating opportunities for non-taxation or reduced taxation through tax evasion or avoidance, including through treaty shopping.
- Under paragraph 3 – An additional statement referring to the desire of the Contracting States to further develop their economic relationship and to enhance cooperation in tax matters.

174. Paragraph 3 of the preamble language is included only with respect to CTAs that do not already contain preamble language referring to a desire to develop an economic

168. Refer Article by Jonathan Schwarz Titled 'The Impact of the New Preamble on the Interpretation of Old and New Treaties and on the Policy of Abuse Prevention' https://research.ibfd.org/#/doc?url=/collections/bit/html/bit_2020_04_o2_1.html (s. 1) accessed on 3 August 2020.

relationship or to enhance cooperation in tax matters. Also, given that including this portion of the preamble of the OECD MTC is not required in order to meet a minimum standard, this paragraph is an optional provision, and, as provided in paragraph 6, will modify a CTA only where all Contracting Jurisdictions agree to such modification by choosing to apply paragraph 3. This statement has not been opted in by Albania, Armenia, Austria, Bosnia and Herzegovina, Bulgaria, Burkina Faso, Canada, Colombia, Cote d'Ivoire, the Czech Republic, Denmark, Estonia, Finland, Gabon, Germany, Guernsey, Iceland, India, Indonesia, the Isle of Man, Israel, Italy, Jersey, Kazakhstan, Korea, Latvia, Lithuania, Malaysia, Morocco, New Zealand, Oman, Poland, Portugal, Sweden.

175. The UN Model (2017) includes both the language of the mandatory text in Article 6(1) and the optional language in Article 6(3) of the MLI. In fact, their order is reversed, and the desire to develop an economic relationship is expressed as the primary purpose in the UN version.[169] However, in the footnote of the Preamble of the UN Model (2017), it is stated that the preamble shall be drafted in accordance with the constitutional procedures of the Contracting States.

Compatibility Clause

176. The compatibility clause in paragraph 2 of Article 6 provides that the preamble text in paragraph 1 replaces existing preamble language of CTAs that refers to an intent to eliminate double taxation (whether or not that language also refers to an intent not to create opportunities for non-taxation or reduced taxation), or is added to the preamble of CTAs where such language does not exist in the preamble of the CTAs.[170] Some CTAs may contain preamble language that refers to intent to eliminate double taxation without creating opportunities for non-taxation or reduced taxation but does not include a reference to tax evasion or avoidance or to treaty shopping. Paragraph 1 is intended to cover these examples and replace them with the preamble language in paragraph 1, though such language may be preserved through the reservation set out in paragraph 4.[171]

177. It would suffice to mention here that there is no specific compatibility clause for paragraph 3 of Article 6 of the MLI.

Reservation under Paragraph 4

178. Since paragraph 1 reflects the minimum standard for protection against the abuse of tax treaties under Action 6, paragraph 4 permits a Party to opt out of applying paragraph 1 only with respect to CTAs that already satisfy the minimum standard. Paragraph 4 is intended to permit Parties to preserve preamble language in their CTAs

169. Refer Article by Jonathan Schwarz Titled 'The Impact of the New Preamble on the Interpretation of Old and New Treaties and on the Policy of Abuse Prevention' https://research.ibfd.org/#/doc?url=/collections/bit/html/bit_2020_04_o2_1.html (s. 5.2) accessed on 3 August 2020.
170. Refer Explanatory Statement to the MLI, para. 81.
171. *Id.*, para. 82.

that already refers to the intent to eliminate double taxation without creating opportunities for non-taxation or reduced taxation, whether or not such language is limited to cases of tax evasion or avoidance (including cases of treaty shopping) or applies more broadly.[172]

Notifications

179. Depending upon the position taken by various jurisdictions, the following notifications are required to be made under Article 6 of the MLI:

(i) Notification to the Depositary of CTAs under paragraph 4 which already contain the preamble language that is within the scope of the reservation under paragraph 4.

(ii) Notification to the Depositary of CTAs under paragraph 5 which are not within the scope of the reservation under paragraph 4 to ensure clarity about which existing preamble language will be replaced by the text described in paragraph 1. Paragraph 5 requires each Party to notify the Depositary of whether each of its CTAs, other than those that are within the scope of a reservation under paragraph 4, contains preamble language referring to an intent to eliminate double taxation, and if so, the text of the relevant preamble paragraph. Existing preamble language would be replaced by the text described in paragraph 1 where all Contracting Jurisdictions have made such a notification with respect to the existing preamble language. In other cases, the text described in paragraph 1 would be included in addition to the existing preamble language.

(iii) Notification to the Depositary under paragraph 6 of the choice to apply paragraph 3 of Article 6. To ensure clarity about whether the text described in paragraph 3 will be included in a particular CTA, such notification shall also include the list of its CTAs that do not already contain preamble language referring to a desire to develop an economic relationship or to enhance cooperation in tax matters. The text described in paragraph 3 will be included in a CTA only where all Contracting Jurisdictions have chosen to apply that paragraph and have made such a notification with respect to the CTA.

Denmark's Position[173] under the MLI

180. Denmark has not made any reservation under Article 6(4) in respect of paragraph 1 of Article 6 of the MLI. In any case, paragraph 1 comprises a minimum standard.

Notification has been made by Denmark under paragraph 5 of Article 6 of the MLI, wherein it has notified all its 64 CTAs under the MLI and has also identified the text of the relevant preambular paragraphs. Hence, in Denmark's case, the preamble text described in Article 6(1) of MLI would replace the existing preamble language or get included in addition to the existing preamble language in Denmark's CTAs notified

172. *Id.*, para. 85.
173. Refer Denmark's Position under the MLI http://www.oecd.org/tax/treaties/beps-mli-position-denmark-instrument-deposit.pdf.

under the MLI, depending upon the corresponding position taken by the respective treaty partner.

Further, Denmark has not opted in for paragraph 3 and has made no notification under paragraph 6 of Article 6 of the MLI.

India's Position[174] under the MLI

181. India has not made any reservation under Article 6(4) in respect of paragraph 1 of Article 6 of the MLI as none of its CTAs contain the entire preamble language recommended by the said paragraph. In any case, paragraph 1 comprises a minimum standard.

No notification has been made by India under paragraph 5 of Article 6 of the MLI. Hence, in India's case, the preamble text described in Article 6(1) of MLI would be included in addition to the existing preamble language of India's CTAs notified under the MLI. A probable factor stimulating India's decision of not replacing the entirety of existing preamble text in its DTAAs with the MLI provisions may have been the desire to retain '*prevention of fiscal evasion with respect to taxes on income*' provisions in the DTAAs, which are enshrined in India's domestic laws as well.

Further, India has not opted in for paragraph 3 and has made no notification under paragraph 6. A probable factor stimulating this decision could have been to ensure that there are no claims and consequent unintended grant of treaty benefits arising, *inter alia*, with the presence of statement referring to the desire of the Contracting States to further develop their economic relationship.

The Netherlands' Position[175] under the MLI

182. The Netherlands has not made any reservation under Article 6(4) in respect of paragraph 1 of Article 6 of the MLI. In any case, paragraph 1 comprises a minimum standard.

Notification has been made by the Netherlands under paragraph 5 of Article 6 of the MLI, wherein it has notified all its CTAs under the MLI (except CTAs with Canada, France, Sweden, US) and has also identified the text of the relevant preambular paragraphs. Hence, in the Netherlands' case, the preamble text described in Article 6(1) of MLI would replace the existing preamble language or get included in addition to the existing preamble language in the Netherlands' CTAs notified under the MLI, depending upon the corresponding position taken by the respective treaty partner.

Further, the Netherlands has opted in for paragraph 3 and has made the requisite notification under paragraph 6 of Article 6 of the MLI by notifying all its CTAs under the MLI (except CTAs with Germany, Ghana, Hungary, Uzbekistan). The text described in paragraph 3 of Article 6 of the MLI shall be included in the notified CTAs only when there is a matching notification by the corresponding treaty partner.

174. Refer India's Position under the MLI http://www.oecd.org/tax/treaties/beps-mli-position-india-instrument-deposit.pdf.
175. Refer The Netherlands' Position under the MLI http://www.oecd.org/tax/treaties/beps-mli-position-netherlands-instrument-deposit.pdf.

Few Snapshots of Positions[176] Taken by Other Countries under the MLI

183. Jurisdictions that have made reservation under paragraph 4 of Article 6 are, namely, Argentina, Bulgaria, Chile, Colombia, Germany, Hong Kong, Japan, Luxembourg, Mexico, Senegal, Spain, Turkey and UK.

184. Jurisdictions that have opted in for paragraph 3 of Article 6 by making a notification under paragraph 6 of Article 6 of the MLI are, namely, Andorra, Argentina, Australia, Bahrain, Barbados, Belgium, Belize, Cameroon, Chile, China, Costa Rica, Croatia, Curaçao, Cyprus, Egypt, Fiji, France, Georgia, Greece, Hong Kong, Hungary, Ireland, Jamaica, Japan, Jordan, Kenya, Kuwait, Liechtenstein, Luxembourg, Malta, Mauritius, Mexico, Monaco, the Netherlands, Nigeria, North Macedonia, Norway, Pakistan, Panama, Papua New Guinea, Peru, Qatar, Romania, Russia, San Marino, Saudi Arabia, Senegal, Serbia, Seychelles, Singapore, the Slovak Republic, Slovenia, South Africa, Spain, Switzerland, Tunisia, Turkey, Ukraine, the United Arab Emirates, UK, Uruguay.

185. Notifications under Article 6 by some countries and modification by the MLI on such CTAs are illustratively given hereunder:

<table>
<tr><th>Jurisdiction</th><th>Position Taken</th><th>Treaty Partner</th><th>Position Taken</th><th>Outcome under the MLI</th></tr>
<tr><td rowspan="2">Japan</td><td rowspan="2">Reservation under Article 6(4) in respect of CTA with Germany</td><td rowspan="2">Germany</td><td>Reservation under Article 6(4) in respect of CTA with Japan</td><td>Article 6(1) would not apply</td></tr>
<tr><td colspan="2">Existing Preamble Text of Japan-Germany CTA
'Desiring to further develop their economic relationship and to enhance their cooperation in tax matters,
Intending to conclude a new Agreement for the elimination of double taxation with respect to taxes on income and to certain other taxes without creating opportunities for non-taxation or reduced taxation through tax evasion or avoidance (including through treaty-shopping arrangements aimed at obtaining reliefs provided in this Agreement for the indirect benefit of residents of third States)'</td></tr>
</table>

176. Refer OECD – Signatories and Parties to the MLI http://www.oecd.org/tax/treaties/beps-mli-signatories-and-parties.pdf.

Jurisdiction	*Position Taken*	*Treaty Partner*	*Position Taken*	*Outcome under the MLI*
	Opted in for Article 6(3) but CTA with Germany not notified under Article 6(6)		Did not opt in for Article 6(3)	Article 6(3) would not apply
Spain	Notification under Article 6(5) and notified the CTA with Australia	Australia	Notification under Article 6(5) and notified the CTA with Spain	As there is matching notification, the preamble language of CTA would be replaced by the text described in Article 6(1) of MLI
	Opted in for Article 6(3) and notified the CTA with Australia under Article 6(6)		Opted in for Article 6(3) and notified the CTA with Spain	As there is matching notification, the preamble text described in Article 6(3) of MLI would be included in the CTA
Turkey	Notification under Article 6(5) and notified CTA with Sweden	Sweden	Notification under Article 6(5) but did not notify CTA with Turkey	As there is notification mismatch, the preamble text described in Article 6(1) of MLI would be included in addition to the existing preamble language of the CTA
	Opted in for Article 6(3) and notified CTA with Sweden		Did not opt in for Article 6(3)	Article 6(3) of MLI would not apply
United Kingdom	Reservation under Article 6(4) and notified the CTA with Ukraine	Ukraine	No reservation under Article 6(4)	Article 6(1) of MLI would not apply
	Opted in for Article 6(3) and notified CTA with Ukraine	Ukraine	Opted in for Article 6(3) and notified CTA with UK	As there is matching notification, the preamble text described in Article 6(3) would be included in the CTA

Jurisdiction	*Position Taken*	*Treaty Partner*	*Position Taken*	*Outcome under the MLI*
	Notification under Article 6(5) and notified CTA with Australia	Australia	Notification under Article 6(5) and notified CTA with UK	As there is matching notification, the preamble language of CTA would be replaced by the text described in Article 6(1) of MLI
	Opted in for Article 6(3) and notified CTA with Australia	Australia	Opted in for Article 6(3) and notified CTA with UK	As there is matching notification, the preamble text described in Article 6(3) would be included in the CTA
	Notification under Article 6(5) and notified CTA with Latvia	Latvia	No notification	As there is notification mismatch, the preamble text described in Article 6(1) of MLI would be included in the CTA in addition to the existing preamble language
	Opted in for Article 6(3) and notified CTA with Canada	Canada	Did not opt in for Article 6(3)	Article 6(3) of MLI would not apply

The various notifications made by treaty partners under Article 6 of the MLI and impact/outcome thereof on the respective CTAs are provided in Figure 7.

Figure 7 Article 6: Purpose of a CTA – Flowchart on Notifications & Their Impact

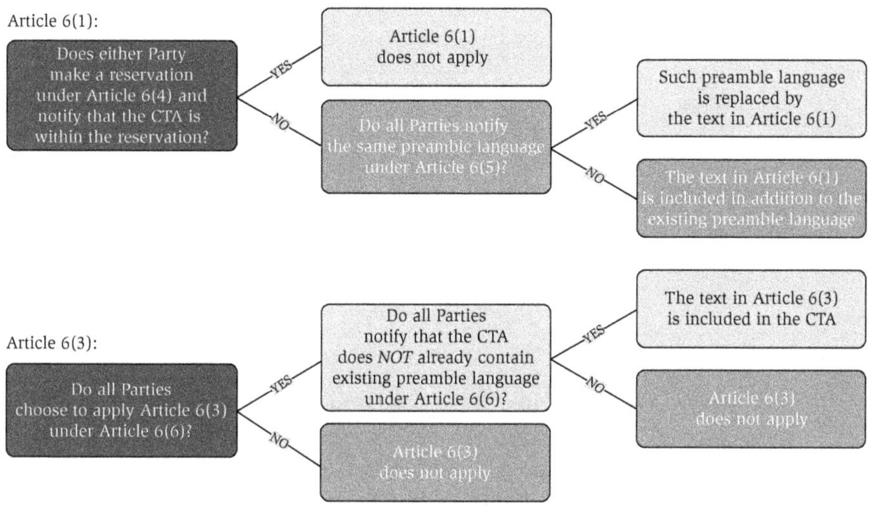

Source: OECD – Toolkit for Application of the Multilateral Instrument for BEPS Tax Treaty Related Measures https://www.oecd.org/tax/treaties/application-toolkit-multilateral-instrument-for-beps-tax-treaty-measures.htm.

3.6.2 Article 7 of MLI: Prevention of Treaty Abuse

186. The interplay between Article 7 of MLI, corresponding BEPS Report and the resulting provisions incorporated in OECD MTC 2017 is represented in a table as below:

MLI		*BEPS Final Report*		*OECD MTC 2017*	
Article	*Title of Article*	*BEPS Action Plan*	*Title of BEPS Action Plan*	*Article*	*Title of Article*
7	Prevention of Treaty Abuse	Action 6	Preventing the Granting of Treaty Benefits in Inappropriate Circumstances	29(1)-(7), (9)	Entitlement to Benefits

187. The article at a glance is as below:

Substantive (BEPS) Provisions under Para(s)	*Opt-In Provisions under Para*	*Alternative Provisions under Para*	*Compatibility Clause*		*Reservations under Para*	*Notifications under Para*
			Para	*Type*		
1, 4, 8-13	3-5, 6-14, Statement in paragraph (17)(a)	None	2, 5, 14	'in place of or in the absence of' and 'applies to'	15, 16	15, 16, 17

Status in Pre-BEPS Project Era

188. Treaty abuse, and in particular treaty shopping, was, and is, one of the most important sources of BEPS concerns. Tax administrations across the globe noticed that taxpayers engaged in treaty shopping and other treaty abuse strategies undermine tax sovereignty by claiming treaty benefits in situations where these benefits were not intended to be granted, which may give rise to double non-taxation, thereby depriving countries of tax revenues. In this light, it became imperative for countries to include anti-abuse provisions in their tax treaties, including a minimum standard to counter treaty shopping.

BEPS Action 6 Report

189. The new treaty anti-abuse rules first address treaty shopping, which involves strategies through which a person who is not a resident of a State attempts to obtain benefits that a tax treaty concluded by that State grants to residents of that State, for example, by establishing a letterbox company in that State. The Action 6 minimum standard includes a commitment to prevent treaty abuse by adopting anti-abuse rules in tax treaties under which jurisdictions should at a minimum include in their tax treaties:

(i) a PPT rule only;
(ii) a PPT rule and either a simplified or detailed LOB provision; or
(iii) a detailed LOB provision, supplemented by a mechanism that would deal with conduit arrangements not already dealt with in tax treaties.

At the same time, some flexibility in the implementation of the minimum standard was proposed as these provisions need to be adapted to each country's specificities and to the circumstances of the negotiation of bilateral conventions.

Article 7 of MLI

190. Article 7 of the MLI prescribes a minimum standard in the shape of PPT. In addition, the said article also provides for the Simplified Limitation of Benefits (S-LoB) provisions. Since a PPT rule is the only approach that can satisfy the Action 6 minimum standard on its own, it is presented as the default option in Article 7.

191. The detailed LOB[177] rule supplemented by a mechanism that would deal with conduit financing arrangements not already dealt with in tax treaties (one of the recommendations of the BEPS Action 6 Report) is not being implemented through the MLI, given that the detailed LOB provision requires substantial bilateral customisation, which would be challenging in the context of a multilateral instrument; hence, the MLI does not include a detailed LOB provision. Instead, Parties are permitted to opt out of the PPT rule, as per reservation under Article 7(15)(a), and agree instead to endeavour to reach a bilateral agreement that satisfies the minimum standard.

Principal Purpose Test Provisions

192. A PPT rule is the only approach that can satisfy the Action 6 minimum standard on its own; hence, it is presented as the default option under paragraph 1 of Article 7 of the MLI. Paragraph 1 provides that the benefits of a tax convention should not be available where one of the principal purposes of certain transactions or arrangements is to secure a benefit under a tax treaty and obtaining that benefit in such circumstances would be contrary to the object and purpose of the relevant provisions of the tax convention. Paragraph 1 incorporates these principles into the CTA itself (through the MLI) in order to allow certain jurisdictions to address cases of improper use of the CTA even if their domestic law does not allow them to do so, whereas it also confirms the application of these principles for certain jurisdictions whose domestic law already allows them to address such cases.

193. At the same time, the last part of paragraph 1 allows the person to whom the benefit would otherwise be denied the possibility of establishing that obtaining the benefit in certain circumstances would be in accordance with the object and purpose of the relevant provisions of this CTA (bona fide escape clause, which complies with the Principles of Natural Justice). This provision is intended to ensure that DTAAs apply in accordance with the purpose for which they were entered into, i.e. to provide benefits in respect of bona fide exchanges of goods and services, and movements of capital and persons as opposed to arrangements whose principal objective is to secure a more favourable tax treatment.

194. Existing PPTs vary in terms of whether they cover all benefits of CTAs or only the benefits under specific articles such as dividends, interest, royalties, income from employment, other income and elimination of double taxation. In this regard, the reference in paragraph 2 to provisions that deny 'all or part of the benefits' is intended to ensure that narrower provisions will also be replaced[178] with the broader provision in paragraph 1. A mismatch is found in India-UK notifications, where, under Article 7(17)(a) of the MLI, India has notified only Article 28C of the DTAA (to be replaced by paragraph 1 of Article 7 of MLI), whereas, on the other hand, UK has notified Articles

177. Refer Explanatory Statement to the MLI, para. 90.
178. *Id.*, para. 94.

11(6), 12(11), 13(9), 28C of the DTAA (to be replaced by paragraph 1 of Article 7 of MLI). Accordingly, this differing view of the two sides has been addressed in the synthesised text[179] of India-UK CTA by incorporating *inter alia* the following comments:

> India understands that the UK considers that paragraph 1 of Article 7 of the MLI replaces Article 28C and supersedes paragraph 6 of Article 11, paragraph 11 of Article 12 and paragraph 9 of Article 13 of the Convention and accordingly in its version of synthesised text makes such reference to paragraph 1 of Article 7 of the MLI in relation to those paragraph of the Convention and places the PPT provisions after Article 29 of the Convention. However, India considers that paragraph 1 of Article 7 of MLI only replaces the provisions of Article 28C of the Convention and in its version of synthesised text places the box containing PPT provisions below the Article 28C of the Convention and excludes the reference to paragraph 1 of Article 7 of the MLI in relation to paragraph 6 of Article 11, paragraph 11 of Article 12 and paragraph 9 of Article 13 of the Convention.

195. Some existing PPTs may include existing procedural requirements such as notification or consultation between the CAs when the PPTs are applied. The compatibility clause in paragraph 2 would replace the existing PPTs including such notification or consultation provisions.[180]

196. Where Parties have not made any reservation under Article 7(15)(a), (b) of the MLI, they are required to notify the relevant article and paragraph of their respective CTAs. In cases where such notifications match, such notified provisions of the CTAs would be 'replaced' by paragraph 1 of Article 7 of MLI. In cases where such notifications do not match, provisions of paragraph 1 of Article 7 of MLI shall 'supersede' the provisions of the CTA only to the extent that those provisions are incompatible with paragraph 1 of Article 7 of MLI. Since PPT is a minimum standard, the provisions of paragraph 1 of Article 7 of MLI shall apply in all situations even if there is a mismatch in notifications of a CTA by the Parties involved, as clarified under 'in place of or in the absence of' provisions in paragraph 15 on page 6 of the Explanatory Statement to the MLI, wherein, it is *inter alia* stated that '*Where the Contracting Jurisdictions do not notify the existence of a provision, the provision of the Convention will still apply*'.

Discretionary Relief Provisions

197. Pursuant to the discretionary relief provisions under Article 7(3)-(5) of the MLI, when treaty benefits are denied due to the PPT rule or the anti-abuse rules of the CTAs, the CA may still grant treaty benefits if it determines that such benefits would have been granted to that person in the absence of the transaction or arrangement that triggered the application of paragraph 1 of the MLI. This alternative provision grants broad discretion to the CA for the purposes of the determinations of benefits.

179. Refer India-UK Synthesised Text https://www.incometaxindia.gov.in/Pages/international-taxation/dtaa.aspx accessed on 1 September 2020.
180. Refer Explanatory Statement to the MLI, para. 96.

198. The 'discretionary relief' provisions require that the CA must consider the relevant facts and circumstances before reaching a decision and must consult the CA of the other Contracting State before rejecting a request to grant benefits if that request was made by a resident of that other State. The first requirement seeks to ensure that the CA will consider each request on its own merits while the requirement that the CA of the other Contracting State be consulted if the request is made by a resident of that other State should ensure that Contracting States treat similar cases in a consistent manner and can justify their decision on the basis of the facts and circumstances of the particular case. This consultation process does not, however, require that the CA to which the request was presented obtains the agreement of the CA that is consulted.

Simplified Limitation on Benefits Provisions

199. Article 7(8) through (13) of the MLI contains the substantive provisions of S-LoB. These provisions restrict the general scope of the other provisions of the CTA, including those of Article 1 of CTA which applies to 'persons' who are residents of a Contracting State. A brief description of S-LoB provisions under the MLI is as below:

- Paragraph 8 of Article 7 of the MLI provides that a resident of a Contracting State shall not be entitled to the benefits of the CTA (except under Articles 4(3), 9(2) and 25) unless it constitutes a 'qualified person' under paragraph 9 or unless specific benefits are granted under the provisions of paragraphs 10, 11 or 12 of Article 7 of the MLI.
- Paragraph 9 of Article 7 of MLI determines who constitutes a 'qualified person' by reference to the nature or attributes of various categories of persons; any person to which that paragraph applies is entitled to all the benefits of the CTA.
- Under paragraph 10 of Article 7 of MLI, a person is entitled to the benefits of the CTA with respect to an item of income even if it does not constitute a 'qualified person' under paragraph 9 as long as that item of income emanates from, or is incidental to, the active conduct of a business in that person's State of residence (subject to certain exceptions).
- Paragraph 11 of Article 7 of MLI is a 'derivative benefits' test that allows certain entities owned by residents of third States to obtain treaty benefits provided that these residents would have been entitled to equivalent benefits if they had invested directly. This derivative benefits test entitles companies and entities that are residents of a Contracting State but that are not qualifying persons under paragraph 9 to be entitled to treaty benefits with respect to an item of income if, at the time that the benefit would otherwise be granted with respect to that item of income and on at least half of the days of any twelve-month period that includes that time, at least 75% of the shares (as defined in paragraph 13) of that company or entity are owned, directly or indirectly, by persons that satisfy the definition of 'equivalent beneficiary' found in paragraph 13. The definition of 'equivalent beneficiary', which is crucial for the application of paragraph 12, basically refers to persons who would have been entitled to equivalent or more favourable benefits from the

State of source if they had received the same income directly (subject to the conditions included in that definition).
- Paragraph 12 of Article 7 of MLI includes the provisions that allow the CA of a Contracting State to grant treaty benefits where the other provisions of the article would otherwise deny these benefits.
- Paragraph 13 of Article 7 of MLI includes a number of definitions that apply for the purposes of the article.

200. Article 7(6) allows Parties to choose to apply the S-LoB provision as a supplement to the PPT provision in Article 7(1). Where one Party chooses to apply the S-LoB provision pursuant to Article 7(6) and the other does not, the S-LoB provision would not apply.[181]

201. Article 7(7), however, allows the possibility to apply the S-LoB provision if the other Party agrees to apply the S-LoB Provision symmetrically or asymmetrically pursuant to Article 7(7)(a) or (b), respectively. In respect of Article 7(7)(a) of the MLI, notifications under Article 7(17)(d) have been made by few States (Denmark, Iceland, Jamaica and Norway) in such a way which allows symmetrical application of S-LoB provisions if their corresponding treaty partner intends to apply S-LoB. If the corresponding treaty partner does not choose to apply S-LoB provisions, these four States shall also apply PPT only. On the other hand, in respect of Article 7(7)(b) of the MLI, notifications under Article 7(17)(d) have been made by few States (Greece and Côte d'Ivoire) in such a way which allows asymmetrical application of S-LoB provisions by their corresponding treaty partner, whereas these two States shall apply PPT only.

Compatibility Clauses

202. The compatibility clause as contained in Article 7(2) provides that the PPT Provision in Article 7(1) replaces existing provisions of CTAs that deny all or part of the benefits otherwise provided under the CTA where the principal purpose or one of the principal purposes of any arrangement or transaction, or of the Parties to an arrangement or transaction, was to obtain those benefits, or is added to CTAs that do not contain such provisions.[182]

203. The compatibility clause under Article 7(5) of the MLI provides that when the Parties to a CTA have chosen to apply Article 7(4), it will be 'applied' to the PPT provisions of a CTA (as modified by the MLI). Thus, paragraph 4 will apply in conjunction[183] with paragraph 1.

204. The compatibility clause under Article 7(14) provides that the S-LoB provision would replace existing provisions of CTAs that would limit the benefits of the CTAs only to a resident that qualifies for such benefits by meeting one or more categorical tests, or would be added to CTAs that do not contain such provisions. It is not,

181. *Id.*, para. 100 and para. 101 (1st sentence).
182. *Id.*, para. 93.
183. *Id.*, para. 99, last sentence.

however, intended to restrict the scope or application of other types of anti-abuse rules in CTAs.[184]

Reservations under Paragraphs 15, 16

205. Paragraphs 15 and 16 provide the reservations under Article 7 of the MLI. These reservations are discussed as below:

(i) Under paragraph 15(a), a Party may opt out of Article 7(1) and the PPT provision entirely with respect to all CTAs. A Party can only opt out and make a reservation under Article 7(15)(a) if it intends to adopt a combination of a detailed LOB provision and either rules to address conduit financing structures or a PPT and endeavours to reach a mutually satisfactory solution with its treaty partners which meets the minimum standard.

(ii) Under paragraph 15(b), a Party may opt out of Article 7(1) (and Article 7(4), if chosen) with respect to CTAs that already contain PPT provisions, as described in Article 7(2) of MLI. This would apply only with respect to a comprehensive PPT denying all treaty benefits, and would not[185] apply to a PPT-type test that applies only with respect to benefits under specific articles such as dividends, interest, royalties, income from employment, other income and elimination of double taxation.

(iii) Under paragraph 15(c), a Party may opt out of the S-LoB provision with respect to CTAs that already contain LoB provisions, as described in Article 7(14) of MLI.

(iv) Under paragraph 16, a Party may opt out of Article 7 entirely, except if an option in Article 7(7) applies, if it wishes to apply the S-LoB Provision with respect to CTAs concluded with Contracting Jurisdictions that do not wish to apply the S-LoB provision under Article 7(6). Hence, where the Contracting Jurisdiction preferring the PPT alone has not chosen to apply paragraph 7(a) or (b), paragraph 16 therefore allows Parties that choose pursuant to paragraph 6 to apply the S-LoB Provision, to opt out of Article 7 entirely with respect to their CTAs. When the reservation under Article 7(16) applies to some CTAs, the Contracting Jurisdictions to these CTAs shall endeavour to reach a mutually satisfactory solution which meets the minimum standard for preventing treaty abuse under the OECD/G20 BEPS package.

Notifications

206. Depending upon the position taken by various jurisdictions, the following notifications are required to be made under Article 7 of the MLI:

(i) Notification to the Depositary of its choice of reservations under sub-paragraphs (a), (b) and (c) of paragraph 15 and paragraph 16 of Article 7 of the MLI.

184. *Id.*, para. 108.
185. *Id.*, para. 111.

(ii) Paragraph 17(a) requires Parties that have not opted out of the application of paragraph 1 under paragraph 15(a) to notify the Depositary of each of its CTAs that is not subject to a reservation under paragraph 15(b), along with the article and paragraph number of each such provision. An existing provision of a CTA would be replaced by the provisions of paragraph 1 (and paragraph 4, where applicable) where all Contracting Jurisdictions to that CTA have made such a notification with respect to the existing provision. In other cases, paragraph 1 (and paragraph 4, where applicable) would apply to the CTA, but would supersede the existing provisions of the CTA only to the extent that those provisions are incompatible with paragraph 1 (and paragraph 4, where applicable).

(iii) Statement of acceptance under paragraph 17(a) of PPT as an interim measure as well as the intention to adopt LoB provisions, where possible. Such Parties may then seek, through bilateral negotiation, to adopt a simplified or detailed LoB provision to supplement paragraph 1, or to replace paragraph 1 with a detailed LoB provision supplemented by rules to address conduit financing structures.

(iv) Notification to the Depositary under paragraph 17(b) of its choice to apply paragraph 4 (discretionary relief provisions).

(v) Notification to the Depositary under paragraph 17(c) of its choice to apply paragraph 6 (S-LoB provisions). Such Party shall also notify list of its CTAs that contain a provision described in paragraph 14 as well as the article and paragraph number of each such provision. Paragraph 17(e) ensures clarity about which existing provisions will be replaced by the S-LoB Provision. An existing provision of a CTA would be replaced by the S-LoB Provision where all Contracting Jurisdictions have made such a notification under paragraph 17(c) with respect to the existing provision. In other cases, the S-LoB Provision would apply to the CTA, but would supersede the existing provisions of the CTA only to the extent that those provisions are incompatible with the S-LoB Provision.

(vi) Each Party that does not choose to apply the S-LoB Provision pursuant to paragraph 6 shall provide notification to the Depositary under paragraph 17(d) of its choice to apply paragraph 7 (symmetrical or asymmetrical application of S-LoB provisions). Such Party shall also notify list of its CTAs that contain a provision described in paragraph 14 as well as the article and paragraph number of each such provision. Paragraph 17(e) ensures clarity about which existing provisions will be replaced by the S-LoB Provision. An existing provision of a CTA would be replaced by the S-LoB Provision where all Contracting Jurisdictions have made such a notification under paragraph 17(d) with respect to the existing provision. In other cases, the S-LoB Provision would apply to the CTA, but would supersede the existing provisions of the CTA only to the extent that those provisions are incompatible with the S-LoB Provision. In the case where paragraph 7(b) applies, such modification would be made asymmetrically only with respect to the application of the S-LoB Provision by the Contracting Jurisdiction that has chosen pursuant to paragraph 6 to apply the S-LoB Provision.

Denmark's Position[186] under the MLI

207. Denmark's positions under Article 7 of the MLI are briefly stated as below:

- Denmark has not made any reservation under Article 7(15), (16) of the MLI. PPT provisions to apply, being a minimum standard.
- Under Article 7(17)(a), Denmark has given notification of those treaties (namely, Chile, China, Israel, Malta, Mexico, Taiwan, Ukraine, UK, Venezuela) which contain provisions similar to PPT to enable Article 7(1) of MLI to replace or supersede such CTA provisions, depending upon corresponding notification made by the respective treaty partner.
- Denmark has not opted for Article 7(4), allowing discretionary relief; hence, no such notification is given in Article 7(17)(b).
- No notification has been made by Denmark under Article 7(17)(c).
- Pursuant to Article 7(17)(d) of the MLI, Denmark has chosen to apply Article 7(7)(a) (so that S-LoB provisions apply symmetrically) and has notified its CTA with US.

India's Position[187] under the MLI

208. India's positions under Article 7 of the MLI are briefly stated as below:

- India has not made any reservation under Article 7(15), (16) of the MLI.
- PPT plus S-LoB provisions to apply by adopting paragraph 1 and paragraph 6 of Article 7, respectively.
- In pursuance to Article 7(17)(a) of the MLI, India has made a statement that while it accepts the application of Article 7(1) alone as an interim measure, it intends where possible to adopt a LOB provision, in addition to or in replacement of Article 7(1), through bilateral negotiation.
- Under Article 7(17)(a), India has given notification of those treaties (namely, Albania, Bhutan, Colombia, Estonia, Ethiopia, Fiji, Finland, Georgia, Iceland, Indonesia, Israel, Kazakhstan, Kenya, Korea, Kuwait, Latvia, Lithuania, Luxembourg, Macedonia, Malaysia, Malta, Mexico, Mozambique, Myanmar, Nepal, Norway, Poland, Romania, Sri Lanka, Syria, Tajikistan, Tanzania, the United Arab Emirates, UK, Uruguay, Uzbekistan) which contain provisions similar to PPT to enable Article 7(1) of MLI to replace or supersede such CTA provisions.
- India has not opted for Article 7(4), allowing discretionary relief; hence, no such notification is given in Article 7(17)(b). This alternative provision grants broad discretion to the CA for the purposes of the determinations of benefits. A probable factor stimulating India's decision to not opt in for discretionary

186. Refer Denmark's Position under the MLI http://www.oecd.org/tax/treaties/beps-mli-position-denmark-instrument-deposit.pdf.
187. Refer India's Position under the MLI http://www.oecd.org/tax/treaties/beps-mli-position-india-instrument-deposit.pdf.

relief by CAs may have stemmed from a conviction to avoid dilution of PPT provisions.
- Under Article 7(17)(c), India has chosen to apply S-LoB provisions under paragraph 6 and given notification of those treaties (namely, Albania, Armenia, Iceland, Mexico, Sri Lanka, Tajikistan, Tanzania, Uruguay, US) which contain provisions similar to S-LoB to enable Article 7(8)-(13) of MLI to replace or supersede such CTA provisions.

The Netherlands' Position[188] under the MLI

209. The Netherlands' positions under Article 7 of the MLI are briefly stated as below:

- The Netherlands has not made any reservation under Article 7(15), (16) of the MLI. PPT provisions to apply, being a minimum standard.
- Under Article 7(17)(a), the Netherlands has given notification of those treaties (namely, Azerbaijan, China, Croatia, Egypt, Estonia, Ghana, Jordan, Kazakhstan, Kenya, Latvia, Lithuania, Malawi, Malta, Mexico, Morocco, Qatar, Romania, Suriname, South Africa, Tunisia, the United Arab Emirates, UK, Uzbekistan, Zambia) which contain provisions similar to PPT to enable Article 7(1) of MLI to replace or supersede such CTA provisions, depending upon corresponding notification made by the respective treaty partner.
- The Netherlands has opted for Article 7(4), allowing discretionary relief; hence, notification is made in Article 7(17)(b).
- No notification has been made by the Netherlands under Article 7(17)(c).
- No notification has been made by the Netherlands under Article 7(17)(d).

Few Snapshots of Positions[189] Taken by Other Countries under the MLI

210. No jurisdiction has made any reservation under Article 7(15)(a) of the MLI, which indicates that all Parties intend to speedily implement the minimum standard under BEPS Action 6 Report through Article 7(1) of the MLI (as similar provisions may already exist in some treaties) and that, none of the Parties intend to adopt the route of bilateral treaty negotiations so as to introduce detailed LoB provisions and either anti-conduit provisions or a PPT in order to meet the minimum standards. Also, no jurisdiction has made any reservation under Article 7(16) of the MLI.

211. Jurisdictions that have made reservations under Article 7(15)(b) of the MLI are, namely, Andorra, Argentina, Chile, Germany, Hong Kong, Italy, Luxembourg, Mexico, San Marino, Senegal, Spain, Turkey and have notified their relevant CTA provisions. The notifications made by some of these countries and the impact on their CTAs are *inter alia* tabulated as below:

188. Refer The Netherlands' Position under the MLI http://www.oecd.org/tax/treaties/beps-mli-position-netherlands-instrument-deposit.pdf.
189. Refer OECD – Signatories and Parties to the MLI http://www.oecd.org/tax/treaties/beps-mli-signatories-and-parties.pdf.

Jurisdiction	*Position Taken*	*Treaty Partner*	*Position Taken*	*Outcome under the MLI*
Argentina	Reservation under Article 7(15)(b) and relevant provision of CTA with Chile notified	Chile	Reservation under Article 7(15)(b) and relevant provision of CTA with Argentina notified	Article 7(1) of MLI would not apply
Argentina	Reservation under Article 7(15)(b) and relevant provision of CTA with Mexico notified	Mexico	Reservation under Article 7(15)(b) and relevant provision of CTA with Argentina notified	Article 7(1) of MLI would not apply
Spain	Reservation under Article 7(15)(b) and relevant provision of CTA with Mexico notified	Mexico	Reservation under Article 7(15)(b) and relevant provision of CTA with Spain notified	Article 7(1) of MLI would not apply

212. Jurisdictions that have made reservations under Article 7(15)(c) of the MLI are, namely, Argentina, Bulgaria, Chile, Italy, Mexico and Russia for some of their specific CTAs. At the same time, jurisdictions which have made notifications under Article 7(17)(c) choosing to apply S-LoB provisions are, namely, Argentina, Armenia, Bulgaria, Chile, Colombia, India, Kazakhstan, Kenya, Mexico, Pakistan, Russia, Senegal, the Slovak Republic, Uruguay. The notifications made by some of these countries and the impact on their CTAs are *inter alia* tabulated as below:

Jurisdiction	*Position Taken*	*Treaty Partner*	*Position Taken*	*Outcome under the MLI*
Chile	- Reservation under Article 7(15)(c) & notified CTAs with Argentina, China, US, Uruguay only - Notification under Article 7(17)(c) choosing to apply S-LoB	Russia	- Reservation under Article 7(15)(c) & notified CTAs with China, Ecuador & US only - Notification under Article 7(17)(c) choosing to apply S-LoB	The S-LoB provision would apply and supersede the provisions of the Chile-Russia CTA to the extent of incompatibility

Jurisdiction	*Position Taken*	*Treaty Partner*	*Position Taken*	*Outcome under the MLI*
Chile	-do-	Colombia	- Notification under Article 7(17)(c) choosing to apply S-LoB	S-LoB provisions under the MLI would apply
Chile	-do-	South Africa	- No notification under 7(17)(c), (d)	S-LoB provisions under the MLI would not apply
India	- Notification under Article 7(17)(c) choosing to apply S-LoB and notified CTA with Uruguay	Uruguay	- Notification under Article 7(17)(c) choosing to apply S-LoB and notified CTA with India	Relevant provisions of India-Uruguay CTA would be replaced by the S-LoB provisions under the MLI
India	- Notification under Article 7(17)(c) choosing to apply S-LoB (no provision of CTA with Kazakhstan notified, as no such provision exists in CTA similar to Article 7(14))	Kazakhstan	- Notification under Article 7(17)(c) choosing to apply S-LoB (no provision of CTA with India notified, as no such provision exists in CTA similar to Article 7(14))	S-LoB provisions under the MLI would apply
India	- Notification under Article 7(17)(c) choosing to apply S-LoB (no provision of CTA with the Slovak Republic notified, as no such provision exists in CTA similar to Article 7(14))	The Slovak Republic	- Notification under Article 7(17)(c) choosing to apply S-LoB (no provision of CTA with India notified, as no such provision exists in CTA similar to Article 7(14))	S-LoB provisions under the MLI would apply
India	- Notification under Article 7(17)(c) choosing to apply S-LoB (relevant provisions of CTA with Iceland notified)	Iceland	- Notification to apply sub-paragraph (a) of Article 7(7) under Article 7(17)(d) wherein it has notified its CTA with India only	Relevant CTA provisions shall be replaced by the S-LoB provisions of the MLI

Jurisdiction	*Position Taken*	*Treaty Partner*	*Position Taken*	*Outcome under the MLI*
The Netherlands	- No notification under Article 7(17)(c)	Australia	- No notification under Article 7(17)(c)	S-LoB provisions under the MLI would not apply
The Netherlands	- No notification under Article 7(17)(c)	Iceland	- Notification to apply sub-paragraph (a) of Article 7(7) under Article 7(17)(d) wherein it has notified its CTA with India only	S-LoB provisions under the MLI would not apply

213. Jurisdictions that have made a statement under Article 7(17)(a) of the MLI that, while they accept the application of Article 7(1) alone as an interim measure, they intend where possible to adopt a simplified or detailed LOB[190] provision, in addition to or in replacement of Article 7(1), through bilateral negotiation are, namely, Canada, Chile, Colombia, India, Kuwait, Norway, Peru, Poland, Senegal and Seychelles.

214. Jurisdictions that have made notifications under Article 7(17)(b) choosing to apply discretionary relief provisions under Article 7(4) are, namely, Andorra, Australia, Bahrain, Belgium, Côte d'Ivoire, Curaçao, Cyprus, the Czech Republic, Fiji, Gabon, Guernsey, Hungary, Ireland, the Isle of Man, Jersey, Liechtenstein, Lithuania, Luxembourg, Malta, Mauritius, the Netherlands, New Zealand, Papua New Guinea, San Marino, Senegal, Seychelles, Singapore, Ukraine, the United Arab Emirates, UK, Uruguay. The notifications made by some of these countries and the impact on their CTAs are *inter alia* tabulated as below:

Jurisdiction	*Position Taken*	*Treaty Partner*	*Position Taken*	*Outcome under the MLI*
Australia	- Notification under Article 7(17)(b)	Belgium	- Notification under Article 7(17)(b)	Discretionary relief provisions under Article 7(4) of MLI would apply and supersede the provisions of the Australia-Belgium CTA to the extent of incompatibility
Australia	- Notification under Article 7(17)(b)	Canada	- No notification under Article 7(17)(b)	Article 7(4) of MLI would not apply to Australia-Canada CTA

190. Refer Explanatory Statement to the MLI, para. 90 (last sentence) and para. 115.

215. Jurisdictions that have chosen sub-paragraph (a) of Article 7(7) and notified the same under Article 7(17)(d) of MLI are, namely, Denmark, Iceland, Jamaica and Norway, choosing to symmetrically apply S-LoB provisions, provided the treaty partner opts for S-LoB provisions; else, these four jurisdictions will apply PPT provisions only. The notifications made by some of the countries and the impact on their CTAs are *inter alia* tabulated as below:

Jurisdiction	*Position Taken*	*Treaty Partner*	*Position Taken*	*Outcome under the MLI*
Denmark	- Notification to apply sub-paragraph (a) of Article 7(7) under Article 7(17)(d)	Jamaica	- Notification to apply sub-paragraph (a) of Article 7(7) under Article 7(17)(d)	S-LoB provision would not apply
Denmark	- Notification to apply sub-paragraph (a) of Article 7(7) under Article 7(17)(d)	India	- Notification under Article 7(17)(c) choosing to apply S-LoB	S-LoB provision would apply and supersede the provisions of the Denmark-India CTA to the extent of incompatibility

216. Jurisdictions that have applied sub-paragraph (b) of Article 7(7) and notified under Article 7(17)(d) of MLI are, namely, Greece and Côte d'Ivoire, allowing asymmetrical application of S-LoB provisions, if the treaty partner opts for S-LoB provisions to be applied to their residents, whereas these two jurisdictions will apply PPT provisions only. The notifications made by some of the countries and the impact on their CTAs are *inter alia* tabulated as below:

Jurisdiction	*Position Taken*	*Treaty Partner*	*Position Taken*	*Outcome under the MLI*
Greece	- Notification to apply sub-paragraph (b) of Article 7(7) under Article 7(17)(d)	Denmark	- Notification to apply sub-paragraph (a) of Article 7(7) under Article 7(17)(d)	S-LoB provisions would not apply

Jurisdiction	*Position Taken*	*Treaty Partner*	*Position Taken*	*Outcome under the MLI*
Greece	-do-	India	– Notification under Article 7(17)(c) choosing to apply S-LoB	S-LoB provisions would apply and supersede the provisions of the Greece-India CTA to the extent of incompatibility (asymmetrical application by India)
Greece	-do-	The Netherlands	– No notification under Article 7(17)(c)	S-LoB provisions would not apply
Greece	-do-	The Slovak Republic	– Notification under Article 7(17)(c) choosing to apply S-LoB	S-LoB provisions would apply and supersede the provisions of the Greece-Slovak Republic CTA to the extent of incompatibility (asymmetrical application by the Slovak Republic)

The various notifications made by treaty partners under Article 7 of the MLI and impact/outcome thereof on the respective CTAs are provided in Figure 8.

Figure 8 Article 7: Prevention of Treaty Abuse – Flowchart on Notifications & Their Impact

PPT

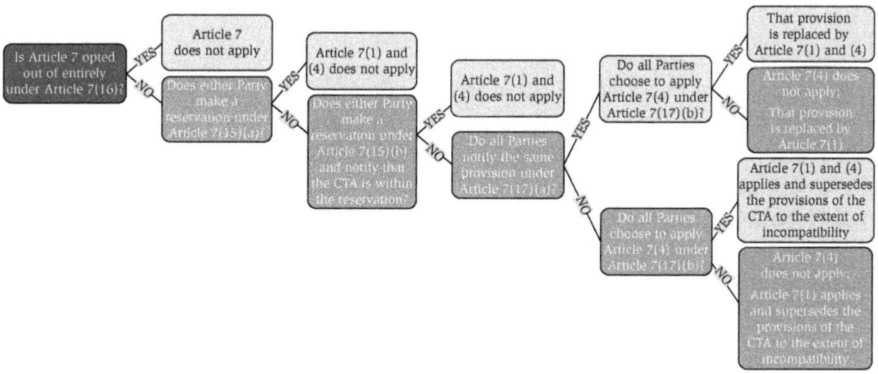

S-LoB

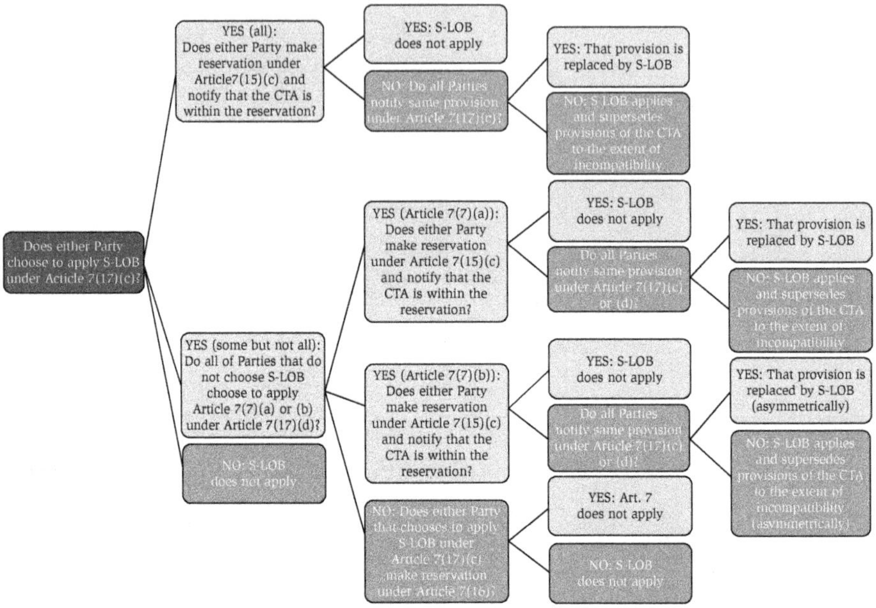

Source: OECD – Toolkit for Application of the Multilateral Instrument for BEPS Tax Treaty Related Measures https://www.oecd.org/tax/treaties/application-toolkit-multilateral-instrument-for-beps-tax-treaty-measures.htm.

3.6.2.1 Interaction Between PPT and S-LoB

217. Most countries which have signed the MLI have gravitated towards the PPT as the default measure in order to meet the minimum standards, with only a handful of countries having chosen to apply the PPT in combination with the S-LoB Provision, which implies that only a few treaties would stand modified to include both the PPT and the S-LoB, while an overwhelming majority of them would include a stand-alone PPT.

218. It is evident from paragraph 20 of BEPS Action 6 Report that a combination of the LoB provision and the PPT was envisioned as the ideal approach to addressing treaty abuse, recognising that each rule has its strengths and weaknesses. The idea was to combine the objectivity and certainty offered by the LoB test in addressing treaty shopping arrangements with the flexibility of the PPT, which can be used to tackle other forms of treaty abuse as well as some forms of treaty shopping such as conduit financing arrangements (defined as, participation of one or more intermediate entities in a financing arrangement where such entities are acting as conduit entities), which are out of scope for the LoB.

219. Paragraph 1 of Article 7 supplements and does not restrict in any way the scope or application of the S-LoB provisions. Conversely, the fact that a person is entitled to benefits under S-LoB provisions does not mean that these benefits cannot be denied under paragraph 1. This is evident on reading of paragraph 172 of the OECD MTC 2017 Commentary on Article 29, which provides that PPT provisions may override S-LoB provisions.

220. A view posits that this privilege provided to PPT provisions and more so, when an arrangement has been classified as legal under S-LoB, appears to collide with the principle of legal certainty and the bona fide application of tax treaty provisions because when an arrangement is within the ambits of Specific Anti-avoidance Rules (SAAR), it may be argued that it should not be considered abusive, thereby, rendering S-LoB provisions as irrelevant. The LoB, while not foolproof in the interpretation and application of its own tests, is more objective and serves the purpose of legal certainty better than the PPT.[191]

221. Another view posits that the S-LoB rules have their own limitations, as they focus primarily on the legal nature, ownership in, and general activities of, residents of a Contracting State and these rules do not ensure that a transaction or arrangement entered into by such a resident cannot constitute an improper use of a treaty provision. The LoB proves inadequate as a stand-alone measure because of its restricted scope, which only covers nexus abuse and leaves treaty shopping resulting from abusive transactions unaddressed. For the latter, the LoB requires additional measures which, under the MLI framework, could be either the PPT or other domestic mechanisms to combat conduit arrangements. This is where paragraph 1 of Article 7 of the MLI steps in and is designed in a manner that it is read in the context of S-LoB provisions and the rest of the CTA, including its preamble. This is particularly important for the purposes of determining the object and purpose of the relevant provisions of the CTA. Hence, it may be inferred that these attributes of the PPT provisions have been carefully introduced into the tax treaties through the MLI (following BEPS Action 6 Report) as S-LoB provisions and other SAAR provisions under the tax treaties are not equipped, by themselves, to address all cases of treaty abuse and treaty shopping.

3.6.2.2 More Discussions on PPT

222. The Commentaries on the OECD MTC have consistently indicated that tax treaty abuse is considered inappropriate for three main reasons. First, tax treaty benefits negotiated between the Contracting States are extended to persons resident in a third country in a way unintended by these jurisdictions. As a result, the principle of reciprocity is breached and the balance of the tax treaty gets disturbed. Second, income flowing internationally may be exempted from taxation altogether or be subjected to

191. Refer Article by Ameya Mithe Titled 'Critical Analysis of the Principal Purpose Test and the Limitation on Benefits Rule: A World Divided but It Takes Two to Tango' https://research.ibfd.org/#/doc?url=/collections/wtj/html/wtj_2020_01_in_1.html (s. 5) accessed on 3 August 2020.

inadequate taxation in a way unintended by the Contracting States. This situation is unacceptable because the granting by a country of treaty benefits is based, except in specific circumstances, on the fact that the respective income is taxed in the other State or at least falls under the normal tax regime of that State. Third, the State of residence of the ultimate income beneficiary has little incentive to enter into a tax treaty with the source country because its residents can indirectly receive tax treaty benefits from the source State without the need for the country of residence to provide reciprocal benefits.[192]

223. To prevent abuse of tax treaties, one of the prominent BEPS anti-abuse measures being introduced through the MLI is the PPT, as contained in paragraph 1 of Article 7 of the MLI. The PPT provision is a minimum standard and shall apply to all DTAAs, depending upon appropriate notifications under the MLI. It states as below:

> Notwithstanding *any provisions of the Agreement, a* benefit *under the Agreement shall not be granted in respect of an item of income* if it is reasonable to conclude, *having regard to all relevant facts and circumstances, that obtaining that benefit was* one of the principal purposes of any arrangement or transaction *that resulted directly or indirectly in that benefit, unless it is established that granting that benefit in these circumstances would be in accordance with the object and purpose of the relevant provisions of the Agreement.*

The above provisions deny all or part of the benefits that would otherwise be provided under the CTA where the principal purpose or one of the principal purposes of any arrangement or transaction, or of any person concerned with an arrangement or transaction, was to obtain those benefits.

224. Ever since the introduction of PPT provisions, various stakeholders have viewed their concerns in various fora over:

- characteristics embedded in PPT provisions;
- consistent and harmonious application of the PPT provisions by the tax officers;
- interface between PPT provisions in tax treaties and General Anti-avoidance Rule (GAAR) provisions under domestic laws.

Some have gone on to posit that the PPT is a vague standard riddled with interpretational issues at every level of its design. Therefore, pending global homogeneity in its interpretation and application, it risks creating divergent judicial precedents and placing excessive discretion with the revenue authorities of individual countries.

192. Refer: OECD, Double Taxation Conventions and the Use of Conduit Companies, in OECD, Model Tax Convention on Income and on Capital: Full Version, R (6), Vol. I and II, para. 7 (OECD 2010) https://read.oecd-ilibrary.org/taxation/model-tax-convention-on-income-and-on-capital-2014-full-version/r-6-double-taxation-conventions-and-the-use-of-conduit-companies_9789264239081-99-en#page4.

The resulting uncertainty has the potential to stifle genuine business arrangements.[193] The PPT consists of two separate prongs: (i) the subjective test, which determines whether one of the principal purposes of the arrangement is to obtain a treaty benefit; and (ii) the objective test, which determines whether the object and purpose of the relevant treaty provisions is to grant that benefit regardless of the principal purpose. The subjective element is the main rule, while the objective element is the exception that safeguards the treaty benefits denied under the main rule. The subjective element involves an enquiry into the intention of the taxpayer, either by way of direct evidence of the taxpayer's state of mind or by reference to all the surrounding circumstances. The objective test essentially ensures treaty benefits to the taxpayer even though it is reasonable to conclude that one of the principal purposes of the transaction was to obtain a treaty benefit, provided the taxpayer is able to establish that granting such benefits would be in accordance with the object and purpose of the relevant provisions of the treaty. On failing the subjective test, the taxpayer may not be successfully able to establish that granting treaty benefits is in accordance with the object and purpose of the treaty. Also, a broad interpretation of the objective test may induce an exclusion of lawful tax planning from treaty benefits.[194]

225. The concerns raised by various stakeholders have been more specifically as below:

(a) PPT provisions begin with '*Notwithstanding any provisions of the Agreement*' giving it wide powers.
(b) The use of the phrase '*if it is reasonable to conclude*' does not specify the gravity of the term 'reasonable' and may lead to arbitrary interpretations.
(c) Use of the phrase '*one of the principal purposes of any arrangement or transaction*' does not align with the phrase '*the main purpose*' used in GAAR provisions (e.g., under India's domestic law). Also, the 'signalling function'[195] of Article 29(9) of the OECD Model is to remind those who are applying the law of the need for a careful establishing of facts and a purposive interpretation, especially in those cases in which one of the principal purposes of the taxpayer's transaction is to obtain the benefit.
(d) Meaning of the term '*benefit*' is unclear.

226. Before making specific comments on the concerns mentioned supra, it is expedient to again highlight the circumstances which prompted introduction of PPT provisions, as succinctly mentioned hereunder:

193. Refer Article by Ameya Mithe Titled 'Critical Analysis of the Principal Purpose Test and the Limitation on Benefits Rule: A World Divided but It Takes Two to Tango' https://research.ibfd.org/#/doc?url=/collections/wtj/html/wtj_2020_01_in_1.html (s. 5) accessed on 3 August 2020.
194. *Id.*, s. 3.2.5.
195. Refer Article by Michael Lang Titled 'The Signalling Function of Article 29(9) of the OECD Model – The Principal Purpose Test' https://research.ibfd.org/#/doc?url=/collections/bit/html/bit_2020_04_o2_5.html (s. 2) accessed on 4 August 2020.

(1) Aggressive tax planning by MNEs leading to abuse of tax treaties. It has been appropriately described in 1987 by the UN Ad Hoc Group of Experts:

- The term 'abuse of tax treaties' may be defined loosely as the use of tax treaties by persons the treaties were not designed to benefit, in order to derive benefits the treaties were not designed to give them.[196]

(2) MNEs have taken advantage of the tilt in granting of treaty benefits which are based on 'residence-based' taxation over 'source-based' taxation.
(3) Limitations in tax treaties in combating conduit arrangements and in prevention of treaty benefits to such abusive transactions.

In order to combat treaty abuse, the aim of PPT rule is to enable to:

- close gaps with a general approach providing extensive powers to tax authorities to act in relation to abusive tax planning;
- provide an enabler to tax authorities to investigate artificial structures which have been put in place primarily for tax advantage in the host country;
- provide a tool to tax authorities to apply primacy of 'substance over form' principle.

227. On having reminisced various constraints of tax treaties in tackling erosion of tax base through treaty shopping and the important role entrusted to PPT provisions to address the same, the specific concerns raised by various stakeholders are discussed as below:

(a) PPT provisions begin with '*Notwithstanding any provisions of the Agreement*' thereby implying that these provisions may override and prevail over all provisions of the CTA including S-LoB provisions, as even the latter are not fully equipped to combat all forms of treaty abuse. In fact, PPT provisions are designed to act as an enabler to establish the primacy of 'substance over form' principle.
(b) The use of the phrase '*if it is reasonable to conclude*' may be a subject matter of different interpretations and hence indicates uncertainty which is contrary to the principle of legal certainty. No doubt, invocation of PPT rule requires an in-depth study of facts and circumstances of the case, and this is where the taxpayers themselves have to discharge their roles, by putting enough, robust and irrefutable documentary evidence on the table in support of their contentions. The PPT requires the tax authorities to discharge their burden of proof only with regard to the subjective element, i.e. '*whether one of the principal purposes of the arrangement is to obtain a treaty benefit*' while the burden is shifted on to the taxpayer with regard to

196. United Nations Ad Hoc Group of Experts, Contributions to International Co-operation in Tax Matters: Treaty Shopping, Thin Capitalization, Co-operation Between Tax Authorities, Resolving International Tax Disputes, para. 8 (1988).

the objective element, i.e. '*whether the object and purpose of the relevant treaty provisions is to grant that benefit regardless of the principal purpose*'. The standard of proof is evidently higher for the taxpayer, who is required to establish that granting the benefit would be in accordance with the object and purpose of the treaty provision. In this situation, 'onus' lies on the taxpayers and their representatives to establish the bona fides of a transaction so as to enable tax officers to draw 'reasonable' conclusions. The term 'arrangement or transaction' as used under the PPT provision should be interpreted broadly and include any agreement, understanding, scheme, transaction or series of transactions, whether or not they are legally enforceable.[197] A person cannot avoid the application of PPT provisions by merely asserting that the 'arrangement or transaction' was not undertaken or not arranged to obtain the benefits of the CTA. All of the evidence must be weighed to determine whether it is 'reasonable' to conclude that an arrangement or transaction was undertaken or arranged for the purpose to obtain the benefits of the CTA.[198] Hence, the purpose of an arrangement is presented as a question of fact, mandating a case-by-case analysis that considers all the facts and circumstances.

(c) Use of the phrase '*one of the principal purposes of any arrangement or transaction that resulted directly or indirectly in that benefit*' in the PPT provisions appears to have wide ranging powers in comparison to GAAR provisions, as contained, for example, under India's domestic law, wherein, under section 96(1) of the Income Tax Act, 1961, an impermissible avoidance arrangement means an arrangement, '*the main purpose of which is to obtain a tax benefit*'. It is perceived that this variance in PPT and GAAR provisions could be a cause of conflict in application of domestic GAAR to international treaties. Use of '*one of the principal purposes*' under PPT provisions implies that PPT may apply even in a situation where the taxpayer could demonstrate that the arrangement has commercial reasons and is justified from an economic perspective. No one can deny that all tax treaty abusive transactions have commercial reasons attached to them; hence, this argument alone cannot be a determinant of passing the PPT test. To determine whether or not '*one of the principal purposes*' of an arrangement or transaction is to obtain benefits under the CTA, it is important to undertake an objective analysis of the aims and objects of all persons involved in putting that arrangement or transaction in place or being a Party to it. What are the purposes of an arrangement or transaction is a question of fact which can only be answered by considering all circumstances surrounding the arrangement or event on a case-by-case basis. It is not necessary to find conclusive proof of the intent of a person concerned with an arrangement or transaction, but it must be reasonable to

197. Refer OECD MTC 2017, para. 177 of the Commentary on Art. 29.
198. *Id.*, para. 179 of the Commentary on Art. 29.

conclude, after an objective analysis of the relevant facts and circumstances, that one of the principal purposes of the arrangement or transaction was to obtain the benefits of the tax convention. It should not be lightly assumed, however, that obtaining a benefit under a tax treaty was one of the principal purposes of an arrangement or transaction and merely reviewing the effects of an arrangement will not usually enable a conclusion to be drawn about its purposes. Where, however, an arrangement can only be reasonably explained by a benefit that arises under a treaty, it may be concluded that one of the principal purposes of that arrangement was to obtain the benefit.[199] Therefore, reference to 'one of the principal purposes' means that obtaining the benefit under a CTA need not be the sole or dominant purpose of a particular arrangement or transaction. It is sufficient that at least one of the principal purposes was to obtain the benefit.[200]

The Australian Taxation Office (ATO), vide Law Administration Practice Statement (PSLA) 2020/2[201] on 'Administering general anti-abuse rules, such as a principal or main purposes test, included in any of Australia's tax treaties', has explained the meaning of '*one of the principal purposes*' as below:

> An arrangement may be reasonably explained by a number of purposes and it may have more than one principal purpose. In this context, 'principal' does not mean strictly 'first or highest in rank', but rather 'among the most important, prominent, leading, main'. The reference to 'one of the principal purposes' means that obtaining the benefit under the CTA need not be the sole, or even the dominant, purpose of the particular arrangement. It is sufficient that at least one of the principal purposes was to obtain the treaty benefit, even if that was not the dominant purpose. This means that an arrangement may attract the operation of the MLI PPT even where it attains commercial objectives and is consistent with commercial gain. It is not necessary to show that the arrangement has no commercial substance or that its only effect is to obtain the benefit that arises under the CTA (obtaining the treaty benefit need not be the only reasonable explanation of the arrangement). Also, where one of the principal purposes of an arrangement is to obtain the relevant treaty benefit and another of its principal purposes is to achieve a particular commercial objective, the test will be met, without the need to determine which purpose is dominant. The text, context and purpose of the MLI PPT make clear that it is not a sole, dominant or primary purpose test.

The Central Board of Direct Taxes (CBDT), India vide Circular No. 7 of 2017[202] has clarified that '*if a case of avoidance is sufficiently addressed by LOB in the treaty, there shall not be an occasion to invoke GAAR*'. Following

199. *Id.*, para. 178 of the Commentary on Art. 29.
200. *Id.*, para. 180 of the Commentary on Art. 29.
201. Refer ATO's PSLA 2020/2 https://www.ato.gov.au/law/view/view.htm?docid=%22PSR%2FPS20202%2FNAT%2FATO%2F00001%22 accessed on 20 November 2020.
202. Refer CBDT's Circular No. 7 of 2017 Providing Clarification on Implementation of GAAR (Question No. 2) https://www.incometaxindia.gov.in/communications/circular/circular7_2017.pdf accessed on 3 September 2020.

this lead, it may be inferred that if PPT rule in the treaty is satisfied, there may not be an occasion to invoke GAAR.

(d) The term 'benefit' in the context of the PPT is likely to be broadly interpreted. The term 'benefit' as alluded to under the PPT provisions includes all limitations (e.g., a tax reduction, exemption, deferral or refund) on taxation imposed on the State of source under Articles 6 through 22 of the OECD MTC, the relief from double taxation provided by Article 23, and the protection afforded to residents and nationals of a Contracting State under Article 24 or any other similar limitations. This includes, for example, limitations on the taxing rights of a Contracting State in respect of dividends, interest or royalties arising in that State, and paid to a resident of the other State (who is the beneficial owner) under Articles 10, 11 or 12. It also includes limitations on the taxing rights of a Contracting State over a capital gain derived from the alienation of movable property located in that State by a resident of the other State under Article 13. When a tax convention includes other limitations (such as a tax sparing provision), the PPT provisions also apply to that benefit.[203] The phrase 'that resulted directly or indirectly in that benefit' has been kept deliberately broad and is intended to include situations where the person who claims the application of the benefits under a tax treaty may do so with respect to a transaction that is not the one that was undertaken for one of the principal purposes of obtaining that treaty benefit. PPT provisions refer to '*benefit under the Agreement*', i.e. to a CTA, and thus PPT shall have no impact on unilateral benefits under domestic laws, where only GAAR provisions will apply.
The ATO, vide PSLA 2020/2, has *inter alia* explained 'benefits to which the MLI PPT may apply' as below:

> The MLI PPT can potentially apply to any 'benefit' under a CTA. Depending on the relevant arrangement being considered, it may include a limitation on the taxing rights of a source jurisdiction (such as a tax reduction, exemption, deferral or refund), or the relief from double taxation provided to residents. It may also include the protection afforded to residents and nationals of a jurisdiction under non-discrimination articles or any other similar limitations.

228. It is beyond doubt that the interpretation of Article 29(9) of the OECD Model (2017) is subject to the principles of Article 31 of the Vienna Convention (1969) just like any other treaty provision. This has several consequences. First of all, in accordance with the principle of effectiveness, both the subjective and objective component of the PPT should be given weight and applied in this order. According to Article 29(9) of the OECD MTC 2017, a denial of tax treaty benefits by the source State may come into play where 'one of the principal purposes' of the arrangement or transaction was to obtain these benefits. In accordance with the 'reasonableness' test of the PPT, it is, therefore,

203. Refer OECD MTC 2017, para. 175 of the Commentary on Art. 29.

not necessary to find conclusive proof of the intent of a person concerned with an arrangement or transaction. Where an arrangement can only be reasonably explained by a benefit that arises under a treaty, it may be concluded that one of the principal purposes of that arrangement was to obtain the benefit. The reference to 'one of the principal purposes' means that obtaining the benefit under a tax convention need not be the sole or dominant purpose of a particular arrangement or transaction. In the examples given by the OECD Commentary on Article 29, treaty benefits would still have to be granted if the taxpayer manages to demonstrate that the object and purpose of articles of the OECD MTC 2017 is not defeated. The objective element of the PPT takes the form of an escape clause. Where it is established that 'one of the principal purposes of any arrangement or transaction' was to claim a treaty benefit, the taxpayer may still claim such benefit if he establishes that granting such benefit would be 'in accordance with the object and purpose of the relevant provisions of this Convention'. It is accepted that the principle of good faith enshrined in Article 26 of the Vienna Convention incorporates a doctrine of abuse of rights, according to which Parties shall abstain from acts calculated to frustrate the object and purpose and, thus, impede the proper execution of the treaty.[204]

229. To sum up, there have been instances of unbridled abuse of tax treaties, following which, after a lot of deliberations, PPT rule has been designed to address such abusive claims of treaty benefits. The consternation among various stakeholders seems to suggest that PPT is kind of a weapon waiting to be unleashed by tax officers with gay abandon. That may not be the case as tax administrations across the world have developed several checks and balances to prevent officers from getting swayed to an extreme. The guidance on invocation of PPT issued by ATO vide PSLA 2020/2 is a step in the right direction to allay the concerns of various stakeholders, as it provides certainty and transparency in the course of invocation of PPT provisions by tax officials. It is expected that more jurisdictions will follow suit and provide similar guidance to their tax officials. To be precise, 60 countries have ratified MLI as of now and for most of these jurisdictions, MLI has entered into effect in recent past only, due to which application of PPT provisions at ground level by tax administrations across the globe is yet to play out in its full glory. It is, therefore, at this stage, too premature to forecast that PPT may lead to abuse of power by tax officers. However, given the checks and balances incorporated in the functioning of Government Institutions, an apprehension in some quarters that PPT may strangulate genuine business sentiments seems exaggerated and highly unlikely to play out.

3.6.3 Article 8 of MLI: Dividend Transfer Transactions

230. The interplay between Article 8 of MLI, corresponding BEPS Report and the resulting provisions incorporated in OECD MTC 2017 is represented in a table as below:

204. Refer Article by Robert J. Danon Titled 'The PPT in Post-BEPS Tax Treaty Law: It is a GAAR but Just a GAAR!' https://research.ibfd.org/#/doc?url=/collections/bit/html/bit_2020_04_o2_9.html (s. 3.3, 4) accessed on 4 August 2020.

MLI		*BEPS Final Report*		*OECD MTC 2017*	
Article	*Title of Article*	*BEPS Action Plan*	*Title of BEPS Action Plan*	*Article*	*Title of Article*
8	Dividend Transfer Transactions	Action 6	Preventing the Granting of Treaty Benefits in Inappropriate Circumstances	10(2)(a)	Dividends

231. The article at a glance is as below:

Substantive (BEPS) Provisions under Para(s)	*Opt-In Provisions under Para*	*Alternative Provisions under Para*	*Compatibility Clause*		*Reservations under Para*	*Notifications under Para*
			Para	*Type*		
1	None	None	2	'in place of or in the absence of'	3	3, 4

Status in Pre-BEPS Project Era

232. Sub-paragraph (a) of paragraph 2 of Article 10 of OECD MTC 2014 did not require that the company receiving the dividend at a reduced rate must have owned at least 25% of the capital for a relatively long time before the date of the distribution. It was felt that the exempt or reduced dividend rate envisaged in sub-paragraph (a) of paragraph 2 should not be granted in cases of abuse of this provision, for example, where a company with a holding of less than 25% has, shortly before the dividends become payable, increased its holding primarily for the purpose of securing the benefits of the reduced dividend rate, or otherwise, where the qualifying holding was arranged primarily in order to obtain the reduction. To counteract such manoeuvres, BEPS Action 6 Report has recommended the provisions as incorporated under Article 8 of the MLI requiring a minimum shareholding period of 365 days.

Article 8(1) of MLI

233. In line with BEPS Action 6 Report, paragraph 1 of Article 8 of MLI (also referred to as 'dividend stripping' provisions) requires a minimum shareholding period of 365 days to be satisfied in order for a company to be entitled to exempt or a reduced rate of tax on dividends from a subsidiary. Specifically, a minimum shareholding period is added to provisions of a CTA where the recipient company holds more than a certain amount of the capital or voting power of the company paying the dividends. Therefore, this paragraph does not affect existing provisions that give a preferential rate for dividends without the condition of holding a certain amount of the capital of the company paying the dividends.[205]

234. The 365-day period, referred to in paragraph 1, shall be computed by counting the period before and after the date of declaration of dividend, including the day of the payment of dividend. This 365-day holding requirement may be met either at the time of payment of the dividend or after the time the dividend is paid.[206] Whereas, no account shall be taken of the changes of ownership that would directly result from a corporate reorganisation, such as a merger or divisive reorganisation, of the company that holds the shares or that pays the dividends.

235. Paragraph 1 is intended to add a minimum shareholding period to existing provisions of CTAs without modifying the other elements of such provisions, such as tax rates, ownership thresholds and form of ownership (e.g., directly and/or indirectly). This paragraph also would not modify any other conditions, such as provisions requiring that:

- the amount of investment is more than a certain monetary value;
- profits out of which dividends are paid are subject to tax in the residence jurisdiction; or
- not more than a certain amount of the gross income of the paying company consists of interest or dividends.[207]

Compatibility Clause

236. The compatibility clause contained in paragraph 2 describes the interaction between paragraph 1 and provisions of CTAs. This paragraph clarifies that the 365-day minimum shareholding period in paragraph 1 replaces the minimum shareholding periods already contained in provisions of CTAs, or is added where such periods do not exist in provisions of CTAs.[208]

Reservations under Paragraph 3

237. Even though the compatibility clause contained in paragraph 2 provides that the 365-day minimum shareholding period in paragraph 1 replaces the minimum shareholding periods already contained in provisions of CTAs, or is added where such periods do not exist in provisions of CTAs, if Parties prefer to preserve existing minimum shareholding periods, paragraph 3(b) allows the possibility to opt out of Article 8 with respect to provisions of CTAs that already include a minimum shareholding period.

238. The various options for making reservations are as below:

205. Refer Explanatory Statement to the MLI, para. 119 (last sentence).
206. Refer UN MDTC 2017, para. 6.1 of the Commentary on Art. 10.
207. Refer Explanatory Statement to the MLI, para. 122.
208. *Id.*, para. 124.

- The provisions addressing dividend transfer transactions are not required to meet a minimum standard; hence, Parties may opt out of Article 8 entirely, as per paragraph 3(a).
- Parties may opt out of Article 8 entirely with respect to CTAs to the extent that the provisions described in paragraph 1 already include a minimum shareholding period, as per paragraph 3(b)(i). This reservation is intended to apply on a provision basis instead of on an agreement basis. As a result, if a CTA contains the provisions described in paragraph 1 that provide two split rates, and one includes a minimum shareholding period and the other does not, this clause would preserve the first provisions alone, while paragraph 1 of Article 8 of MLI would add a minimum shareholding period to the latter provisions of the CTA.[209]
- A Party may choose to preserve a minimum shareholding period included in provisions of a CTA that is shorter or longer than 365 days, as per paragraphs 3(b)(ii), (iii).

Notifications

239. Depending upon the position taken by various jurisdictions, the following notifications are required to be made under Article 8 of the MLI:

(i) Jurisdictions intending to make reservations under paragraph 3 are required to make notifications under sub-paragraph (a) or (b)(i), (ii), (iii), as the case may be.
(ii) Under paragraph 4, jurisdictions that have not made the reservation described in paragraph 3 shall make notifications whether each of its CTAs contains a provision described in paragraph 1, and if so, the article and paragraph number of each such provision. Paragraph 1 would apply with respect to an existing provision of a CTA only where all Contracting Jurisdictions have made such a notification with respect to the existing provision.

Denmark's Position[210] under the MLI

240. Notifications have been provided under Article 8(4) of the MLI by Denmark. The application of paragraph 1 of Article 8 of MLI in respect of CTAs which have been notified by Denmark under Article 8(4) is provided hereunder:

209. *Id.*, para. 126.
210. Refer Denmark's Position under the MLI http://www.oecd.org/tax/treaties/beps-mli-position-denmark-instrument-deposit.pdf.

Denmark's Treaty Partner	*Position Taken by Treaty Partner*	*Outcome under the MLI*
Argentina	- Has notified Article 10(2)(a) of the CTA	Denmark has notified Article 10(2) of the CTA. Barring this mismatch, Article 8(1) would apply
Austria	- Has not notified Denmark as a CTA under the MLI	Article 8 would not apply
Azerbaijan	- Not a Signatory to MLI	-
Bangladesh	- Not a Signatory to MLI	-
Belgium	- Has notified Article 10(2(2)) of the CTA	Denmark has notified Article 10(2) of the CTA. Barring this mismatch, Article 8(1) would apply
Bulgaria	- Has made reservation under Article 8(3)(a) of MLI	Article 8 would not apply
Canada	- Has notified Article 10(2)(a) of the CTA	Denmark has notified Article 10(2) of the CTA. Barring this mismatch, Article 8(1) would apply
Chile	- Has made reservation under Article 8(3)(a) of MLI	Article 8 would not apply
China	- Has notified Article 10(2)(a) of the CTA	Denmark has notified Article 10(2) of the CTA. Barring this mismatch, Article 8(1) would apply
Croatia	- Has made reservation under Article 8(3)(a) of MLI	Article 8 would not apply
Cyprus	- Has made reservation under Article 8(3)(a) of MLI	Article 8 would not apply
The Czech Republic	- Has made reservation under Article 8(3)(a) of MLI	Article 8 would not apply
Egypt	- Has notified Article 10(2)(a)(i) of the CTA	Denmark has notified Article 10(2) of the CTA. Barring this mismatch, Article 8(1) would apply
Estonia	- Has made reservation under Article 8(3)(a) of MLI	Article 8 would not apply
Georgia	- Has not notified Denmark as a CTA under the MLI	Article 8 would not apply
Ghana	- Not a Signatory to MLI	-
Greece	- Has made reservation under Article 8(3)(a) of MLI	Article 8 would not apply
Hungary	- Has made reservation under Article 8(3)(a) of MLI	Article 8 would not apply

Denmark's Treaty Partner	*Position Taken by Treaty Partner*	*Outcome under the MLI*
India	- Has notified Article 11(2)(a) of the CTA	Denmark has notified Article 11(2) of the CTA. Barring this mismatch, Article 8(1) would apply
Indonesia	- Has not notified Denmark in its position under Article 8(4) of the MLI	Article 8 would not apply
Ireland	- Has not notified Denmark in its position under Article 8(4) of the MLI	Article 8 would not apply
Israel	- Has notified Article 10(2)(a) of the CTA	Denmark has notified Article 10(2) of the CTA. Barring this mismatch, Article 8(1) would apply
Italy	- Has made reservation under Article 8(3)(a) of MLI	Article 8 would not apply
Jamaica	- Matching notification as Denmark's	Article 8(1) would apply
Kenya	- Has made reservation pursuant to Article 8(3)(b)(ii) of the MLI in respect of CTA with Denmark	Article 8 would not apply to the extent that the existing provisions include a minimum shareholding period shorter than a 365-day period
Kuwait	- Has made reservation under Article 8(3)(a) of MLI	Article 8 would not apply
Latvia	- Has made reservation under Article 8(3)(a) of MLI	Article 8 would not apply
Lithuania	- Has made reservation under Article 8(3)(a) of MLI	Article 8 would not apply
Luxembourg	- Has made reservation under Article 8(3)(a) of MLI	Article 8 would not apply
Malta	- Has made reservation under Article 8(3)(a) of MLI	Article 8 would not apply
Mexico	- Has notified Article 10(2)(a) of the CTA	Denmark has notified Article 10(2) of the CTA. Barring this mismatch, Article 8(1) would apply
Montenegro	- Not a Signatory to MLI	-
Morocco	- Has made reservation under Article 8(3)(a) of MLI	Article 8 would not apply
North Macedonia	- Has notified Article 10(2)(a) of the CTA	Denmark has notified Article 10(2) of the CTA. Barring this mismatch, Article 8(1) would apply

Denmark's Treaty Partner	*Position Taken by Treaty Partner*	*Outcome under the MLI*
The Philippines	- Not a Signatory to MLI	-
Poland	- Has made reservation pursuant to Article 8(3)(b)(i) of the MLI in respect of CTA with Denmark	Article 8 would not apply to the extent that the existing provisions include a minimum shareholding period
Romania	- Has notified Article 10(2)(a) of the CTA	Denmark has notified Article 10(2) of the CTA. Barring this mismatch, Article 8(1) would apply
Serbia	- Has notified Article 10(2(1)) of the CTA	Denmark has notified Article 10(2) of the CTA. Barring this mismatch, Article 8(1) would apply
Singapore	- Has made reservation under Article 8(3)(a) of MLI	Article 8 would not apply
Slovenia	- Has notified Article 10(2)(a), (b) of the CTA	Denmark has notified Article 10(2) of the CTA. Barring this mismatch, Article 8(1) would apply
South Africa	- Has notified Article 10(2)(a) of the CTA	Denmark has notified Article 10(2) of the CTA. Barring this mismatch, Article 8(1) would apply
Trinidad & Tobago	- Not a Signatory to MLI	-
Turkey	- Has made reservation under Article 8(3)(a) of MLI	Article 8 would not apply
Uganda	- Not a Signatory to MLI	-
Ukraine	- Has made reservation under Article 8(3)(a) of MLI	Article 8 would not apply
United Kingdom	- Has made reservation under Article 8(3)(a) of MLI	Article 8 would not apply
United States	- Not a Signatory to MLI	-
Venezuela	- Not a Signatory to MLI	-
Vietnam	- Not a Signatory to MLI	-

India's Position[211] under the MLI

241. A two-step notification has been done by India in this Article:

211. Refer India's Position under the MLI http://www.oecd.org/tax/treaties/beps-mli-position-india-instrument-deposit.pdf.

(a) Reservation has been taken under Article 8(3)(b)(iii) of the MLI; as in Article 10(2) of India-Portugal CTA, a period of two years (i.e., more than the threshold holding period of 365 days provided in Article 8(1) of the MLI) has been specified. On the other hand, Portugal has taken a reservation in respect of the said CTA under 8(3)(b)(i) of the MLI (as the CTA already has a minimum holding period), implying that in regard to India-Portugal CTA, Article 8(1) of the MLI shall not apply.

(b) Notifications have been provided in Article 8(4) of the MLI in respect of those treaties where Two-Tier WHT rate on dividend is provided. This provision is not intended to apply to existing dividend provisions of those CTAs that do not give a preferential rate based on holding a certain amount of shares of company paying the dividend. In all, 24 CTAs have been notified by India under Article 8(4) and the application of paragraph 1 of Article 8 of MLI in respect of these CTAs is provided hereunder:

India's Treaty Partner	*Position Taken by Treaty Partner*	*Outcome under the MLI*
Bangladesh	- Not a Signatory to MLI	-
Belarus	- Not a Signatory to MLI	-
Botswana	- Not a Signatory to MLI	-
Canada	- Matching notification as India's	Article 8(1) would apply
Croatia	- Has made reservation under Article 8(3)(a) of MLI	Article 8 would not apply
Denmark	- Has notified Article 11(2) of the CTA	India has notified Article 11(2)(a). Barring this mismatch, Article 8(1) would apply
Italy	- Has made reservation under Article 8(3)(a) of MLI	Article 8 would not apply
Lithuania	- Has made reservation under Article 8(3)(a) of MLI	Article 8 would not apply
Mauritius	- Has not notified India as a CTA under the MLI	Article 8 would not apply
Montenegro	- Not a Signatory to MLI	-

India's Treaty Partner	*Position Taken by Treaty Partner*	*Outcome under the MLI*
Nepal	- Not a Signatory to MLI	-
Oman	- Has not notified India as a CTA under the MLI	Article 8 would not apply
The Philippines	- Not a Signatory to MLI	-
Qatar	- Has made reservation under Article 8(3)(a) of MLI	Article 8 would not apply
Serbia	- Matching notification as India's	Article 8(1) would apply
Singapore	- Has made reservation under Article 8(3)(a) of MLI	Article 8 would not apply
The Slovak Republic	- Matching notification as India's	Article 8(1) would apply
Slovenia	- Matching notification as India's	Article 8(1) would apply
Syria	- Not a Signatory to MLI	-
Tajikistan	- Not a Signatory to MLI	-
Tanzania	- Not a Signatory to MLI	-
Ukraine	- Has made reservation under Article 8(3)(a) of MLI	Article 8 would not apply
US	- Not a Signatory to MLI	-
Zambia	- Not a Signatory to MLI	-

The Netherlands' Position[212] under the MLI

242. Notifications have been provided under Article 8(4) of the MLI by the Netherlands. The application of paragraph 1 of Article 8 of MLI in respect of CTAs which have been notified by the Netherlands under Article 8(4) is provided hereunder:

212. Refer The Netherlands' Position under the MLI http://www.oecd.org/tax/treaties/beps-mli-position-netherlands-instrument-deposit.pdf.

The Netherlands' Treaty Partner	*Position Taken by Treaty Partner*	*Outcome under the MLI*
Albania	- Matching notification as the Netherlands'	Article 8(1) would apply
Argentina	- Matching notification as the Netherlands'	Article 8(1) would apply
Armenia	- Matching notification as the Netherlands'	Article 8(1) would apply
Austria	- Has made reservation under Article 8(3)(a) of MLI	Article 8 would not apply
Azerbaijan	- Not a Signatory to MLI	-
Bahrain	- Has made reservation under Article 8(3)(a) of MLI	Article 8 would not apply
Bangladesh	- Not a Signatory to MLI	-
Barbados	- Has made reservation under Article 8(3)(a) of MLI	Article 8 would not apply
Belarus	- Not a Signatory to MLI	-
Bosnia & Herzegovina	- Has made reservation under Article 8(3)(a) of MLI	Article 8 would not apply
Canada	- Matching notification as the Netherlands'	Article 8(1) would apply
China	- Matching notification as the Netherlands'	Article 8(1) would apply
Croatia	- Has made reservation under Article 8(3)(a) of MLI	Article 8 would not apply
The Czech Republic	- Has made reservation under Article 8(3)(a) of MLI	Article 8 would not apply
Egypt	- Matching notification as the Netherlands'	Article 8(1) would apply
Estonia	- Has made reservation under Article 8(3)(a) of MLI	Article 8 would not apply
Ethiopia	- Not a Signatory to MLI	-
Finland	- Has made reservation under Article 8(3)(a) of MLI	Article 8 would not apply
France	- Matching notification as the Netherlands'	Article 8(1) would apply
Georgia	- Matching notification as the Netherlands'	Article 8(1) would apply
Germany	- Has not notified the Netherlands as a CTA under the MLI	Article 8 would not apply
Ghana	- Not a Signatory to MLI	-
Greece	- Has made reservation under Article 8(3)(a) of MLI	Article 8 would not apply

The Netherlands' Treaty Partner	*Position Taken by Treaty Partner*	*Outcome under the MLI*
Hong Kong	- Has made reservation under Article 8(3)(a) of MLI	Article 8 would not apply
Hungary	- Has made reservation under Article 8(3)(a) of MLI	Article 8 would not apply
Iceland	- Has made reservation under Article 8(3)(a) of MLI	Article 8 would not apply
Indonesia	- Matching notification as the Netherlands'	Article 8(1) would apply
Israel	- Matching notification as the Netherlands'	Article 8(1) would apply
Italy	- Has made reservation under Article 8(3)(a) of MLI	Article 8 would not apply
Japan	- Has made reservation under Article 8(3)(a) of MLI	Article 8 would not apply
Jordan	- Matching notification as the Netherlands'	Article 8(1) would apply
Kazakhstan	- Matching notification as the Netherlands'	Article 8(1) would apply
Kenya	- Has notified Article 10(2) of the CTA	The Netherlands has notified Article 10(3)(a) of the CTA. Barring this mismatch, Article 8(1) would apply
Korea	- Has made reservation under Article 8(3)(a) of MLI	Article 8 would not apply
Kuwait	- Has made reservation under Article 8(3)(a) of MLI	Article 8 would not apply
Latvia	- Has made reservation under Article 8(3)(a) of MLI	Article 8 would not apply
Lithuania	- Has made reservation under Article 8(3)(a) of MLI	Article 8 would not apply
Luxembourg	- Has made reservation under Article 8(3)(a) of MLI	Article 8 would not apply
Malawi	- Not a Signatory to MLI	-
Malaysia	- Has made reservation under Article 8(3)(a) of MLI	Article 8 would not apply
Malta	- Has made reservation under Article 8(3)(a) of MLI	Article 8 would not apply
Mexico	- Matching notification as the Netherlands'	Article 8(1) would apply
Moldova	- Not a Signatory to MLI	-
Montenegro	- Not a Signatory to MLI	-

The Netherlands' Treaty Partner	*Position Taken by Treaty Partner*	*Outcome under the MLI*
Morocco	– Has made reservation under Article 8(3)(a) of MLI	Article 8 would not apply
Nigeria	– Has made reservation under Article 8(3)(a) of MLI	Article 8 would not apply
North Macedonia	– Matching notification as the Netherlands'	Article 8(1) would apply
Norway	– Matching notification as the Netherlands'	Article 8(1) would apply
Oman	– Has made reservation under Article 8(3)(a) of MLI	Article 8 would not apply
Pakistan	– Matching notification as the Netherlands'	Article 8(1) would apply
Panama	– Has made reservation under Article 8(3)(a) of MLI	Article 8 would not apply
The Philippines	– Not a Signatory to MLI	–
Qatar	– Has made reservation under Article 8(3)(a) of MLI	Article 8 would not apply
Romania	– Matching notification as the Netherlands'	Article 8(1) would apply
Russia	– Matching notification as the Netherlands'	Article 8(1) would apply
Saudi Arabia	– Has made reservation under Article 8(3)(a) of MLI	Article 8 would not apply
Serbia	– Matching notification as the Netherlands'	Article 8(1) would apply
Singapore	– Has made reservation under Article 8(3)(a) of MLI	Article 8 would not apply
The Slovak Republic	– Matching notification as the Netherlands'	Article 8(1) would apply
Slovenia	– Matching notification as the Netherlands'	Article 8(1) would apply
South Africa	– Matching notification as the Netherlands'	Article 8(1) would apply
Sri Lanka	– Not a Signatory to MLI	–
Suriname	– Not a Signatory to MLI	–
Sweden	– Has made reservation under Article 8(3)(a) of MLI	Article 8 would not apply
Thailand	– Not a Signatory to MLI	–
Tunisia	– Matching notification as the Netherlands'	Article 8(1) would apply

The Netherlands' Treaty Partner	*Position Taken by Treaty Partner*	*Outcome under the MLI*
Turkey	- Has made reservation under Article 8(3)(a) of MLI	Article 8 would not apply
Uganda	- Not a Signatory to MLI	-
The United Arab Emirates	- Has made reservation under Article 8(3)(a) of MLI	Article 8 would not apply
United Kingdom	- Has made reservation under Article 8(3)(a) of MLI	Article 8 would not apply
United States	- Not a Signatory to MLI	-
Uzbekistan	- Not a Signatory to MLI	-
Venezuela	- Not a Signatory to MLI	-
Vietnam	- Not a Signatory to MLI	-
Zambia	- Not a Signatory to MLI	-
Zimbabwe	- Not a Signatory to MLI	-

Few Snapshots of Positions[213] Taken by Other Countries under the MLI

243. Jurisdictions that have made reservation under Article 8(3)(a) of the MLI are, namely, Andorra, Austria, Bahrain, Barbados, Belize, Bosnia and Herzegovina, Bulgaria, Chile, Croatia, Curaçao, Cyprus, the Czech Republic, Estonia, Finland, Gabon, Georgia, Greece, Guernsey, Hong Kong, Hungary, Iceland, the Isle of Man, Italy, Japan, Jersey, Korea, Kuwait, Latvia, Liechtenstein, Lithuania, Luxembourg, Malaysia, Malta, Mauritius, Monaco, Morocco, Nigeria, Oman, Panama, Papua New Guinea, Qatar, San Marino, Saudi Arabia, Seychelles, Singapore, Sweden, Switzerland, Turkey, Ukraine, the United Arab Emirates, UK.

244. Jurisdictions that have made reservations under Article 8(3)(b)(i) of the MLI are, namely, Armenia, Germany, Norway, Poland, Portugal, Russia and have notified their respective CTAs therein by reserving the right for the entirety of Article 8 not to apply to their respective CTAs to the extent that the provisions described in Article 8(1) already include a minimum holding period.

245. Kenya is the only jurisdiction as of now that has made reservation under Article 8(3)(b)(ii) of the MLI wherein it has notified its CTAs with Canada, Denmark, Italy, Norway and Sweden.

246. Jurisdictions that have made reservations under Article 8(3)(b)(iii) of the MLI are, namely, India (notified CTA with Portugal) and Slovak Republic (notified CTAs with Poland and Portugal).

213. Refer OECD – Signatories and Parties to the MLI http://www.oecd.org/tax/treaties/beps-mli-signatories-and-parties.pdf.

247. As an illustration, the impact of MLI on a few CTAs on account of notifications made by certain jurisdictions is tabulated as below:

Jurisdiction	*Position Taken*	*Treaty Partner*	*Position Taken*	*Outcome under the MLI*
Armenia	- Reservation under Article 8(3)(b)(i)	Croatia	- Reservation under Article 8(3)(a)	Article 8 would not apply
Armenia	- Reservation under Article 8(3)(b)(i) and has notified Article 10(2)(b)(ii) of the CTA with Spain	Spain	- Notified Article 10(2) of the CTA with Armenia under Article 8(4) of MLI	Article 8 of MLI would not apply to the extent that the existing provisions of the CTA include a minimum shareholding period (of two years)[214]
Russia	- Reservation under Article 8(3)(b)(i) and notified CTA with Portugal	Portugal	- Reservation under Article 8(3)(b)(i) and notified CTA with Russia	Article 8 of MLI would not apply to the extent that the existing provisions in the CTA include a minimum shareholding period (of two years)[215]
Kenya	- Reservation under Article 8(3)(b)(ii) and notified CTA with Canada	Canada	- Notified CTA with Kenya under Article 8(4) of MLI	Article 8 MLI would not apply to the extent that the existing provisions under Article 10(2)(a) of the Kenya-Canada CTA[216] include a minimum shareholding period shorter than a 365-day period (period of six months provided in the CTA)
Kenya	- Reservation under Article 8(3)(b)(ii) and notified CTA with Italy	Italy	- Reservation under Article 8(3)(a)	Article 8 would not apply

214. Refer Armenia-Spain CTA https://research.ibfd.org/#/doc?url=/linkresolver/static/tt_am-es_02_eng_2010_tt accessed on 3 September 2020.
215. Refer Russia-Portugal CTA https://research.ibfd.org/#/doc?url=/linkresolver/static/tt_pt-ru_01_eng_2000_tt accessed on 3 September 2020.
216. Refer Kenya-Canada CTA https://research.ibfd.org/#/doc?url=/linkresolver/static/tt_ca-ke_02_eng_1983_tt accessed on 3 September 2020.

Jurisdiction	*Position Taken*	*Treaty Partner*	*Position Taken*	*Outcome under the MLI*
The Slovak Republic	- Reservation under Article 8(3)(b)(iii) and notified CTA with Portugal	Portugal	- Reservation under Article 8(3)(b)(i) and notified CTA with the Slovak Republic	Article 8(1) would not apply
The Slovak Republic	- Notified CTA with Canada under Article 8(4) of MLI	Canada	- Notified CTA with the Slovak Republic under Article 8(4)	As there is a matching notification, Article 8(1) of MLI would apply with respect to Article 10(2)(a) of the CTA

The various notifications made by treaty partners under Article 8 of the MLI and impact/outcome thereof on the respective CTAs are provided in Figure 9.

Figure 9 Article 8: Dividend Transfer Transactions – Flowchart on Notifications & Their Impact

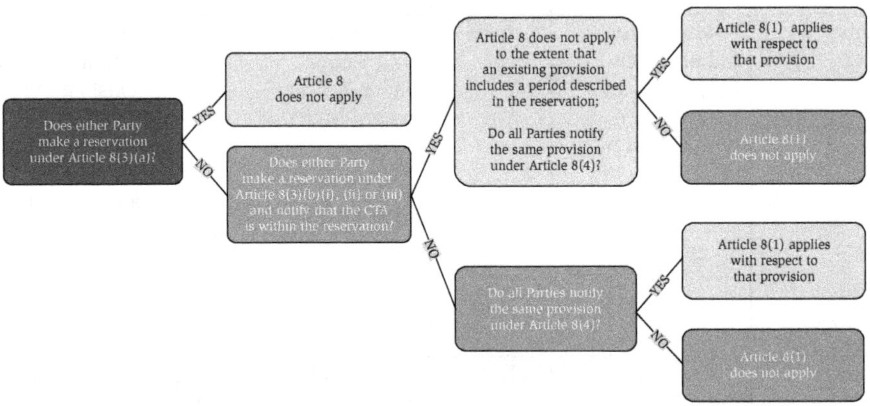

Source: OECD – Toolkit for Application of the Multilateral Instrument for BEPS Tax Treaty Related Measures https://www.oecd.org/tax/treaties/application-toolkit-multilateral-instrument-for-beps-tax-treaty-measures.htm.

3.6.4 Article 9 of MLI: Capital Gains from Alienation of Shares or Interests of Entities Deriving Their Value Principally from Immovable Property

248. The interplay between Article 9 of MLI, corresponding BEPS Report and the resulting provisions incorporated in OECD MTC 2017 is represented in a table as below:

MLI		*BEPS Final Report*		*OECD MTC 2017*	
Article	*Title of Article*	*BEPS Action Plan*	*Title of BEPS Action Plan*	*Article*	*Title of Article*
9	Capital Gains from Alienation of Shares or Interests of Entities Deriving Their Value Principally from Immovable Property	Action 6	Preventing the Granting of Treaty Benefits in Inappropriate Circumstances	13(4)	Capital Gains

249. The article at a glance is as below:

Substantive (BEPS) Provisions under Para(s)	*Opt-In Provisions under Para*	*Alternative Provisions under Para*	*Compatibility Clause*		*Reservations under Para*	*Notifications under Para*
			Para	*Type*		
1, 4	3-5	None	2*,5	'in place of or in the absence of'	6	6, 7, 8

*Paragraph 2 is the compatibility clause of paragraph 1(a) of Article 9 as paragraph 1(b) of Article 9 already describes the relationship with shares or rights covered by existing provisions.

Status in Pre-BEPS Project Era

250. Paragraph 4 of Article 13 of OECD MTC 2014 did not specifically address situations where assets were contributed to an entity shortly before the sale of shares or comparable interests (such as interests in a partnership or trust) in that entity in order to dilute the proportion of the value of the entity that is derived from immovable property; with the result, taxation of capital gain on sale of shares or comparable interests was artificially shifted to the State of residence, thereby depriving the State of source, where the immovable property is situated, of its rightful share of tax. In the OECD MTC 2014, though Article 13(4) per se did not mention about interests in a partnership or trust, paragraph 28.5 of the Commentary did recognise that jurisdictions may, in their bilateral treaties, broaden paragraph 4 by covering not only gains from shares but also gains from the alienation of interests in other entities, such as partnerships and trusts, that do not issue shares, as long as the value of these interests is similarly derived principally from immovable property. Therefore, it was agreed under BEPS Action 6 Report that Article 13(4) should be amended to include such wording. Now, 'comparable interests' have been included in Article 13(4) itself. It was also agreed that Article 13(4) should be amended to refer to situations where shares or similar interest derive their value primarily from immovable property at any time during a certain period as opposed to at the time of the alienation only.

Article 9(1) of MLI

251. On following the BEPS Action 6 Report, Article 9 of MLI was articulated to address tax treaty abuse related to the taxation of capital gain realised from the alienation of shares of companies that derive their value principally from immovable property (real property), by introducing a testing period for determining whether the shares derive their value principally from immovable property (in Article 9(1)(a)) and to expand the scope of interests covered to include interests comparable to shares, such as interests in a partnership or trust (in Article 9(1)(b)). Hence, Article 9(1) of the MLI establishes a 365-day holding period for capital gains from the alienation of shares or comparable interests, such as interests in partnership or trust, deriving a certain part of their value from immovable property.

252. The term 'comparable interests' has been replaced with 'other rights of participation in an entity' in the chapeau to make sure that paragraph 1 applies with respect to existing provisions that may describe the ownership interests more broadly than 'comparable interests'. This change is intended to broadly capture existing provisions to be modified by this paragraph, but (except to the extent provided in sub-paragraph (b)) not to expand the scope of the interests covered.[217]

253. Since the purpose of this provision is to introduce a testing period and to ensure that the provision addresses interests comparable to shares (such as interest in a partnership or trust), the threshold provided in existing provisions would be preserved, and where CTAs contain exceptions to the application of the existing provisions (e.g., some CTAs may exclude gains derived from the alienation of shares of companies that are listed on an approved stock exchange of one of the Contracting Jurisdictions), those exceptions would continue to apply. Also, some existing provisions may use the terms 'income' and 'profits' in addition to or instead of 'gains'; such provisions would also be within the scope of the application of paragraph 1.[218]

Opt-In Provisions under Article 9(4) of MLI

254. Article 9(4) was established to modify CTAs that do not contain a treaty provision similar or equivalent to Article 13(4) of the OECD MTC (2014) dealing with gains derived by a resident of a Contracting State from the alienation of shares or other rights of participation in an entity situated in the other Contracting State when such shares or rights derived a certain part of their value from immovable property. The said complementary provision modifies CTAs only when corresponding Parties have opted in to the provision. In addition to this, paragraph 4 provides an option for Parties that prefer to apply Article 13(4) of the OECD MTC, as produced in the Action 6 Report, to their CTAs, rather than to incorporate a testing period in existing capital gains provisions and to expand the types of interest covered by those existing provisions

217. Refer Explanatory Statement to the MLI, para. 130(i).
218. *Id.*, para. 131.

through paragraph 1. Where paragraph 4 applies to a CTA, paragraph 1 would not apply.[219]

255. The 365-day period, referred to in paragraph 1 and paragraph 4 of Article 9, shall be computed by counting the period before alienation of shares or comparable interests, in contrast to Article 8(1) of MLI, where the 365-day period is computed by counting the period before and after the date of declaration of dividend, including the day of the payment of dividend.

Compatibility Clauses

256. Paragraph 2 is the compatibility clause of paragraph 1(a) which describes the interaction between paragraph 1(a) and provisions of CTAs. This paragraph clarifies that the 365-day testing period in paragraph 1(a) replaces the testing periods already contained in existing provisions, or is added where such testing periods do not exist in existing provisions. If Parties prefer to preserve existing testing periods, paragraph 6(d) allows the possibility to opt out of paragraph 1(a) with respect to provisions of CTAs that already include a testing period. Since paragraph 1(b) already describes the relationship with shares or rights covered by existing provisions, paragraph 2 does not describe the compatibility of paragraph 1(b) with existing provisions.[220]

257. Paragraph 5 is the compatibility clause of paragraph 4 which describes the interaction between paragraph 4 and provisions of CTAs. This paragraph clarifies that the provision in paragraph 4 replaces existing provisions of CTAs addressing capital gains from the alienation of shares or interests in entities deriving their value principally from immovable property, or is added where such provisions do not exist in CTAs. If Parties prefer to preserve existing provisions of their CTAs, paragraph 6(f) allows the possibility to opt out of paragraph 4 with respect to the CTAs.

Reservations under Paragraph 6

258. The following reservations are provided for under paragraph 6:

(i) Under paragraph 6(a), Parties may opt out of Article 9(1) entirely, as the same is not a minimum standard.
(ii) Under paragraphs 6(b), (d), Parties may opt out of Article 9(1)(a) (the testing period) either for all CTAs or for CTAs that already contain a provision that includes a testing period.
(iii) Under paragraphs 6(c), (e), Parties may opt out of Article 9(1)(b) (expanded scope of interest covered) either for all CTAs or for CTAs that already contain a provision that applies to interests other than shares.
(iv) Under paragraph 6(f), Parties may opt out of the option of Article 9(4) of MLI for CTAs that already contain a provision as described in Article 9(5) of MLI. As a result, such existing provisions would be preserved, and paragraph 4

219. *Id.*, para. 133.
220. *Id.*, para. 132.

would apply only with respect to CTAs that do not contain provisions described in paragraph 5. Since this reservation is intended to work in the situation where paragraph 4 applies (in other words, paragraph 1 does not apply), it would have no effect on the application of paragraph 1. On the other hand, Parties that choose to apply paragraph 4 would be able to make the reservations described in sub-paragraphs (a) through (e) in addition to sub-paragraph (f) with respect to cases where paragraph 1, and not paragraph 4, applies.[221]

Notifications

259. Depending upon the position taken by various jurisdictions, the following notifications are required to be made under Article 9 of the MLI:

(i) Jurisdictions intending to make reservations under paragraph 6 are required to make notifications under sub-paragraphs (a)-(f), as the case may be.
(ii) Under paragraph 7, jurisdictions which have not made the reservation described in sub-paragraph (a) of paragraph 6 shall make notifications whether each of its CTAs contains a provision described in paragraph 1, and if so, the article and paragraph number of each such provision. Given that paragraph 1(a) or (b) could apply even in the case where the other paragraph is opted out of under the reservations described in paragraphs 6(b) through (e), paragraph 7 does not exclude Parties that have made those reservations from the notification requirement. Paragraph 1 would apply with respect to a provision of a CTA only where all Contracting Jurisdictions have made such a notification with respect to the existing provision.[222]
(iii) Jurisdictions that choose to apply paragraph 4 shall make notifications of its choice under paragraph 8 of Article 9 of the MLI. A Party that has not reserved the right under paragraph 6(a) for paragraph 1 not to apply to its CTAs will have included in its notifications under paragraph 7 a list of CTAs containing a relevant existing provision. A Party that has made such a reservation, however, will be required to include such a list in its notification under paragraph 8, except where such Party has reserved the right under paragraph 6(f) to preserve existing provisions. It then describes the relationship between paragraph 4 and paragraph 1. Where all Contracting Jurisdictions have chosen to apply paragraph 4 by making a notification under this paragraph, paragraph 1 would not apply with respect to that CTA, and instead paragraph 4 would apply. An existing provision of a CTA would be replaced by the provisions of paragraph 4 where all Contracting Jurisdictions have made a notification under paragraph 7 or 8 with respect to the existing provision. In other cases, paragraph 4 would

221. *Id.*, para. 139.
222. *Id.*, para. 140.

supersede the provisions of the CTA only to the extent that those provisions are incompatible with paragraph 4.[223]

Interplay Between Paragraph 1 and Paragraph 4

260. Where paragraph 4 applies to a CTA, paragraph 1 would not apply. In contrast, if one Contracting Jurisdiction chooses to apply paragraph 4 and one or more of the other Contracting Jurisdictions do not (or neither Contracting Jurisdiction chooses to apply it), paragraph 4 would not apply to that CTA, and paragraph 1 would apply.[224]

261. Article 9(4) applies only where all Contracting Jurisdictions choose to apply it. Therefore, if either Contracting Jurisdiction does not choose to apply Article 9(4), Article 9(4) does not apply, and then, Article 9(1) would apply as a default rule. As described in paragraph 139 of the Explanatory Statement, Parties choosing to apply Article 9(4) would be able to make the reservations described in Article 9(6)(a) through (e) with respect to such cases where paragraph 1, and not paragraph 4, applies.

262. If all Contracting Jurisdictions choose to apply Article 9(4), Article 9(4) would apply and Article 9(1) is switched off entirely. To make clear the relationship between Article 9(4) and Article 9(1), the third sentence of Article 9(8) provides '*In such case, paragraph 1 shall not apply with respect to that Covered Tax Agreement.*' With respect to this sentence, paragraph 141 of the Explanatory Statement explains '*It then describes the relationship between paragraph 4 and paragraph 1. Where all Contracting Jurisdictions have chosen to apply paragraph 4 by making a notification under this paragraph, paragraph 1 would not apply with respect to that Covered Tax Agreement, and instead paragraph 4 would apply.*'

263. Where all Contracting Jurisdictions have chosen to apply Article 9(4) by making a notification under Article 9(8), Article 9(4) would apply and Article 9(1) would no longer apply. As a result, even if either Contracting Jurisdiction makes a reservation under Article 9(6)(f), Article 9(1) would not apply. Reason thereof is described in paragraph 139 of the Explanatory Statement, which provides that the reservation in Article 9(6)(f) was introduced to allow Parties choosing to apply Article 9(4) to preserve existing provisions rather than modifying them. Therefore, where all Contracting Jurisdictions have chosen to apply Article 9(4), existing provisions that are within the scope of the reservation would be preserved without any modification by Article 9.[225]

264. Further, it is possible to make a reservation under Article 9(6)(a) and to choose to apply Article 9(4) because Article 9(6)(a) provides opting out of Article 9(1) alone (not Article 9(4)).[226]

---

223. *Id.*, para. 141.
224. *Id.*, para. 133.
225. Refer OECD's FAQs on MLI https://community.oecd.org/docs/DOC-113848 accessed on 7 August 2020.
226. *Id.*

Denmark's Position[227] under the MLI

265. Denmark has made a two-step notification in this Article:

(1) Pursuant to Article 9(8), Denmark has chosen to apply Article 9(4) of the MLI, which implies, in Denmark's CTAs where provisions similar to Article 13(4) of the OECD MTC 2017 are not present, Article 9(4) of the MLI would be inserted, provided the corresponding treaty partner also makes similar notification.
(2) Pursuant to Article 9(7), Denmark has notified 28 of its 64 CTAs, which contain a provision described in Article 9(1) of the MLI.

266. In view of the two-step notification made by Denmark, as an illustration, the application of paragraph 1 or paragraph 4 of Article 9 of the MLI to some of Denmark's CTAs is provided hereunder:

227. Refer Denmark's Position under the MLI http://www.oecd.org/tax/treaties/beps-mli-position-denmark-instrument-deposit.pdf.

<table>
<tr><th>Jurisdiction</th><th>Position Taken</th><th>Treaty Partner</th><th>Position Taken</th><th>Outcome under the MLI</th></tr>
<tr><td rowspan="2">Denmark</td><td>– Denmark has chosen to apply Article 9(4) of the MLI</td><td>Argentina</td><td>– Argentina has chosen to apply Article 9(4) of the MLI</td><td rowspan="2">– Article 9(1) would not apply
– Article 9(4) would apply</td></tr>
<tr><td colspan="3">– A provision described in Article 9(1) of the MLI is not present in Denmark-Argentina CTA, hence, no notification by Denmark or Argentina under Article 9(7) of MLI</td></tr>
<tr><td>Denmark</td><td>– Denmark has chosen to apply Article 9(4) of the MLI
– Denmark has notified Article 13(2) of CTA with Australia under Article 9(7) of the MLI</td><td>Australia</td><td>– No similar notification to apply Article 9(4) by Australia
– Australia has notified Article 13(1), 13(2)(a)(iii) and (b)(iii) of CTA with Denmark under Article 9(7) of the MLI</td><td>– Barring the notification mismatch, Article 9(1) would apply
– Article 9(4) would not apply</td></tr>
</table>

Jurisdiction	*Position Taken*	*Treaty Partner*	*Position Taken*	*Outcome under the MLI*
Denmark	- Denmark has chosen to apply Article 9(4) of the MLI - Denmark has notified Article 13(4) of CTA with Canada under Article 9(7) of the MLI	Canada	- Canada has chosen to apply Article 9(4) of the MLI - Pursuant to Article 9(6)(e), Canada has made a reservation in respect of CTA with Denmark - Canada has notified Article 13(4) of CTA with Denmark under Article 9(7) of the MLI	- Article 9(1) would not apply - Article 9(4) would replace relevant provisions of the CTA
Denmark	- Denmark has chosen to apply Article 9(4) of the MLI - Denmark has notified Article 13(4) of CTA with Egypt under Article 9(7) of the MLI	Egypt	- Egypt has chosen to apply Article 9(4) of the MLI - Egypt has notified Article 13(4) of CTA with Denmark under Article 9(7) of the MLI	- Article 9(1) would not apply - Article 9(4) would replace relevant provisions of the CTA

Jurisdiction	*Position Taken*	*Treaty Partner*	*Position Taken*	*Outcome under the MLI*
Denmark	– Denmark has chosen to apply Article 9(4) of the MLI – Denmark has notified Article 13(5) of CTA with Israel under Article 9(7) of the MLI	Israel	– Israel has chosen to apply Article 9(4) of the MLI – Israel has taken a reservation under Article 9(6)(a)	– Article 9(1) would not apply – Article 9(4) would replace relevant provisions of the CTA
Denmark	– Denmark has chosen to apply Article 9(4) of the MLI – Denmark has notified Article 15(1) of CTA with Jamaica under Article 9(7) of the MLI	Jamaica	– Jamaica has taken a reservation under Article 9(6)(a) – No similar notification to apply Article 9(4)	– Article 9(1) would not apply – Article 9(4) would not apply

Jurisdiction	*Position Taken*	*Treaty Partner*	*Position Taken*	*Outcome under the MLI*
Denmark	– Denmark has chosen to apply Article 9(4) of the MLI – Denmark has notified Article 13(2) of CTA with Singapore under Article 9(7) of the MLI	Singapore	– Singapore has taken a reservation under Article 9(6)(a) – No similar notification to apply Article 9(4)	– Article 9(1) would not apply – Article 9(4) would not apply
Denmark	– Denmark has chosen to apply Article 9(4) of the MLI – Denmark has notified Article 13(2) of CTA with Ukraine under Article 9(7) of the MLI	Ukraine	– Ukraine has chosen to apply Article 9(4) of the MLI – Ukraine has notified Article 13(2) of CTA with Denmark under Article 9(7) of the MLI	– Article 9(1) would not apply – Article 9(4) would replace relevant provisions of the CTA

India's Position[228] under the MLI

267. India has made a two-step notification in this Article:

(1) Pursuant to Article 9(8), India has chosen to apply Article 9(4) of the MLI, which implies, in India's CTAs where provisions similar to Article 13(4) of the OECD MTC 2017 are not present, Article 9(4) of the MLI would be inserted, provided the corresponding treaty partner also makes similar notification.
(2) Pursuant to Article 9(7), India has notified 71 of its 93 CTAs, which contain a provision described in Article 9(1) of the MLI.

268. In view of the two-step notification made by India, as an illustration, the application of paragraph 1 or paragraph 4 of Article 9 of the MLI to some of India's CTAs is provided hereunder:

228. Refer India's Position under the MLI http://www.oecd.org/tax/treaties/beps-mli-position-india-instrument-deposit.pdf.

Jurisdiction	*Position Taken*	*Treaty Partner*	*Position Taken*	*Outcome under the MLI*
India	– India has chosen to apply Article 9(4) of the MLI	Albania	– No similar notification to apply Article 9(4) by Albania	– Article 9(1) would not apply – Article 9(4) would not apply
	– A provision described in Article 9(1) of the MLI is not present in India-Albania CTA, hence, no notification by India or Albania under Article 9(7) of MLI			
India	– India has chosen to apply Article 9(4) of the MLI – India has notified CTA with Australia under Article 9(7) of the MLI	Australia	– No similar notification to apply Article 9(4) by Australia – Australia has notified CTA with India under Article 9(7) of the MLI	– Article 9(1) would apply – Article 9(4) would not apply
India	– India has chosen to apply Article 9(4) of the MLI – India has notified CTA with Austria under Article 9(7) of the MLI	Austria	– No similar notification to apply Article 9(4) by Austria – Austria has taken reservation under Article 9(6)(a) and opted out of Article 9(1) of MLI	– Article 9(1) would not apply – Article 9(4) would not apply
India	– India has chosen to apply Article 9(4) of the MLI – India has notified CTA with Belgium under Article 9(7) of the MLI	Belgium	– No similar notification to apply Article 9(4) by Belgium – Belgium has taken reservation under Article 9(6)(b) and opted out of Article 9(1)(a) of MLI	– Article 9(1)(a) would not apply – Article 9(1)(b) would apply – Article 9(4) would not apply

Jurisdiction	*Position Taken*	*Treaty Partner*	*Position Taken*	*Outcome under the MLI*
India	– India has chosen to apply Article 9(4) of the MLI	Canada	– Similar notification to apply Article 9(4) by Canada	– Article 9(1) would not apply – Article 9(4) would apply
	– A provision described in Article 9(1) of the MLI is not present in India-Canada CTA, hence, no notification by India or Canada under Article 9(7) of MLI			
India	– India has chosen to apply Article 9(4) of the MLI – India has notified CTA with Croatia under Article 9(7) of the MLI	Croatia	– Similar notification to apply Article 9(4) by Croatia – Croatia has taken reservation under Article 9(6)(a) and opted out of Article 9(1) of MLI – Croatia has notified CTA with India under Article 9(8) of the MLI	– Article 9(1) would not apply – Article 9(4) would replace relevant provisions of the CTA
India	– India has chosen to apply Article 9(4) of the MLI – India has notified CTA with Denmark under Article 9(7) of the MLI	Denmark	– Similar notification to apply Article 9(4) by Denmark – Denmark has notified CTA with India under Article 9(7) of the MLI	– Article 9(1) would not apply – Article 9(4) would replace relevant provisions of the CTA
India	– India has chosen to apply Article 9(4) of the MLI	Japan	– Similar notification to apply Article 9(4) by Japan	– Article 9(1) would not apply – Article 9(4) would apply
	– A provision described in Article 9(1) of the MLI is not present in India-Japan CTA, hence, no notification by India or Japan under Article 9(7) of MLI			

The Netherlands' Position[229] under the MLI

269. The Netherlands has made a one-step notification in this Article, whereby, pursuant to Article 9(7), the Netherlands has notified 24 of its 81 CTAs, which contain a provision described in Article 9(1) of the MLI. In this light, there will not be any application of Article 9(4) of the MLI in any of the CTAs of the Netherlands.

270. In view of the one-step notification made by the Netherlands, as an illustration, the application of paragraph 1 of Article 9 of the MLI to some of the Netherlands' CTAs is provided hereunder:

229. Refer The Netherlands' Position under the MLI http://www.oecd.org/tax/treaties/beps-mli-position-netherlands-instrument-deposit.pdf.

Jurisdiction	*Position Taken*	*Treaty Partner*	*Position Taken*	*Outcome under the MLI*
The Netherlands	– The Netherlands has notified Article 13(4) of CTA with Albania under Article 9(7) of the MLI	Albania	– Albania has notified Article 13(4) of CTA with the Netherlands under Article 9(7) of the MLI	– Article 9(1) would apply
The Netherlands	– The Netherlands has notified Article 13(4) of CTA with China under Article 9(7) of the MLI	China	– Pursuant to Article 9(6)(b) of the MLI, China has made a reservation to not apply Article 9(1)(a) – China has notified Article 13(4) of CTA with the Netherlands under Article 9(7) of the MLI	– Article 9(1)(a) would not apply – Article 9(1)(b) would apply with respect to Article 13(4) of the CTA
The Netherlands	– The Netherlands has notified Article 13(1) of CTA with France under Article 9(7) of the MLI	France	– France has notified Article 13(1) of CTA with the Netherlands under Article 9(7) of the MLI – France has chosen to apply Article 9(4) of the MLI	– Article 9(1) would apply – Article 9(4) would not apply
The Netherlands	– The Netherlands has notified Article 13(4) of CTA with Hong Kong under Article 9(7) of the MLI	Hong Kong	– Pursuant to Article 9(6)(a) of the MLI, Hong Kong has made a reservation for Article 9(1) not to apply to its CTAs	– Article 9(1) would not apply
The Netherlands	– The Netherlands has notified Article 13(2) of CTA with Kazakhstan under Article 9(7) of the MLI	Kazakhstan	– Kazakhstan has notified Article 13(2) of CTA with the Netherlands under Article 9(7) of the MLI – Has chosen to apply Article 9(4) of the MLI	– Article 9(1) would apply – Article 9(4) would not apply

Jurisdiction	*Position Taken*	*Treaty Partner*	*Position Taken*	*Outcome under the MLI*
The Netherlands	– The Netherlands has notified Article 13(6) of CTA with Panama under Article 9(7) of the MLI	Panama	– Pursuant to Article 9(6)(a) of the MLI, Panama has made a reservation for Article 9(1) not to apply to its CTAs	– Article 9(1) would not apply
The Netherlands	– The Netherlands has notified Article 13(4) of CTA with Slovenia under Article 9(7) of the MLI	Slovenia	– Slovenia has notified Article 13(4) of CTA with the Netherlands under Article 9(7) of the MLI – Slovenia has made a reservation under Article 9(6)(e) of the MLI; however, CTA with the Netherlands has not been notified therein – Slovenia has chosen to apply Article 9(4) of the MLI	– Article 9(1) would apply – Article 9(4) would not apply
The Netherlands	– The Netherlands has notified Article 13(4) of CTA with United Kingdom under Article 9(7) of the MLI	United Kingdom	– Pursuant to Article 9(6)(a) of the MLI, United Kingdom has made a reservation for Article 9(1) not to apply to its CTAs	– Article 9(1) would not apply

Few Snapshots of Positions[230] Taken by Other Countries under the MLI

271. Jurisdictions that have made reservations under Article 9(6)(a) of the MLI (for paragraph 1 not to apply) are, namely, Austria, Bahrain, Barbados, Belize, Bulgaria, Curaçao, Cyprus, the Czech Republic, Finland, Georgia, Greece, Guernsey, Hong Kong, Hungary, Iceland, the Isle of Man, Israel, Italy, Jamaica, Jersey, Jordan, Korea, Kuwait, Latvia, Liechtenstein, Lithuania, Luxembourg, Malaysia, Malta, Mauritius, Monaco, Morocco, Norway, Oman, Panama, Papua New Guinea, Qatar, Romania, San Marino, Saudi Arabia, Seychelles, Singapore, South Africa, Sweden, Switzerland, the United Arab Emirates, UK.

272. Jurisdictions that have made reservation under Article 9(6)(b) of the MLI (for paragraph 1(a) not to apply) are Belgium and China.

273. There is no jurisdiction as of now that has made reservation under Article 9(6)(c) of the MLI (for paragraph 1(b) not to apply).

274. Chile and Senegal have made reservations under Article 9(6)(d) of the MLI. Application of MLI provisions in respect of certain jurisdictions that have made reservation under Article 9(6)(d) of the MLI (for paragraph 1(a) not to apply to CTAs which already contain the relevant provision under certain CTAs notified to the Depositary) is *inter alia* as below:

Jurisdiction	*Position Taken*	*Treaty Partner*	*Position Taken*	*Outcome under the MLI*
Chile	- Opting out of Article 9(1)(a) of MLI for CTA with Argentina	Argentina	- Notification of Chile under Article 9(7)	- Article 9(1)(a) would not apply - Article 9(1)(b) would apply to the relevant provision of the CTA
Chile	- Opting out of Article 9(1)(a) of MLI for CTA with Uruguay	Uruguay	- Notification of Chile under Article 9(7)	- Article 9(1)(a) would not apply - Article 9(1)(b) would apply to the relevant provision of the CTA
Senegal	- Opting out of Article 9(1)(a) of MLI for CTA with UK	UK	- Reservation under Article 9(6)(a) for paragraph 1 not to apply	- Article 9(1) would not apply

275. Australia, Canada, Ireland, Russia and Slovenia have made reservations under Article 9(6)(e) of the MLI. Application of MLI provisions in respect of jurisdictions that

230. Refer OECD – Signatories and Parties to the MLI http://www.oecd.org/tax/treaties/beps-mli-signatories-and-parties.pdf.

have made reservation under Article 9(6)(e) of the MLI (for paragraph 1(b) not to apply to CTAs which already contain the relevant provision under certain CTAs notified to the Depositary) is *inter alia* as below:

Jurisdiction	*Position Taken*	*Treaty Partner*	*Position Taken*	*Outcome under the MLI*
Australia	- Opting out of Article 9(1)(b) of MLI for CTA with Canada - Australia has notified CTA with Canada under Article 9(7) of the MLI	Canada	- Similar Notification & opting out of Article 9(1)(b) of MLI for CTA with Australia - Similar Notification & Canada has notified CTA with Australia under Article 9(7) of the MLI	- Article 9(1)(b) would not apply - Article 9(1)(a) would apply
Australia	- Opting out of Article 9(1)(b) of MLI for CTA with Ireland - Australia has notified CTA with Ireland under Article 9(7) of the MLI	Ireland	- Similar Notification & opting out of Article 9(1)(b) of MLI for CTA with Australia - Similar Notification & Ireland has notified CTA with Australia under Article 9(7) of the MLI	- Article 9(1)(b) would not apply - Article 9(1)(a) would apply
Australia	- Opting out of Article 9(1)(b) of MLI for CTA with Russia - Australia has notified CTA with Russia under Article 9(7) of the MLI	Russia	- Similar Notification & opting out of Article 9(1)(b) of MLI for CTA with Australia - Similar Notification & Russia has notified CTA with Australia under Article 9(7) of the MLI	- Article 9(1)(b) would not apply - Article 9(1)(a) would apply

276. No Signatory, as of now, has made any reservation under Article 9(6)(f) of the MLI for paragraph 4 not to apply to CTAs that already contain the relevant provisions.

277. Jurisdictions that have made notifications under Article 9(8) of the MLI, choosing to apply paragraph 4, are, namely, Argentina, Armenia, Bosnia and Herzegovina, Burkina Faso, Cameroon, Canada, Colombia, Costa Rica, Cote d'Ivoire, Croatia, Denmark, Egypt, Estonia, France, Germany, India, Indonesia, Ireland, Israel, Italy, Japan, Kazakhstan, Kenya, Malta, Mexico, New Zealand, Nigeria, North Macedonia, Pakistan, Papua New Guinea, Peru, Poland, Portugal, Russia, San Marino, Senegal, Serbia, the Slovak Republic, Slovenia, South Africa, Spain, Tunisia, Turkey, Ukraine, Uruguay.

The various notifications made by treaty partners under Article 9 of the MLI and impact/outcome thereof on the respective CTAs are provided in Figure 10.

Figure 10 Article 9: Capital Gains from Alienation of Shares or Interests of Entities Deriving Their Value Principally from Immovable Property – Flowchart on Notifications & Their Impact

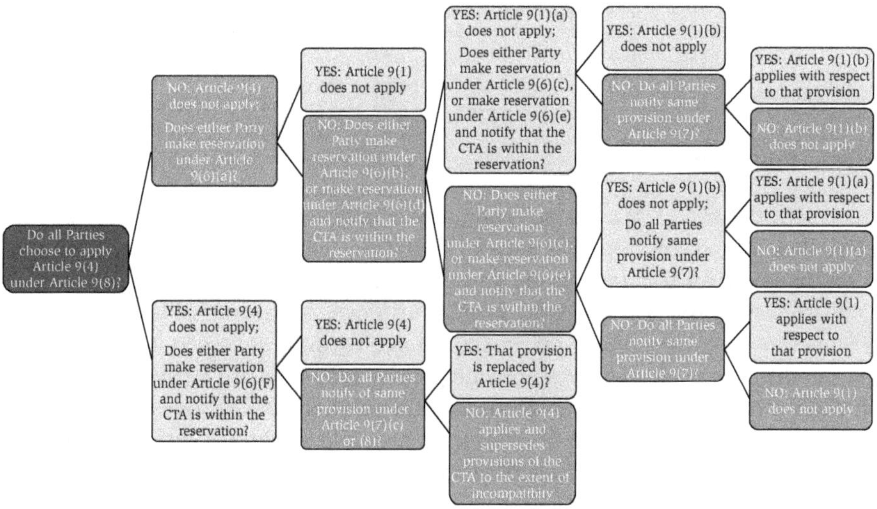

Source: OECD – Toolkit for Application of the Multilateral Instrument for BEPS Tax Treaty Related Measures https://www.oecd.org/tax/treaties/application-toolkit-multilateral-instrument-for-beps-tax-treaty-measures.htm.

3.6.5 Article 10 of MLI: Anti-abuse Rule for Permanent Establishments Situated in Third Jurisdictions

278. The interplay between Article 10 of MLI, corresponding BEPS Report and the resulting provisions incorporated in OECD MTC 2017 is represented in a table as below:

MLI		*BEPS Final Report*		*OECD MTC 2017*	
Article	*Title of Article*	*BEPS Action Plan*	*Title of BEPS Action Plan*	*Article*	*Title of Article*
10	Anti-abuse Rule for Permanent Establishments Situated in Third Jurisdictions	Action 6	Preventing the Granting of Treaty Benefits in Inappropriate Circumstances	29(8)	Entitlement to Benefits

279. The article at a glance is as below:

Substantive (BEPS) Provisions under Para(s)	*Opt-In Provisions under Para*	*Alternative Provisions under Para*	*Compatibility Clause*		*Reservations under Para*	*Notifications under Para*
			Para	*Type*		
1-3	None	None	4	'in place of or in the absence of'	5	5, 6

Status in Pre-BEPS Project Era

280. The OECD MTC 2014 did not expressly contain provisions to address potential abuses that, first, result from the transfer of shares, debt-claims, rights or property to PEs set up solely for that purpose in countries that offer preferential treatment to the income from such assets and second, from an artificial transfer of residence by an entity to a State that has a favourable tax treaty in force with the source State, but, retains a PE in the third State to which the income-generating assets are attributable. Thus, in such cases where the State of residence exempts, or taxes at low rates, profits of such PEs situated in third States, the State of source should not be expected to grant treaty benefits with respect to that income. Though paragraph 71 of the Commentary on Article 24 of the OECD MTC 2014 made recommendations for incorporation of anti-abuse rule during bilateral negotiation of tax treaties, it was concluded during the BEPS Project that a specific anti-abuse provision should be included in the MTC itself to deal with that and similar triangular cases where income attributable to the PE in a third State is subject to low taxation. Against this backdrop, it is fair to conclude that the purpose[231] of Article 29(8) of the OECD MTC 2017 is to address potential abuse in PE triangular structures pursuant to which profits attributable to the PE are exempt in the Residence State and bear little or no tax in the PE State.

231. Refer Jean-Philippe Van West's 'The Anti-abuse Rule for Permanent Establishments Situated in Third States – A Legal Analysis of Article 29(8) OECD Model' – WU Institute for Austrian and International Tax Law – Tax Law and Policy Series 16, IBFD, p. 121.

Article 10(1)-(3) of the MLI

281. Article 10 of the MLI establishes the anti-abuse rule for PEs situated in third jurisdictions where jurisdictions follow 'territorial system' of taxation. The rule under paragraph 1 tackles situations in which the income of an enterprise is attributed to a PE located in a third jurisdiction (is not taxed normally in that third State) and is treated as exempt from tax in the State of residence of the enterprise. That income, as attributable to a PE located in a third jurisdiction, if subjected to low taxation (tax on that income is less than 60% of the tax on that income in the State of residence) or if subjected to nil taxation in the third jurisdiction where the PE is located, then, as a consequence, by invocation of the anti-abuse rules enshrined in Article 10, such income shall be taxable in the State of source and no treaty benefit shall be granted by the State of source. Thus, State of source is able to protect its right to tax such income and situations of double non-taxation or reduced taxation are avoided.

282. As per paragraph 2 of Article 10, paragraph 1 thereof shall not apply if the income emanates from, or is incidental to, the active conduct of a business through the PE, excluding an investment business that is not carried on by a bank, insurance enterprise or registered securities dealer. Paragraph 1 shall also apply to investment activity comprising restructuring of business or transfer of shares.

283. As per paragraph 3 of Article 10, in a case where benefits are denied under paragraph 1, the resident of a Contracting State who derives the relevant income may request that the CA of the other Contracting State grants these benefits. The CA who receives such a request may, at its discretion, grant these benefits if it determines that doing so would be justified; it shall, however, consult with the CA of the other Contracting State before granting or denying the request.

284. The following example[232] illustrates the type of situation in which the provisions of Article 10(1)-(3) of MLI are intended to apply:

> An enterprise of a Contracting State sets up a permanent establishment in a third jurisdiction that imposes no or low tax on the profits of the permanent establishment. The profits attributable to the permanent establishment are exempt from tax by the first-mentioned State either pursuant to a provision similar to Article 23 A included in a tax treaty between that State and the jurisdiction where the permanent establishment is located or pursuant to the first-mentioned State's domestic law. The enterprise derives interest arising from the other Contracting State which is included in the profits attributable to the permanent establishment. Assuming that the conditions for the application of Article 11 of the treaty are met, the State in which the interest arises would, in the absence of provisions equivalent to Article 10(1)-(3) of the MLI, be obliged to grant the benefits of the limitation of tax provided for in paragraph 2 of Article 11 of the treaty despite the fact that the interest is exempt from tax in the first-mentioned State and is subject to little or no tax in the third jurisdiction in which the permanent establishment is situated. With the introduction of Article 10(1) of the MLI, the benefits of the tax treaty will be denied with respect to that income unless the exception of para 2 of

232. Refer OECD MTC 2017, para. 163 of the Commentary on Art. 29(8).

Article 10 of MLI applicable to income that emanates from, or is incidental to, the active conduct of a business applies to the relevant income or unless these benefits are granted, under the discretionary relief provision of para 3 of Article 10 of MLI, by the competent authority of the State in which the interest arises.

Scope of 'Anti-abuse Rule for Permanent Establishments Situated in Third Jurisdictions' Vis-à-Vis 'S-LoB'

285. Article 3(1)(c) of the OECD MTC 2017 connects the term 'enterprise' with the term 'business'. It follows from Article 3(1)(h) of the OECD MTC 2017 that individuals carrying on a business fall under the scope of the term 'enterprise'. Consequently, in this regard, the scope of Article 29(8) is wider than the S-LoB provision contained in Article 29(1)-(7), which excludes individuals from its scope.[233] Article 29(8) functions in parallel with the S-LoB provisions.[234] A taxpayer that is a qualified person under Article 29(1)-(7) of the OECD MTC can still be denied treaty benefit under Article 29(8). In addition, a taxpayer that does not fall within the scope of Article 29(8) can still be denied treaty benefit under S-LoB provisions.

Scope of 'Anti-abuse Rule for Permanent Establishments Situated in Third Jurisdictions' Vis-à-Vis 'PPT'

286. According to its wording, Article 29(9) of the OECD MTC 2017 is applicable 'notwithstanding the other provisions of this Convention'. This wording indicates that Article 29(9) is a self-standing provision that applies in parallel with Article 29(8). It is meant to make it clear that a more specific anti-abuse rule should not prevent the application of Article 29(9) and consequently, if a taxpayer falls outside the scope of Article 29(8), treaty benefits could still be denied under Article 29(9) in so far as the conditions for this provision to apply are fulfilled. However, some scholars take a more nuanced view that if a certain arrangement falls outside the scope of a specific anti-abuse rule, the PPT should be applicable only to the extent that the abusive behaviour lies completely outside the scope of the type of treaty abuse the specific rule intends to counter; i.e., when a certain factual situation is covered by a specific anti-abuse rule, that situation should no longer be tested against the PPT.[235]

Compatibility Clause

287. Paragraph 4 is the compatibility clause which describes the interaction between paragraphs 1 through 3 of Article 10 and provisions of CTAs. This paragraph provides that the provisions in paragraphs 1 through 3 replace existing provisions of CTAs that deny or limit benefits available to an enterprise of a Contracting Jurisdiction which derives income from the other Contracting Jurisdiction that is attributable to a PE of the

---

233. Refer Jean-Philippe Van West's 'The Anti-abuse Rule for Permanent Establishments Situated in Third States – A Legal Analysis of Article 29(8) OECD Model' – WU Institute for Austrian and International Tax Law – Tax Law and Policy Series 16, IBFD, p. 128.
234. *Id.*, p. 234.
235. *Id.*, pp. 235, 236.

enterprise situated in a third jurisdiction, or is added where such provisions do not exist in CTAs.[236]

Reservations under Paragraph 5

288. The following reservations are provided for under paragraph 5:

(i) Under paragraph 5(a), Parties may opt out of Article 10 entirely, as the same is not a minimum standard.
(ii) Under paragraph 5(b), Parties may opt out of Article 10 entirely with respect to CTAs that already contain the provisions described in Article 10(4).
(iii) Under paragraph 5(c), Parties may opt out of Article 10 entirely and apply Article 10 only to CTAs that already contain the provisions described in Article 10(4).

Notifications

289. Depending upon the position taken by various jurisdictions, the following notifications are required to be made under Article 10 of the MLI:

(i) Jurisdictions intending to make reservations under paragraph 5 are required to make notifications under sub-paragraphs (a)-(c), as the case may be.
(ii) Under paragraph 6, jurisdictions which have not made the reservation described in sub-paragraphs (a), (b) of paragraph 5 shall make notifications whether each of its CTAs contains a provision described in paragraph 4, and if so, the article and paragraph number of each such provision. An existing provision of a CTA would be replaced by the provisions of paragraphs 1 through 3 where all Contracting Jurisdictions have made such a notification with respect to the existing provision. In other cases, paragraphs 1 through 3 would supersede the provisions of the CTA only to the extent that those provisions are incompatible with those paragraphs.

Denmark's Position[237] under the MLI

290. No notification of similar provisions described in paragraph 4 has been made by Denmark under paragraph 6 of Article 10 of the MLI. Also, no reservation has been made by Denmark under paragraph 5 of Article 10 of the MLI. The application of paragraphs 1-3 of Article 10 of the MLI to some of Denmark's CTAs is provided hereunder:

236. Refer Explanatory Statement to the MLI, para. 144.
237. Refer Denmark's Position under the MLI http://www.oecd.org/tax/treaties/beps-mli-position-denmark-instrument-deposit.pdf.

Denmark's Treaty Partner	*Position Taken by Treaty Partner*	*Outcome under the MLI*
Argentina, Chile, India, Israel, Jamaica, Kenya, Mexico, New Zealand, Pakistan, Romania, Russia, the Slovak Republic, Slovenia, Ukraine	- No notification under paragraph 5 or 6 of Article 10 of MLI concerning Denmark	Article 10(1) through (3) of MLI would apply to Denmark's CTA with these countries
Australia, Belgium, Bulgaria, Canada, China, Croatia, Cyprus, the Czech Republic, Egypt, Estonia, Greece, Hungary, Indonesia, Ireland, Italy, Korea, Kuwait, Latvia, Lithuania, Luxembourg, Malaysia, Malta, Morocco, North Macedonia, Poland, Portugal, Serbia, Singapore, South Africa, Tunisia, Turkey, United Kingdom	- Reservation under Article 10(5)(a) and opting out of Article 10 for all CTAs	Article 10 of MLI would not apply to Denmark's CTA with these countries

India's Position[238] under the MLI

291. No notification of similar provisions described in paragraph 4 has been made by India under paragraph 6 of Article 10 of the MLI, as such provisions are not presently there in any of India's DTAAs. Also, no reservation has been made by India under paragraph 5 of Article 10 of the MLI. The application of paragraphs 1-3 of Article 10 of the MLI to some of India's CTAs is provided hereunder:

India's Treaty Partner	*Position Taken by Treaty Partner*	*Outcome under the MLI*
Albania, Armenia, Austria, Denmark, Fiji, Israel, Japan, Kazakhstan, Kenya, Mexico, the Netherlands, New Zealand, Romania, Russia, the Slovak Republic, Slovenia, Spain, Ukraine, Uruguay	- No notification under paragraph 5 or 6 of Article 10 of MLI concerning India	Article 10(1) through (3) of MLI would apply to India's CTA with these countries

238. Refer India's Position under the MLI http://www.oecd.org/tax/treaties/beps-mli-position-india-instrument-deposit.pdf.

India's Treaty Partner	*Position Taken by Treaty Partner*	*Outcome under the MLI*
Australia, Belgium, Bulgaria, Canada, Colombia, Croatia, Cyprus, the Czech Republic, Egypt, Estonia, Finland, France, Georgia, Greece, Hungary, Iceland, Indonesia, Ireland, Italy, Jordan, Korea, Kuwait, Latvia, Lithuania, Luxembourg, Malaysia, Malta, Morocco, North Macedonia, Norway, Poland, Portugal, Qatar, Saudi Arabia, Serbia, Singapore, South Africa, Sweden, Turkey, UAE, UK	- Reservation under Article 10(5)(a) and opting out of Article 10 for all CTAs	Article 10 of MLI would not apply to India's CTA with these countries

The Netherlands' Position[239] under the MLI

292. Notification of similar provisions described in paragraph 4 has been made by the Netherlands under paragraph 6 of Article 10 of the MLI in respect of its CTAs with UK and US only. Also, no reservation has been made by the Netherlands under paragraph 5 of Article 10 of the MLI. The application of paragraphs 1-3 of Article 10 of the MLI to some of the Netherlands' CTAs is provided hereunder:

The Netherlands' Treaty Partner	*Position Taken by Treaty Partner*	*Outcome under the MLI*
Albania, Argentina, Armenia, Austria, India, Israel, Japan, Kazakhstan, Kenya, Mexico, New Zealand, Nigeria, Pakistan, Romania, Russia, the Slovak Republic, Slovenia	- No notification under paragraph 5 or 6 of Article 10 of MLI concerning the Netherlands	Article 10(1) through (3) of MLI would apply to the Netherlands' CTA with these countries

239. Refer The Netherlands' Position under the MLI http://www.oecd.org/tax/treaties/beps-mli-position-netherlands-instrument-deposit.pdf.

The Netherlands' Treaty Partner	*Position Taken by Treaty Partner*	*Outcome under the MLI*
Australia, Bahrain, Barbados, Bosnia & Herzegovina, Canada, China, Croatia, the Czech Republic, Egypt, Estonia, Finland, France, Georgia, Greece, Hong Kong, Hungary, Iceland, Indonesia, Italy, Jordan, Korea, Kuwait, Latvia, Lithuania, Luxembourg, Malaysia, Malta, Morocco, North Macedonia, Norway, Oman, Panama, Portugal, Qatar, Saudi Arabia, Serbia, Singapore, South Africa, Sweden, Tunisia, Turkey, the United Arab Emirates, United Kingdom	- Reservation under Article 10(5)(a) and opting out of Article 10 for all CTAs	Article 10 of MLI would not apply to the Netherlands' CTA with these countries

Few Snapshots of Positions[240] Taken by Other Countries under the MLI

293. The jurisdictions that have made reservation under Article 10(5)(a) of the MLI (for the entirety of Article 10 of MLI not to apply) are, namely, Australia, Bahrain, Barbados, Belgium, Belize, Bosnia and Herzegovina, Bulgaria, Burkina Faso, Cameroon, Canada, China, Colombia, Costa Rica, Cote d'Ivoire, Croatia, Curaçao, Cyprus, the Czech Republic, Egypt, Estonia, Finland, France, Gabon, Georgia, Greece, Guernsey, Hong Kong, Hungary, Iceland, Indonesia, Ireland, the Isle of Man, Italy, Jersey, Jordan, Korea, Kuwait, Latvia, Liechtenstein, Lithuania, Luxembourg, Malaysia, Malta, Mauritius, Monaco, Morocco, North Macedonia, Norway, Oman, Panama, Papua New Guinea, Poland, Portugal, Qatar, San Marino, Saudi Arabia, Serbia, Seychelles, Singapore, South Africa, Sweden, Switzerland, Tunisia, Turkey, the United Arab Emirates, UK.

294. There are two jurisdictions that have made reservation under Article 10(5)(b) for the entirety of Article 10 not to apply to its CTAs that already contain the provisions described in paragraph 4, namely Argentina and Chile. Both jurisdictions have notified Article 24(8) of Argentina-Chile CTA[241] under Article 10(5)(b); with the result, Article 10 of MLI would not apply to the said CTA. In fact, apart from Argentina, Chile has notified some more treaties under Article 10(5)(b) also and the consequent impact of MLI on such CTAs is as below (i.e., Article 10 would not apply in any of the CTAs):

240. Refer OECD – Signatories and Parties to the MLI http://www.oecd.org/tax/treaties/beps-mli-signatories-and-parties.pdf.

241. Refer Argentina-Chile CTA https://research.ibfd.org/#/doc?url=/linkresolver/static/tt_ar-cl_02_eng_2015_tt#tt_ar-cl_02_eng_2015_tt__td1_a24.

Chile's Treaty Partner	*Position Taken by Treaty Partner*	*Outcome under the MLI*
Austria	– Notification under Article 10(6) of the MLI in respect of CTA with Chile	Article 10 would not apply
China	– Did not notify CTA with Chile under the MLI	-do-
The Czech Republic	– Reservation under Article 10(5)(a) and opting out of Article 10 for all CTAs	-do-
Italy	– Did not notify CTA with Chile under the MLI	-do-
Uruguay	– Notification under Article 10(6) of the MLI in respect of CTA with Chile	-do-
US	– Not a Signatory to the MLI	–

295. There is no jurisdiction, as of now, that has made a reservation under Article 10(5)(c) of the MLI.

The various notifications made by treaty partners under Article 10 of the MLI and impact/outcome thereof on the respective CTAs are provided in Figure 11.

Figure 11 Article 10: Anti-abuse Rule for PEs Situated in Third Jurisdictions – Flow-chart on Notifications & Their Impact

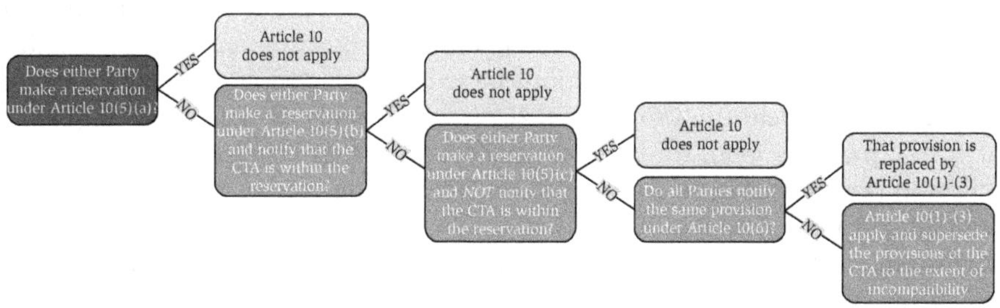

Source: OECD – Toolkit for Application of the Multilateral Instrument for BEPS Tax Treaty Related Measures https://www.oecd.org/tax/treaties/application-toolkit-multilateral-instrument-for-beps-tax-treaty-measures.htm.

3.6.6 Article 11 of MLI: Application of Tax Agreements to Restrict a Party's Right to Tax Its Own Residents

296. The interplay between Article 11 of MLI, corresponding BEPS Report and the resulting provisions incorporated in OECD MTC 2017 is represented in a table as below:

MLI		*BEPS Final Report*		*OECD MTC 2017*	
Article	*Title of Article*	*BEPS Action Plan*	*Title of BEPS Action Plan*	*Article*	*Title of Article*
11	Application of Tax Agreements to Restrict a Party's Right to Tax Its Own Residents	Action 6	Preventing the Granting of Treaty Benefits in Inappropriate Circumstances	1(3)	Persons Covered

297. The article at a glance is as below:

Substantive (BEPS) Provisions under Para(s)	*Opt-In Provisions under Para*	*Alternative Provisions under Para*	*Compatibility Clause*		*Reservations under Para*	*Notifications under Para*
			Para	*Type*		
1	None	None	2	'in place of or in the absence of'	3	3, 4

Status in Pre-BEPS Project Era

298. The majority of the provisions included in tax treaties are intended to restrict the right of a Contracting State to tax the residents of the other Contracting State. In some limited cases, however, it has been argued that some provisions that are aimed at the taxation of non-residents could be interpreted as limiting a Contracting State's right to tax its own residents. Such interpretations have been rejected in paragraph 6.1 of the Commentary on Article 1 in OECD MTC 2014, which deals with a Contracting State's right to tax partners who are its own residents on their share of the income of a partnership that is treated as a resident of the other Contracting State. Paragraph 6.1 states that in such a case it would not affect the right of State of residence to tax its residents under its domestic law. Similarly, paragraph 23 of the Commentary on Article 1 and paragraph 14 of the Commentary on Article 7 in OECD MTC 2014 address the case of CFC rules, wherein it is stated that the State of residence cannot be restricted to tax income of its own residents by applying CFC rules, even though, treaty provisions grant exclusive right of taxation of such income to State of source.

299. It was concluded during the BEPS Project that the principle reflected in paragraph 6.1 of the Commentary on Article 1 of OECD MTC 2014 (which deals with a Contracting State's right to tax partners who are its own residents on their share of the income of a partnership that is treated as a resident of the other Contracting State) should be applicable to the vast majority of the provisions of the MTC in order to prevent interpretations intended to circumvent the application of a Contracting State's domestic anti-abuse rules. This corresponds to the practice long followed by the US in its tax treaties, where a so-called saving clause confirms the Contracting States' right to tax their residents (and citizens, in the case, of the US) notwithstanding the provisions of the treaty except those, such as the rules on relief of double taxation, that are clearly intended to apply to residents.

Article 11(1) of the MLI

300. Article 11 of the MLI provides for the 'saving clause' whereby the Contracting States' right to tax their own residents gets confirmed, and the State of residence passes on the taxing rights to the State of source only in respect of situations listed in clauses (a)-(j) of paragraph 1 of Article 11. The exceptions so listed are intended to cover all cases where it is envisaged in the CTA that a Contracting State may have to provide treaty benefits to its own residents (whether or not these or similar benefits are provided under the domestic law of that State).

301. References to certain provisions in the OECD MTC have been replaced with various sub-paragraphs (a)-(j) in paragraph 1 of Article 11 of the MLI as below:

(1) Paragraph 3 of Article 7 (Business Profits) and paragraph 2 of Article 9 (Associated Enterprises) in the OECD MTC replaced with sub-paragraph (a) of Article 11(1) of MLI.
(2) Article 19 (Government Service) replaced with sub-paragraph (b) of Article 11(1) of MLI.
(3) Article 20 (Students) or teacher, professor, etc. who meet the conditions of the CTA replaced with sub-paragraph (c) of Article 11(1) of MLI.
(4) Articles 23A (Exemption Method) and 23B (Credit Method) replaced with sub-paragraph (d) of Article 11(1) of MLI.
(5) Article 24 (Non-discrimination) replaced with sub-paragraph (e) of Article 11(1) of MLI.
(6) Article 25 (MAP) replaced with sub-paragraph (f) of Article 11(1) of MLI.
(7) Article 28 (Members of Diplomatic Missions and Consular Posts) replaced with sub-paragraph (g) of Article 11(1) of MLI.
(8) Pensions or other payments made under the social security legislation of the other Contracting Jurisdiction shall be taxable only in that other Contracting Jurisdiction, replaced with sub-paragraph (h) of Article 11(1) of MLI.
(9) Provisions that provide for exclusive taxation at source of pensions and similar payments, annuities, alimony payments, etc. arising in the other Contracting Jurisdiction shall be taxable only in that other Contracting Jurisdiction, replaced with sub-paragraph (i) of Article 11(1) of MLI.
(10) Sub-paragraph (j)[242] in Article 11(1) has been included as additional exception to the saving clause, to broadly cover provisions that expressly limit taxation rights of the residence jurisdiction or expressly allow taxation rights exclusively to the source jurisdiction. This sub-paragraph would also

242. Refer Explanatory Statement to the MLI, para. 150.

cover provisions that provide for exemption of income in both jurisdictions (e.g., in the case of child support payments under some existing treaties). It would also cover, for example, the following types of provisions:

- provisions which allow the CA of a Contracting Jurisdiction that has made or is to make an initial adjustment to the profits of an enterprise of that Contracting Jurisdiction to provide relief from double taxation;
- provisions which require a Contracting Jurisdiction to consider the acquisition value of a property owned by its resident to be its fair market value at the time when he ceases to be a resident of the other Contracting Jurisdiction and becomes a resident of the first-mentioned Contracting Jurisdiction; or
- provisions which grant deductions for contributions made by a resident of a Contracting Jurisdiction to a retirement plan in the other Contracting Jurisdiction in computing income in the first-mentioned Contracting Jurisdiction.

302. The term 'resident', as used in paragraph 1 of Article 11 of the MLI, is defined in Article 4 of the OECD MTC 2017. Where, under paragraph 1 of Article 4 of the OECD MTC 2017, a person is considered to be a resident of both Contracting States based on the domestic laws of these States, paragraphs 2 and 3 of that Article make it generally possible to determine a single State of residence for the purposes of the CTA. Thus, paragraph 1 of Article 11 of the MLI does not apply to an individual or legal person who is a resident of one of the Contracting States under the laws of that State but who, for the purposes of the CTA, is deemed to be a resident only of the other Contracting State.[243]

Compatibility Clause

303. Paragraph 2 is the compatibility clause which describes the interaction between paragraph 1 and provisions of CTAs. This paragraph clarifies that the provision in paragraph 1 replaces existing provisions of CTAs stating that the CTAs would not affect the taxation by a Contracting Jurisdiction of its residents, or is added where such provisions do not exist in CTAs.[244]

Reservations under Paragraph 3

304. The following reservations are provided for under paragraph 3:

(i) Under paragraph 3(a), Parties may opt out of Article 11 entirely with respect to all CTAs, as the same is not a minimum standard. Where either Party makes a reservation under Article 11(3)(a), the provisions of Article 3(1) of the MLI will be modified under Article 3(3) of the MLI to ensure that its application will not interfere with the taxation by a Contracting Jurisdiction of its residents.[245]

243. Refer OECD MTC 2017, para. 21 of the Commentary on Art. 1(3).
244. Refer Explanatory Statement to the MLI, para. 152.
245. *Id.*, para. 154.

(ii) Under paragraph 3(b), Parties may opt out of Article 11 entirely with respect to CTAs that already contain the provisions described in Article 11(2).

Notifications

305. Depending upon the position taken by various jurisdictions, the following notifications are required to be made under Article 11 of the MLI:

(i) Jurisdictions intending to make reservations under paragraph 3 are required to make notifications under sub-paragraphs (a) and (b), as the case may be.
(ii) Under paragraph 4, jurisdictions that have not made the reservation described in sub-paragraph (a) or (b) of paragraph 3 shall make notifications whether each of its CTAs contains a provision described in paragraph 2, and if so, the article and paragraph number of each such provision. An existing provision of a CTA would be replaced by the provisions of paragraph 1 where all Contracting Jurisdictions have made such a notification with respect to the existing provision. In other cases, paragraph 1 would supersede the provisions of the CTA only to the extent that those provisions are incompatible with paragraph 1.

Denmark's Position[246] under the MLI

306. Pursuant to Article 11(4) of the MLI, Denmark has notified its CTAs with Canada, Egypt, Indonesia, Kuwait, Malaysia, Sri Lanka, Thailand and US which contain a provision described in Article 11(2) of the MLI. Depending upon the MLI position of its treaty partners, the application of paragraph 1 of Article 11 of the MLI to some of Denmark's CTAs is provided hereunder:

Denmark's Treaty Partner	*Position Taken by Treaty Partner*	*Outcome under the MLI*
Argentina, Australia, Belgium, Chile, China, Croatia, India, Indonesia, Jamaica, Kenya, Mexico, New Zealand, Pakistan, Poland, Portugal, Romania, Russia, the Slovak Republic, South Africa, United Kingdom	– No notification under paragraph 3 or 4 of Article 11 concerning Denmark	Article 11(1) of MLI would apply to Denmark's CTA with these countries
Bulgaria, Canada, Cyprus, the Czech Republic, Egypt, Estonia, Greece, Hungary, Ireland, Israel, Italy, Korea, Kuwait, Latvia, Lithuania, Luxembourg, Malaysia, Malta, Morocco, North Macedonia, Serbia, Singapore, Slovenia, Tunisia, Turkey, Ukraine	– Reservation under Article 11(3)(a) and opting out of Article 11 for all CTAs	Article 11 of MLI would not apply to Denmark's CTA with these countries

246. Refer Denmark's Position under the MLI http://www.oecd.org/tax/treaties/beps-mli-position-denmark-instrument-deposit.pdf.

India's Position[247] under the MLI

307. No notification of similar provisions described in paragraph 2 has been made by India under paragraph 4 of Article 11 of the MLI, as such provisions are not presently there in any of India's DTAAs. Also, no reservation has been made by India under paragraph 3 of Article 11 of the MLI. The application of paragraph 1 of Article 11 of the MLI to some of India's CTAs is provided hereunder:

India's Treaty Partner	*Position Taken by Treaty Partner*	*Outcome under the MLI*
Armenia, Australia, Belgium, Colombia, Croatia, Denmark, Fiji, Indonesia, Kenya, Mexico, New Zealand, Norway, Poland, Portugal, Romania, Russia, the Slovak Republic, South Africa, United Kingdom	- No notification under paragraph 3 or 4 of Article 11 concerning India	Article 11(1) of MLI would apply to India's CTA with these countries
Albania, Austria, Bulgaria, Canada, Cyprus, the Czech Republic, Egypt, Estonia, Finland, France, Georgia, Greece, Hungary, Iceland, Ireland, Israel, Italy, Japan, Jordan, Kazakhstan, Korea, Kuwait, Latvia, Lithuania, Luxembourg, Macedonia, Malaysia, Malta, Morocco, the Netherlands, Qatar, Saudi Arabia, Serbia, Singapore, Slovenia, Spain, Sweden, Turkey, Ukraine, the United Arab Emirates, Uruguay	- Reservation under Article 11(3)(a) and opting out of Article 11 for all CTAs	Article 11 of MLI would not apply to India's CTA with these countries

The Netherlands' Position[248] under the MLI

308. Pursuant to Article 11(3)(a) of the MLI, the Netherlands has made a reservation for the entirety of Article 11 not to apply to its CTAs.

Few Snapshots of Positions[249] Taken by Other Countries under the MLI

309. Jurisdictions that have made reservation under Article 11(3)(a) of the MLI (for the entirety of Article 11 of MLI not to apply) are, namely, Albania, Austria, Bahrain, Barbados, Belize, Bosnia and Herzegovina, Bulgaria, Burkina Faso, Cameroon, Canada, Costa Rica, Cote d'Ivoire, Curaçao, Cyprus, the Czech Republic, Egypt, Estonia, Finland, France, Georgia, Germany, Greece, Guernsey, Hong Kong, Hungary, Iceland, Ireland, the Isle of Man, Israel, Italy, Japan, Jersey, Jordan, Kazakhstan, Korea, Kuwait, Latvia, Liechtenstein, Lithuania, Luxembourg, Malaysia, Malta, Mauritius, Monaco, Morocco, the Netherlands, Nigeria, North Macedonia, Oman, Panama,

247. Refer India's Position under the MLI http://www.oecd.org/tax/treaties/beps-mli-position-india-instrument-deposit.pdf.
248. Refer The Netherlands' Position under the MLI http://www.oecd.org/tax/treaties/beps-mli-position-netherlands-instrument-deposit.pdf.
249. Refer OECD – Signatories and Parties to the MLI http://www.oecd.org/tax/treaties/beps-mli-signatories-and-parties.pdf.

Papua New Guinea, Peru, Qatar, San Marino, Saudi Arabia, Serbia, Seychelles, Singapore, Slovenia, Spain, Sweden, Switzerland, Turkey, Ukraine, the United Arab Emirates, Uruguay.

310. Jurisdictions that have made reservation under Article 11(3)(b) of the MLI are, namely, Chile, Mexico and Portugal. The various notifications by these countries and resultant impact on their CTAs under the MLI are *inter alia* depicted as below:

Jurisdiction	*Position Taken*	*Treaty Partner*	*Position Taken*	*Outcome under the MLI*
Chile	- Reservation under Article 11(3)(b) of MLI made in respect of CTA with US only	Mexico	- Reservation under Article 11(3)(b) of MLI made in respect of CTA with US only	- Article 11(1) of MLI would apply to Chile-Mexico CTA
Chile	-do-	Portugal	-do-	- Article 11(1) of MLI would apply to Chile-Portugal CTA
Mexico	-do-	Portugal	-do-	- Article 11(1) of MLI would apply to Mexico-Portugal CTA

The various notifications made by treaty partners under Article 11 of the MLI and impact/outcome thereof on the respective CTAs are provided in Figure 12.

Figure 12 Article 11: Application of Tax Agreements to Restrict a Party's Right to Tax Its Own Residents – Flowchart on Notifications & Their Impact

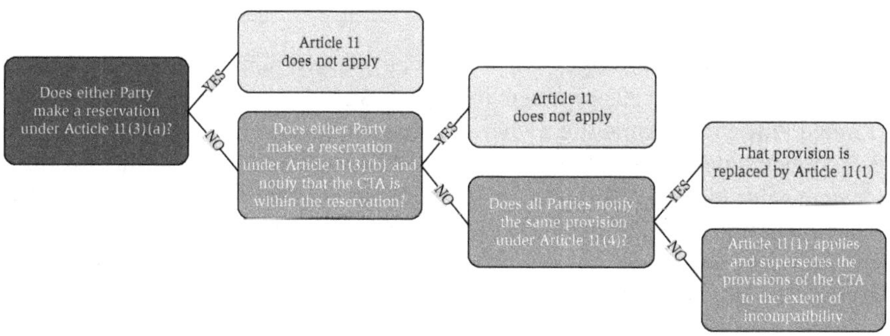

Source: OECD – Toolkit for Application of the Multilateral Instrument for BEPS Tax Treaty Related Measures https://www.oecd.org/tax/treaties/application-toolkit-multilateral-instrument-for-beps-tax-treaty-measures.htm.

3.7 PART IV OF MLI: AVOIDANCE OF PERMANENT ESTABLISHMENT STATUS

3.7.1 Article 12 of MLI: Artificial Avoidance of Permanent Establishment Status Through Commissionaire Arrangements and Similar Strategies

311. The interplay between Article 12 of MLI, corresponding BEPS Report and the resulting provisions incorporated in OECD MTC 2017 is represented in a table as below:

MLI		*BEPS Final Report*		*OECD MTC 2017*	
Article	*Title of Article*	*BEPS Action Plan*	*Title of BEPS Action Plan*	*Article*	*Title of Article*
12	Artificial Avoidance of Permanent Establishment Status Through Commissionaire Arrangements and Similar Strategies	Action 7	Preventing the Artificial Avoidance of Permanent Establishment Status	5(5), 5(6)	Permanent Establish-ment

312. The article at a glance is as below:

Substantive (BEPS) Provisions under Para(s)	*Opt-In Provisions under Para*	*Alternative Provisions under Para*	*Compatibility Clause*		*Reservations under Para*	*Notifications under Para*
			Para	*Type*		
1, 2	None	None	3(a), (b)	'in place of'	4	4, 5, 6

313. A commissionaire arrangement[250] may be loosely defined as an arrangement through which a person sells products in a given State in its own name but on behalf of a foreign enterprise that is the owner of these products. Through such an arrangement, a foreign enterprise is able to sell its products in a State without having a PE to which such sales may be attributed for tax purposes; since the person that concludes the sales does not own the products that it sells, it cannot be taxed on the profits derived from such sales and may only be taxed on the remuneration that it receives for its services (usually a commission).

250. Refer Action 7: BEPS 2015 Final Report, OECD/G20 Base Erosion and Profit Shifting Project, para. 5, s. A, p. 15.

Status in Pre-BEPS Project Era

314. BEPS concerns arising from commissionaire arrangements may involve situations where Article 5(5) of the OECD MTC 2014 is unable to address artificial arrangements where an entity, hitherto, working as an entrepreneur and selling goods of its AE, would transform itself to the status of a commission agent of its AE, thereby leading to substantial reduction in its taxable profits in its state of operations. Similar strategies that sought to avoid the application of Article 5(5) of the OECD MTC 2014 involved situations where contracts which were substantially negotiated in a State were not concluded in that State because they were finalised or authorised abroad, or where the person that habitually exercised an authority to conclude contracts constituted an 'independent agent' to which the exception of Article 5(6) of the OECD MTC 2014 applied even though it was closely related to the foreign enterprise on behalf of which it was acting. It was clear that in many cases commissionaire arrangements and similar strategies were put in place primarily so as to erode the taxable base of the State where sales took place. Prior to BEPS Action 7 Report, the provisions in place in most of the CTAs recognised the existence of an agency PE only when the agent habitually exercised the authority to conclude contracts in the name of the principal. Changes to the wording of Article 5(5) and 5(6) of the OECD MTC 2014 were therefore needed in order to address such strategies. The same was achieved through the BEPS Action 7 Report which *inter alia* recommended that where the activities that an intermediary exercises in a country are intended to result in the regular conclusion of contracts to be performed by a foreign enterprise, that enterprise should be considered to have a sufficient taxable nexus in that country unless the intermediary is performing these activities in the course of an independent business.

Article 12 of the MLI

315. Article 12 of the MLI addresses the avoidance of PE status through commissionaire arrangements and similar strategies. The same is accomplished by modifying the provisions dealing with agency PEs – articles equivalent to Article 5(5) of the OECD MTC (2014) – and independent agents – articles equivalent to Article 5(6) of the OECD MTC (2014). Article 12 specifically addresses abuses of the dependent agent PE in Article 5(5) and Article 5(6) of the OECD Model PE definition, pursuant to which an enterprise is deemed to have a PE in a country in respect of an activity which a person other than an agent of an independent status undertakes for that enterprise. The changes contemplated through Article 12 aim at increasing the number of cases in which an agency PE can be deemed to be a PE of a non-resident person.

Paragraph 1 of Article 12 of the MLI

316. Paragraph 1 addresses the artificial avoidance of PE status through commissionaire arrangements by change in article provisions related to Dependent Agent Permanent Establishment (DAPE). Article 12(1) of MLI redefines DAPE in view of work under Action 7. DAPE would exist if the person acts in a Contracting State on behalf of an enterprise (parent), habitually concludes contracts or habitually plays the principal role to the conclusion of contracts that are routinely concluded without material modification by the (parent) enterprise and such contracts are:

- in the name of the (parent) enterprise. The reference to contracts 'in the name of' does not restrict the application of the phrase to contracts that are literally in the name of the enterprise; it may apply, for example, to certain situations where the name of the enterprise is undisclosed in a written contract;[251]
- for transfer of any right, property, etc. owned or under the right to use by the (parent) enterprise. Parts of the contracts that relate to the transfer of the ownership or use of property will be performed by the enterprise as opposed to the person that acts on the enterprise's behalf;[252]
- for provision of services by the (parent) enterprise. Parts of the contracts that relate to the provision of services will be performed by the enterprise as opposed to the person that acts on the enterprise's behalf.[253]

317. Persons whose activities may create a PE for the enterprise are persons, whether or not employees of the enterprise, who act on behalf of the enterprise and are not doing so in the course of carrying on a business as an independent agent falling under paragraph 2 of Article 12 of MLI. Such persons may be either individuals or companies and need not be residents of, nor have a place of business in, the State in which they act for the enterprise. Paragraph 1 proceeds on the basis that only persons habitually concluding contracts that are in the name of the enterprise or that are to be performed by the enterprise, or habitually playing the principal role leading to the conclusion of such contracts which are routinely concluded without material modification by the enterprise, can lead to a PE for the enterprise. In such a case, the person's actions on behalf of the enterprise, since they result in the conclusion of such contracts and go beyond mere promotion or advertising, are sufficient to conclude that the enterprise participates in a business activity in the State concerned. The use of the term 'permanent establishment' in this context presupposes, of course, that the conclusion of contracts by that person, or as a direct result of the actions of that person, takes place repeatedly and not merely in isolated cases.[254] Similarly, the maintenance of a fixed place of business solely for the purposes of preparatory or auxiliary activities is deemed not to constitute a PE; hence, a person acting on behalf of the enterprise, whose activities are restricted to such purposes (of preparatory or auxiliary activities), should not create a PE either.[255]

318. The phrase 'concludes contracts' used in paragraph 1 of Article 12 of the MLI focusses on situations where, under the relevant law governing contracts, a contract is considered to have been concluded by a person. A contract may be concluded without any active negotiation of the terms of that contract; this would be the case, for example,

251. Refer OECD MTC 2017, para. 93 of the Commentary on Art. 5(5).
252. *Id.*, para. 94 of the Commentary on Art. 5(5).
253. *Id.*
254. Refer OECD MTC 2017, para. 83 of the Commentary on Art. 5(5).
255. *Id.*, para. 85 of the Commentary on Art. 5(5).

where the relevant law provides that a contract is concluded by reason of a person accepting, on behalf of an enterprise, the offer made by a third party to enter into a standard contract with that enterprise. Also, a contract may, under the relevant law, be concluded in a State even if that contract is signed outside that State; where, for example, the conclusion of a contract results from the acceptance, by a person acting on behalf of an enterprise, of an offer to enter into a contract made by a third party, it does not matter that the contract is signed outside that State. In addition, a person who negotiates in a State all elements and details of a contract in a way binding on the enterprise can be said to conclude the contract in that State even if that contract is signed by another person outside that State.[256]

319. The phrase 'or habitually plays the principal role leading to the conclusion of contracts that are routinely concluded without material modification by the enterprise' is aimed at situations where the conclusion of a contract directly results from the actions that the person performs in a Contracting State on behalf of the enterprise even though, under the relevant law, the contract is not concluded by that person in that State. The phrase must be interpreted in the light of the object and purpose of paragraph 1, which is to cover cases where the activities that a person exercises in a State are intended to result in the regular conclusion of contracts to be performed by a foreign enterprise, i.e. where that person acts as the sales force of the enterprise. The principal role leading to the conclusion of the contract will therefore typically be associated with the actions of the person who convinced the third party to enter into a contract with the enterprise. The words 'contracts that are routinely concluded without material modification by the enterprise' clarify that where such principal role is performed in that State, the actions of that person will fall within the scope of paragraph 1 even if the contracts are not formally concluded in the State, for example where the contracts are routinely subject, outside that State, to review and approval without such review resulting in a modification of the key aspects of these contracts.[257]

Paragraph 2 of Article 12 of the MLI

320. Article 12(2) of MLI defines where DAPE provisions may not apply, i.e. where an entity acts as an independent agent and acts for the enterprise in the ordinary course of that business. The activities of such an agent, who represents a separate and independent enterprise, should not result in the finding of a PE of the foreign enterprise. However, the last line of paragraph 2 provides that DAPE provisions may apply where a person acts exclusively or almost exclusively on behalf of one or more enterprises to which it is *closely related* (definition of closely related is provided in Article 15 of MLI); thus, that person shall not be considered to be an independent agent within the meaning of this paragraph with respect to any such enterprise.

321. An independent agent will typically be responsible to his principal for the results of his work but not subject to significant control with respect to the manner in which

256. *Id.*, para. 87 of the Commentary on Art. 5(5).
257. *Id.*, para. 88 of the Commentary on Art. 5(5).

that work is carried out. He will not be subject to detailed instructions from the principal as to the conduct of the work. The fact that the principal is relying on the special skill and knowledge of the agent is an indication of independence.[258] All the facts and circumstances must be taken into account to determine whether the agent's activities constitute an autonomous business conducted by him in which he bears risk and receives reward through the use of his entrepreneurial skills and knowledge.

Compatibility Clauses

322. Article 12(3)(a) provides that Article 12(1) replaces provisions of a CTA that describe the conditions under which an enterprise shall be deemed to have a DAPE, but only to the extent that such provisions address the situation in which the person who undertakes an activity for that enterprise has, and habitually exercises, an authority to conclude contracts in the name of the enterprise.

323. Article 12(1) is not intended to apply to a provision or part of a provision under which an enterprise can be deemed to have a PE for a reason other than an authority to conclude contracts that are binding on another enterprise. For example, Article 12(1) would not apply to a provision modelled after Article 5(5)(b) of the 2011 version of the UN MTC and a provision that provides that a person shall be deemed to have a PE where the person secures orders for the enterprise. Such provisions would not be affected by the application of Article 12.[259] Similarly, Article 12(1) of the MLI would not apply to provisions where the person habitually maintains in the State stock of goods or merchandise from which that person regularly delivers goods or merchandise on behalf of the enterprise, as per formulation present in certain treaties and Article 5(5)(b) of the UN Model Double Taxation Convention 2017.

324. Article 12(3)(b) provides that Article 12(2) replaces provisions of a CTA that provide that an enterprise shall not be deemed to have a PE in a Contracting Jurisdiction in respect of an activity which an agent of an independent status undertakes for the enterprise. Such provisions of a CTA would include those modelled after, for example, Article 5(6) of the 2014 version of the OECD MTC or Article 5(7) of the 2011 version of the UN MTC, as well as bilaterally negotiated provisions of the same type.[260]

Reservation under Paragraph 4

325. A jurisdiction may opt out of Article 12 entirely (paragraphs 1 and 2) with respect to all CTAs, as the same is not a minimum standard.

---

258. *Id.*, para. 106 of the Commentary on Art. 5(6).
259. Refer Explanatory Statement to the MLI, para. 163.
260. *Id.*, para. 164.

Notifications

326. Depending upon the position taken by various jurisdictions, the following notifications are required to be made under Article 12 of the MLI:

(i) Jurisdictions intending to make reservation under paragraph 4 are required to make notifications, as the case may be.

(ii) Under paragraph 5, each Party (other than a Party that has opted out of the entirety of Article 12) is required to notify the Depositary of each of its CTAs that contains an existing provision of the same type as the provision in paragraph 1, and the article and paragraph number of each such provision. Paragraph 1 would apply with respect to a provision of a CTA only where all Contracting Jurisdictions to the CTA have made such a notification.

(iii) Under paragraph 6, each Party (other than a Party that has opted out of the entirety of Article 12) to notify the Depositary of each of its CTAs that contains an existing provision of the same type as the provision in paragraph 2, and the article and paragraph number of each such provision. Paragraph 2 would apply with respect to a provision of a CTA only where all Contracting Jurisdictions to the CTA have made such a notification.

Denmark's Position[261] under the MLI

327. No reservation has been made by Denmark under paragraph 4 of Article 12 of the MLI.

328. Paragraph 1 of Article 12 modifies paragraph 5 of Article 5 of OECD MTC. Accordingly, Denmark has notified under paragraph 5 of Article 12 of MLI such provisions in all of its 64 notified CTAs which it wants to be replaced with paragraph 1 of Article 12.

329. Paragraph 2 of Article 12 modifies paragraph 6 of Article 5 of OECD MTC. Accordingly, Denmark has notified under paragraph 6 of Article 12 of MLI such provisions in all of its 64 notified CTAs which it wants to be replaced with paragraph 2 of Article 12.

330. The application of paragraphs 1, 2 of Article 12 of the MLI to some of Denmark's CTAs is provided hereunder:

261. Refer Denmark's Position under the MLI http://www.oecd.org/tax/treaties/beps-mli-position-denmark-instrument-deposit.pdf.

Denmark's Treaty Partner	*Position Taken by Treaty Partner*	*Outcome under the MLI*
Argentina, Belgium, Chile, Croatia, Egypt, India*, Indonesia*, Israel, Jamaica, Kenya, Lithuania, Malaysia*, Mexico, New Zealand, North Macedonia, Pakistan*, Romania, Russia, Serbia, the Slovak Republic, Slovenia, Tunisia*, Turkey*, Ukraine	- Matching notification concerning Denmark	Article 12(1), (2) of MLI would apply to Denmark's CTA with these countries
Australia, Bulgaria, Canada, China, Cyprus, the Czech Republic, Estonia, Greece, Hungary, Ireland, Italy, Korea, Kuwait, Latvia, Luxembourg, Malta, Morocco, Poland, Portugal, Singapore, South Africa, United Kingdom	- Reservation under Article 12(4) for Article 12 not to apply to its CTAs	Article 12 of MLI would not apply to Denmark's CTA with these countries

* Barring notification mismatch by Denmark and its treaty partner, Article 12 of MLI to apply to Denmark's CTA with the said treaty partner.

India's Position[262] under the MLI

331. No reservation has been made by India under paragraph 4 of Article 12 of the MLI.

332. Paragraph 1 of Article 12 modifies paragraph 5 of Article 5 of OECD MTC. Accordingly, India has notified under paragraph 5 of Article 12 of MLI such provisions in all of its 93 notified CTAs which it wants to be replaced with paragraph 1 of Article 12.

333. Paragraph 2 of Article 12 modifies paragraph 6 of Article 5 of OECD MTC. Accordingly, India has notified under paragraph 6 of Article 12 of MLI such provisions in all of its 93 notified CTAs which it wants to be replaced with paragraph 2 of Article 12.

334. The application of paragraphs 1, 2 of Article 12 of the MLI to some of India's CTAs is provided hereunder:

India's Treaty Partner	*Position Taken by Treaty Partner*	*Outcome under the MLI*
Albania, Armenia, Belgium, Colombia, Denmark*, Egypt, Fiji, France, Indonesia, Israel, Japan, Jordan, Kazakhstan, Lithuania, Macedonia, Malaysia, Mexico, New Zealand, Norway, Romania, Russia, Serbia, the Slovak Republic, Slovenia, Spain, Turkey, Ukraine, Uruguay	- Matching notification concerning India	Article 12(1), (2) of MLI would apply to India's CTA with these countries

262. Refer India's Position under the MLI http://www.oecd.org/tax/treaties/beps-mli-position-india-instrument-deposit.pdf.

India's Treaty Partner	*Position Taken by Treaty Partner*	*Outcome under the MLI*
Australia, Austria, Bulgaria, Canada, Cyprus, the Czech Republic, Estonia, Finland, Georgia, Greece, Hungary, Iceland, Ireland, Italy, Korea, Kuwait, Latvia, Luxembourg, Malta, Morocco, the Netherlands, Poland, Portugal, Qatar, Singapore, South Africa, Sweden, the United Arab Emirates, United Kingdom	- Reservation under Article 12(4) for Article 12 not to apply to its CTAs	Article 12 of MLI would not apply to India's CTA with these countries

* Barring notification mismatch under Article 12(5) of MLI by India and Denmark, Article 12(1) of MLI to apply to the said CTA.

The Netherlands' Position[263] under the MLI

335. Pursuant to Article 12(4) of the MLI, the Netherlands has made a reservation for the entirety of Article 12 not to apply to its CTAs.

Few Snapshots of Positions[264] Taken by Other Countries under the MLI

336. Jurisdictions that have made reservation under Article 12(4) of the MLI (for the entirety of Article 12 of MLI not to apply) are, namely, Andorra, Australia, Austria, Bahrain, Barbados, Belize, Bulgaria, Canada, China, Curaçao, Cyprus, the Czech Republic, Estonia, Finland, Georgia, Germany, Greece, Guernsey, Hong Kong, Hungary, Iceland, Ireland, the Isle of Man, Italy, Jersey, Korea, Kuwait, Latvia, Liechtenstein, Luxembourg, Malta, Mauritius, Monaco, Morocco, the Netherlands, Oman, Panama, Poland, Portugal, Qatar, San Marino, Seychelles, Singapore, South Africa, Sweden, Switzerland, the United Arab Emirates, UK.

337. Application of Article 12 of MLI, *inter alia*, to CTAs of some jurisdictions as per their mutual notifications is as below:

Jurisdiction	*Position Taken*	*Treaty Partner*	*Position Taken*	*Outcome under the MLI*
Albania	- Notification made under Article 12(5), (6)	Austria	- Did not notify CTA with Albania under the MLI	-
Albania	-do-	Belgium	- Matching notification made under Article 12(5), (6)	Article 12(1), (2) of MLI would apply

263. Refer The Netherlands' Position under the MLI http://www.oecd.org/tax/treaties/beps-mli-position-netherlands-instrument-deposit.pdf.
264. Refer OECD – Signatories and Parties to the MLI http://www.oecd.org/tax/treaties/beps-mli-signatories-and-parties.pdf.

Jurisdiction	*Position Taken*	*Treaty Partner*	*Position Taken*	*Outcome under the MLI*
Egypt	- Notification made under Article 12(5), (6)	Canada	- Reservation under Article 12(4) for Article 12 not to apply to its CTAs	Article 12 of MLI would not apply
Egypt	-do-	France	- Matching notification made under Article 12(5), (6)	Article 12(1), (2) of MLI would apply
Indonesia	- Notification made under Article 12(5), (6)	Finland	- Reservation under Article 12(4) for Article 12 not to apply to its CTAs	Article 12 of MLI would not apply
Indonesia	-do-	New Zealand	- Matching notification made under Article 12(5), (6)	Article 12(1), (2) of MLI would apply

The various notifications made by treaty partners under Article 12 of the MLI and impact/outcome thereof on the respective CTAs are provided in Figure 13.

Figure 13 Article 12: Artificial Avoidance of PE Status Through Commissionaire Arrangements and Similar Strategies – Flowchart on Notifications & Their Impact

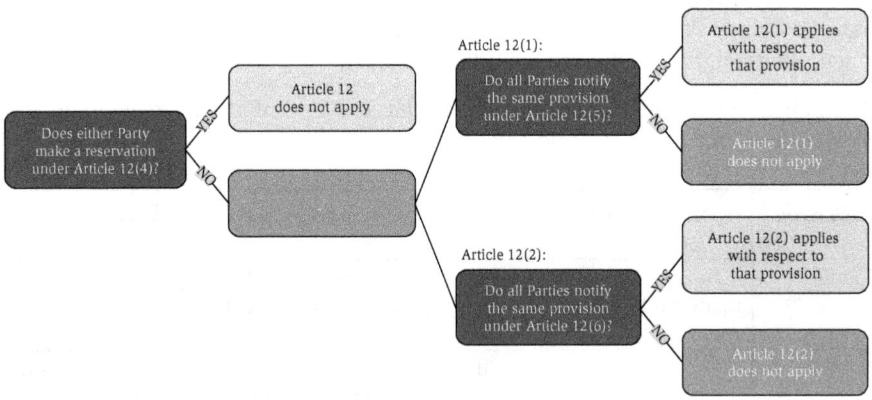

Source: OECD – Toolkit for Application of the Multilateral Instrument for BEPS Tax Treaty Related Measures https://www.oecd.org/tax/treaties/application-toolkit-multilateral-instrument-for-beps-tax-treaty-measures.htm.

3.7.2 Article 13 of MLI: Artificial Avoidance of Permanent Establishment Status Through the Specific Activity Exemptions

338. The interplay between Article 13 of MLI, corresponding BEPS Report and the resulting provisions incorporated in OECD MTC 2017 is represented in a table as below:

MLI		*BEPS Final Report*		*OECD MTC 2017*	
Article	*Title of Article*	*BEPS Action Plan*	*Title of BEPS Action Plan*	*Article*	*Title of Article*
13	Artificial Avoidance of Permanent Establishment Status Through the Specific Activity Exemptions	Action 7	Preventing the Artificial Avoidance of Permanent Establishment Status	5(4)#, 5(4.1)	Permanent Establish-ment

Option A under Article 13(2) of the MLI corresponds to Article 5(4) of the OECD MTC 2017, whereas Option B under Article 13(3) of the MLI is contained in paragraph 78 of the Commentary on Article 5(4) of OECD MTC 2017.

339. The article at a glance is as below:

Substantive (BEPS) Provisions under Para(s)	*Opt-In Provisions under Para*	*Alternative Provisions under Para*	*Compatibility Clause*		*Reservations under Para*	*Notifications under Para*
			Para	*Type*		
1-4	None	2, 3	5(a), (b)	'in place of' and 'applies to'	6	6, 7, 8

Status in Pre-BEPS Project Era

340. Earlier, in 2014 version of the OECD MTC, an interpretation was being taken that activities described in 5(4)(a) through (d) shall not be deemed to be a PE even if they were *not* of preparatory or auxiliary character, as proviso stating 'provided that the overall activity of the fixed place of business resulting from this combination is of a preparatory or auxiliary character' was embedded in clause (f) of Article 5(4) of the OECD MTC and it was being sometimes interpreted that this proviso applies only to clause (f) and not to clauses (a)-(d). Thus, earlier, under Article 5, paragraph 4 applied automatically where one of the activities listed in sub-paragraphs (a)-(d) was the only activity carried on at a fixed place of business; with the result, PE provisions were deemed not to apply. Invocation of PE provisions could therefore be avoided by taking advantage of the exceptions listed in sub-paragraphs (a)-(d). Hence, regardless of the purpose of the exceptions included in sub-paragraphs (a)-(d) of paragraph 4, it was envisaged to address situations where these sub-paragraphs give rise to BEPS concerns. It was, therefore, agreed to modify Article 5(4) so that each of the exceptions included in that provision is restricted to activities that are otherwise of a 'preparatory or auxiliary' character.

341. On the other hand, some jurisdictions considered that BEPS concerns related to Article 5(4) essentially arose where there was fragmentation of activities between closely related Parties and that these concerns will be appropriately addressed by the inclusion of the anti-fragmentation rule. They considered that some of the activities referred to in paragraph 4 are intrinsically preparatory or auxiliary and, in order to provide greater certainty for both tax administrations and taxpayers, were of the view that these activities listed as exceptions in sub-paragraphs (a)-(d) of paragraph 4 should not be subject to the condition that they be of a preparatory or auxiliary character. These jurisdictions, therefore, considered that there was no need to modify Article 5(4) as long as the anti-fragmentation rules were included.

Article 13 of the MLI

342. Article 13 of the MLI addresses the avoidance of PE status through specific activity exemptions on applying two different alternatives:

(1) Option A modifies the list of auxiliary exceptions to PE status – articles equivalent to Article 5(4) of the OECD MTC (2014) – by explicitly stating that those activities or the combination of several of them will be deemed not to create a PE only if they effectively fulfil the further condition of being of a preparatory or auxiliary nature.[265] In order to elaborate, through Option A (paragraph 2) under Article 13 of MLI, proviso at the end of Article 5(4) stating '*provided that such activity or, in the case of subparagraph (c), the overall activity of the fixed place of business, is of a preparatory or auxiliary character*' corresponds to all clauses, namely, (a)-(c) of paragraph 2 of Article 13 of MLI, which means that all individual activities under these clauses, if preparatory or auxiliary in character, shall tantamount to no PE. However, if such activities listed in clauses (a)-(c) of paragraph 2 of Article 13 of MLI are not preparatory or auxiliary in character, PE status of that entity shall be held.
(2) Option B does not modify the list of activities but merely reaffirms that even auxiliary activities are intrinsically exceptions[266] to the PE status.

Article 13 also establishes an anti-fragmentation rule, which applies by default and complements both Options A and B, so as to prevent the fragmentation of a cohesive business operation into several small operations (in order to contend that

265. Action 7: BEPS 2015 Final Report, OECD/G20 Base Erosion and Profit Shifting Project, pp. 28-29.
266. *Id.*, p. 38.

each is merely engaged in preparatory or auxiliary activity), leading to abuse of the specific activity exemptions.

Option A under Paragraph 2

343. The effect of applying Article 13(2) of the MLI would be to preserve the exceptions for activities described in Article 5(4)(a) through (d) of the CTA, but to make those activities subject to the condition that the activity be of a preparatory or auxiliary character.[267]

Option B under Paragraph 3

344. The effect of applying Article 13(3) of the Convention would be to preserve the exceptions for activities described in Article 5(4)(a) through (d) of the CTA, and to ensure that those exceptions will apply irrespective of whether the activity is of a preparatory or auxiliary character. An exception is provided in Article 13(3)(a) of the MLI, however, in order to preserve existing provisions of a CTA that explicitly provide that a specific activity shall be deemed not to constitute a PE provided that the activity is of a preparatory or auxiliary character.[268]

Difference Between Option A and Option B[269]

345. Article 13(1) provides that a Party may choose to apply Option A or Option B or not to apply either of these Options. Options A and B have been produced as part of the Action 7 Report. The text of Article 5(4) of the OECD MTC 2017 is equivalent to the principles reflected in Option A, while provisions contained in paragraph 78 of the Commentary on Article 5 of the OECD MTC 2017 are equivalent to Option B.

346. The provisions in Option A provide that the activities listed therein will be deemed not to constitute a PE only if they are of a preparatory or auxiliary character. On the other hand, the alternative provisions in Option B provide that only the activities listed in sub-paragraphs (e) and (f) are subject to the condition that they be of a preparatory or auxiliary character. This reflects the view in Option B that the activities listed in sub-paragraphs (a) through (d) are intrinsically preparatory or auxiliary and, in order to provide greater certainty for both tax administrations and taxpayers, these activities should not be subject to the condition that they be of a preparatory or auxiliary character.

347. Sub-paragraph (a) of Option A is reflected in Article 5(4)(a) through (d) of the OECD MTC 2017. Also, sub-paragraphs (b) and (c) of Option A correspond to Article 5(4)(e) and (f) of the OECD MTC. Similarly, sub-paragraphs (a)-(c) of Option B are reflected in paragraph 78 of the Commentary on Article 5 of the OECD MTC 2017. The effect of applying Option A would be to preserve the exceptions for activities described

267. Refer Explanatory Statement to the MLI, para. 171.
268. *Id.*, para. 173.
269. Refer OECD's FAQs on MLI https://community.oecd.org/docs/DOC-113848 accessed on 13 August 2020.

in Article 5(4)(a) through (d) of the CTAs, but to make those activities subject to the condition that the activity be of a preparatory or auxiliary character. In contrast, the effect of applying Option B would be to preserve the exceptions for activities described in Article 5(4)(a) through (d) of the CTAs, and to ensure that those exceptions will apply irrespective of whether the activity is of a preparatory or auxiliary character.

Anti-fragmentation Provisions under Paragraph 4

348. Sub-paragraph (c) of paragraphs 2, 3 in Article 13 of the MLI is of no importance in a case where an enterprise maintains several fixed places of business within the meaning of sub-paragraphs (a) and (b) provided that they are separated from each other locally and organisationally, as in such a case each place of business has to be viewed separately and in isolation for deciding whether a PE exists. Places of business are not 'separated organisationally' where they each perform in Contracting State complementary functions such as receiving and storing goods in one place, distributing those goods through another, etc. An enterprise cannot fragment a cohesive operating business into several small operations in order to argue that each is merely engaged in a preparatory or auxiliary activity. This criterion should not be restricted to cases where the same enterprise maintains different places of business in a country but should be extended to cases where these places of business belong to closely related enterprises. Some BEPS concerns related to Article 5(4) will therefore be addressed by the rule which will take account not only of the activities carried on by the same enterprise at different places but also of the activities carried on by closely related enterprises (as defined in Article 15 of the MLI) at different places or at the same place. This new rule is the logical consequence of the decision to restrict the scope of Article 5(4) to activities that have a 'preparatory and auxiliary' character because, in the absence of that rule, it would be relatively easy to use closely related enterprises in order to segregate activities which, when taken together, go beyond that threshold.

Meaning of 'Preparatory' and 'Auxiliary'

349. As a general rule, an activity that has a preparatory character is one that is carried on in contemplation of the carrying on of what constitutes the essential and significant part of the activity of the enterprise as a whole. Since a preparatory activity precedes another activity, it will often be carried on during a relatively short period, the duration of that period being determined by the nature of the core activities of the enterprise. This, however, will not always be the case as it is possible to carry on an activity at a given place for a substantial period of time in preparation for activities that take place somewhere else. An activity that has an auxiliary character, on the other hand, generally corresponds to an activity that is carried on to support, without being part of, the essential and significant part of the activity of the enterprise as a whole. It is unlikely that an activity that requires a significant proportion of the assets or employees of the enterprise could be considered as having an auxiliary character.[270]

270. Refer OECD MTC 2017, para. 60 of the Commentary on Art. 5(4).

Compatibility Clauses

350. The compatibility clause in Article 13(5)(a) provides that Option A or B shall apply in place of the relevant parts of provisions of a CTA that list specific activities deemed not to constitute a PE even if the activity is carried on through a fixed place of business.

351. The compatibility clause in Article 13(5)(b) provides that Article 13(4) shall apply to provisions of a CTA (as they may be modified by Option A or B) that list specific activities deemed not to constitute a PE even if the activity is carried on through a fixed place of business.

352. The phrase '*provisions of a Covered Tax Agreement that operate in a comparable manner*' contained in paragraphs 5(a) and (b) would include, for example, provisions of a CTA that describe specific activities which are deemed not to constitute a PE in a single sentence, rather than by listing those activities, but would not include, for example, specific provisions that provide that a project or activity constitutes a PE only if a time period test is met.[271]

Reservations under Paragraph 6

353. The following reservations are provided for under paragraph 6:

(i) Under paragraph 6(a), Parties may opt out of Article 13 entirely with respect to all CTAs, as the same is not a minimum standard.
(ii) Under paragraph 6(b), Parties may opt out of Article 13(2) (Option A) with respect to CTAs that explicitly state that a list of specific activities shall be deemed not to constitute a PE only if each of the activities is of a preparatory or auxiliary character.
(iii) Under paragraph 6(c), Parties may opt out of Article 13(4) with respect to all CTAs, as the same is not a minimum standard.

Notifications

354. Depending upon the position taken by various jurisdictions, the following notifications are required to be made under Article 13 of the MLI:

(i) Jurisdictions intending to make reservations under paragraph 6 are required to make notifications, as the case may be.
(ii) Under paragraph 7, Parties that opted for Option A (Article 13(2)) or Option B (Article 13(3)) shall notify the Depositary of their choice of Option. That notification would also include a list of each of CTAs that includes specific activity exemptions, including those that are subject to a reservation under paragraph 6(b), as well as the article and paragraph number of each such provision. An Option would apply to a provision only where all Contracting

271. Refer Explanatory Statement to the MLI, para. 177.

Jurisdictions have chosen to apply the same Option and have made such a notification with respect to that provision.

(iii) Under paragraph 8, Party that has not opted out of applying paragraph 4 (or the entirety of Article 13) to notify the Depositary of each of its CTAs that includes specific activity exemptions as well as the article and paragraph number of each such provision. To avoid duplication, this notification is not required of Parties that have chosen to apply an Option under paragraph 1, as they are required to make a notification under paragraph 7 which would include a list of each of its CTAs that includes specific activity exemptions even if they have made a reservation under paragraph 6(b). Paragraph 4 will apply to a provision of a CTA only where all Contracting Jurisdictions have made such a notification with respect to that provision pursuant to either paragraph 7 or paragraph 8.

Denmark's Position[272] under the MLI

355. No reservation has been made by Denmark under paragraph 6 of Article 13 of the MLI.

356. Pursuant to Article 13(7) of the MLI, Denmark has chosen Option A under Article 13(1) of the MLI and has notified all of its 64 CTAs, wherein relevant provisions shall be replaced with paragraph 2 of Article 13, provided the respective treaty partners provide matching notifications. At the same time, since no reservation has been taken by Denmark under Article 13(6)(c) of the MLI, paragraph 4 of Article 13 shall apply to all of Denmark's CTAs, provided the treaty partners also do not make a reservation.

357. As an illustration, the application of paragraph 2 (Option A) and paragraph 4 (anti-fragmentation rule) of Article 13 of the MLI to some of Denmark's CTAs is provided hereunder:

Denmark's Treaty Partner	*Position Taken by Treaty Partner*	*Outcome under the MLI*
Argentina	- Matching notification under Article 13(7)	Paragraph 2 (Option A) and paragraph 4 (anti-fragmentation rule) would apply
Australia	- Matching notification under Article 13(7)	Paragraph 2 (Option A) and paragraph 4 (anti-fragmentation rule) would apply
Austria	- Did not notify CTA with Denmark under the MLI	-
Azerbaijan	- Not a Signatory to the MLI	-
Bangladesh	- Not a Signatory to the MLI	-

272. Refer Denmark's Position under the MLI http://www.oecd.org/tax/treaties/beps-mli-position-denmark-instrument-deposit.pdf.

Denmark's Treaty Partner	*Position Taken by Treaty Partner*	*Outcome under the MLI*
Belgium	- Notified Option B under Article 13(7)	- Neither Option A nor Option B would apply - Paragraph 4 (anti-fragmentation rule) would apply
Brazil	- Not a Signatory to the MLI	-
Bulgaria	- Reservation under Article 13(6)(a)	Article 13 would not apply
Canada	- Reservation under Article 13(6)(a)	Article 13 would not apply
Chile	- Notification under Article 13(8)	- Neither Option A nor Option B would apply - Paragraph 4 (anti-fragmentation rule) would apply
China	- Reservation under Article 13(6)(a)	Article 13 would not apply
Croatia	- Matching notification under Article 13(7)	Paragraph 2 (Option A) and paragraph 4 (anti-fragmentation rule) would apply
Cyprus	- Reservation under Article 13(6)(a)	Article 13 would not apply
The Czech Republic	- Reservation under Article 13(6)(a)	Article 13 would not apply
Egypt	- Matching notification under Article 13(7)	Paragraph 2 (Option A) and paragraph 4 (anti-fragmentation rule) would apply
Estonia	- Reservation under Article 13(6)(a)	Article 13 would not apply
Georgia	- Did not notify CTA with Denmark under the MLI	-
Ghana	- Not a Signatory to the MLI	-
Greece	- Reservation under Article 13(6)(a)	Article 13 would not apply
Hungary	- Reservation under Article 13(6)(a)	Article 13 would not apply
India	- Matching notification under Article 13(7)	Paragraph 2 (Option A) and paragraph 4 (anti-fragmentation rule) would apply
Indonesia	- Matching notification under Article 13(7)	Paragraph 2 (Option A) and paragraph 4 (anti-fragmentation rule) would apply

Denmark's Treaty Partner	*Position Taken by Treaty Partner*	*Outcome under the MLI*
Ireland	- Notified Option B under Article 13(7)	- Neither Option A nor Option B would apply - Paragraph 4 (anti-fragmentation rule) would apply
Israel	- Matching notification under Article 13(7)	Paragraph 2 (Option A) and paragraph 4 (anti-fragmentation rule) would apply
Italy	- Matching notification under Article 13(7)	Paragraph 2 (Option A) and paragraph 4 (anti-fragmentation rule) would apply
Jamaica	- Matching notification under Article 13(7)	Paragraph 2 (Option A) and paragraph 4 (anti-fragmentation rule) would apply
Kenya	- Matching notification under Article 13(7)	Paragraph 2 (Option A) and paragraph 4 (anti-fragmentation rule) would apply
Korea	- Reservation under Article 13(6)(a)	Article 13 would not apply
Kuwait	- Matching notification under Article 13(7)	Paragraph 2 (Option A) and paragraph 4 (anti-fragmentation rule) would apply
Latvia	- Reservation under Article 13(6)(a)	Article 13 would not apply
Lithuania	- Notified Option B under Article 13(7)	- Neither Option A nor Option B would apply - Paragraph 4 (anti-fragmentation rule) would apply
Luxembourg	- Reservation under Article 13(6)(c) - Notified Option B under Article 13(7)	Neither paragraphs 2, 3 (Options A, B) nor paragraph 4 (anti-fragmentation rule) would apply
Malta	- Reservation under Article 13(6)(a)	Article 13 would not apply
Mexico	- Matching notification under Article 13(7)	Paragraph 2 (Option A) and paragraph 4 (anti-fragmentation rule) would apply
Montenegro	- Not a Signatory to the MLI	-
Morocco	- Reservation under Article 13(6)(a)	Article 13 would not apply
New Zealand	- Matching notification under Article 13(7)	Paragraph 2 (Option A) and paragraph 4 (anti-fragmentation rule) would apply

Denmark's Treaty Partner	*Position Taken by Treaty Partner*	*Outcome under the MLI*
North Macedonia	- Matching notification under Article 13(7)	Paragraph 2 (Option A) and paragraph 4 (anti-fragmentation rule) would apply
Pakistan	- Matching notification under Article 13(7)	Paragraph 2 (Option A) and paragraph 4 (anti-fragmentation rule) would apply
The Philippines	- Not a Signatory to the MLI	-
Poland	- Reservation under Article 13(6)(a)	Article 13 would not apply
Portugal	- Notification under Article 13(8)	- Neither Option A nor Option B would apply - Paragraph 4 (anti-fragmentation rule) would apply
Romania	- Matching notification under Article 13(7)	Paragraph 2 (Option A) and paragraph 4 (anti-fragmentation rule) would apply
Russia	- Matching notification under Article 13(7)	Paragraph 2 (Option A) and paragraph 4 (anti-fragmentation rule) would apply
Serbia	- Matching notification under Article 13(7)	Paragraph 2 (Option A) and paragraph 4 (anti-fragmentation rule) would apply
Singapore	- Reservation under Article 13(6)(c) - Notified Option B under Article 13(7)	Neither paragraphs 2, 3 (Options A, B) nor paragraph 4 (anti-fragmentation rule) would apply
The Slovak Republic	- Matching notification under Article 13(7)	Paragraph 2 (Option A) and paragraph 4 (anti-fragmentation rule) would apply
Slovenia	- Matching notification under Article 13(7)	Paragraph 2 (Option A) and paragraph 4 (anti-fragmentation rule) would apply
South Africa	- Matching notification under Article 13(7)	Paragraph 2 (Option A) and paragraph 4 (anti-fragmentation rule) would apply
Trinidad & Tobago	- Not a Signatory to the MLI	-
Tunisia	- Matching notification under Article 13(7)	Paragraph 2 (Option A) and paragraph 4 (anti-fragmentation rule) would apply
Turkey	- Matching notification under Article 13(7)	Paragraph 2 (Option A) and paragraph 4 (anti-fragmentation rule) would apply
Uganda	- Not a Signatory to the MLI	-

Denmark's Treaty Partner	*Position Taken by Treaty Partner*	*Outcome under the MLI*
Ukraine	- Matching notification under Article 13(7)	Paragraph 2 (Option A) and paragraph 4 (anti-fragmentation rule) would apply
United Kingdom	- Notification under Article 13(8)	- Neither Option A nor Option B would apply - Paragraph 4 (anti-fragmentation rule) would apply
Venezuela	- Not a Signatory to the MLI	-

India's Position[273] under the MLI

358. No reservation has been made by India under paragraph 6 of Article 13 of the MLI.

359. Pursuant to Article 13(7) of the MLI, India has chosen Option A under Article 13(1) of the MLI and has notified all of its 93 CTAs, wherein relevant provisions shall be replaced with paragraph 2 of Article 13, provided the respective treaty partners provide matching notifications. At the same time, since no reservation has been made by India under Article 13(6)(c) of the MLI, paragraph 4 of Article 13 shall apply to all of India's CTAs, provided the treaty partners also do not make a reservation.

360. As an illustration, the application of paragraph 2 (Option A) and paragraph 4 (anti-fragmentation rule) of Article 13 of the MLI to some of India's CTAs is provided hereunder:

India's Treaty Partner	*Position Taken by Treaty Partner*	*Outcome under the MLI*
Albania	- Reservation under Article 13(6)(a)	Article 13 would not apply
Armenia	- Matching notification under Article 13(7)	Paragraph 2 (Option A) and paragraph 4 (anti-fragmentation rule) would apply
Australia	- Matching notification under Article 13(7)	Paragraph 2 (Option A) and paragraph 4 (anti-fragmentation rule) would apply
Austria	- Reservation under Article 13(6)(c) - Matching notification under Article 13(7)	- Paragraph 2 (Option A) would apply - Paragraph 4 (anti-fragmentation rule) would not apply

273. Refer India's Position under the MLI http://www.oecd.org/tax/treaties/beps-mli-position-india-instrument-deposit.pdf.

India's Treaty Partner	*Position Taken by Treaty Partner*	*Outcome under the MLI*
Belgium	- Notified Option B under Article 13(7)	- Neither Option A nor Option B would apply - Paragraph 4 (anti-fragmentation rule) would apply
Bulgaria	- Reservation under Article 13(6)(a)	Article 13 would not apply
Canada	- Reservation under Article 13(6)(a)	Article 13 would not apply
Colombia	- Matching notification under Article 13(7)	Paragraph 2 (Option A) and paragraph 4 (anti-fragmentation rule) would apply
Croatia	- Matching notification under Article 13(7)	Paragraph 2 (Option A) and paragraph 4 (anti-fragmentation rule) would apply
Cyprus	- Reservation under Article 13(6)(a)	Article 13 would not apply
The Czech Republic	- Reservation under Article 13(6)(a)	Article 13 would not apply
Denmark	- Matching notification under Article 13(7)	Paragraph 2 (Option A) and paragraph 4 (anti-fragmentation rule) would apply
Egypt	- Matching notification under Article 13(7)	Paragraph 2 (Option A) and paragraph 4 (anti-fragmentation rule) would apply
Estonia	- Reservation under Article 13(6)(a)	Article 13 would not apply
Fiji	- Matching notification under Article 13(7)	Paragraph 2 (Option A) and paragraph 4 (anti-fragmentation rule) would apply
Finland	- Reservation under Article 13(6)(a)	Article 13 would not apply
France	- Notified Option B under Article 13(7)	- Neither Option A nor Option B would apply - Paragraph 4 (anti-fragmentation rule) would apply
Georgia	- Reservation under Article 13(6)(a)	Article 13 would not apply
Greece	- Reservation under Article 13(6)(a)	Article 13 would not apply
Hungary	- Reservation under Article 13(6)(a)	Article 13 would not apply

India's Treaty Partner	*Position Taken by Treaty Partner*	*Outcome under the MLI*
Iceland	- Reservation under Article 13(6)(a)	Article 13 would not apply
Indonesia	- Matching notification under Article 13(7)	Paragraph 2 (Option A) and paragraph 4 (anti-fragmentation rule) would apply
Ireland	- Notified Option B under Article 13(7)	- Neither Option A nor Option B would apply - Paragraph 4 (anti-fragmentation rule) would apply
Israel	- Matching notification under Article 13(7)	Paragraph 2 (Option A) and paragraph 4 (anti-fragmentation rule) would apply
Italy	- Matching notification under Article 13(7)	Paragraph 2 (Option A) and paragraph 4 (anti-fragmentation rule) would apply
Japan	- Matching notification under Article 13(7)	Paragraph 2 (Option A) and paragraph 4 (anti-fragmentation rule) would apply
Jordan	- Matching notification under Article 13(7)	Paragraph 2 (Option A) and paragraph 4 (anti-fragmentation rule) would apply
Kazakhstan	- Matching notification under Article 13(7)	Paragraph 2 (Option A) and paragraph 4 (anti-fragmentation rule) would apply
Korea	- Reservation under Article 13(6)(a)	Article 13 would not apply
Kuwait	- Matching notification under Article 13(7)	Paragraph 2 (Option A) and paragraph 4 (anti-fragmentation rule) would apply
Latvia	- Reservation under Article 13(6)(a)	Article 13 would not apply
Lithuania	- Notified Option B under Article 13(7)	- Neither Option A nor Option B would apply - Paragraph 4 (anti-fragmentation rule) would apply
Luxembourg	- Reservation under Article 13(6)(c) - Notified Option B under Article 13(7)	Neither paragraphs 2, 3 (Options A, B) nor paragraph 4 (anti-fragmentation rule) would apply
Malaysia	- Matching notification under Article 13(7)	Paragraph 2 (Option A) and paragraph 4 (anti-fragmentation rule) would apply

India's Treaty Partner	*Position Taken by Treaty Partner*	*Outcome under the MLI*
Malta	– Reservation under Article 13(6)(a)	Article 13 would not apply
Mexico	– Matching notification under Article 13(7)	Paragraph 2 (Option A) and paragraph 4 (anti-fragmentation rule) would apply
Morocco	– Reservation under Article 13(6)(a)	Article 13 would not apply
The Netherlands	– Matching notification under Article 13(7)	Paragraph 2 (Option A) and paragraph 4 (anti-fragmentation rule) would apply
New Zealand	– Matching notification under Article 13(7)	Paragraph 2 (Option A) and paragraph 4 (anti-fragmentation rule) would apply
Norway	– Matching notification under Article 13(7)	Paragraph 2 (Option A) and paragraph 4 (anti-fragmentation rule) would apply
Poland	– Reservation under Article 13(6)(a)	Article 13 would not apply
Portugal	– Notification under Article 13(8)	– Neither Option A nor Option B would apply – Paragraph 4 (anti-fragmentation rule) would apply
Qatar	– Reservation under Article 13(6)(a)	Article 13 would not apply
Romania	– Matching notification under Article 13(7)	Paragraph 2 (Option A) and paragraph 4 (anti-fragmentation rule) would apply
Russia	– Matching notification under Article 13(7)	Paragraph 2 (Option A) and paragraph 4 (anti-fragmentation rule) would apply
Saudi Arabia	– Matching notification under Article 13(7)	Paragraph 2 (Option A) and paragraph 4 (anti-fragmentation rule) would apply
Serbia	– Matching notification under Article 13(7)	Paragraph 2 (Option A) and paragraph 4 (anti-fragmentation rule) would apply
Singapore	– Reservation under Article 13(6)(c) – Notified Option B under Article 13(7)	Neither paragraphs 2, 3 (Options A, B) nor paragraph 4 (anti-fragmentation rule) would apply
The Slovak Republic	– Matching notification under Article 13(7)	Paragraph 2 (Option A) and paragraph 4 (anti-fragmentation rule) would apply

India's Treaty Partner	*Position Taken by Treaty Partner*	*Outcome under the MLI*
Slovenia	- Matching notification under Article 13(7)	Paragraph 2 (Option A) and paragraph 4 (anti-fragmentation rule) would apply
South Africa	- Matching notification under Article 13(7)	Paragraph 2 (Option A) and paragraph 4 (anti-fragmentation rule) would apply
Spain	- Matching notification under Article 13(7)	Paragraph 2 (Option A) and paragraph 4 (anti-fragmentation rule) would apply
Sweden	- Reservation under Article 13(6)(a)	Article 13 would not apply
Turkey	- Matching notification under Article 13(7)	Paragraph 2 (Option A) and paragraph 4 (anti-fragmentation rule) would apply
Ukraine	- Matching notification under Article 13(7)	Paragraph 2 (Option A) and paragraph 4 (anti-fragmentation rule) would apply
UAE	- Reservation under Article 13(6)(a)	Article 13 would not apply
United Kingdom	- Notification under Article 13(8)	- Neither Option A nor Option B would apply - Paragraph 4 (anti-fragmentation rule) would apply
Uruguay	- Matching notification under Article 13(7)	Paragraph 2 (Option A) and paragraph 4 (anti-fragmentation rule) would apply

The Netherlands' Position[274] under the MLI

361. No reservation has been made by the Netherlands under paragraph 6 of Article 13 of the MLI.

362. Pursuant to Article 13(7) of the MLI, the Netherlands has chosen Option A under Article 13(1) of the MLI and has notified all of its 81 CTAs, wherein relevant provisions shall be replaced with paragraph 2 of Article 13, provided the respective treaty partners provide matching notifications. At the same time, since no reservation has been taken by the Netherlands under Article 13(6)(c) of the MLI, paragraph 4 of Article 13 shall apply to all of the Netherlands' CTAs, provided the treaty partners also do not make a reservation.

274. Refer The Netherlands' Position under the MLI http://www.oecd.org/tax/treaties/beps-mli-position-netherlands-instrument-deposit.pdf.

363. As an illustration, the application of paragraph 2 (Option A) and paragraph 4 (anti-fragmentation rule) of Article 13 of the MLI to some of the Netherlands' CTAs is provided hereunder:

The Netherlands' Treaty Partner	*Position Taken by Treaty Partner*	*Outcome under the MLI*
Albania	- Reservation under Article 13(6)(a)	Article 13 would not apply
Argentina	- Matching notification under Article 13(7)	Paragraph 2 (Option A) and paragraph 4 (anti-fragmentation rule) would apply
Australia	- Matching notification under Article 13(7)	Paragraph 2 (Option A) and paragraph 4 (anti-fragmentation rule) would apply
Austria	- Reservation under Article 13(6)(c) - Matching notification under Article 13(7)	- Paragraph 2 (Option A) would apply - Paragraph 4 (anti-fragmentation rule) would not apply
Azerbaijan	- Not a Signatory to the MLI	-
Bahrain	- Reservation under Article 13(6)(a)	Article 13 would not apply
Barbados	- Reservation under Article 13(6)(a)	Article 13 would not apply
Belarus	- Not a Signatory to the MLI	-
Bosnia & Herzegovina	- Reservation under Article 13(6)(a)	Article 13 would not apply
Canada	- Reservation under Article 13(6)(a)	Article 13 would not apply
China	- Reservation under Article 13(6)(a)	Article 13 would not apply
Croatia	- Matching notification under Article 13(7)	Paragraph 2 (Option A) and paragraph 4 (anti-fragmentation rule) would apply
The Czech Republic	- Reservation under Article 13(6)(a)	Article 13 would not apply
Egypt	- Matching notification under Article 13(7)	Paragraph 2 (Option A) and paragraph 4 (anti-fragmentation rule) would apply
Estonia	- Reservation under Article 13(6)(a)	Article 13 would not apply
Finland	- Reservation under Article 13(6)(a)	Article 13 would not apply

The Netherlands' Treaty Partner	*Position Taken by Treaty Partner*	*Outcome under the MLI*
France	- Notified Option B under Article 13(7)	- Neither Option A nor Option B would apply - Paragraph 4 (anti-fragmentation rule) would apply
Georgia	- Reservation under Article 13(6)(a)	Article 13 would not apply
Germany	- Did not notify CTA with the Netherlands under the MLI	-
Greece	- Reservation under Article 13(6)(a)	Article 13 would not apply
Hong Kong	- Reservation under Article 13(6)(a)	Article 13 would not apply
Hungary	- Reservation under Article 13(6)(a)	Article 13 would not apply
Iceland	- Reservation under Article 13(6)(a)	Article 13 would not apply
India	- Matching notification under Article 13(7)	Paragraph 2 (Option A) and paragraph 4 (anti-fragmentation rule) would apply
Indonesia	- Matching notification under Article 13(7)	Paragraph 2 (Option A) and paragraph 4 (anti-fragmentation rule) would apply
Israel	- Matching notification under Article 13(7)	Paragraph 2 (Option A) and paragraph 4 (anti-fragmentation rule) would apply
Italy	- Matching notification under Article 13(7)	Paragraph 2 (Option A) and paragraph 4 (anti-fragmentation rule) would apply
Japan	- Matching notification under Article 13(7)	Paragraph 2 (Option A) and paragraph 4 (anti-fragmentation rule) would apply
Jordan	- Matching notification under Article 13(7)	Paragraph 2 (Option A) and paragraph 4 (anti-fragmentation rule) would apply
Kenya	- Matching notification under Article 13(7)	Paragraph 2 (Option A) and paragraph 4 (anti-fragmentation rule) would apply
Korea	- Reservation under Article 13(6)(a)	Article 13 would not apply
Kuwait	- Matching notification under Article 13(7)	Paragraph 2 (Option A) and paragraph 4 (anti-fragmentation rule) would apply
Latvia	- Reservation under Article 13(6)(a)	Article 13 would not apply

The Netherlands' Treaty Partner	*Position Taken by Treaty Partner*	*Outcome under the MLI*
Lithuania	- Notified Option B under Article 13(7)	- Neither Option A nor Option B would apply - Paragraph 4 (anti-fragmentation rule) would apply
Luxembourg	- Reservation under Article 13(6)(c) - Notified Option B under Article 13(7)	Neither paragraphs 2, 3 (Options A, B) nor paragraph 4 (anti-fragmentation rule) would apply
Malaysia	- Matching notification under Article 13(7)	Paragraph 2 (Option A) and paragraph 4 (anti-fragmentation rule) would apply
Malta	- Reservation under Article 13(6)(a)	Article 13 would not apply
Mexico	- Matching notification under Article 13(7)	Paragraph 2 (Option A) and paragraph 4 (anti-fragmentation rule) would apply
Montenegro	- Not a Signatory to the MLI	-
Morocco	- Reservation under Article 13(6)(a)	Article 13 would not apply
New Zealand	- Matching notification under Article 13(7)	Paragraph 2 (Option A) and paragraph 4 (anti-fragmentation rule) would apply
Nigeria	- Matching notification under Article 13(7)	Paragraph 2 (Option A) and paragraph 4 (anti-fragmentation rule) would apply
North Macedonia	- Matching notification under Article 13(7)	Paragraph 2 (Option A) and paragraph 4 (anti-fragmentation rule) would apply
Norway	- Matching notification under Article 13(7)	Paragraph 2 (Option A) and paragraph 4 (anti-fragmentation rule) would apply
Oman	- Reservation under Article 13(6)(a)	Article 13 would not apply
Pakistan	- Matching notification under Article 13(7)	Paragraph 2 (Option A) and paragraph 4 (anti-fragmentation rule) would apply
Panama	- Reservation under Article 13(6)(a)	Article 13 would not apply
The Philippines	- Not a Signatory to the MLI	-
Portugal	- Notification under Article 13(8)	- Neither Option A nor Option B would apply - Paragraph 4 (anti-fragmentation rule) would apply

The Netherlands' Treaty Partner	*Position Taken by Treaty Partner*	*Outcome under the MLI*
Qatar	– Reservation under Article 13(6)(a)	Article 13 would not apply
Romania	– Matching notification under Article 13(7)	Paragraph 2 (Option A) and paragraph 4 (anti-fragmentation rule) would apply
Russia	– Matching notification under Article 13(7)	Paragraph 2 (Option A) and paragraph 4 (anti-fragmentation rule) would apply
Serbia	– Matching notification under Article 13(7)	Paragraph 2 (Option A) and paragraph 4 (anti-fragmentation rule) would apply
Singapore	– Reservation under Article 13(6)(c) – Notified Option B under Article 13(7)	Neither paragraphs 2, 3 (Options A, B) nor paragraph 4 (anti-fragmentation rule) would apply
The Slovak Republic	– Matching notification under Article 13(7)	Paragraph 2 (Option A) and paragraph 4 (anti-fragmentation rule) would apply
Slovenia	– Matching notification under Article 13(7)	Paragraph 2 (Option A) and paragraph 4 (anti-fragmentation rule) would apply
South Africa	– Matching notification under Article 13(7)	Paragraph 2 (Option A) and paragraph 4 (anti-fragmentation rule) would apply
Sweden	– Reservation under Article 13(6)(a)	Article 13 would not apply
Thailand	– Not a Signatory to the MLI	–
Tunisia	– Matching notification under Article 13(7)	Paragraph 2 (Option A) and paragraph 4 (anti-fragmentation rule) would apply
Turkey	– Matching notification under Article 13(7)	Paragraph 2 (Option A) and paragraph 4 (anti-fragmentation rule) would apply
The United Arab Emirates	– Reservation under Article 13(6)(a)	Article 13 would not apply
United Kingdom	– Notification under Article 13(8)	– Neither Option A nor Option B would apply – Paragraph 4 (anti-fragmentation rule) would apply

Few Snapshots of Positions[275] Taken by Other Countries under the MLI

364. Jurisdictions that have made reservation under Article 13(6)(a) of the MLI for the entirety of Article 13 not to apply to their CTAs are, namely, Albania, Andorra, Bahrain, Barbados, Belize, Bosnia and Herzegovina, Bulgaria, Canada, China, Cyprus, the Czech Republic, Estonia, Finland, Georgia, Greece, Guernsey, Hong Kong, Hungary, Iceland, the Isle of Man, Jersey, Korea, Latvia, Liechtenstein, Malta, Mauritius, Monaco, Morocco, Oman, Panama, Poland, Qatar, Seychelles, Sweden, Switzerland, the United Arab Emirates.

365. Jurisdictions that have made reservation under Article 13(6)(b) of the MLI are, namely, Argentina (in respect of CTA with Chile only), Australia (in respect of CTAs with Finland, New Zealand and South Africa only), Kenya (in respect of CTAs with India, Norway, Qatar, South Africa, Sweden).

366. Jurisdictions that have made reservation under Article 13(6)(c) of the MLI are, namely, Austria, Germany, Luxembourg and Singapore.

367. Under Article 13(7), jurisdictions that have exercised their choice of Option A or B are listed as below:

Jurisdictions Choosing Option A	*Jurisdictions Choosing Option B*
Argentina, Armenia, Australia, Austria, Burkina Faso, Cameroon, Colombia, Costa Rica, Côte d'Ivoire, Croatia, Curaçao, Denmark, Egypt, Fiji, Gabon, Germany, India, Indonesia, Israel, Italy, Jamaica, Japan, Jordan, Kazakhstan, Kenya, Kuwait, Malaysia, Mexico, the Netherlands, New Zealand, Nigeria, North Macedonia, Norway, Pakistan, Papua New Guinea, Peru, Romania, Russia, Saudi Arabia, Senegal, Serbia, the Slovak Republic, Slovenia, South Africa, Spain, Tunisia, Turkey, Ukraine, Uruguay	Belgium, France, Ireland, Lithuania, Luxembourg, San Marino, Singapore

The various notifications made by treaty partners under Article 13 of the MLI and impact/outcome thereof on the respective CTAs are provided in Figure 14.

275. Refer OECD – Signatories and Parties to the MLI http://www.oecd.org/tax/treaties/beps-mli-signatories-and-parties.pdf.

Figure 14 Article 13: Artificial Avoidance of PE Status Through the Specific Activity Exemptions – Flowchart on Notifications & Their Impact

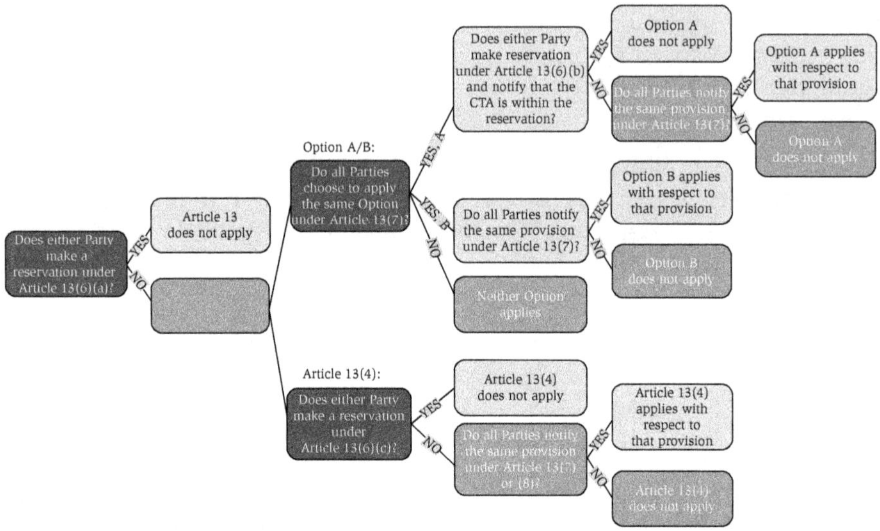

Source: OECD – Toolkit for Application of the Multilateral Instrument for BEPS Tax Treaty Related Measures https://www.oecd.org/tax/treaties/application-toolkit-multilateral-instrument-for-beps-tax-treaty-measures.htm.

3.7.3 Article 14 of MLI: Splitting-Up of Contracts

368. The interplay between Article 14 of MLI, corresponding BEPS Report and the resulting provisions incorporated in OECD MTC 2017 is represented in a table as below:

MLI		*BEPS Final Report*		*OECD MTC 2017*	
Article	*Title of Article*	*BEPS Action Plan*	*Title of BEPS Action Plan*	*Article*	*Title of Article*
14	Splitting-Up of Contracts	Action 7	Preventing the Artificial Avoidance of Permanent Establishment Status	5(3) (paragraph 52 of Commentary)	Permanent Establishment

369. The article at a glance is as below:

Substantive (BEPS) Provisions under Para(s)	*Opt-In Provisions under Para*	*Alternative Provisions under Para*	*Compatibility Clause*		*Reservations under Para*	*Notifications under Para*
			Para	*Type*		
1	None	None	2	'in place of or in the absence of'	3	3, 4

Status in Pre-BEPS Project Era

370. The 12-month threshold as mentioned in Article 5(3) of the OECD MTC 2014 (or 6-month threshold in some CTAs based on UN Model) has given rise to abuses. In order to artificially circumvent the 12-month threshold, for PE provisions not to apply under paragraph 3 of Article 5 of the OECD MTC 2014, it has been found that enterprises (mainly contractors or subcontractors working on the continental shelf or engaged in activities connected with the exploration and exploitation of the continental shelf) divided their contracts up into several parts, each covering a period less than 12 months and attributed to a different company which was, however, owned by the same group. Commensurate changes in provisions were needed to address specifically the splitting-up of contracts and abuses of the exception in Article 5(3) of the OECD Model PE definition, pursuant to which a building site or construction or installation project constitutes a PE only if it lasts more than 12 months.

Article 14 of MLI

371. The BEPS Action 7 Report noted that the PPT provision will address BEPS concerns related to the abusive splitting-up of contracts and included a draft provision specifically addressing the splitting-up of contracts for use in treaties that would not include the PPT, or for Contracting Jurisdictions that wish to address such abuses explicitly. Article 14 of the MLI provides for the implementation of the said provision of BEPS Action 7 Report.[276]

Paragraph 1 of Article 14

372. Paragraph 1 of Article 14 of the MLI addresses the splitting-up of contracts, through an anti-abuse rule that allows the aggregation of different periods of time for the purpose of determining whether or not the activities conducted in the State of source can be deemed to constitute a project or construction PE (provisions of Article 14(1) of the MLI do not apply to service PE provisions present in certain treaties akin to Article 5(3)(b) of UN Model Double Taxation Convention, 2017). The various

276. Refer Explanatory Statement to the MLI, para. 182.

activities envisaged in paragraph 1 of Article 14 which are to be taken into account for determining the 'period' are as below:

(i) building site;
(ii) construction project;
(iii) installation project;
(iv) other specific projects;
(v) supervisory or consultancy activities in connection with the above.

373. The terms 'building site', 'construction project', 'installation project' include not only the construction of buildings but also the construction of roads, bridges or canals, the renovation (involving more than mere maintenance or redecoration) of buildings, roads, bridges or canals, the laying of pipelines and excavating and dredging. Additionally, the term 'installation project' is not restricted to an installation related to a construction project; it also includes the installation of new equipment, such as a complex machine, in an existing building or outdoors. On-site planning and supervision of the erection of a building are also covered.[277]

374. Under paragraph 1 of Article 14, for the purposes of determining the 'period' referred to in the relevant CTA provisions commensurate to Article 5(3) of the OECD MTC, the following different periods of time are to be added to the aggregate period of time during which an enterprise has carried out activities:

- paragraph 1(a) of Article 14 – Activities carried on by an enterprise of a Contracting Jurisdiction in the other Contracting Jurisdiction, during one or more periods of time which in aggregate exceed 30 days but remain below the threshold limit prescribed in the relevant provisions of the CTA; and
- paragraph 1(b) of Article 14 – Connected activities carried on in that other Contracting Jurisdiction by one or more closely related enterprises (as defined in Article 15 of the MLI) of the first-mentioned enterprise, during different periods of time, each exceeding 30 days.

375. The determination of whether activities are 'connected' (as mentioned in paragraph 1(b) of Article 14 of the MLI) will depend on the facts and circumstances of each case. Factors[278] that may be relevant for such determination include:

- whether the contracts covering the different activities were concluded with the same person or related persons;
- whether the conclusion of additional contracts with a person is a logical consequence of a previous contract concluded with that person or related persons;
- whether the activities would have been covered by a single contract absent tax planning considerations;

277. Refer OECD MTC 2017, para. 50 of the Commentary on Art. 5(3).
278. *Id.*, para. 53 of the Commentary on Art. 5(3).

- whether the nature of the work involved under the different contracts is the same or similar;
- whether the same employees are performing the activities under the different contracts.

Compatibility Clause

376. The compatibility clause in Article 14(2) provides that the splitting-up of contracts rule shall apply in place of or in the absence of provisions in CTAs to the extent that such provisions address the division of contracts into multiple parts to avoid the application of a time period or periods in relation to the existence of a PE for specific projects or activities. Many treaties feature anti-splitting rules that apply to a wide variety of activities, only some of which may be covered by the provision in Article 14. Paragraph 2 is intended to replace those existing rules only to the extent that they relate to the activities described in paragraph 1, and to leave those rules intact with respect to activities that are not within the scope of paragraph 1. This would be the case, for example, where the same anti-splitting rule is used for a provision relating to construction activities carried on through a fixed place of business and for a provision deeming a PE to exist in the case of provision of services that are not tied to a specific place of business.[279]

Reservations under Paragraph 3

377. The following reservations are provided for under paragraph 3:

(i) Under paragraph 3(a), Parties may opt out of Article 14 entirely with respect to all CTAs, as the same is not a minimum standard.
(ii) Under paragraph 3(b), Parties may opt out of Article 14 entirely with respect to provisions of CTAs relating to the exploration for or exploitation of natural resources so as to preserve such carefully negotiated anti-contract splitting rules in their respective CTAs.

Notifications

378. Depending upon the position taken by various jurisdictions, the following notifications are required to be made under Article 14 of the MLI:

(i) Jurisdictions intending to make reservations under paragraph 3 are required to make notifications, as the case may be.
(ii) Under paragraph 4, Parties (other than those that have opted out of the entirety of the article) are required to notify the Depositary of whether each of its CTAs contains an existing anti-contract splitting provision that is not subject to a reservation under paragraph 3(b), and if so, the article and paragraph number of each such provision. Paragraph 1 will replace such provisions to the extent

279. Refer Explanatory Statement to the MLI, para. 185.

provided in paragraph 2 where all Contracting Jurisdictions to the CTA have made such a notification. In other cases, paragraph 1 will apply to the CTA, but will supersede the existing provisions of the CTA only to the extent that those provisions are incompatible with paragraph 1.

Denmark's Position[280] under the MLI

379. Pursuant to Article 14(4) of the MLI, Denmark has notified its CTAs which contain a provision described in Article 14(2) that is not subject to a reservation under Article 14(3)(b). The application of paragraph 1 of Article 14 of the MLI to some of Denmark's CTAs notified by it under Article 14(4) is provided hereunder:

Denmark's Treaty Partner	*Position Taken by Treaty Partner*	*Outcome under the MLI*
Argentina, India, Indonesia, Kuwait, Russia, Ukraine	- No notification under paragraph 3 or 4 of Article 14 concerning Denmark	Article 14(1) would apply and supersede the relevant provisions of Denmark's CTA with these countries to the extent of incompatibility
Belgium, Canada, Chile, China, the Czech Republic, Estonia, Italy, Jamaica, Latvia, Malta, Mexico, Portugal, Singapore, Slovenia, South Africa	- Reservation under Article 14(3)(a) and opting out of Article 14 for all CTAs	Article 14 of MLI would not apply to Denmark's CTA with these countries
Pakistan	- Matching notification under Article 14(4)	Article 14(1) would replace the relevant provisions of the CTA
Ireland, Lithuania	- Reservation under Article 14(3)(b) concerning Denmark	- Article 14(1) of MLI would apply and supersede the relevant provisions of Denmark's CTAs with these countries to the extent of incompatibility - However, Article 14 of MLI would not apply with respect to the existing provisions relating to the exploration for or exploitation of natural resources (as Ireland, Lithuania have made a reservation)

280. Refer Denmark's Position under the MLI http://www.oecd.org/tax/treaties/beps-mli-position-denmark-instrument-deposit.pdf.

Denmark's Treaty Partner	*Position Taken by Treaty Partner*	*Outcome under the MLI*
Austria	- Did not notify CTA with Denmark under the MLI	-

380. The application of paragraph 1 of Article 14 of the MLI to some of Denmark's CTAs which are not notified by it under Article 14(4) is provided hereunder:

Denmark's Treaty Partner	*Position Taken by Treaty Partner*	*Outcome under the MLI*
Australia, Egypt, Serbia, the Slovak Republic	- No notification under paragraph 3 or 4 of Article 14 concerning Denmark	Article 14(1) would apply and supersede the provisions of the CTA to the extent of incompatibility
Bulgaria, Croatia, Cyprus	- Reservation under Article 14(3)(a) and opting out of Article 14 for all CTAs	Article 14 of MLI would not apply to Denmark's CTA with these countries

India's Position[281] under the MLI

381. No reservation has been made by India under paragraph 3 of Article 14 of the MLI. Also, no notification of similar provisions described in paragraph 2 has been made by India under paragraph 4 of Article 14 of the MLI, as such provisions are not presently there in India's DTAAs. The application of paragraph 1 of Article 14 of the MLI to some of India's CTAs is provided hereunder:

India's Treaty Partner	*Position Taken by Treaty Partner*	*Outcome under the MLI*
Armenia, Australia, Egypt, Fiji, Indonesia, Ireland, Israel, Jordan, Kazakhstan, Kenya, Kuwait, the Netherlands, New Zealand, Romania, Russia, Saudi Arabia, Serbia, the Slovak Republic, Ukraine, Uruguay	- No notification under paragraph 3 or 4 of Article 14 concerning India	Article 14(1) of MLI would apply to India's CTA with these countries

281. Refer India's Position under the MLI http://www.oecd.org/tax/treaties/beps-mli-position-india-instrument-deposit.pdf.

India's Treaty Partner	*Position Taken by Treaty Partner*	*Outcome under the MLI*
Albania, Austria, Belgium, Bulgaria, Canada, Croatia, Cyprus, the Czech Republic, Estonia, Finland, France, Georgia, Greece, Hungary, Iceland, Italy, Japan, Korea, Latvia, Luxembourg, Malaysia, Malta, Mexico, Morocco, Macedonia, Poland, Portugal, Qatar, Singapore, Slovenia, South Africa, Spain, Sweden, Turkey, UAE, UK	- Reservation under Article 14(3)(a) and opting out of Article 14 for all CTAs	Article 14 of MLI would not apply to India's CTA with these countries
Denmark	- Notified relevant provisions of CTA with India pursuant to Article 14(4) of the MLI	Article 14(1) of MLI would apply and supersede the relevant provisions of CTA to the extent of incompatibility
Lithuania	- Reservation under Article 14(3)(b) concerning India	Article 14(1) of MLI would apply to Article 5(3)(a) of India-Lithuania CTA and not to Article 5(3)(c) of CTA that pertains to exploration for or exploitation of natural resources (as Lithuania has made a reservation)

The Netherlands' Position[282] under the MLI

382. Pursuant to Article 14(3)(b) of the MLI, the Netherlands has made a reservation for the entirety of Article 14 not to apply with respect to provisions of its CTAs relating to the exploration for or exploitation of natural resources. The application of paragraph 1 of Article 14 of the MLI to some of the Netherlands' CTAs notified by it under Article 14(3)(b) is provided hereunder:

282. Refer The Netherlands' Position under the MLI http://www.oecd.org/tax/treaties/beps-mli-position-netherlands-instrument-deposit.pdf.

The Netherlands' Treaty Partner	*Position Taken by Treaty Partner*	*Outcome under the MLI*
Argentina, Armenia, Kazakhstan, Kuwait, Romania, Saudi Arabia	- No notification under paragraph 3 or 4 of Article 14 concerning the Netherlands	- Article 14(1) of MLI would apply and supersede the relevant provisions of the Netherlands' CTAs with these countries to the extent of incompatibility - However, Article 14 of MLI would not apply with respect to the existing provisions relating to the exploration for or exploitation of natural resources (as the Netherlands has made a reservation)
Albania, Bahrain, Barbados, Bosnia & Herzegovina, Canada, Croatia, Estonia, Finland, Georgia, Hong Kong, Iceland, Latvia, North Macedonia, Panama, Portugal, Qatar, Slovenia, South Africa, Sweden, United Kingdom	- Reservation under Article 14(3)(a) and opting out of Article 14 for all CTAs	- Article 14 of MLI would not apply to the Netherlands' CTA with these countries
Egypt, Lithuania, Russia	- Treaty partner has also made a reservation under Article 14(3)(b) concerning the Netherlands	- Article 14(1) of MLI would apply and supersede the relevant provisions of the Netherlands' CTAs with these countries to the extent of incompatibility - However, Article 14 of MLI would not apply with respect to the existing provisions relating to the exploration for or exploitation of natural resources (as both, the Netherlands and its treaty partner, have made a reservation)
Indonesia, Jordan	- Notified relevant provisions of CTA with the Netherlands pursuant to Article 14(4) of the MLI	- Article 14(1) of MLI would apply and supersede the relevant provisions of the Netherlands' CTA with these countries to the extent of incompatibility - However, Article 14 of MLI would not apply with respect to the existing provisions relating to the exploration for or exploitation of natural resources (as the Netherlands has made a reservation)

383. The Netherlands has notified its treaties with Germany, Norway and Suriname (which is not a Signatory to the MLI) pursuant to Article 14(4) of the MLI which contain a provision described in Article 14(2) and are not subject to a reservation under Article 14(3)(b). At the same time, the Netherlands has notified its treaties with Germany, Norway pursuant to Article 14(3)(b) of the MLI for the entirety of Article 14 not to apply with respect to provisions of its CTAs relating to the exploration for or exploitation of natural resources. Accordingly, applicability of provisions of Article 14 of the MLI on its CTAs with Germany, Norway is as below:

The Netherlands' Treaty Partner	*Position Taken by Treaty Partner*	*Outcome under the MLI*
Germany	- Did not notify CTA with the Netherlands under the MLI	Article 14 of MLI would not apply
Norway	- Matching notification (as done by the Netherlands) wherein Article 24(3) of the CTA has been notified under Article 14(3)(b) of the MLI and Protocol (III) of the CTA has been notified under Article 14(4) of the MLI	- Article 14 of MLI would not apply with respect to the existing provisions relating to the exploration for or exploitation of natural resources (as both, the Netherlands and its treaty partner, have made a reservation) - Protocol (III) of the CTA would be replaced by Article 14(1) of the MLI

384. The application of paragraph 1 of Article 14 of the MLI to some of the Netherlands' CTAs which are not notified by it under Article 14(3)(b) or Article 14(4) is provided hereunder:

The Netherlands' Treaty Partner	*Position Taken by Treaty Partner*	*Outcome under the MLI*
Australia, India, Israel, Kenya, New Zealand, Nigeria, Pakistan, Serbia, the Slovak Republic, Tunisia	- No notification under paragraph 3 or 4 of Article 14 concerning the Netherlands	Article 14(1) would apply and supersede the provisions of the CTA to the extent of incompatibility
Austria, China, the Czech Republic, France, Greece, Hungary, Italy, Japan, Korea, Luxembourg, Malaysia, Malta, Mexico, Morocco, Oman, Singapore, Turkey, the United Arab Emirates	- Reservation under Article 14(3)(a) and opting out of Article 14 for all CTAs	Article 14 of MLI would not apply to the Netherlands' CTA with these countries

Few Snapshots of Positions[283] Taken by Other Countries under the MLI

385. Jurisdictions that have made reservation under Article 14(3)(a) of the MLI for the entirety of Article 14 not to apply to their CTAs are, namely, Albania, Andorra, Austria, Bahrain, Barbados, Belgium, Belize, Bosnia and Herzegovina, Bulgaria, Canada, Chile, China, Costa Rica, Croatia, Curaçao, Cyprus, the Czech Republic, Estonia, Finland, France, Georgia, Germany, Greece, Guernsey, Hong Kong, Hungary, Iceland, the Isle of Man, Italy, Jamaica, Japan, Jersey, Korea, Latvia, Liechtenstein, Luxembourg, Malaysia, Malta, Mauritius, Mexico, Monaco, Morocco, North Macedonia, Oman, Panama, Peru, Poland, Portugal, Qatar, San Marino, Seychelles, Singapore, Slovenia, South Africa, Spain, Sweden, Switzerland, Turkey, the United Arab Emirates, UK.

386. There are eight jurisdictions that have made reservation under Article 14(3)(b) of the MLI (for the entirety of Article 14 not to apply with respect to provisions of its CTAs relating to the exploration for or exploitation of natural resources), namely:

(i) Australia (in respect of CTA with Norway).
(ii) Egypt (in respect of CTAs with Ireland, the Netherlands).
(iii) Ireland (in respect of CTAs with Armenia, Bahrain, Bosnia and Herzegovina, Botswana, Canada, Denmark, Estonia, Ethiopia, Finland, Ghana, Greece, Iceland, Kazakhstan, Latvia, Lithuania, Norway, Pakistan, Panama, Poland, Romania, Serbia, Singapore, South Africa, Sweden, US, Uzbekistan, Zambia).
(iv) Lithuania (in respect of CTAs with Armenia, Austria, Azerbaijan, Belgium, Bulgaria, Canada, China, Croatia, Cyprus, Denmark, Estonia, Finland, Georgia, Germany, Greece, Hungary, Iceland, India, Ireland, Israel, Italy, Kazakhstan, Kuwait, Kyrgyzstan, Latvia, Luxembourg, Malta, Mexico, Moldova, Morocco, the Netherlands, North Macedonia, Norway, Poland, Portugal, Romania, Russia, Serbia, the Slovak Republic, Slovenia, Spain, Sweden, Ukraine, the United Arab Emirates Article, UK, US, Uzbekistan).
(v) The Netherlands (in respect of CTAs with Albania, Argentina, Armenia, Azerbaijan, Bahrain, Barbados, Belarus, Canada, Croatia, Egypt, Estonia, Ethiopia, Finland, Georgia, Germany, Hong Kong, Iceland, Indonesia, Jordan, Kazakhstan, Kuwait, Latvia, Lithuania, North Macedonia, Moldova, Norway, Panama, Portugal, Qatar, Romania, the Russian Federation, Saudi Arabia, Slovenia, South Africa, Sweden, Uganda, UK, US, Uzbekistan, Venezuela, Zambia).
(vi) Norway (in respect of CTAs with Argentina, Australia, Bulgaria, China, Cyprus, the Czech Republic, Estonia, India, Ireland, Japan, Latvia, Lithuania, Luxembourg, Malta, Mexico, the Netherlands, Poland, Portugal, Romania, Russia, Serbia, Slovenia, South Africa, Turkey, UK).
(vii) Russia (in respect of CTAs with Iceland, Latvia, Lithuania, the Netherlands, New Zealand, Norway).
(viii) Serbia (in respect of CTA with Norway).

283. Refer OECD – Signatories and Parties to the MLI http://www.oecd.org/tax/treaties/beps-mli-signatories-and-parties.pdf.

387. Application of provisions under Article 14 of MLI in CTAs of some jurisdictions, as per their mutual notifications, is *inter alia* as below:

Jurisdiction	*Position Taken*	*Treaty Partner*	*Position Taken*	*Outcome under the MLI*
Australia	- Reservation under Article 14(3)(b) concerning CTA with Norway - No notification made concerning CTA with Canada	Canada	- Reservation under Article 14(3)(a) for Article 14 not to apply to its CTAs	Article 14 of MLI would not apply
Australia	- Reservation under Article 14(3)(b) concerning CTA with Norway - Notification made under Article 14(4) concerning CTA with Chile	Chile	- Reservation under Article 14(3)(a) for Article 14 not to apply to its CTAs	Article 14 of MLI would not apply
Australia	- Reservation under Article 14(3)(b) concerning CTA with Norway - Notification made under Article 14(4) concerning CTA with New Zealand	New Zealand	- Similar notification under Article 14(4) concerning CTA with Australia	Article 14 of MLI would replace relevant provisions (Article 5(6))[284] of Australia-New Zealand CTA
Australia	- Reservation under Article 14(3)(b) concerning CTA with Norway - Notification made under Article 14(4)	Norway	- Similar Reservation under Article 14(3)(b) concerning CTA with Australia - Similar notification made	Article 14(1) of MLI would replace relevant provisions (Article 5(4))[285] of Australia-Norway CTA, and not apply on provisions (Article 20(3)

284. Refer Australia-New Zealand CTA https://research.ibfd.org/#/doc?url=/linkresolver/static/tt_au-nz_01_eng_2009_tt accessed on 5 September 2020.
285. Refer Australia-Norway CTA https://research.ibfd.org/#/doc?url=/linkresolver/static/tt_au-no_01_eng_2006_tt accessed on 5 September 2020.

Jurisdiction	*Position Taken*	*Treaty Partner*	*Position Taken*	*Outcome under the MLI*
	concerning CTA with Norway		under Article 14(4) concerning CTA with Australia	of the CTA) that pertain to exploration for or exploitation of natural resources (as both sides have made a reservation)

The various notifications made by treaty partners under Article 14 of the MLI and impact/outcome thereof on the respective CTAs are provided in Figure 15.

Figure 15 Article 14: Splitting-Up of Contracts – Flowchart on Notifications & Their Impact

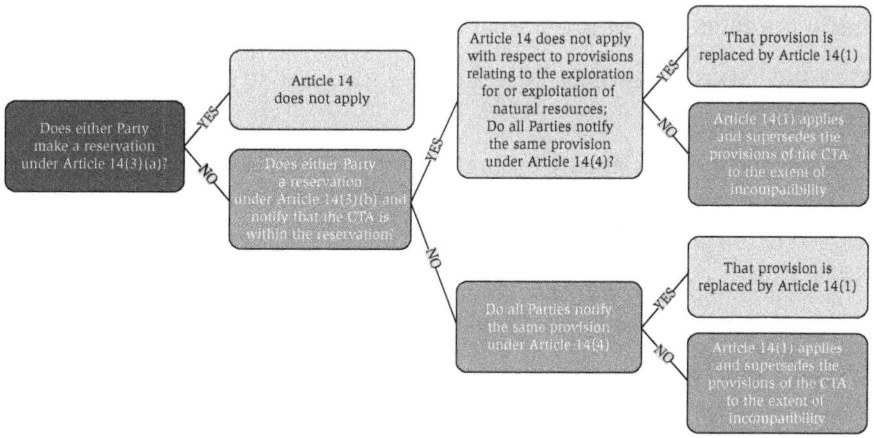

Source: OECD – Toolkit for Application of the Multilateral Instrument for BEPS Tax Treaty Related Measures https://www.oecd.org/tax/treaties/application-toolkit-multilateral-instrument-for-beps-tax-treaty-measures.htm.

3.7.4 Article 15 of MLI: Definition of a Person Closely Related to an Enterprise

388. The interplay between Article 15 of MLI, corresponding BEPS Report and the resulting provisions incorporated in OECD MTC 2017 is represented in a table as below:

MLI		*BEPS Final Report*		*OECD MTC 2017*	
Article	*Title of Article*	*BEPS Action Plan*	*Title of BEPS Action Plan*	*Article*	*Title of Article*
15	Definition of a Person Closely Related to an Enterprise	Action 7	Preventing the Artificial Avoidance of Permanent Establishment Status	5(8)	Permanent Establishment

389. The article at a glance is as below:

Substantive (BEPS) Provisions under Para(s)	*Opt-In Provisions under Para*	*Alternative Provisions under Para*	*Compatibility Clause*		*Reservations under Para*	*Notifications under Para*
			Para	*Type*		
1	None	None	None	–	2	2

Status in Pre-BEPS Project Era

390. Earlier, MNEs were able to deliberately circumvent the applicability of PE provisions by:

- conducting their agency business in other countries through closely related persons/enterprises that were dubbed as independent agents; or
- fragmenting their specific activities among closely related persons/enterprises; or
- splitting-up of contracts of connected activities among closely related persons/enterprises so as to avoid the threshold period.

Such deliberate measures intended to artificially avoid PE status, which led to base erosion, are envisaged to be addressed by the BEPS Action 7 Report by introducing the concept of a 'person closely related to an enterprise'.

Paragraph 1 of Article 15 of MLI

391. Article 15 of the MLI provides the definition of 'a person closely related to an enterprise' relevant for the application of Articles 12(2) (ascertain status of independent agents), 13(4) (anti-fragmentation rule) and 14(1)(b) (splitting-up of contract provisions) of the MLI. Hence, there is no compatibility clause in this Article, as found in other substantive provisions of the MLI.

392. The definition of 'a person closely related to an enterprise' provided in Article 15(1) of the MLI is divided into two parts:

(1) The first part consists of '*a person is closely related to an enterprise if, based on all the relevant facts and circumstances, one has control of the other or both are under the control of the same persons or enterprises*'. This general

rule would cover situations where a person or enterprise controls an enterprise by virtue of a special arrangement that allows that person or enterprise to exercise rights that are similar to those that it would hold if it possessed directly or indirectly more than 50% of the beneficial interests in the enterprise.

(2) The second part comprises of '*In any case, a person shall be considered to be closely related to an enterprise if one possesses directly or indirectly more than 50 per cent of the beneficial interest in the other (or, in the case of a company, more than 50 per cent of the aggregate vote and value of the company's shares or of the beneficial equity interest in the company) or if another person possesses directly or indirectly more than 50 per cent of the beneficial interest (or, in the case of a company, more than 50 per cent of the aggregate vote and value of the company's shares or of the beneficial equity interest in the company) in the person and the enterprise.*' The second part of the definition provides that the requirements of the definition of a person or enterprise closely related to an enterprise are automatically met in certain circumstances.

393. The concept 'a person closely related to an enterprise' is to be distinguished from the concept of 'AEs' which is used for the purposes of Article 9; although the two concepts overlap to a certain extent, they are not intended to be equivalent.[286]

Reservation under Paragraph 2

394. A jurisdiction may opt out of Article 15 entirely with respect to CTAs for which it has made reservations under Article 12(4), Article 13(6)(a) or (c), and Article 14(3)(a) of the MLI.

Notifications

395. Depending upon the position taken by various jurisdictions in terms of reservation made under this Article, they are required to make notification under paragraph 2 of Article 15 of the MLI.

Denmark's Position[287] under the MLI

396. No reservation has been made by Denmark under paragraph 2 of Article 15 of the MLI. The application of paragraph 1 of Article 15 of the MLI to some of Denmark's CTAs is provided hereunder:

286. Refer OECD MTC 2017, para. 119 of the Commentary on Art. 5(8).
287. Refer Denmark's Position under the MLI http://www.oecd.org/tax/treaties/beps-mli-position-denmark-instrument-deposit.pdf.

Denmark's Treaty Partner	*Position Taken by Treaty Partner*	*Outcome under the MLI*
Argentina, Australia, Belgium, Chile, Croatia, Egypt, India, Indonesia, Ireland, Israel, Italy, Jamaica, Kenya, Kuwait, Lithuania, Malaysia, Mexico, New Zealand, North Macedonia, Pakistan, Portugal, Romania, Russia, Serbia, the Slovak Republic, Slovenia, South Africa, Turkey, Ukraine, United Kingdom	- No notification under paragraph 2 of Article 15 concerning Denmark	Article 15(1) of MLI would apply to Denmark's CTA with these countries
Bulgaria, Canada, China, Cyprus, the Czech Republic, Estonia, Greece, Hungary, Korea, Latvia, Luxembourg, Malta, Morocco, Poland, Singapore	- Reservation under paragraph 2 of Article 15 concerning Denmark	Article 15(1) of MLI would not apply to Denmark's CTA with these countries

India's Position[288] under the MLI

397. No reservation has been made by India under paragraph 2 of Article 15 of the MLI. The application of paragraph 1 of Article 15 of the MLI to some of India's CTAs is provided hereunder:

India's Treaty Partner	*Position Taken by Treaty Partner*	*Outcome under the MLI*
Albania, Armenia, Australia, Belgium, Colombia, Croatia, Denmark, Egypt, Fiji, France, Indonesia, Ireland, Israel, Italy, Japan, Jordan, Kazakhstan, Kenya, Kuwait, Lithuania, Malaysia, Mexico, the Netherlands, New Zealand, Macedonia, Norway, Portugal, Romania, Russia, Saudi Arabia, Serbia, the Slovak Republic, Slovenia, South Africa, Spain, Turkey, Ukraine, UK, Uruguay	- No notification under paragraph 2 of Article 15 concerning India	Article 15(1) of MLI would apply to India's CTA with these countries
Austria, Bulgaria, Canada, Cyprus, the Czech Republic, Estonia, Finland, Georgia, Greece, Hungary, Iceland, Korea, Latvia, Luxembourg, Malta, Morocco, Poland, Qatar, Singapore, Sweden, the United Arab Emirates	- Reservation under paragraph 2 of Article 15 concerning India	Article 15(1) of MLI would not apply to India's CTA with these countries

288. Refer India's Position under the MLI http://www.oecd.org/tax/treaties/beps-mli-position-india-instrument-deposit.pdf.

The Netherlands' Position[289] under the MLI

398. No reservation has been made by the Netherlands under paragraph 2 of Article 15 of the MLI. The application of paragraph 1 of Article 15 of the MLI to some of the Netherlands' CTAs is provided hereunder:

The Netherlands' Treaty Partner	*Position Taken by Treaty Partner*	*Outcome under the MLI*
Albania, Argentina, Armenia, Australia, Bosnia & Herzegovina, Croatia, Egypt, France, India, Indonesia, Israel, Italy, Japan, Jordan, Kazakhstan, Kenya, Kuwait, Lithuania, Malaysia, Mexico, New Zealand, Nigeria, North Macedonia, Norway, Pakistan, Portugal, Romania, Russia, Saudi Arabia, Serbia, the Slovak Republic, Slovenia, South Africa, Turkey, United Kingdom	- No notification under paragraph 2 of Article 15 concerning the Netherlands	Article 15(1) of MLI would apply to the Netherlands' CTA with these countries
Austria, Bahrain, Barbados, Canada, China, the Czech Republic, Estonia, Finland, Georgia, Greece, Hong Kong, Hungary, Iceland, Korea, Latvia, Luxembourg, Malta, Morocco, Oman, Panama, Qatar, Singapore, Sweden, the United Arab Emirates	- Reservation under paragraph 2 of Article 15 concerning the Netherlands	Article 15(1) of MLI would not apply to the Netherlands' CTA with these countries

Few Snapshots of Positions[290] Taken by Other Countries under the MLI

399. As of now, certain jurisdictions have reserved the right for the entirety of Article 15 not to apply to their CTAs. A summary of reservations made by some of the jurisdictions under Article 12(4), Article 13(6)(a) or (c), Article 14(3)(a) and Article 15(2) of the MLI is provided hereunder:

Name of the Jurisdiction	*Reservation under Article 12(4)*	*Reservation under Article 13(6)(a)*	*Reservation under Article 13(6)(c)*	*Reservation under Article 14(3)(a)*	*Reservation under Article 15(2)*
Andorra	√	√		√	√
Austria	√		√	√	√
Bahrain	√	√		√	√
Barbados	√	√		√	√

289. Refer The Netherlands' Position under the MLI http://www.oecd.org/tax/treaties/beps-mli-position-netherlands-instrument-deposit.pdf.
290. Refer OECD – Signatories and Parties to the MLI http://www.oecd.org/tax/treaties/beps-mli-signatories-and-parties.pdf.

Name of the Jurisdiction	*Reservation under Article 12(4)*	*Reservation under Article 13(6)(a)*	*Reservation under Article 13(6)(c)*	*Reservation under Article 14(3)(a)*	*Reservation under Article 15(2)*
Belize	√	√		√	√
Bulgaria	√	√		√	√
Canada	√	√		√	√
China	√	√		√	√
Cyprus	√	√		√	√
The Czech Republic	√	√		√	√
Estonia	√	√		√	√
Finland	√	√		√	√
Georgia	√	√		√	√
Germany	√		√	√	√
Greece	√	√		√	√
Guernsey	√	√		√	√
Hong Kong	√	√		√	√
Hungary	√	√		√	√
Iceland	√	√		√	√
The Isle of Man	√	√		√	√
Jersey	√	√		√	√
Korea	√	√		√	√
Latvia	√	√		√	√
Liechtenstein	√	√		√	√
Luxembourg	√		√	√	√
Malta	√	√		√	√
Mauritius	√	√		√	√
Monaco	√	√		√	√
Morocco	√	√		√	√
Oman	√	√		√	√
Panama	√	√		√	√
Poland	√	√		√	√
Qatar	√	√		√	√
Seychelles	√	√		√	√
Singapore	√		√	√	√
Sweden	√	√		√	√
Switzerland	√	√		√	√
UAE	√	√		√	√

The notifications made by treaty partners under Article 15 of the MLI and impact/outcome thereof on the respective CTAs are provided in Figure 16.

Figure 16 Article 15: Definition of a Person Closely Related to an Enterprise – Flow-chart on Notifications & Their Impact

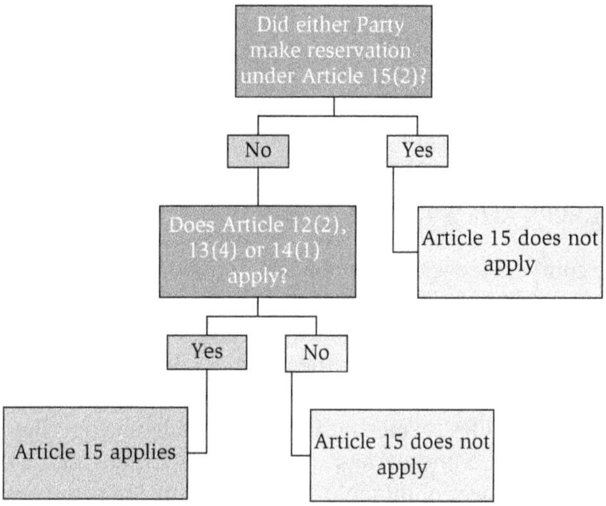

3.8 PART V OF MLI: IMPROVING DISPUTE RESOLUTION

3.8.1 Article 16 of MLI: Mutual Agreement Procedure

400. The interplay between Article 16 of MLI, corresponding BEPS Report and the resulting provisions incorporated in OECD MTC 2017 is represented in a table as below:

MLI		*BEPS Final Report*		*OECD MTC 2017*	
Article	*Title of Article*	*BEPS Action Plan*	*Title of BEPS Action Plan*	*Article*	*Title of Article*
16	Mutual Agreement Procedure	Action 14	Making Dispute Resolution Mechanisms More Effective	25(1)-(3)	Mutual Agreement Procedure

401. The article at a glance is as below:

Substantive (BEPS) Provisions under Para(s)	*Opt-In Provisions under Para*	*Alternative Provisions under Para*	*Compatibility Clause*		*Reservations under Para*	*Notifications under Para*
			Para	*Type*		
1-3	None	None	4	'in place of or in the absence of', 'in place of' and 'in the absence of'	5	5, 6

Raison d'etre of BEPS Action 14 Plan

402. During the course of developing the BEPS Action Plan, countries agreed that the introduction of measures being developed to address BEPS should not lead to unnecessary uncertainty for compliant taxpayers and to unintended double taxation. Improving dispute resolution mechanisms was, therefore, made an integral component of the work on BEPS issues, leading to development of the BEPS Action 14 Report. Article 25 of the OECD MTC provides a mechanism, independent from the ordinary legal remedies available under domestic law, through which the CAs of the Contracting States may resolve differences or difficulties regarding the interpretation or application of the CTA on a mutually agreed basis. This mechanism, called the MAP, is of fundamental importance to the proper application and interpretation of tax treaties, notably to ensure that taxpayers entitled to the benefits of the treaty are not subject to taxation by either of the Contracting States which is not in accordance with the terms of the treaty. The measures developed under BEPS Action 14 Report aim to strengthen the effectiveness and efficiency of the MAP process. They aim to minimise the risks of uncertainty and unintended double taxation by ensuring the consistent and proper implementation of tax treaties, including the effective and timely resolution of disputes regarding their interpretation or application through the MAP.

403. Through the adoption of BEPS Action 14 Report, countries have agreed to important changes in their approach to dispute resolution, in particular by having developed a minimum standard (complemented by a set of Best Practices) with respect to the resolution of treaty-related disputes, committed to its rapid implementation and agreed to ensure its effective implementation. The objective of the minimum standard is to ensure:

(a) that treaty obligations related to the MAP are fully implemented in good faith and that MAP cases are resolved in a timely manner;
(b) the implementation of administrative processes that promote the prevention and timely resolution of treaty-related disputes; and
(c) that taxpayers can access the MAP when eligible.

404. In addition to the commitment to implement the minimum standard by all countries adhering to the outcomes of the BEPS Project, the following countries have declared their commitment to provide for mandatory binding MAP arbitration[291] in their bilateral tax treaties as a mechanism to guarantee that treaty-related disputes will be resolved within a specified time frame: Australia, Austria, Belgium, Canada, France, Germany, Ireland, Italy, Japan, Luxembourg, the Netherlands, New Zealand, Norway, Poland, Slovenia, Spain, Sweden, Switzerland, UK, US.

Article 16 of the MLI

405. Element 1.1 of the Action 14 minimum standard requires jurisdictions to include Article 25(1) through (3) of the OECD MTC in their tax treaties, and subject to the variations in these paragraphs provided for under Elements 3.1 and 3.3 of the Action 14 minimum standard.

406. Article 16 of the MLI implements the minimum standards. It introduces changes to the MAP provisions, equivalent to Article 25(1) through (3) of the OECD Model (2014), as per the following:

(a) The possibility of presenting a MAP case before the CA of '*either*' of the Contracting States. A number of countries have made a reservation over MAP submission to '*either*' of the Contracting States and are of the view that it may be submitted by a resident or national to its CA only. Hence, the minimum standard in this regard can be implemented under Element 3.1 (BEPS Action 14 Report), through implementation of a bilateral notification or consultation process for cases in which the CA to which the MAP case was presented does not consider the taxpayer's objection to be justified.
(b) MAP case can be presented within three years from the first notification of the action resulting in taxation not in accordance with the provisions of the CTA.
(c) The CAs shall endeavour to arrive at a satisfactory solution by means of a MAP.
(d) If an agreement is reached under MAP, the CAs are required to implement it, notwithstanding any time limits existing in their respective domestic laws.
(e) The CAs are under obligation to endeavour to resolve, by means of a MAP, any doubts arising over the interpretation or application of the CTA.
(f) The CAs may also consult each other for the elimination of double taxation in cases not provided for in the CTA.

407. Although, BEPS Action 15 anticipated implementation of multilateral MAP, however, Article 16 of MLI on MAP provides for bilateral MAP only, as evident from the use of expressions in the first sentence of Article 16(1) stating '*present the case to the*

291. Action 14: BEPS 2015 Final Report, OECD/G20 Base Erosion and Profit Shifting Project (p. 10).

competent authority of either Contracting Jurisdiction'; expressions in the first sentence of Article 16(2) stating '*resolve the case by mutual agreement with the competent authority of the other Contracting Jurisdiction*'.

The co-relation of MAP provisions under paragraphs 1-3 of Article 16 of the MLI and paragraphs 1-3 of Article 25 of the OECD MTC is provided in Figure 17.

Figure 17 Article 16: MAP – Flowchart on Application of MLI Provisions Vis-à-Vis OECD MTC

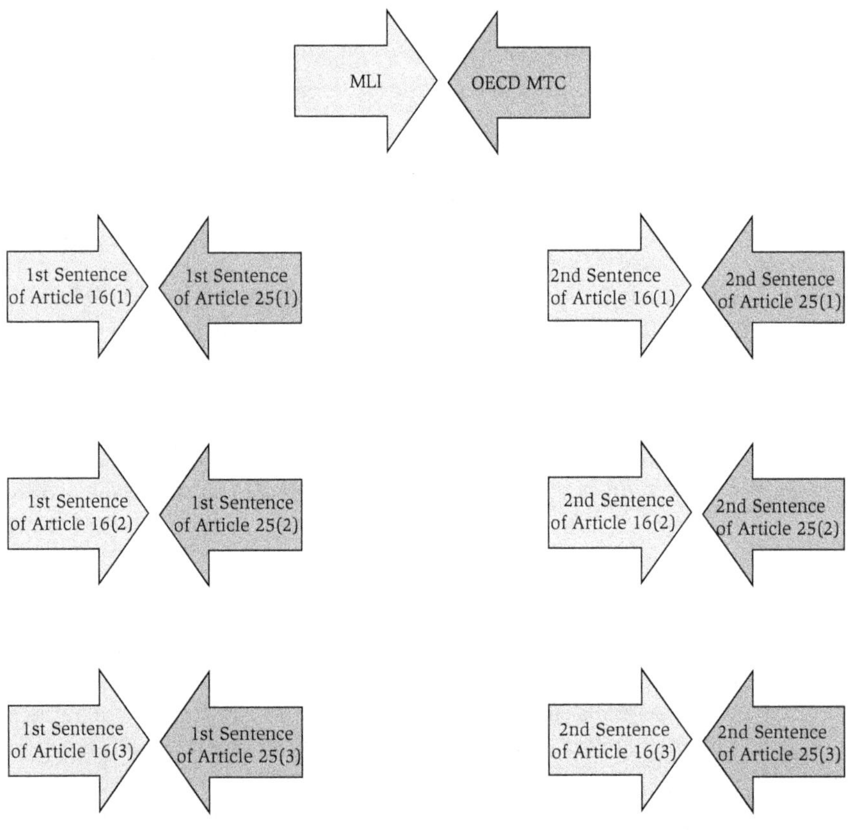

First Sentence of Paragraph 1 of Article 16 of MLI

408. The option provided to the taxpayer to present his case to the CA of *either* Contracting State is intended to reinforce the general principle that access to the MAP should be as widely available as possible and to provide flexibility. This option is also intended to ensure that the decision as to whether a case should proceed to the second stage of the MAP (i.e., be discussed by the CAs of both Contracting States) is open to consideration by both CAs. On the other hand, Contracting States may consider that taxpayers should not have the option of presenting their cases to the CA of either State, but should, in the first instance, be required to present their cases to the CA of the State of which they are resident. Also, where a person who is a national of one State, but a resident of the other, complains of having been subjected in that other State to taxation (or any requirement connected therewith) which is discriminatory under paragraph 1 of Article 24, he is allowed by way of exception to the alternative rule which obliges the taxpayer to present his case to the CA of his State of residence, to present his objection to the CA of the Contracting State of which he is a national. When jurisdictions do not adopt measures allowing taxpayers to have the option of presenting their cases to the CA of *either* State, the minimum standard in such situations can be implemented under Element 3.1 (BEPS Action 14 Report), through implementation of a bilateral notification or consultation process for cases in which the CA to which the MAP case was presented does not consider the taxpayer's objection to be justified.

409. With reference to Sentence 1 of Article 16(1) of the MLI, a number of countries, namely, Albania, Armenia, Austria, Bosnia and Herzegovina, Canada, Chile, China, Croatia, Curaçao, Germany, Hungary, India, Indonesia, Israel, Italy, Kenya, Latvia, Monaco, North Macedonia, Peru, Poland, Portugal, Romania, San Marino, Serbia, Singapore, the Slovak Republic, Slovenia, South Africa, Spain, have made reservation under Article 16(5)(a) in respect of all CTAs so as to allow MAP reference to be made to the CA of the jurisdiction where the applicant is resident (or national), rather than to *either* CA. A probable factor stimulating this decision could have been to prevent a situation where the CA of a jurisdiction becomes another appellate authority and adjudicates over the addition/adjustment to income made by an assessing authority in that very jurisdiction.

Second Sentence of Paragraph 1 of Article 16 of MLI

410. The time limit of three years set by the second sentence of paragraph 1 for presenting objections is intended to protect administrations against late objections. Contracting States may omit the second sentence of paragraph 1 if they concur that their respective domestic regulations apply automatically to such objections and are more favourable in their effects to the taxpayers affected, because they allow a longer time for presenting objections.

First Sentence of Paragraph 2 of Article 16 of MLI

411. The determination whether the objection *'appears … to be justified'* requires the CA to which the case was presented to make a preliminary assessment of the taxpayer's objection in order to determine whether the taxation in both Contracting States is consistent with the terms of the CTA. If the CA duly approached recognises that the MAP application is justified and considers that the taxation complained of is due wholly or in part to a measure taken in that State itself, it must give the MAP applicant satisfaction as speedily as possible by making such adjustments or allowing such reliefs as appear to be justified. In this situation, the issue can be resolved without moving beyond the first (unilateral) stage of the MAP. If, however, it appears to that CA that the taxation complained of is due wholly or in part to a measure taken in the other State, it will be incumbent on it, to set in motion the second (bilateral) stage of the MAP.

Second Sentence of Paragraph 2 of Article 16 of MLI

412. The purpose of the second sentence of paragraph 2 is to enable countries with time limits relating to adjustments of assessments and tax refunds in their domestic law to give effect to an agreement (under MAP) despite such time limits. Due to constitutional or other legal grounds, countries that cannot include the second sentence in their tax treaties should, as per Element 3.3 of BEPS Action 14 Report, be willing to accept alternative treaty provisions that limit the time during which a Contracting State may make an adjustment pursuant to Article 9(1) or Article 7(2), in order to avoid late adjustments with respect to which MAP relief will not be available.

First Sentence of Paragraph 3 of Article 16 of MLI

413. These provisions authorise the CAs to resolve, if possible, difficulties of interpretation or application by means of mutual agreement. These are essentially difficulties of a general nature which may concern a category of taxpayers, even if they have arisen in connection with an individual case normally coming under the procedure defined in paragraphs 1 and 2. Mutual agreements resolving general difficulties of interpretation or application are binding on administrations as long as the CAs do not agree to modify or rescind the mutual agreement.

Second Sentence of Paragraph 3 of Article 16 of MLI

414. The second sentence of paragraph 3 enables the CAs to deal with such cases of double taxation which do not come within the scope of the provisions of the CTA, for example, as in the case of a resident of a third State having PEs in both Contracting States. The second sentence of paragraph 3 allows the CAs of the Contracting States to consult with each other in order to eliminate double taxation that may occur with respect to dealings between the PEs. This could, for instance, be the case where one or both of the Contracting States have no bilateral tax convention with the third State. The second sentence of paragraph 3 does not, however, allow the Contracting States to eliminate double taxation where the provision of such relief would contravene their respective domestic laws or is not authorised by the provisions of other applicable tax treaties.

Compatibility Clauses

415. Paragraph 4(a)(i) provides that the first sentence of Article 16(1) of the MLI would replace provisions of a CTA that provide that where a person considers that the actions of one or both of the Contracting Jurisdictions result or will result for that person in taxation not in accordance with the provisions of the CTA, that person may, irrespective of the remedies provided by the domestic law of those Contracting Jurisdictions, present the case to the CA of the Contracting Jurisdiction of which that person is a resident, including provisions under which, if the case presented by that person comes under the article of the CTA relating to non-discrimination based on nationality, the case may be presented to the CA of the Contracting Jurisdiction of which that person is a national. Paragraph 4(a)(i) would also apply in the absence of such a provision in a tax treaty.[292]

416. Paragraph 4(a)(ii) provides that the second sentence of Article 16(1) of the MLI would replace provisions of a CTA that provide that the MAP case must be presented within a specific time period that is shorter than three years from the first notification of the action resulting in taxation not in accordance with the provisions of a CTA. This would preserve longer time periods provided in CTAs without necessitating a reservation not to apply to the second sentence of Article 25(1) to these CTAs. Paragraph 4(a)(ii) would also add the second sentence of Article 16(1) to CTAs in the absence of a provision describing a time period within which a case must be presented.[293]

417. The compatibility clause in paragraph (4)(a)(ii) is unique in itself, as it contains two different compatibility clauses, i.e. 'in place of' or 'in the absence of', which apply separately depending on the CTA provisions, which, in turn, will get impacted in not two but in three different ways. To explain this point, it would be pertinent at this juncture to state the provisions contained in Article 16(4)(a)(ii) of the MLI as below:

> ii) The second sentence of paragraph 1 shall apply *in place of* provisions of a Covered Tax Agreement that provide that a case referred to in the first sentence of paragraph 1 must be presented within a specific time period that is shorter than three years from the first notification of the action resulting in taxation not in accordance with the provisions of the Covered Tax Agreement, or *in the absence of* a provision of a Covered Tax Agreement describing the time period within which such a case must be presented.

The three different ways of impact on CTAs by the compatibility clause in paragraph (4)(a)(ii) are:

(1) '*In place of*' shall apply where the treaty provisions equivalent to the second sentence of paragraph 1 of Article 16 contain time period shorter than three years.
(2) '*In the absence of*' shall apply where the treaty provisions equivalent to the second sentence of paragraph 1 of Article 16 contain no time period, and hence, time period of three years shall get introduced.
(3) The impact of the said compatibility clause on the CTAs in the third possible way would be to preserve longer time periods (more than three years) provided in certain DTAAs, for example:
    - In the Netherlands' DTAC with Serbia, a period of five years is provided.
    - In India's DTAAs with Brazil and Turkey, a period of five years is provided.

292. Refer Explanatory Statement to the MLI, para. 196(i).
293. *Id.*, para. 196(ii).

- In US's DTACs with the Netherlands and Canada, a period of six years is provided.
- In US's DTACs with Portugal and Slovenia, a period of five years is provided.
- The Germany-US DTAC provides that the case must be presented within four years.

418. Paragraph 4(b)(i) provides that the first sentence of Article 16(2) of MLI would apply to CTAs that do not contain a provision that provides that the CA that is presented with the case by the person referred to in Article 16(1) shall endeavour, if the objection appears to it to be justified and if it is not itself able to arrive at a satisfactory solution, to resolve the case by mutual agreement with the CA of the other Contracting Jurisdiction, with a view to the avoidance of taxation which is not in accordance with the CTA.[294]

419. Paragraph 4(b)(ii) provides that the second sentence of Article 16(2) would apply to CTAs that do not contain a provision that provides that any agreement reached via the MAP shall be implemented notwithstanding any time limits in the domestic law of the Contracting Jurisdictions.[295]

420. Paragraph 4(c)(i) provides that the first sentence of Article 16(3) of MLI would apply to CTAs that do not contain a provision that provides that the CAs of the Contracting Jurisdictions shall endeavour to resolve by mutual agreement any difficulties or doubts arising as to the interpretation or application of the CTA.[296]

421. Paragraph 4(c)(ii) provides that the second sentence of Article 16(3) of MLI would apply to CTAs that do not contain a provision which provides that the CAs of the Contracting Jurisdictions may also consult together for the elimination of double taxation in cases not provided for in the tax treaty.[297]

Reservations under Paragraph 5

422. Paragraph 5 of Article 16 of MLI recognises that Parties are also permitted to implement Element 1.1 of the Action 14 minimum standard (requiring jurisdictions to include Article 25(1) through (3) of the OECD MTC in their tax treaties) through administrative measures, as provided under Elements 3.1 and 3.3 of the Action 14 minimum standard. Accordingly, the following reservations are provided for under paragraph 5:

(i) Under paragraph 5(a), Parties may opt out of the first sentence of paragraph 1 (presentation of MAP cases to the CA of either Contracting State) entirely for all CTAs and meet Element 3.1 of the Action 14 minimum standard through the

294. *Id.*, para. 197(i).
295. *Id.*, para. 197(ii).
296. *Id.*, para. 198(i).
297. *Id.*, para. 198(ii).

implementation of a bilateral notification or consultation process. Accordingly, reservation under Article 16(5)(a) allows a Party to opt out of applying the first sentence of Article 16(1), and thus not modify its CTA to allow the taxpayer to present a case to the CA of '*either*' Contracting Jurisdiction. Such a reservation is allowed only on the basis that for the purposes of each of its CTAs, the taxpayer may present its case to the CA of the Contracting Jurisdiction of which it is a resident (or a national in cases involving the non-discrimination provision based on nationality) and that Contracting Jurisdiction will implement a bilateral notification or consultation process with the CA of the other Contracting Jurisdiction for cases presented by the taxpayers to its CA in which its CA does not consider the taxpayer's objection to be justified (with the understanding that such notification or consultation should not be interpreted as consultation as to how to resolve the case). Such an approach is allowed under Element 3.1 of the Action 14 minimum standard.[298]

(ii) Under paragraph 5(b), Parties may opt out of the second sentence of paragraph 1 (presentation of MAP cases within three years) entirely for all CTAs and meet Element 1.1 of the Action 14 minimum standard through other means that ensure taxpayers are allowed to present MAP cases within a period of at least three years. Recognising that Contracting Jurisdictions are left free to agree in their tax treaties to omit the second sentence of Article 25(1) of the OECD MTC if their respective domestic regulations apply automatically and are more favourable in their effects to the taxpayer, either because they allow a longer time for presenting objections or because they do not set any time limits for such purpose, Article 16(5)(b) allows a Party to reserve on the application of the second sentence of Article 16(1) in instances where its tax treaty does not contain a provision stipulating the time period for the taxpayer to present the case for CA discussion under the MAP. A Party may make such a reservation only if it intends to ensure that even in the absence of such a provision, a taxpayer would be permitted to present its case within a period of at least three years from the first notification of the action resulting in taxation not in accordance with the provisions of the CTA. It is anticipated, therefore, that this reservation would only be made by a Contracting Jurisdiction to a CTA if its domestic regulations apply automatically and are more favourable in their effects to the taxpayer, either because they allow a longer time for presenting objections or because they do not set any time limits for such purpose.[299]

(iii) Under paragraph 5(c), Parties may opt out of the second sentence of paragraph 2 (agreements reached through the MAP are implemented notwithstanding any time limits in domestic law) for all CTAs and meet Element 3.3 of the Action 14 minimum standard through other means or through bilateral treaty negotiations. Such a reservation is allowed only on the basis that for the purposes of all of its CTAs, either: (i) all agreements reached via MAP shall be implemented notwithstanding any time limits in the domestic law of the

298. Refer Explanatory Statement to the MLI, para. 200.
299. *Id.*, para. 201.

Contracting Jurisdictions; or (ii) it intends to meet the minimum standard by accepting, in its bilateral treaty negotiations, alternative treaty provisions that limit the time during which a Contracting Jurisdiction may make an adjustment pursuant to provisions modelled after Article 9(1) or Article 7(2) of the OECD MTC, in order to avoid late adjustments with respect to which MAP relief will not be available. Such an approach is allowed under Element 3.3 of the Action 14 minimum standard.[300]

Notifications

423. Depending upon the position taken by various jurisdictions, the following notifications are required to be made under Article 16 of the MLI:

(i) Jurisdictions intending to make reservations under paragraph 5 are required to make notifications, as the case may be.

(ii) Under paragraph 6(a), each Party (other than a Party that has reserved the right not to apply the first sentence of paragraph 1) is required to notify the Depositary of whether each of its CTAs contains an existing provision that provides that a taxpayer may present its case to the CA of the Contracting Jurisdiction of which that person is a resident (or a national, if the issue involves non-discrimination based on nationality), and if so, the article and paragraph number of each such provision. When all Contracting Jurisdictions to a CTA have made a notification with respect to a provision of a CTA, the first sentence of paragraph 1 of Article 16 of MLI replaces that provision. In other cases (except where one of the Contracting States has reserved the right not to apply the first sentence of paragraph 1), the first sentence of paragraph 1 shall apply to the CTA, but shall supersede the existing provision of the CTA only to the extent that those provisions are incompatible with that sentence.

(iii) Paragraph 6(b)(i) requires each Party that has not reserved the right not to apply the second sentence of paragraph 1 to notify the Depositary of the list of its CTAs which provide that a case referred to in the first sentence of Article 16(1) must be presented within a specific time period that is shorter than three years from the first notification of the action resulting in taxation not in accordance with the provisions of the CTA, as well as the article and paragraph number of each such provision. Paragraph 6(b)(ii) requires each Party that has not reserved the right not to apply the second sentence of paragraph 1 to notify the Depositary of the list of its CTAs (as well as the article and paragraph number of each such provision) which include a provision that provides that a case referred to in the first sentence of Article 16(1) must be presented within a specific time period that is at least three years from the first notification of the action resulting in taxation not in accordance with the provisions of the CTA. The combined effect of paragraphs 6(b)(i) and 6(b)(ii) is that the second sentence of paragraph 1 will apply to a CTA if either:

300. *Id.*, para. 202.

- all Contracting Jurisdictions to a CTA make such a notification that the CTA provides for a time period shorter than three years; or
- no Contracting Jurisdiction to a CTA makes such a notification that the CTA provides for a time period of at least three years.

In all other cases, the second sentence of paragraph 1 shall apply to the CTA, but shall supersede the existing provisions of the CTA only to the extent that those provisions are incompatible with the second sentence of paragraph 1.

(iv) Paragraph 6(c)(i) requires each Party to notify the Depositary of the list of its CTAs which do not contain provisions that provide that the CA that is presented with the case by the person referred to in paragraph 1 shall endeavour, if the objection appears to it to be justified and if it is not itself able to arrive at a satisfactory solution, to resolve the case by mutual agreement with the CA of the other Contracting Jurisdiction, with a view to the avoidance of taxation which is not in accordance with the CTA. The first sentence of paragraph 2 shall apply to a CTA only where all Contracting Jurisdictions to a CTA have made such a notification.

(v) Paragraph 6(c)(ii) provides that each Party (other than a Party that has reserved the right not to apply the second sentence of paragraph 2) shall notify the Depositary of the list of its CTAs which do not contain provisions that require any agreement reached to be implemented notwithstanding any time limits in the domestic law of the Contracting Jurisdictions. The second sentence of paragraph 2 shall apply to a CTA only where all Contracting Jurisdictions to a CTA have made such a notification.

(vi) Paragraph 6(d)(i) requires each Party to notify the Depositary of the list of its CTAs which do not contain provisions that require the CAs of the Contracting Jurisdictions to endeavour to resolve by mutual agreement any difficulties or doubts arising as to the interpretation or application of the CTA. The first sentence of paragraph 3 shall apply to a CTA only where all Contracting Jurisdictions to a CTA have made such a notification.

(vii) Paragraph 6(d)(ii) requires each Party to notify the Depositary of the list of its CTAs which do not contain provisions that provide that the CAs may also consult together for the elimination of double taxation in cases not provided for in the CTA. The second sentence of paragraph 3 shall apply to a CTA only where all Contracting Jurisdictions to a CTA have made such a notification.

Denmark's Position[301] under the MLI

424. The following notifications have been made by Denmark under Article 16 of the MLI:

301. Refer Denmark's Position under the MLI http://www.oecd.org/tax/treaties/beps-mli-position-denmark-instrument-deposit.pdf.

(a) With reference to sentence 1 of paragraph 1 of Article 16 of MLI, Denmark has not made a reservation under Article 16(5)(a) and has notified all its 64 CTAs so as to provide that MAP reference to be made to 'either' CA.

(b) Under Article 16(6)(b)(i) of the MLI, Denmark has notified two treaties where invocation period for MAP is less than three years, namely Belgium, Italy (with reference to the second sentence of Article 16(1) of MLI). As a result of this notification, a period of three years for invoking MAP shall get introduced in these CTAs through the MLI.

(c) Under Article 16(6)(b)(ii) of the MLI, Denmark has notified those treaties where invocation period for MAP is at least three years (with reference to the second sentence of Article 16(1) of MLI). Notably, the following treaties have not been notified under this provision:

    (i) Belgium, Italy - period is less than three years (already notified/covered under Article 16(6)(b)(i) of MLI).

    (ii) Brazil, Canada, Korea, Malaysia, Mexico, Trinidad and Tobago, UK, US, Zambia - no period is mentioned in these CTAs.

    As a result of this notification, the following effect shall be made by MLI on Denmark's CTAs:

    (i) The CTAs notified under Article 16(6)(b)(ii) shall not be impacted by the MLI (as they already have a period of at least three years).

    (ii) In Denmark's CTAs with Brazil, Canada, Korea, Malaysia, Mexico, Trinidad and Tobago, UK, US and Zambia, a period of three years for invoking MAP shall get introduced through the MLI.

(d) Under Article 16(6)(c)(i) of the MLI, Denmark has notified the treaty which does not contain provision corresponding to the first sentence of Article 16(2) of the MLI, namely Mexico. As a result of this notification, provision corresponding to the first sentence of Article 16(2) shall get introduced in this CTA through the MLI only when matching notification is made by the treaty partner.

(e) Under Article 16(6)(c)(ii) of the MLI, Denmark has notified those treaties which do not contain provision corresponding to the second sentence of Article 16(2) of MLI, namely Argentina, Belgium, Brazil, Bulgaria, Canada, Chile, Greece, Kenya, Korea, Malaysia, Mexico, Montenegro, Morocco, New Zealand, Pakistan, Romania, the Slovak Republic, Sri Lanka, Thailand, Trinidad and Tobago, UK and Zambia. As a result of this notification, provision corresponding to the second sentence of Article 16(2) shall get introduced in these CTAs through the MLI (subject to matching notifications).

(f) Under Article 16(6)(d)(i) of the MLI, Denmark has notified those treaties which do not contain provision corresponding to the first sentence of Article 16(3) of MLI, namely Australia, Belgium and Vietnam. As a result of this notification, provision corresponding to the first sentence of Article 16(3) shall get introduced in these CTAs through the MLI only when similar notification is made by the treaty partners.

(g) Under Article 16(6)(d)(ii) of the MLI, Denmark has notified those treaties which do not contain provision corresponding to the second sentence of Article 16(3) of MLI, namely Australia, Belgium, Chile, Indonesia, Italy, Malaysia, Ukraine and UK. As a result of this notification, provision corresponding to the second sentence of Article 16(3) shall get introduced in these CTAs through the MLI only when a similar notification is made by the treaty partners.

425. The application of Article 16 of the MLI to some of Denmark's CTAs is provided hereunder:

Jurisdiction	*Position Taken*	*Treaty Partner*	*Position Taken*	*Outcome under the MLI*
Denmark	- Notification of existing provisions - Article 16(1), 1st sentence - Denmark has notified under Article 16(6)(b)(ii) relevant provisions of CTA with Argentina - Denmark has notified under Article 16(6)(c)(ii) CTA with Argentina	Argentina	- Notification of existing provisions – Article 16(1), 1st sentence - Argentina has notified under Article 16(6)(b)(ii) relevant provisions of CTA with Denmark - Argentina has notified under Article 16(6)(c)(ii) CTA with Denmark	No provision of Article 16 of MLI would apply to Denmark-Argentina CTA except: - 1st sentence of Article 16(1) - 2nd sentence of Article 16(2)
Denmark	- Notification of existing provisions - Article 16(1), 1st sentence - Denmark has notified under Article 16(6)(b)(i) relevant provisions of CTA with Belgium	Belgium	- Notification of existing provisions – Article 16(1), 1st sentence - Belgium has notified under Article 16(6)(b)(i) relevant provisions of CTA with Denmark	All provisions of Article 16 of MLI would apply to Denmark-Belgium CTA except: - 1st sentence of Article 16(2)

Jurisdiction	*Position Taken*	*Treaty Partner*	*Position Taken*	*Outcome under the MLI*
	- Denmark has not notified under Article 16(6)(c)(i) CTA with Belgium - Denmark has notified under Article 16(6)(c)(ii) CTA with Belgium - Denmark has notified under Article 16(6)(d)(i) CTA with Belgium - Denmark has notified under Article 16(6)(d)(ii) CTA with Belgium		- Belgium has notified under Article 16(6)(c)(i) CTA with Denmark - Belgium has notified under Article 16(6)(c)(ii) CTA with Denmark - Belgium has notified under Article 16(6)(d)(i) CTA with Denmark - Belgium has notified under Article 16(6)(d)(ii) CTA with Denmark	
Denmark	- Notification of existing provisions - Article 16(1), 1st sentence - Denmark has notified under Article 16(6)(b)(ii) relevant provisions of CTA with New Zealand - Denmark has notified under Article 16(6)(c)(ii) CTA with New Zealand	New Zealand	- Notification of existing provisions – Article 16(1), 1st sentence - New Zealand has notified under Article 16(6)(b)(ii) relevant provisions of CTA with Denmark - New Zealand has notified under Article 16(6)(c)(ii) CTA with Denmark	No provision of Article 16 of MLI would apply to Denmark-New Zealand CTA except: - 1st sentence of Article 16(1) - 2nd sentence of Article 16(2)

Jurisdiction	*Position Taken*	*Treaty Partner*	*Position Taken*	*Outcome under the MLI*
Denmark	- Notification of existing provisions - Article 16(1), 1st sentence - Denmark has notified under Article 16(6)(b)(ii) relevant provisions of CTA with Romania - Denmark has notified under Article 16(6)(c)(ii) CTA with Romania	Romania	- Romania has made reservation under Article 16(5)(a) - Romania has notified under Article 16(6)(b)(ii) relevant provisions of CTA with Denmark - Romania has notified under Article 16(6)(c)(ii) CTA with Denmark	No provision of Article 16 of MLI would apply to Denmark-Romania CTA except: - 2nd sentence of Article 16(2)

India's Position[302] under the MLI

426. The following notifications have been made by India under Article 16 of the MLI:

(a) With reference to sentence 1 of paragraph 1 of Article 16 of MLI, India has made a reservation under Article 16(5)(a) in respect of all CTAs so as to provide that MAP reference to be made to CA of the 'resident' or 'national', rather than to 'either' CA.

(b) Under Article 16(6)(b)(i) of MLI, India has notified four treaties where invocation period for MAP is less than three years, namely Belgium, Canada, Italy and UAE (with reference to the second sentence of Article 16(1) of MLI). As a result of this notification, a period of three years for invoking MAP shall get introduced in these CTAs through the MLI.

(c) Under Article 16(6)(b)(ii) of MLI, India has notified those treaties where invocation period for MAP is at least three years (with reference to the second sentence of Article 16(1) of MLI). Notably, the following treaties have not been notified under this provision:

   (i) Belgium, Canada, Italy, UAE – period is less than three years (already notified/covered under Article 16(6)(b)(i) of MLI).

   (ii) Egypt, Greece, Libya, UK – no period is mentioned in these CTAs.

   As a result of this notification, the following effect shall be made by MLI on India's CTAs:

   (i) The CTAs notified under Article 16(6)(b)(ii) shall not be impacted by the MLI (as they already have a period of at least three years, which

302. Refer India's Position under the MLI http://www.oecd.org/tax/treaties/beps-mli-position-india-instrument-deposit.pdf.

includes CTAs with Brazil and Turkey, where period longer than three years, i.e., five years is provided and this period of five years, therefore, shall be retained in India's CTAs with Brazil and Turkey).

(ii) In India's CTAs with Egypt, Greece, Libya, UK a period of three years for invoking MAP shall get introduced through the MLI.

(d) Under Article 16(6)(c)(i) of MLI, India has notified those treaties which do not contain provision corresponding to the first sentence of Article 16(2) of the MLI, namely Greece and Mexico. As a result of this notification, provision corresponding to the first sentence of Article 16(2) shall get introduced in these CTAs through the MLI only when a similar notification is made by the treaty partners.

(e) Under Article 16(6)(c)(ii) of MLI, India has notified those treaties which do not contain provision corresponding to the second sentence of Article 16(2) of MLI, namely Canada, Egypt, Greece, Italy, Libya, Mexico, the Philippines, Swiss Confederation, Turkey and UK. As a result of this notification, provision corresponding to the second sentence of Article 16(2) shall get introduced in these CTAs through the MLI (subject to matching notifications).

(f) Under Article 16(6)(d)(i) of MLI, India has notified those treaties which do not contain provision corresponding to the first sentence of Article 16(3) of MLI, namely Australia and Greece. As a result of this notification, provision corresponding to the first sentence of Article 16(3) shall get introduced in these CTAs through the MLI only when a similar notification is made by the treaty partners.

(g) Under Article 16(6)(d)(ii) of MLI, India has notified those treaties which do not contain provision corresponding to the second sentence of Article 16(3) of MLI, namely Australia, Belgium, Greece, the Philippines, Ukraine and UK. As a result of this notification, provision corresponding to the second sentence of Article 16(3) shall get introduced in these CTAs through the MLI only when a similar notification is made by the treaty partners.

427. The application of Article 16 of the MLI to some of India's CTAs is provided hereunder:

Jurisdiction	*Position Taken*	*Treaty Partner*	*Position Taken*	*Outcome under the MLI*
India	- India has made reservation under Article 16(5)(a) - India has notified under Article 16(6)(b)(ii) relevant provisions of CTA with Albania	Albania	- Similar notification under Article 16(5)(a) and Article 16(6)(b)(ii)	- Article 16 would not apply
India	- India has made reservation under Article 16(5)(a) - India has notified under Article 16(6)(b)(ii), 16(6)(d)(i) & 16(6)(d)(ii) CTA with Australia	Australia	- Relevant provisions of CTA with India notified under Article 16(6)(a) - Australia has notified under Article 16(6)(b)(ii), 16(6)(d)(i) & 16(6)(d)(ii) CTA with India	No provision of Article 16 of MLI would apply to India-Australia CTA except: - 1st sentence of Article 16(3) - 2nd sentence of Article 16(3)
India	- India has made reservation under Article 16(5)(a) - India has notified under Article 16(6)(b)(i) & 16(6)(c)(ii) CTA with Canada	Canada	- Canada has made reservation under Article 16(5)(a), (c)* - Canada has notified under Article 16(6)(b)(i) relevant provisions of CTA with India	No provision of Article 16 of MLI would apply to India-Canada CTA except: - 2nd sentence of Article 16(1)
India	- India has made reservation under Article 16(5)(a) - India has notified under Article 16(6)(c)(ii) & 16(6)(d)(ii) CTA with UK	UK	- Relevant provisions of CTA with India notified under Article 16(6)(a) - UK has notified under Article 16(6)(c)(ii) & 16(6)(d)(ii) CTA with India	No provision of Article 16 of MLI would apply to India-UK CTA except: - 2nd sentence of Article 16(1) - 2nd sentence of Article 16(2) - 2nd sentence of Article 16(3)

* On making reservation under Article 16(5)(c), Canada has taken the position to achieve the minimum standard on inclusion of the second sentence of Article 16(2) of MLI through alternative provided in Element 3.3 of Action 14 minimum standard by limiting time limit of making adjustment under Article 9(1) or Article 7(2) of the India-Canada CTA. Presently, in India-Canada CTA,[303] while there is time limit of five years provided in Article 9(3) to limit time of adjustment in Article 9(1), however, there is no such time limit for adjustment under Article 7(2). This may need bilateral amendment in India-Canada DTAA to achieve the minimum standard.

The Netherlands' Position[304] under the MLI

428. The following notifications have been made by the Netherlands under Article 16 of the MLI:

(a) With reference to sentence 1 of paragraph 1 of Article 16 of MLI, the Netherlands has not made a reservation under Article 16(5)(a) and has notified all its 81 CTAs so as to provide that MAP reference to be made to 'either' CA.

(b) Under Article 16(6)(b)(i) of the MLI, the Netherlands has notified treaties where invocation period for MAP is less than three years, namely Canada, Italy, Malaysia, the Philippines, Qatar, Venezuela (with reference to the second sentence of Article 16(1) of MLI). As a result of this notification, a period of three years for invoking MAP shall get introduced in these CTAs through the MLI.

(c) Under Article 16(6)(b)(ii) of the MLI, the Netherlands has notified those treaties where invocation period for MAP is at least three years (with reference to the second sentence of Article 16(1) of MLI). Notably, the following treaties have not been notified under this provision:
   (i) Canada, Italy, Malaysia, the Philippines, Qatar, Venezuela – period is less than three years (already notified/covered under Article 16(6)(b)(i) of MLI).
   (ii) Austria, the Czech Republic, Israel, Korea, Luxembourg, Morocco, Singapore, the Slovak Republic, Suriname, Thailand, Turkey, US – no period is mentioned in these CTAs.

   As a result of this notification, the following effect shall be made by MLI on the Netherlands' CTAs:
   (i) The CTAs notified under Article 16(6)(b)(ii) shall not be impacted by the MLI (as they already have a period of at least three years).
   (ii) In the Netherlands' CTAs with Austria, the Czech Republic, Israel, Korea, Luxembourg, Morocco, Singapore, the Slovak Republic, Suriname, Thailand, Turkey, US, a period of three years for invoking MAP shall get introduced through the MLI.

303. Refer India-Canada Synthesised Text https://research.ibfd.org/#/doc?url=/data/treaty/docs/html/tt_ca-in_02_eng_1996_tt__td2.html#tt_ca-in_02_eng_1996_tt__td2_a9.
304. Refer The Netherlands' Position under the MLI http://www.oecd.org/tax/treaties/beps-mli-position-netherlands-instrument-deposit.pdf.

(d) Under Article 16(6)(c)(ii) of the MLI, the Netherlands has notified those treaties which do not contain provision corresponding to the second sentence of Article 16(2) of MLI, namely Austria, Bosnia and Herzegovina, Canada, the Czech Republic, Indonesia, Israel, Italy, Korea, Luxembourg, Malaysia, Mexico, Montenegro, Morocco, Nigeria, the Philippines, Serbia, Singapore, the Slovak Republic, Suriname, Tajikistan, Thailand, UK. As a result of this notification, provision corresponding to the second sentence of Article 16(2) shall get introduced in these CTAs through the MLI (subject to matching notifications).

(e) Under Article 16(6)(d)(i) of the MLI, the Netherlands has notified those treaties which do not contain provision corresponding to the first sentence of Article 16(3) of MLI, namely Australia, France and Vietnam. As a result of this notification, provision corresponding to the first sentence of Article 16(3) shall get introduced in these CTAs through the MLI only when a similar notification is made by the treaty partners.

(f) Under Article 16(6)(d)(ii) of the MLI, the Netherlands has notified those treaties which do not contain provision corresponding to the second sentence of Article 16(3) of MLI, namely Australia, Italy, Mexico and Nigeria. As a result of this notification, provision corresponding to the second sentence of Article 16(3) shall get introduced in these CTAs through the MLI only when a similar notification is made by the treaty partners.

429. The application of Article 16 of the MLI to some of the Netherlands' CTAs is provided hereunder:

Jurisdiction	*Position Taken*	*Treaty Partner*	*Position Taken*	*Outcome under the MLI*
The Netherlands	- Notification of existing provisions - Article 16(1), 1st sentence - The Netherlands has not notified Israel under Article 16(6)(b)(ii) - The Netherlands has notified under Article 16(6)(c)(ii) CTA with Israel	Israel	- Israel has made reservation under Article 16(5)(a) - Israel has not notified the Netherlands under Article 16(6)(b)(ii) - Israel has notified under Article 16(6)(c)(ii) CTA with the Netherlands	No provision of Article 16 of MLI would apply to the Netherlands-Israel CTA except: - 2nd sentence of Article 16(1) - 2nd sentence of Article 16(2)

Jurisdiction	*Position Taken*	*Treaty Partner*	*Position Taken*	*Outcome under the MLI*
The Netherlands	- Notification of existing provisions - Article 16(1), 1st sentence - The Netherlands has not notified Korea under Article 16(6)(b)(ii) - The Netherlands has notified under Article 16(6)(c)(ii) CTA with Korea	Korea	- Notification of existing provisions - Article 16(1), 1st sentence - Korea has not notified the Netherlands under Article 16(6)(b)(ii) - Korea has notified under Article 16(6)(c)(ii) CTA with the Netherlands	No provision of Article 16 of MLI would apply to the Netherlands-Korea CTA except: - 1st sentence of Article 16(1) - 2nd sentence of Article 16(1) - 2nd sentence of Article 16(2)
The Netherlands	- Notification of existing provisions - Article 16(1), 1st sentence - The Netherlands has not notified Morocco under Article 16(6)(b)(ii) - The Netherlands has notified under Article 16(6)(c)(ii) CTA with Morocco	Morocco	- Notification of existing provisions - Article 16(1), 1st sentence - Morocco has not notified the Netherlands under Article 16(6)(b)(ii) - Morocco has notified under Article 16(6)(c)(ii) CTA with the Netherlands	No provision of Article 16 of MLI would apply to the Netherlands-Morocco CTA except: - 1st sentence of Article 16(1) - 2nd sentence of Article 16(1) - 2nd sentence of Article 16(2)

Jurisdiction	*Position Taken*	*Treaty Partner*	*Position Taken*	*Outcome under the MLI*
The Netherlands	- Notification of existing provisions - Article 16(1), 1st sentence - The Netherlands has notified under Article 16(6)(c)(ii) CTA with Nigeria - The Netherlands has notified under Article 16(6)(d)(ii) CTA with Nigeria	Nigeria	- Notification of existing provisions - Article 16(1), 1st sentence - Nigeria has notified under Article 16(6)(c)(ii) CTA with the Netherlands - Nigeria has notified under Article 16(6)(d)(ii) CTA with the Netherlands	No provision of Article 16 of MLI would apply to the Netherlands-Nigeria CTA except: - 1st sentence of Article 16(1) - 2nd sentence of Article 16(2) - 2nd sentence of Article 16(3)

Few Snapshots of Positions[305] Taken by Other Countries under the MLI

430. Jurisdictions that have made reservation under Article 16(5)(a) of the MLI are, namely, Albania, Armenia, Austria, Bosnia and Herzegovina, Canada, Chile, China, Croatia, Curaçao, Germany, Hungary, India, Indonesia, Israel, Italy, Kenya, Latvia, Monaco, North Macedonia, Peru, Poland, Portugal, Romania, San Marino, Serbia, Singapore, the Slovak Republic, Slovenia, South Africa, Spain.

431. No jurisdiction has made any reservation under Article 16(5)(b) of the MLI as on date.

432. Monaco and Senegal have made reservation under Article 16(5)(c)(i) of the MLI.

433. Canada, Chile, Mexico, Monaco, Senegal and Switzerland have made reservation under Article 16(5)(c)(ii) of the MLI.

The various notifications made by treaty partners under Article 16 of the MLI and impact/outcome thereof on the respective CTAs are provided in Figure 18.

305. Refer OECD – Signatories and Parties to the MLI http://www.oecd.org/tax/treaties/beps-mli-signatories-and-parties.pdf.

Figure 18 Article 16: MAP – Flowchart on Notifications & Their Impact

1st Sentence of Article 16(1)

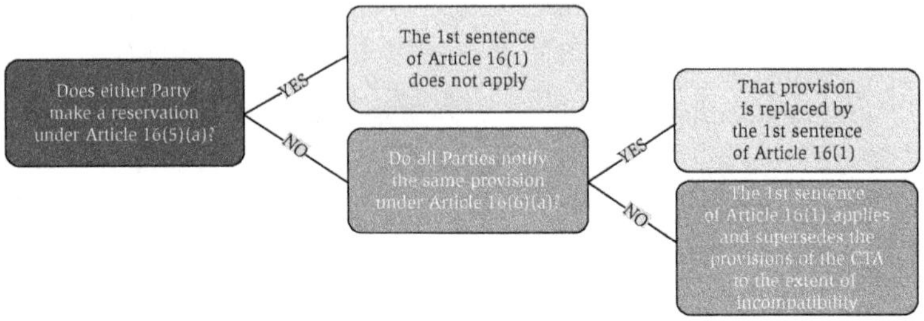

2nd Sentence of Article 16(1)

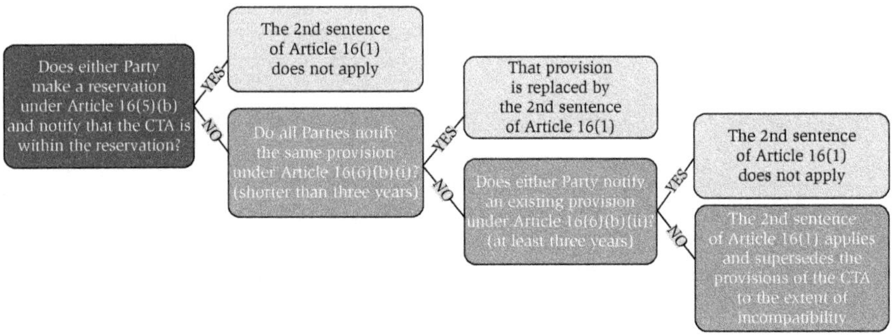

Article 16(2)

1st sentence:

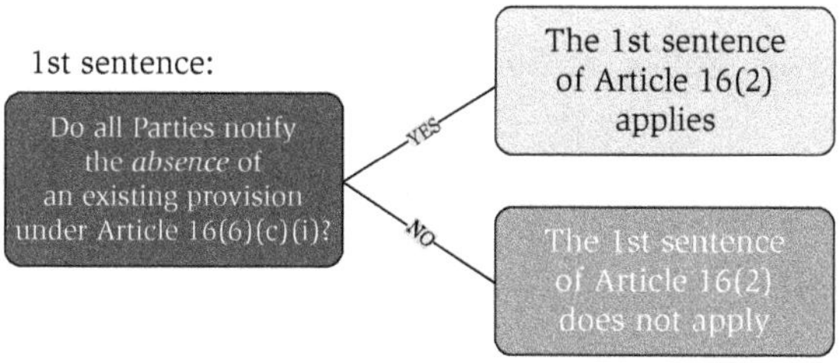

2nd sentence:

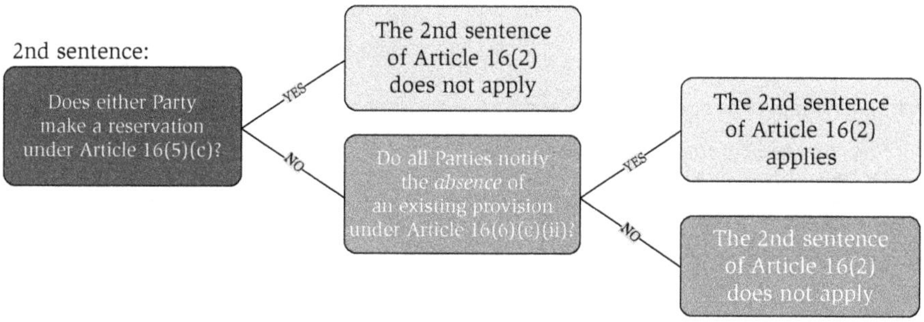

Article 16(3)

1st sentence:

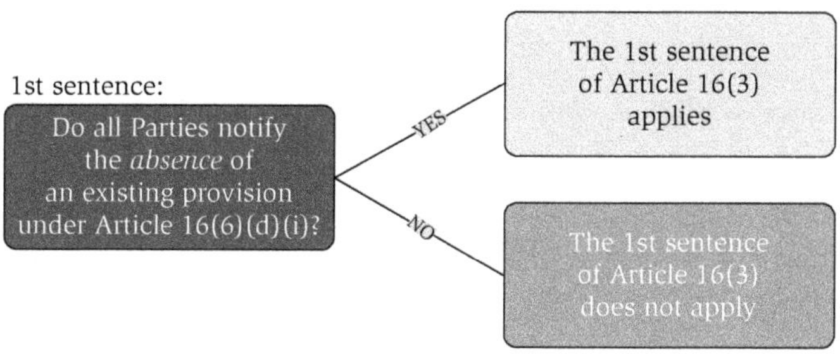

2nd sentence:

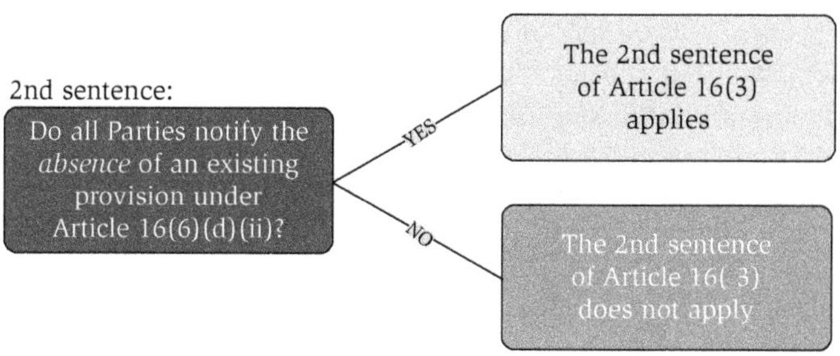

Source: OECD – Toolkit for Application of the Multilateral Instrument for BEPS Tax Treaty Related Measures https://www.oecd.org/tax/treaties/application-toolkit-multilateral-instrument-for-beps-tax-treaty-measures.htm.

3.8.2 Article 17 of MLI: Corresponding Adjustments

434. The interplay between Article 17 of MLI, corresponding BEPS Report and the resulting provisions incorporated in OECD MTC 2017 is represented in a table as below:

MLI		*BEPS Final Report*		*OECD MTC 2017*	
Article	*Title of Article*	*BEPS Action Plan*	*Title of BEPS Action Plan*	*Article*	*Title of Article*
17	Corresponding Adjustments	Action 14	Making Dispute Resolution Mechanisms More Effective	9(2)	Associated Enterprises

435. The article at a glance is as below:

Substantive (BEPS) Provisions under Para(s)	*Opt-In Provisions under Para*	*Alternative Provisions under Para*	*Compatibility Clause*		*Reservations under Para*	*Notifications under Para*
			Para	*Type*		
1	None	None	2	'in place of or in the absence of'	3	3, 4

Recommendation of BEPS Action 14 Report

436. One of the objectives of the minimum standard under BEPS Action 14 Report is for countries to ensure that treaty obligations related to the MAP are fully implemented in good faith and that MAP cases are resolved in a timely manner. In this light, Best Practice 1 under BEPS Action 14 Report provides that countries should include paragraph 2 of Article 9 in their tax treaties.

437. Most countries consider that the economic double taxation resulting from the inclusion of profits of AEs under paragraph 1 of Article 9 is not in accordance with the object and purpose of tax treaties and falls within the scope of the MAP under Article 25. On the other hand, some countries take the position that in the absence of a treaty provision based on paragraph 2 of Article 9, they are not obliged to make corresponding adjustments or to grant access to the MAP with respect to the economic double taxation that may otherwise result from a primary TP adjustment. Such a position frustrates a primary objective of tax treaties – the elimination of double taxation – and prevents bilateral consultation to determine appropriate TP adjustments. Element 1.1 of the minimum standard ensures that access to MAP is provided for in such TP cases.

However, it would be more efficient if countries would also have the possibility to provide for corresponding adjustments unilaterally in cases in which they find the objection of the taxpayer to be justified. BEPS Action 14 Report recommends as a Best Practice that countries should include paragraph 2 of Article 9 in their tax treaties. Article 17 of the MLI provides a mechanism for Parties to implement this Best Practice.

Article 17 of the MLI

438. Article 17 of the MLI introduces the corresponding adjustment provisions in the accounts of an enterprise resident in a State, as a result of TP adjustments in the accounts of an AE of that enterprise in the other State, under provisions akin to Article 9(2) of the OECD MTC. Thus, paragraph 1 of Article 17 of the MLI improves dispute resolution by ensuring treaty partners make corresponding adjustments in TP cases or grant access to the MAP with respect to TP cases. It has been clarified by the OECD through its FAQs[306] on MLI that despite certain CTAs not having Article 9(1) of the OECD MTC and UN MTC, an equivalent to Article 9(1) would not need to be added in order for Article 17 of MLI to function properly, as Article 9(1) is merely a confirmation of a right that would exist with or without that provision and that Article 17(1) of MLI can function as a stand-alone provision also.

Compatibility Clause

439. Paragraph 2 contains a compatibility clause which describes the relationship between Article 17(1) of the MLI and provisions of CTAs. It provides that Article 17(1) of the MLI applies to CTAs in the place or absence of a provision requiring that a Contracting Jurisdiction shall make a corresponding adjustment with respect to the profits of a resident enterprise where the other Contracting Jurisdiction makes an adjustment that reflects the arm's-length profits of an AE resident of that other Contracting Jurisdiction.

Reservations under Paragraph 3

440. The inclusion of Article 9(2) of the OECD MTC in tax treaties is a Best Practice under BEPS Action 14 and is not required as part of the Action 14 minimum standard. Hence, the following reservations are provided for under paragraph 3:

(i) Under paragraph 3(a), Parties may opt out of Article 17 entirely with respect to CTAs that already contain a provision described in Article 17(2) (whether or not the provision adopts the precise language of the OECD MTC or the UN MTC so long as the provision contains a requirement that a Contracting Jurisdiction shall make a corresponding adjustment).

(ii) Under paragraph 3(b), Parties may opt out of Article 17 entirely with respect to CTAs on the basis that in the absence of a provision referred to in Article 17(2):
   - they shall make an appropriate corresponding adjustment, *or*

306. Refer OECD's FAQs on MLI https://community.oecd.org/docs/DOC-113848 accessed on 17 August 2020.

- they shall endeavour to resolve the case under the provisions of a CTA relating to MAP.

Where one Contracting Jurisdiction to a CTA makes such a reservation and the other Contracting Jurisdiction does not, Article 17 will not apply to the CTA, and there is no expectation created under the MLI that the Contracting Jurisdiction that has not made the reservation will make a corresponding adjustment.

(iii) Under paragraph 3(c), Parties may opt out of Article 17 entirely with respect to CTAs in the case of a Contracting Jurisdiction that has made a reservation under Article 16(5)(c)(ii) of the MLI on the basis that in its bilateral treaty negotiations it shall accept a treaty provision of the type contained in paragraph 1, provided that the Contracting Jurisdictions were able to reach agreement on that provision and on the provisions described in Article 16(5)(c)(ii).

Notifications

441. Depending upon the position taken by various jurisdictions, the following notifications are required to be made under Article 17 of the MLI:

(i) Jurisdictions intending to make reservations under paragraph 3 are required to make notifications, as the case may be.

(ii) Under paragraph 4, each Party (other than a Party that has made a reservation under paragraph 3) is required to notify the Depositary of whether each of its CTAs contains an existing requirement to make a corresponding adjustment, and if so, the article and paragraph number of each such provision. The provisions of paragraph 1 will replace such provisions where all Contracting Jurisdictions to a CTA have made such a notification. In other cases, paragraph 1 will apply to the CTA, but will supersede existing provisions of a CTA only to the extent that those provisions are incompatible with paragraph 1. The word 'may' appearing in existing provisions of some CTAs permitting a Contracting Jurisdiction to choose not to make an appropriate adjustment even in the situation in which the adjustment made by the other Contracting Jurisdiction was justified, 'conflicts' with 'shall' in Article 17(1) and is thus incompatible; with the result, provisions of Article 17(1) of MLI will supersede the provisions of such CTAs.

Denmark's Position[307] under the MLI

442. Pursuant to Article 17(3)(a) of MLI, Denmark has made a reservation for the entirety of Article 17 not to apply to its CTAs that already contain a provision described

307. Refer Denmark's Position under the MLI http://www.oecd.org/tax/treaties/beps-mli-position-denmark-instrument-deposit.pdf.

in Article 17(2) and has notified such CTAs to the Depositary which already contain a provision described in Article 17(2) of the MLI.

443. The application of Article 17 of the MLI to some of Denmark's CTAs is provided hereunder:

Jurisdiction	*Position Taken*	*Treaty Partner*	*Position Taken*	*Outcome under the MLI*
Denmark	- Denmark has made reservation under Article 17(3)(a) and notified relevant provisions of CTA with Argentina	Argentina	- Argentina has made notification under Article 17(4) and has notified relevant provisions of CTA with Denmark	Article 17(1) would not apply
Denmark	- Denmark has made reservation under Article 17(3)(a) and notified relevant provisions of CTA with Australia	Australia	- Australia has made reservation under Article 17(3)(a) and has notified relevant provisions of CTA with Denmark	Article 17(1) would not apply
Denmark	- Denmark has made reservation under Article 17(3)(a) but has not notified relevant provisions of CTA with Belgium	Belgium	- Belgium has made notification under Article 17(4) but has not notified relevant provisions of CTA with Denmark	Article 17(1) would apply & supersede the provisions of the CTA to the extent of incompatibility
Denmark	- Denmark has made reservation under Article 17(3)(a) and notified relevant provisions of CTA with Canada	Canada	- Canada has made reservation under Article 17(3)(a) and notified relevant provisions of CTA with Denmark - Canada has also made a reservation under Article 17(3)(c), as it had also made a reservation under Article 16(5)(c)(ii)	Article 17(1) would not apply
Denmark	- Denmark has made reservation under Article 17(3)(a) and notified relevant provisions of CTA with Egypt	Egypt	- Egypt has made reservation under Article 17(3)(b)(i)(ii)	Article 17(1) would not apply

Jurisdiction	*Position Taken*	*Treaty Partner*	*Position Taken*	*Outcome under the MLI*
Denmark	– Denmark has made reservation under Article 17(3)(a) and notified relevant provisions of CTA with Ukraine	Ukraine	– Ukraine has made reservation under Article 17(3)(b)(i)(ii)	Article 17(1) would not apply

India's Position[308] under the MLI

444. Pursuant to Article 17(3)(a) of MLI, India has made a reservation for the entirety of Article 17 not to apply to its CTAs that already contain a provision described in Article 17(2) and has notified such CTAs to the Depositary which already contain a provision described in Article 17(2) of the MLI. A probable factor stimulating this decision could have been that such existing provisions in India's treaties are compliant (or customised in some CTAs ensuring corresponding adjustment) with the provisions of Article 17(1) of the MLI.

445. The application of Article 17 of the MLI to some of India's CTAs is provided hereunder:

Jurisdiction	*Position Taken*	*Treaty Partner*	*Position Taken*	*Outcome under the MLI*
India	– India has made reservation under Article 17(3)(a) and notified relevant provisions of CTA with Armenia	Armenia	– Armenia has made notification under Article 17(4) and has notified relevant provisions of CTA with India	Article 17(1) would not apply
India	– India has made reservation under Article 17(3)(a) but has not notified relevant provisions of CTA with Australia	Australia	– Australia has made reservation under Article 17(3)(a) and has notified relevant provisions of CTA with India	Article 17(1) would not apply
India	– India has made reservation under Article 17(3)(a) but has not notified relevant provisions of CTA with Belgium	Belgium	– Belgium has made notification under Article 17(4) but has not notified relevant provisions of CTA with India	Article 17(1) would apply & supersede the provisions of the CTA to the extent of incompatibility

308. Refer India's Position under the MLI http://www.oecd.org/tax/treaties/beps-mli-position-india-instrument-deposit.pdf.

Jurisdiction	*Position Taken*	*Treaty Partner*	*Position Taken*	*Outcome under the MLI*
India	– India has made reservation under Article 17(3)(a) and notified relevant provisions of CTA with Canada	Canada	– Canada has made reservation under Article 17(3)(a) and notified relevant provisions of CTA with India – Canada has also made a reservation under Article 17(3)(c), as it had also made a reservation under Article 16(5)(c)(ii)	Article 17(1) would not apply
India	– India has made reservation under Article 17(3)(a) but has not notified relevant provisions of CTA with Egypt	Egypt	– Egypt has made reservation under Article 17(3)(b)(i)(ii)	Article 17(1) would not apply
India	– India has made reservation under Article 17(3)(a) but has not notified relevant provisions of CTA with France	France	– France has made notification under Article 17(4) but has not notified relevant provisions of CTA with India	Article 17(1) would apply & supersede the provisions of the CTA to the extent of incompatibility
India	– India has made reservation under Article 17(3)(a) but has not notified relevant provisions of CTA with Japan	Japan	– Japan has made notification under Article 17(4) and has notified relevant provisions of CTA with India	Article 17(1) would apply & supersede the provisions of the CTA to the extent of incompatibility
India	– India has made reservation under Article 17(3)(a) and notified relevant provisions of CTA with Qatar	Qatar	– Qatar has made reservation under Article 17(3)(b)(ii)	Article 17(1) would not apply
India	– India has made reservation under Article 17(3)(a) but has not notified relevant provisions of CTA with Ukraine	Ukraine	– Ukraine has made reservation under Article 17(3)(b)(i)(ii)	Article 17(1) would not apply

The Netherlands' Position[309] under the MLI

446. The Netherlands has made notification under Article 17(4) of the MLI and has notified such CTAs to the Depositary which already contain a provision described in Article 17(2) of the MLI.

447. As an illustration, the application of Article 17 of the MLI to some of the Netherlands' CTAs is provided hereunder:

309. Refer The Netherlands' Position under the MLI http://www.oecd.org/tax/treaties/beps-mli-position-netherlands-instrument-deposit.pdf.

Jurisdiction	*Position Taken*	*Treaty Partner*	*Position Taken*	*Outcome under the MLI*
The Netherlands	– The Netherlands has made notification under Article 17(4) and has notified relevant provisions of CTA with Albania	Albania	– Albania has made notification under Article 17(4) and has notified relevant provisions of CTA with the Netherlands	Article 17(1) would replace relevant provisions of the CTA
The Netherlands	– The Netherlands has made notification under Article 17(4) and has notified relevant provisions of CTA with Barbados	Barbados	– Barbados has made notification under Article 17(4) and has notified relevant provisions of CTA with the Netherlands	Article 17(1) would replace relevant provisions of the CTA
The Netherlands	– The Netherlands has made notification under Article 17(4) and has notified relevant provisions of CTA with Croatia	Croatia	– Croatia has made reservation under Article 17(3)(a) and notified relevant provisions of CTA with the Netherlands	Article 17(1) would not apply
The Netherlands	– The Netherlands has made notification under Article 17(4) and notified relevant provisions of CTA with Estonia	Estonia	– Estonia has made reservation under Article 17(3)(a) and notified relevant provisions of CTA with the Netherlands	Article 17(1) would not apply
The Netherlands	– The Netherlands has made notification under Article 17(4) but has not notified relevant provisions of CTA with France	France	– France has made notification under Article 17(4) but has not notified relevant provisions of CTA with the Netherlands	Article 17(1) would apply and supersede the provisions of the CTA to the extent of incompatibility
The Netherlands	– The Netherlands has made notification under Article 17(4) and has notified relevant provisions of CTA with Georgia	Georgia	– Georgia has made reservation under Article 17(3)(a) and notified relevant provisions of CTA with the Netherlands	Article 17(1) would not apply
The Netherlands	– The Netherlands has made notification under Article 17(4) and has notified relevant provisions of CTA with Iceland	Iceland	– Iceland has made reservation under Article 17(3)(a) and notified relevant provisions of CTA with the Netherlands	Article 17(1) would not apply

Jurisdiction	*Position Taken*	*Treaty Partner*	*Position Taken*	*Outcome under the MLI*
The Netherlands	– The Netherlands has made notification under Article 17(4) and has notified relevant provisions of CTA with Indonesia	Indonesia	– Indonesia has made notification under Article 17(4) and has notified relevant provisions of CTA with the Netherlands	Article 17(1) would replace relevant provisions of the CTA
The Netherlands	– The Netherlands has made notification under Article 17(4) but has not notified relevant provisions of CTA with Morocco	Morocco	– Morocco has made reservation under Article 17(3)(b)(i)(ii)	Article 17(1) would not apply

Few Snapshots of Positions[310] Taken by Other Countries under the MLI

448. Jurisdictions that have made reservation under Article 17(3)(a) of the MLI are, namely, Australia, Bosnia and Herzegovina, Bulgaria, Canada, Chile, Costa Rica, Cote d'Ivoire, Croatia, Denmark, Estonia, Finland, Gabon, Georgia, Germany, Greece, Guernsey, Hong Kong, Hungary, Iceland, India, Ireland, the Isle of Man, Jersey, Korea, Latvia, Liechtenstein, Malaysia, Mexico, Nigeria, Norway, Oman, Panama, Poland, Romania, Russia, San Marino, Serbia, the Slovak Republic, Slovenia, Spain, Sweden, Turkey, Uruguay.

449. Jurisdictions that have made reservation under Article 17(3)(b)(i) of the MLI are, namely, Belize, Curaçao, the Czech Republic, Egypt, Jordan, Latvia, Monaco, Morocco, Papua New Guinea, Seychelles, Ukraine.

450. Jurisdictions that have made reservation under Article 17(3)(b)(ii) of the MLI are, namely, Belize, Curaçao, the Czech Republic, Egypt, Jordan, Latvia, Monaco, Morocco, Papua New Guinea, Qatar, Seychelles, Ukraine.

451. Jurisdictions that have made reservation under Article 17(3)(c) of the MLI are, namely, Canada, Monaco, Senegal. These jurisdictions have also made a reservation under Article 16(5)(c)(ii) of the MLI in line with the requirement of Article 17(3).

The various notifications made by treaty partners under Article 17 of the MLI and impact/outcome thereof on the respective CTAs are provided in Figure 19.

Figure 19 Article 17: Corresponding Adjustments – Flowchart on Notifications & Their Impact

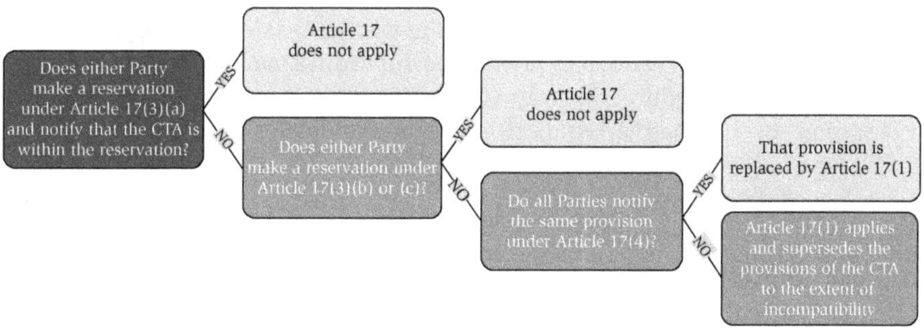

Source: OECD – Toolkit for Application of the Multilateral Instrument for BEPS Tax Treaty Related Measures https://www.oecd.org/tax/treaties/application-toolkit-multilateral-instrument-for-beps-tax-treaty-measures.htm.

310. Refer OECD – Signatories and Parties to the MLI http://www.oecd.org/tax/treaties/beps-mli-signatories-and-parties.pdf.

3.9 PART VI OF MLI: ARBITRATION – ARTICLES 18-26 OF MLI

Mandatory Binding Arbitration of MAP Cases – Background

452. Part VI of the MLI establishes the mandatory binding arbitration procedure as an optional set of provisions. The Subgroup on Arbitration developed provisions for the mandatory binding arbitration of MAP cases when the CAs are unable to reach agreement within a fixed period of time. Although the BEPS Action 14 Report recommended the implementation of the mandatory binding arbitration procedure in tax treaties, it did not recommend the substantive measures. That is why the Subgroup on Arbitration produced all the provisions reflected in Part VI of the MLI, comprising nine articles (Articles 18 through 26 under the MLI), that address both the substance of those provisions and its technical application to CTAs. Part VI is intended to operate as a single cohesive arbitration provision.[311]

453. Articles 18 through 26 of the MLI set out rules relevant for conducting a mandatory binding arbitration procedure, including the initiation of the procedure, the appointment of arbitrators, confidentiality, types of arbitration, costs of the arbitration procedure and implementation of the arbitral award by the CAs. At the same time, the CAs still need to settle, by means of a MAP, the mode of application of the provisions contained in Part VI. Part VI applies only between Parties that expressly choose to apply Part VI with respect to their CTAs. The structure of the articles of Part VI differs from the structure of other Articles of the MLI.

454. Implementation of MAP under Article 16 of MLI is bilateral in nature and so is the obligation to engage in mandatory binding arbitration procedure. The MLI establishes a default procedure for conducting the mandatory binding arbitration provisions of Part VI. The default procedure applies in cases in which the Parties that opted in to Part VI do not make any reservations to prevent its application and do not mutually agree to apply a different procedure; this way, 'final offer' arbitration process (also known as 'last best offer' or 'baseball' arbitration) serves as the default procedure.

3.9.1 Article 18

455. Under Article 18 of the MLI, a Party is given the option to apply Part VI and is required to notify the Depositary accordingly. Part VI shall apply in relation to two Contracting Jurisdictions with respect to a CTA only where both Contracting Jurisdictions have made such a notification. As of now, there are 30 jurisdictions which have made notification under Article 18[312] and have chosen to apply Part VI, namely Andorra, Australia, Austria, Barbados, Belgium, Canada, Curaçao, Denmark, Fiji, Finland, France, Germany, Greece, Ireland, Italy, Japan, Liechtenstein, Luxembourg, Malta, Mauritius, the Netherlands, New Zealand, Papua New Guinea, Portugal,

311. Refer Explanatory Statement to the MLI, para. 20.
312. Refer OECD – Signatories and Parties to the MLI http://www.oecd.org/tax/treaties/beps-mli-signatories-and-parties.pdf.

Singapore, Slovenia, Spain, Sweden, Switzerland, UK. On the other hand, jurisdictions, namely, Albania, Argentina, Armenia, Bahrain, Belize, Bosnia and Herzegovina, Bulgaria, Burkina Faso, Cameroon, Chile, China, Colombia, Costa Rica, Côte d'Ivoire, Croatia, Cyprus, the Czech Republic, Egypt, Estonia, Gabon, Georgia, Guernsey, Hong Kong, Hungary, Iceland, India, Indonesia, the Isle of Man, Israel, Jamaica, Jersey, Jordan, Kazakhstan, Kenya, Korea, Kuwait, Latvia, Lithuania, Malaysia, Mexico, Monaco, Morocco, Nigeria, North Macedonia, Norway, Oman, Pakistan, Panama, Peru, Poland, Qatar, Romania, Russia, San Marino, Saudi Arabia, Senegal, Serbia, Seychelles, the Slovak Republic, South Africa, Tunisia, Turkey, Ukraine, the United Arab Emirates, Uruguay have not opted for Part VI (Arbitration) provisions contained in Articles 18-26 of the MLI.

The various notifications made by treaty partners under Article 18 and certain other provisions of Part VI of the MLI and consequent impact thereof on application of Part VI of the MLI on the respective CTAs are provided in Figure 20.

Figure 20 Article 18: Flowchart on Notifications & Their Impact

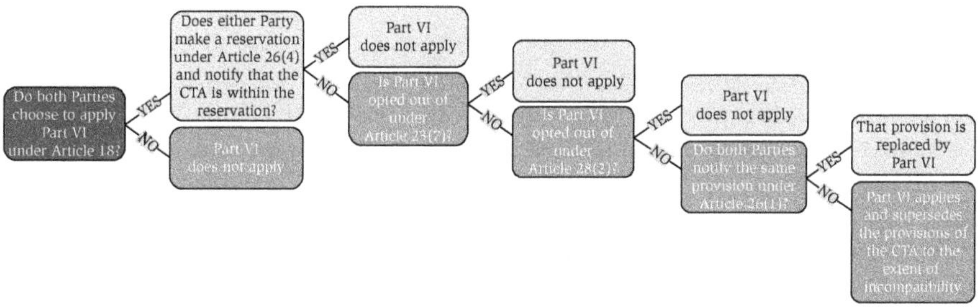

Source: OECD – Toolkit for Application of the Multilateral Instrument for BEPS Tax Treaty Related Measures https://www.oecd.org/tax/treaties/application-toolkit-multilateral-instrument-for-beps-tax-treaty-measures.htm.

3.9.2 Article 19

456. Under Article 19 of the MLI, the following provisions exist which determine the rules through which the Arbitration process shall work:

(i) *Paragraph 1* – It contains the core arbitration provision. It provides that, where the CAs are unable to reach an agreement on a case pursuant to the MAP under the CTA within a period of two years, unresolved issues will, at the request of the person who presented the case, be submitted to arbitration in the manner described in Part VI. The start date for the two-year period is determined pursuant to paragraph 8 or 9, as the case may be. The CAs may, however, agree to a different time period with respect to a particular case, provided that they notify the person who presented the case of such agreement prior to the expiration of the two-year period referred to in sub-paragraph (b) of paragraph

1. This different time period with respect to a particular case could be longer or shorter than the two-year period referred to in sub-paragraph (b). In addition, paragraph 11 permits a Party to reserve the right to substitute a three-year period for the two-year period referred to in sub-paragraph (b) for the purposes of applying Article 19 to its CTAs. A Party is also permitted to formulate reservations with respect to the scope of cases that are eligible for arbitration, as described in Article 28(2) (subject to the acceptance of those reservations by the other Parties).

(ii) *Paragraph 2* – The MAP is available to taxpayers irrespective of the judicial and administrative remedies provided by the domestic law of the Contracting Jurisdictions. Most tax administrations, however, will require that one process takes place before the other, to ensure that a taxpayer's case will not proceed through both the MAP and a domestic court or administrative proceeding at the same time. To accommodate this approach, paragraph 2 provides that the period provided in paragraph 1(b) will stop running where a CA has suspended the mutual agreement process referred to in paragraph 1(a) because a case with respect to one or more of the same issues is pending before a court or administrative tribunal. The period will start running again when a final decision has been rendered by the court or administrative tribunal or the case has been suspended or withdrawn. However, where a Party makes the reservation described in Article 19(12), the arbitration process will terminate if a decision is rendered by the court or administrative tribunal during the period in which the arbitration process is suspended. Paragraph 2 also provides that the period provided in paragraph 1(b) will stop running where a person who presented a case and a CA have agreed to suspend the mutual agreement process for any reason. This would apply, for example, where the taxpayer and the CA have agreed to suspend the MAP due to serious illness or some other personal hardship. The period would start running again once that suspension has been lifted.

(iii) *Paragraph 3* – It provides that the period provided in paragraph 1(b) shall be extended where both CAs agree that a person directly affected by the case has failed to provide in a timely manner any additional material information requested by either CA after the start of the period provided in paragraph 1(b). In that case, the period will be extended for an amount of time equal to the period beginning on the date by which the information was requested, and ending on the date on which that information was ultimately provided.

(iv) *Paragraph 4* – Sub-paragraph (a) of paragraph 4 provides that the arbitration decision shall be final and shall be implemented through the mutual agreement concerning the case referred to in paragraph 1. Sub-paragraph (b) provides that the arbitration decision shall be binding on both Contracting Jurisdictions except in three situations:

(1) if a person directly affected by the case does not accept the mutual agreement that implements the arbitration decision;

(2) if the arbitration decision is held to be invalid by a final decision of the courts of one of the Contracting Jurisdictions; and

(3) if a person directly affected by the case pursues litigation in any court or administrative tribunal on the issues which were resolved in the mutual agreement implementing the arbitration decision.

(v) *Paragraph 5* – It provides that the CA that received the initial request for a MAP must, within two calendar months of receiving the initial request for a MAP, notify the person who presented the case that the request has been received, and send a notification of the request, along with a copy of the request, to the other CA.

(vi) *Paragraph 6* – It provides that a CA must notify the person that presented the case and the other CA that it has received all information necessary to undertake substantive consideration of the case, or request additional information for that purpose from the person that presented the case, within three calendar months from the date on which it received the initial request.

(vii) *Paragraph 7* – It provides that after receiving additional information, the CA requesting the information would have three calendar months to notify the person presenting the case and the other CA that it has received all necessary information, or that requested information is still missing.

(viii) *Paragraph 8* – It provides that the start date of the period referred to in paragraph 1(b) depends on whether such additional information has been requested. Where no request for additional information has been made, paragraph 8 provides that the start date is the earlier of:
- the date on which both CAs have notified the person who presented the case that all necessary information was received (i.e., the date on which the second of the two CAs has made that notification); and
- three calendar months after the date on which the CA to which the request for a MAP was initially made notified the other CA of the request.

(ix) *Paragraph 9* – It provides that where additional information was requested, in general, the start date is the earlier of:
- the latest date on which the CAs that requested additional information have notified the taxpayer and the other CA that the information has been received; and
- the date that is three calendar months after both CAs have received the additional information from the person who presented the case.

If either CA notifies the taxpayer and the other CA that some of the requested information is still missing, such notification shall be treated as a request for additional information.

(x) *Paragraph 10* – It requires that the CAs of the Contracting Jurisdictions settle the mode of application of the arbitration provisions by mutual agreement, including (but not limited to) the minimum information necessary for each CA to undertake substantive consideration of the case, before the date on which unresolved issues in a MAP case are first eligible to be submitted to arbitration.

(xi) *Paragraph 11* – It allows a Party to reserve the right to replace the two-year period set forth in paragraph 1(b) with a three-year period for the purposes of applying Part VI to its CTAs. Like other reservations to the MLI, where a Contracting Jurisdiction to a CTA makes this reservation, it will apply for the purposes of the application of that CTA by both Contracting Jurisdictions. Jurisdictions that have made reservations under paragraph 11[313] of Article 19 are, namely, Austria, France, Germany, Greece, Liechtenstein, Portugal, Slovenia, Sweden, Switzerland.

(xii) *Paragraph 12* - Arbitration process may not be pursued with respect to issues that have been resolved through domestic litigation, either before submission of the issues to arbitration or during the arbitration process. Paragraph 12 permits a Party to reserve the right to exclude from arbitration issues with respect to which a decision has been rendered by a court or administrative tribunal of either Contracting Jurisdiction. Also, the arbitration process will terminate if a decision concerning the unresolved issue is rendered by a court or administrative tribunal of one of the Contracting Jurisdictions at any time after a request for arbitration has been made and before the arbitration decision has been delivered. Jurisdictions that have made a reservation under paragraph 12[314] of Article 19 are, namely, Andorra, Australia, Austria, Belgium, Canada, Denmark, France, Greece, Ireland, Italy, Japan, Luxembourg, Malta, Mauritius, New Zealand, Papua New Guinea, Portugal, Singapore, Slovenia, Spain.

The various notifications made by treaty partners under Article 19 of the MLI and impact thereof on the arbitration process under Part VI of the MLI are provided in Figure 21.

313. Refer OECD – Signatories and Parties to the MLI http://www.oecd.org/tax/treaties/beps-mli-signatories-and-parties.pdf.
314. *Id.*, accessed on 18 August 2020.

Figure 21 Article 19: Flowchart on Notifications & Their Impact

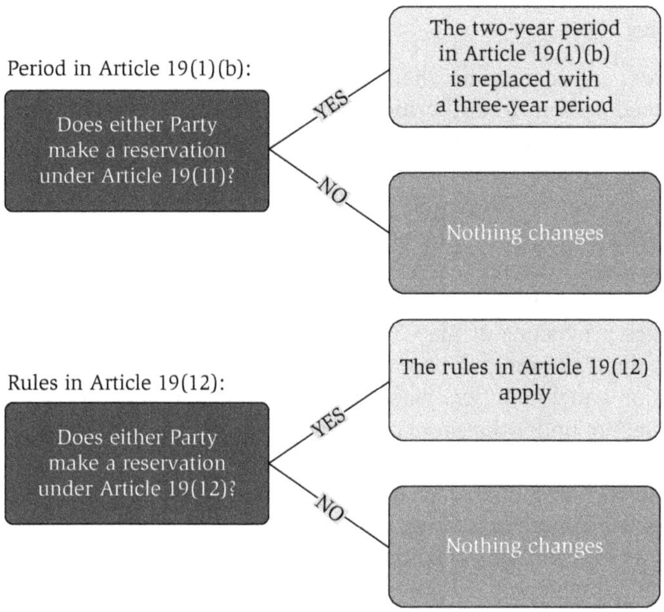

Source: OECD – Toolkit for Application of the Multilateral Instrument for BEPS Tax Treaty Related Measures https://www.oecd.org/tax/treaties/application-toolkit-multilateral-instrument-for-beps-tax-treaty-measures.htm.

3.9.3 Article 20

457. Under Article 20 of the MLI, paragraphs 1 and 2 set out basic rules for the composition of an arbitration panel and the appointment and qualifications of arbitrators. While these rules would apply by default, paragraph 1 also permits the CAs to mutually agree on different rules, either generally or with respect to a particular case. Paragraph 2 governs the appointment of the members of an arbitration panel which shall be composed of three individual members. Paragraphs 3 and 4 describe default rules which would apply in the case in which either CA fails, within the prescribed time periods, to appoint an arbitrator, or in the case in which two initial members of the arbitration panel fail to appoint a chair. These paragraphs provide that, in such cases, the appointment will be made by the highest ranking official of the Centre for Tax Policy and Administration (CTPA) of the OECD that is not a national of either Contracting Jurisdiction. These default rules are intended to ensure that arbitration, and therefore, a resolution of the issues in a MAP case, cannot be unduly delayed by a failure to constitute an arbitration panel.

3.9.4 Article 21

458. Article 21 provides for confidentiality of Arbitration proceedings in the following two paragraphs:

(i) *Paragraph 1* – It provides that the members of the arbitration panel shall be considered persons or authorities to whom information may be disclosed solely for the purposes of Part VI, the CTA and the domestic laws of the Contracting Jurisdictions related to the exchange of information, confidentiality, and administrative assistance. Paragraph 1 additionally provides that information received by the arbitration panel or by prospective arbitrators, as well as any information that the CAs may receive from the arbitration panel, shall be considered information exchanged under the exchange of information and administrative assistance provisions of the CTA. Recognising the need to balance the goal of minimising the number of people to whom information may be disclosed against arbitration panel members' need for staff support, this paragraph also provides for disclosure under the same conditions to a maximum of three staff per panel member.

(ii) *Paragraph 2* – It requires the CAs to ensure that members of the arbitration panel and their staff agree in writing, prior to their acting in an arbitration proceeding, to treat any information relating to the arbitration proceeding consistently with the confidentiality and non-disclosure requirements under the provisions of the CTA related to the exchange of information and administrative assistance and under the applicable laws of the Contracting Jurisdictions. As part of the agreement on the mode of application of Part VI under Article 19(10), the CAs may wish to settle the details of this process, including which CA would obtain such written agreement. The consequences of breaching such an agreement would be determined under the domestic laws of the Contracting Jurisdictions and under the terms of the agreement.

3.9.5 Article 22

459. Article 22 provides that the MAP, as well as the arbitration procedure, will terminate if, during the arbitration process (at any time after a request for arbitration has been made and before the arbitration panel has delivered its decision), either:

- the CAs come to a mutual agreement to resolve the case; or
- the taxpayer withdraws either its request for arbitration or its request for a MAP.

3.9.6 Article 23

460. Article 23 provides for the types of the Arbitration process and rules applicable to arbitration proceedings in the following paragraphs:

(i) *Paragraph 1* – It provides for default rules with respect to the type of arbitration process that will apply for the purposes of arbitration proceedings pursuant to Part VI:

(a) By default, a 'final offer' arbitration process (also known as 'last best offer' or 'baseball' arbitration) will apply, except to the extent that the CAs mutually agree on different rules. Under this approach, the CAs will each submit to the arbitration panel a proposed resolution which addresses all of the unresolved issues in the case in a manner that is consistent with any previous agreements that have been reached in that case by the CAs. For each adjustment or similar issue in the case, the proposed resolution will include only the disposition of specific monetary amounts (e.g., of income or expense) or the maximum rate of tax charged pursuant to the CTA. In some cases, however, unresolved issues will include questions regarding whether the conditions for applying a provision of a CTA have been met. Where the unresolved issues in a case include such a 'threshold question', such as whether a person is a resident of a Contracting Jurisdiction or whether an enterprise of one of the Contracting Jurisdictions has a PE in the other Contracting Jurisdiction, the CAs may submit their proposed answers to the threshold question (i.e., yes or no). If there are other unresolved issues, the disposition of which is contingent on the answer reached with respect to the threshold question, it is expected that the CAs would also submit alternative proposed resolutions of those remaining issues.

(b) The proposed resolutions submitted by the CAs of each Contracting Jurisdiction may be supported by a position paper. Each CA may also submit a reply submission with respect to the proposed resolution and supporting position paper submitted by the other CA. The reply submission and its supporting paper are meant to address only the positions and arguments of the other CA, and are not intended as an opportunity for a CA to advance additional arguments in favour of its own position.

(c) In the 'final offer' arbitration process (also known as 'last best offer' or 'baseball' arbitration), the arbitration panel will select as its decision one of the proposed resolutions submitted by the CAs. In a case involving one or more threshold questions, the arbitration panel will decide the threshold question(s), and then adopt one of the alternative proposed resolutions submitted by the CAs. The decision will be adopted by a simple majority of the panel members, and will not include any rationale or explanation. In light of the purpose of arbitration to act as a streamlined method for resolving disputes between the CAs, the decision will be delivered in writing to the CAs and may not be used as precedent with respect to any other cases.

(ii) *Paragraph 2* – Under paragraph 2, a Party that is not willing to accept the 'final offer' approach described in paragraph 1 as a default rule may reserve the right not to apply paragraph 1 to its CTAs and to adopt the 'independent opinion' approach as the default type of arbitration process, except to the extent that the CAs of the two Contracting Jurisdictions mutually agree on different rules, which may apply to all cases or to a particular case. In such situation, the following rules shall apply to the arbitration proceedings:

   (a) Under the 'independent opinion' approach, each CA must provide to the arbitration panel any information that the panel may consider necessary to reach its decision. As part of the mutual agreement under Article 19(10), the CAs may wish to describe the process they will use to reach agreement on the issues to be resolved by the arbitration panel. The CAs may also agree, as part of the CA agreement entered into pursuant to Article 19(10), that each CA may submit a supporting position paper for consideration by the arbitration panel.

   (b) The arbitration panel will then decide the issues which have been submitted to arbitration in accordance with the applicable provisions of the CTA and, subject to those provisions, those of the domestic laws of the Contracting Jurisdictions. In this regard, the arbitration panel would review the application of domestic law only to the extent necessary to determine whether a Contracting Jurisdiction correctly applied the CTA. The CAs may also, by mutual agreement, identify other sources of law or authority that will be considered by the arbitration panel.

   (c) The decision of the arbitration panel will be presented to the CAs in writing, indicating the sources of law relied upon and the reasoning which led to its result. The adoption of the arbitration decision will be by a simple majority of the panel members. As with the 'final offer' approach, the decision will have no precedential value.

   Jurisdictions that have made reservation under Article 23(2)[315] are, namely, Andorra, Greece, Japan, Malta, Papua New Guinea, Portugal, Slovenia, Sweden.

(iii) *Paragraph 3* – It provides a mechanism to address the situation in which two Parties have differing, firmly held views on their preferred type of arbitration process. Under paragraph 3, a Party that has not reserved the right to apply the 'independent opinion' approach as a default rule under paragraph 2 may reserve the right for the default rules provided in paragraphs 1 and 2 not to apply with respect to its CTAs with Parties that have reserved the right to apply the 'independent opinion' approach as a default rule in place of 'final offer' arbitration. Where a Party has made the reservation permitted by paragraph 3, it would be left to the CA of that Party and the CA of the Party that made a

315. Refer OECD – Signatories and Parties to the MLI http://www.oecd.org/tax/treaties/beps-mli-signatories-and-parties.pdf.

reservation under paragraph 2 to determine the type of arbitration process that would apply as between those two Parties. Where a reservation under paragraph 3 has been made by either Contracting Jurisdiction to a CTA, and where the other Contracting Jurisdiction has made a reservation under paragraph 2, the CAs are required to endeavour to reach an agreement on the type of arbitration process that will apply to all cases arising under the CTA. Until such agreement is reached, Article 19 will not apply. As a result, the CAs are not required to consider a request for arbitration until such an agreement is reached.

Jurisdictions that have made reservation under Article 23(3)[316] are, namely, Canada, Denmark, Italy, Singapore.

(iv) *Paragraphs 4, 5* – Paragraph 4 provides that Parties may choose to apply paragraph 5 to their CTAs. This paragraph is an optional provision which, subject to paragraphs 6 and 7, will apply between two Contracting Jurisdictions to a CTA if either Contracting Jurisdiction chooses to apply it and notifies the Depositary accordingly. Paragraph 5 requires the CAs, prior to the start of arbitration proceedings, to ensure that each taxpayer involved in the case and their advisors agree in writing not to disclose any of the information received during the course of the arbitration proceedings from either CA or from the arbitration panel. Thus, paragraph 5 ensures a non-disclosure agreement prior to arbitration process. A material breach of this agreement between the time at which the request for arbitration was made and before the arbitration panel has delivered its decision will result in the termination of the MAP and the arbitration proceedings with respect to the case.

A characteristic feature of paragraph 4 is that this optional provision applies to a CTA even if one of the Parties has notified its willingness to opt in. Thus, paragraph 4 allows unilateral opt-in provisions.

Jurisdictions that have opted under paragraph 4[317] to apply the non-disclosure rule under paragraph 5 are, namely, Andorra, Australia, Canada, Denmark, Fiji, Finland, France, Germany, Greece, Ireland, Italy, Luxembourg, Malta, Mauritius, New Zealand, Papua New Guinea, Portugal, Singapore, Slovenia, UK.

(v) *Paragraphs 6, 7* – Paragraph 6 allows a Party, other than a Party that has chosen to apply paragraph 5, to reserve the right not to apply paragraph 5 with respect to one or more identified CTAs (or with respect to all of its CTAs). Paragraph 6 is therefore a reservation to block applying the non-disclosure agreement, i.e., opt out of the non-disclosure rule. A Party that has chosen to apply paragraph 5, however, may reserve the right under paragraph 7 for Part VI not to apply at all with respect to any CTA for which the other Contracting Jurisdiction has made the reservation pursuant to paragraph 6. The overall effect of paragraphs 4 through 7 is to ensure that where a Contracting Jurisdiction to a CTA has chosen to apply paragraph 5, taxpayers will be required to keep information received during the arbitration process secret by default. Parties that do not consider this necessary, however, may opt out of this requirement with respect to one or more

316. *Id.*
317. *Id.*

CTAs. Parties that consider it essential to require the taxpayer to maintain strict confidentiality, however, may opt out of arbitration entirely with a Party that has opted out of the non-disclosure rule.

As of now, no jurisdiction has made any reservation under paragraph 6, whereas jurisdictions that have made reservation under paragraph 7[318] are, namely, Andorra, Australia, Canada, Denmark, Finland, Germany, New Zealand, Papua New Guinea, Portugal.

The above data set (notifications) under paragraphs 4-7 shows that jurisdictions are giving primacy to application of non-disclosure rule and attach special importance to confidentiality of the mandatory binding arbitration procedure.

The various notifications made by treaty partners under Article 23 of the MLI and impact thereof on the arbitration process under Part VI of the MLI are provided in Figure 22.

Figure 22 Article 23: Flowchart on Notifications & Their Impact

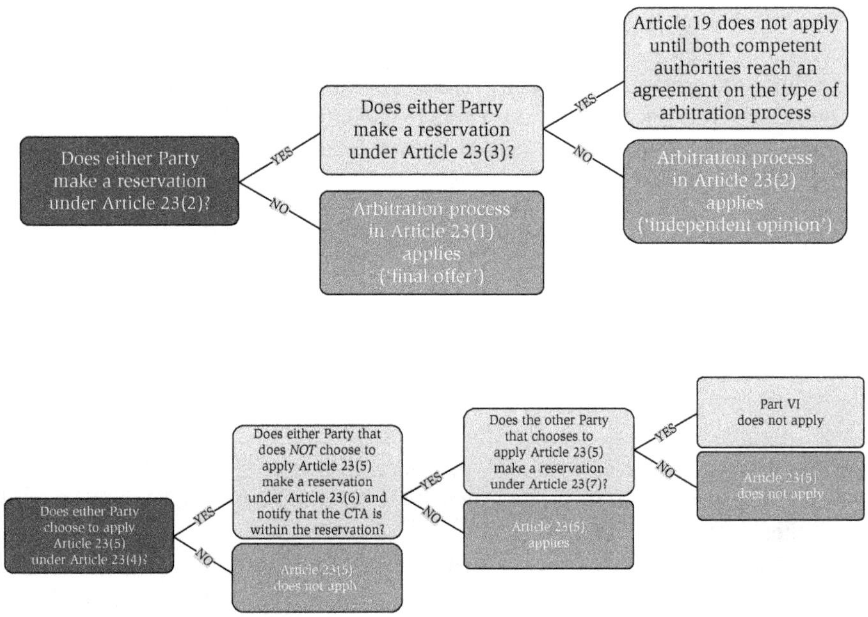

Source: OECD – Toolkit for Application of the Multilateral Instrument for BEPS Tax Treaty Related Measures https://www.oecd.org/tax/treaties/application-toolkit-multilateral-instrument-for-beps-tax-treaty-measures.htm.

318. *Id.*

3.9.7 Article 24

461. Though the arbitration decision is binding (as provided in Article 19(4) of the MLI), contracting jurisdictions may depart from it. Provisions of Article 24 deal with such situations in the following manner:

(i) *Paragraphs 1, 2* – Paragraph 1 permits a Party to choose to apply paragraph 2 with respect to its CTAs. Notwithstanding Article 19(4), which provides that the arbitration decision is binding, paragraph 2 allows the CAs to depart from the arbitration decision and to agree on a different resolution within three calendar months after the decision has been delivered to them. This may arise, for example, if the arbitration panel issues a decision that both CAs consider to be an inappropriate resolution of the issues in the case. Paragraph 2 is an optional provision and will be applied with respect to a CTA only if both Contracting Jurisdictions choose to apply it.

Jurisdictions that have opted in paragraph 1[319] to apply paragraph 2 are, namely, Andorra, Austria, Barbados, Belgium, Denmark, Fiji, Finland, France, Germany, Greece, Ireland, Italy, Liechtenstein, Luxembourg, Malta, Mauritius, New Zealand, Papua New Guinea, Portugal, Singapore, Slovenia, Spain, Sweden, Switzerland, UK.

(ii) *Paragraph 3* – Some jurisdictions consider that Article 24 would be unlikely to be applied where the 'final offer' approach described in Article 23(1) is used, given that under 'final offer' arbitration, the arbitration panel's decision will be the position of one of the two CAs. To accommodate this view, paragraph 3 of Article 24 therefore allows a Party that chooses to apply paragraph 2 of Article 24 to reserve the right for paragraph 2 of Article 24 to apply only with respect to its CTAs for which the 'independent opinion' approach described in Article 23(2) is applied.

Jurisdictions that have made reservation under paragraph 3[320] are, namely, Belgium, Luxembourg, New Zealand, Papua New Guinea, Switzerland.

The various notifications made by treaty partners under Article 24 of the MLI and impact thereof on paragraph 2 of Article 24 under Part VI of the MLI are provided in Figure 23.

319. *Id.*
320. *Id.*

Figure 23 Article 24 Flowchart on Notifications & Their Impact

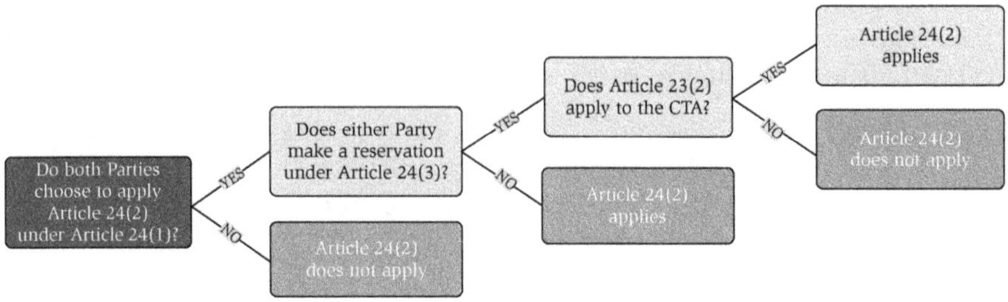

Source: OECD – Toolkit for Application of the Multilateral Instrument for BEPS Tax Treaty Related Measures https://www.oecd.org/tax/treaties/application-toolkit-multilateral-instrument-for-beps-tax-treaty-measures.htm.

3.9.8 Article 25

462. It provides that the CAs of the Contracting Jurisdictions shall settle by mutual agreement rules for the division of the fees and expenses of the members of the arbitration panel (which shall not include those of the staff of such members) as well as any costs incurred in connection with the arbitration proceedings. It also provides that, in the absence of such agreement:

(i) each Contracting Jurisdiction will bear its own expenses and those of its appointed panel member; and
(ii) the cost of the chair of the arbitration panel and the other expenses associated with the conduct of the arbitration proceedings will be borne by the two Contracting Jurisdictions in equal shares.

3.9.9 Article 26

463. Article 26 contains the single compatibility clause in the entire Part VI and operates in the following manner:

(i) *Paragraph 1* – Paragraph 1 is a compatibility clause which describes the interaction between the provisions of Part VI and provisions of CTAs that provide for arbitration of MAP cases. This paragraph provides that the provisions of Part VI will apply to CTAs that do not already provide for arbitration of unresolved issues arising from MAP cases brought to the CAs by taxpayers. Part VI will also apply in place of existing arbitration provisions that apply to issues arising from MAP cases (whether they provide for mandatory binding arbitration or not), subject to the reservation in paragraph 4 of Article 26, which permits a Party to preserve the application of certain existing mandatory binding arbitration provisions. Each Party that chooses to apply Part VI is required to notify the

Depositary whether its CTAs (other than those within the scope of a reservation under paragraph 4 of Article 26) contain arbitration provisions (and, if so, the article and paragraph number of each such provision). Where two Contracting Jurisdictions have made a notification with respect to a provision of a CTA, that provision shall be replaced by the provisions of Part VI of the MLI.

(ii) *Paragraph 2* – Paragraph 2 avoids duplication of efforts by providing that an unresolved issue arising from a MAP case will not be submitted to arbitration under Part VI if an arbitration panel or similar body has previously been set up with respect to the issue under another bilateral or multilateral convention that provides for the mandatory binding arbitration of unresolved issues. Where an arbitration panel has not yet been set up under another convention, however, Part VI would continue to apply to ensure that unresolved issues that arise in MAP cases and that are eligible for submission to arbitration pursuant to Article 19 can be resolved as quickly as possible.

(iii) *Paragraph 3* – Paragraph 3 clarifies that the provisions of Part VI are not intended to affect the fulfilment of wider obligations (e.g., obligations to resolve issues or cases that are not covered by Part VI) with respect to the arbitration of unresolved issues arising in the context of a MAP resulting from any conventions to which the Contracting Jurisdictions are or will become Parties, other than provisions of a CTA which have been superseded by Part VI pursuant to paragraph 1.

(iv) *Paragraph 4* – Paragraph 4 allows a Party to preserve existing mandatory binding arbitration provisions by reserving the right for Part VI not to apply to one or more identified CTAs (or to all of its CTAs) that provide for mandatory binding arbitration of unresolved issues arising in a MAP case. In this context, a CTA would be considered to provide for 'mandatory binding arbitration' if, under specific circumstances (such as a request by a person who presented the case), the CAs are required to submit issues arising in a MAP case that are not resolved after a specific amount of time to arbitration, and the outcome of that arbitration is binding on the CAs.

Jurisdictions that have made reservation under paragraph 4[321] are, namely, Austria, Belgium, Canada, Curaçao, Germany, Italy, Japan, Liechtenstein, Luxembourg, Malta, the Netherlands, Sweden, Switzerland, UK.

Reservations under Part VI

464. The reservations provided for under Part VI of the MLI are summarised as below:

(a) Article 19(11) allows a Party to reserve the right to replace the two-year period set forth in paragraph 1(b) of Article 19 with a three-year period for the purposes of applying Part VI to its CTAs.

321. *Id.*

(b) Article 19(12) permits a Party to reserve the right to exclude from arbitration issues with respect to which a decision has been rendered by a court or administrative tribunal of either Contracting Jurisdiction. Also, the arbitration process will terminate if a decision concerning the unresolved issue is rendered by a court or administrative tribunal of one of the Contracting Jurisdictions at any time after a request for arbitration has been made and before the arbitration decision has been delivered.
(c) Under Article 23(2), a Party that is not willing to accept the 'final offer' approach described in paragraph 1 of Article 23 as a default rule may reserve the right not to apply paragraph 1 to its CTAs and to adopt the 'independent opinion' approach as the default type of arbitration process.
(d) Under Article 23(3), a Party that has not reserved the right to apply the 'independent opinion' approach as a default rule under paragraph 2 may reserve the right for the default rules provided in paragraphs 1 and 2 not to apply with respect to its CTAs with Parties that have reserved the right to apply the 'independent opinion' approach as a default rule in place of 'final offer' arbitration.
(e) Article 23(6) allows a Party, other than a Party that has chosen to apply paragraph 5 (non-disclosure agreement) of Article 23, to reserve the right not to apply paragraph 5 with respect to one or more identified CTAs (or with respect to all of its CTAs).
(f) A Party that has chosen to apply paragraph 5 of Article 23, however, may reserve the right under Article 23(7) for Part VI not to apply at all with respect to any CTA for which the other Contracting Jurisdiction has made the reservation pursuant to paragraph 6. Thus, paragraph 7 blocks arbitration with a Party that has made a reservation under paragraph 6.
(g) Article 24(3) allows a Party that chooses to apply paragraph 2 of Article 24 to reserve the right for paragraph 2 to apply only with respect to its CTAs for which the 'independent opinion' approach described in Article 23(2) is applied.
(h) Article 26(4) allows a Party to preserve existing mandatory binding arbitration provisions by reserving the right for Part VI not to apply to one or more identified CTAs (or to all of its CTAs) that provide for mandatory binding arbitration of unresolved issues arising in a MAP case.

3.9.10 Article 28(2)

465. Article 28(2)(a) provides that any Party that chooses under Article 18 to apply Part VI of the MLI may formulate one or more reservations with respect to the scope of cases that shall be eligible for arbitration under Part VI. These provisions were added to provide Parties committing to arbitration with flexibility to tailor the scope of cases that will be eligible for arbitration to reflect their domestic policies regarding arbitration. A reservation under paragraph 2(a) would generally be made at the time of signature or when depositing the instrument of ratification. For a Party that does not choose to apply Part VI at the time it becomes a Party to the MLI, but chooses later to apply Part VI by making a notification to the Depositary, in such a case, reservations under paragraph 2(a) must be made at the same time as the Party's notification to the Depositary that it chooses to apply Part VI pursuant to Article 18 of the MLI. A Party is free to withdraw a reservation or replace it with a more limited reservation pursuant to Article 28(9) by means of a notification to the Depositary at any time.

466. In accordance with the principles of international law reflected in Article 21 of the VCLT and as confirmed in Article 28(3) of the MLI, unless explicitly provided otherwise in the provisions of the MLI, any reservation made by a Party under the MLI modifies the provisions to which it relates to the same extent for both the reserving Party and the other Party to the relevant CTA. In other words, all reservations, including free-form reservations made under Article 28(2)(a) of the MLI, apply symmetrically unless provided otherwise.[322]

467. Jurisdictions that have made reservations under Article 28(2)(a)[323] are, namely, Australia, Austria, Canada, Denmark, Finland, France, Germany, Greece, Ireland, Italy, Japan, Malta, Mauritius, New Zealand, Portugal, Singapore, Slovenia, Spain, Sweden, Switzerland. As an illustration, reservations made under Article 28(2)(a) by some countries in respect of the scope of application of the mandatory binding arbitration procedure are stated hereunder:

(i) Australia[324]

Pursuant to Article 28(2)(a) of the Convention, Australia formulates the following reservation with respect to the scope of cases that shall be eligible for arbitration under the provisions of Part VI:

> 1. Australia reserves the right to exclude from the scope of Part VI any case to the extent that it involves the application of Australia's general anti-avoidance rules contained in Part IVA of the Income Tax Assessment Act 1936 and section 67 of the Fringe Benefits Tax Assessment Act 1986. Australia also reserves the right to extend the scope of the exclusion for Australia's general anti-avoidance rules to any provisions replacing, amending or updating those rules. Australia shall notify the Depositary of any such provisions that involve substantial changes.

322. Refer Explanatory Statement to the MLI, para. 270.
323. Refer OECD – Signatories and Parties to the MLI http://www.oecd.org/tax/treaties/beps-mli-signatories-and-parties.pdf.
324. Refer Australia's Position under the MLI http://www.oecd.org/tax/treaties/beps-mli-position-australia-instrument-deposit.pdf.

(ii) Denmark[325]

Pursuant to Article 28(2)(a) of the Convention, the Kingdom of Denmark formulates the following reservations with respect to the scope of cases that shall be eligible for arbitration under the provisions of Part VI:

1. Part VI (Arbitration) of the Convention shall not apply to cases that fall within the scope of application of the Convention on the Elimination of Double Taxation in Connection with the Adjustment of Profits of Associated Enterprises (90/436/EEC) as amended, of Council Directive (EU) 2017/1852 on tax dispute resolution mechanisms in the European Union, or subsequent regulation.
2. Part VI (Arbitration) of the Convention shall apply to a tax case only insofar the Parties agree that (a) the Chair of the arbitration panel shall be a judge, and (b) Denmark shall be permitted to publish abstracts of decisions made by the arbitration panel.
3. Part VI (Arbitration) of the Convention shall not apply to cases where penalties were imposed on an individual or a legal person by a Party for tax fraud, willful default or gross negligence.

(iii) Japan[326]

Pursuant to Article 28(2)(a) of the Convention, Japan formulates the following reservations with respect to the scope of cases that shall be eligible for arbitration under the provisions of Part VI of the Convention:

1. Japan reserves the right to exclude from the scope of Part VI of the Convention with respect to a Covered Tax Agreement of Japan cases falling within the provisions of that Covered Tax Agreement which provide rules for determining whether a person other than an individual shall be treated as a resident of one of the Contracting Jurisdictions in cases in which that person would otherwise be treated as a resident of both Contracting Jurisdictions (as they may be modified by the Convention).
2. Where a reservation made by the other Contracting Jurisdiction to a Covered Tax Agreement of Japan pursuant to Article 28(2)(a) of the Convention exclusively excludes, whether or not by referring to its domestic law, from the scope of Part VI of the Convention cases of taxation in that other Contracting Jurisdiction, Japan reserves the right to exclude from the scope of Part VI of the Convention with respect to that Covered Tax Agreement cases of taxation in Japan which are analogous to the cases referred to in that other Contracting Jurisdiction's reservation.

---

325. Refer Denmark's Position under the MLI http://www.oecd.org/tax/treaties/beps-mli-position-denmark-instrument-deposit.pdf.
326. Refer Japan's Position under the MLI http://www.oecd.org/tax/treaties/beps-mli-position-japan-consolidated.pdf.

(iv) Singapore[327]

Pursuant to Article 28(2)(a) of the Convention, the Republic of Singapore formulates the following reservation with respect to the scope of cases that shall be eligible for arbitration under the provisions of Part VI:

a) The Republic of Singapore reserves the right to exclude from the scope of Part VI (Arbitration) cases involving the application of its domestic general anti-avoidance rules contained in Section 33 of the Income Tax Act, case law or juridical doctrines. Any subsequent provisions replacing, amending or updating these anti-avoidance rules would also be comprehended. The Republic of Singapore shall notify the Depositary of any such subsequent provisions.
b) Where a reservation made by the other Contracting Jurisdiction to a Covered Tax Agreement pursuant to Article 28(2)(a) refers exclusively to its domestic law (including legislative provisions, case law, judicial doctrines and penalties), the Republic of Singapore reserves the right to exclude from the scope of Part VI those cases that would be excluded from the scope of Part VI if the other Contracting Jurisdiction's reservation were formulated with reference to any analogous provisions of the Republic of Singapore's domestic law or any subsequent provisions which replace, amend or update those provisions. The competent authority of the Republic of Singapore will consult with the competent authority of the other Contracting Jurisdiction in order to specify any such analogous provisions which exist in the Republic of Singapore's domestic law in the agreement concluded pursuant to Article 19(10).

468. In line with the principles of international law reflected in the 1969 VCLT, Article 28(2)(b) of the MLI provides that the free-form reservations made under Article 28(2)(a) of the MLI are subject to acceptance by the other Parties. In cases where an objection is raised to a free-form reservation pursuant to Article 28(2)(b), the entirety of Part VI is not applicable between an objecting Party and the reserving Party.[328] Paragraph 2(b) specifies that a reservation made under paragraph 2(a) shall be considered to have been accepted by another Party if that other Party has not notified the Depositary that it objects to the reservation by the end of a period of 12 calendar months beginning on the date of notification of the reservation to all Parties and Signatories by the Depositary or by the date on which the Party deposits its instrument of ratification, whichever is later. Article 36(4) of the MLI has specific provision allowing withdrawal of objection to a reservation made under Article 28(2), which would result in a fuller application of the MLI (and arbitration), as the effect of the withdrawal of objection would be equivalent to the acceptance of the reservation taken by another Party under Article 28(2)(a). Thus, Part VI would enter into force between the reserving Party and the Party withdrawing the objection, although subject to the

327. Refer Singapore's Position under the MLI http://www.oecd.org/tax/treaties/beps-mli-position-singapore-instrument-deposit.pdf.
328. Refer Explanatory Statement to the MLI, para. 267.

limitations set out in the reservation. On 2 October 2020, the Depositary has communicated that Australia[329] has made an objection under Article 28(2)(b) of the MLI in respect of paragraph 2 of reservation by Denmark under Article 28(2)(a) of the MLI. Further, on 8 October 2020, the Depositary has communicated that Canada[330] has also made an objection under Article 28(2)(b) of the MLI in respect of paragraph 2 of reservation by Denmark under Article 28(2)(a) of the MLI.

The various notifications made by treaty partners under Article 28(2) of the MLI and impact thereof on the arbitration process under Part VI of the MLI are provided in Figure 24.

Figure 24 Article 28(2): Flowchart on Notifications & Their Impact

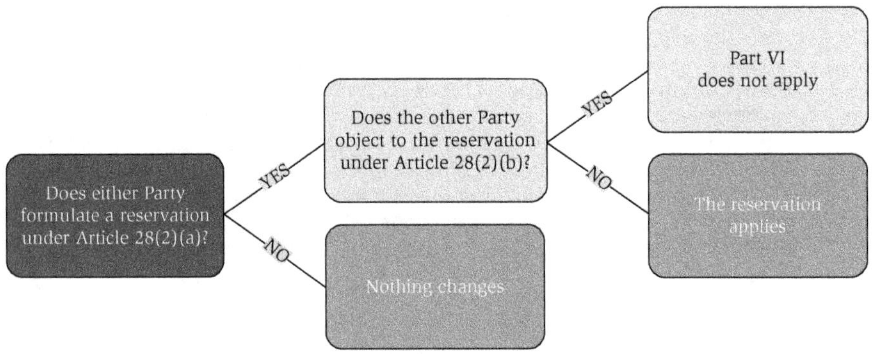

Source: OECD – Toolkit for Application of the Multilateral Instrument for BEPS Tax Treaty Related Measures https://www.oecd.org/tax/treaties/application-toolkit-multilateral-instrument-for-beps-tax-treaty-measures.htm.

Notifications under Part VI

469. Depending upon the position taken by various jurisdictions, the following notifications are required to be made under Articles 18-26 of the MLI:

(i) Jurisdictions intending to make various reservations under Part VI are required to make notifications, as the case may be.
(ii) Under Article 18, each Party opting to apply Part VI shall notify the Depositary of its choice.
(iii) Under paragraph 4 of Article 23, each Party opting in for the non-disclosure rule under paragraph 5 of Article 23 shall notify the Depositary.

329. Refer Australia's objection under Art. 28(2)(b) of the MLI http://www.oecd.org/tax/treaties/beps-mli-objection-australia-to-denmark.pdf.
330. Refer Canada's objection under Art. 28(2)(b) of the MLI http://www.oecd.org/tax/treaties/beps-mli-objection-canada-to-denmark.pdf.

(iv) Under paragraph 1 of Article 24, notwithstanding Article 19(4), each Party opting in for a different resolution under paragraph 2 of Article 24 vis-à-vis an arbitration decision shall make the necessary notification.

(v) Each Party that chooses to apply Part VI is required to notify the Depositary under paragraph 1 of Article 26 whether its CTAs (other than those within the scope of a reservation under paragraph 4 of Article 26) contain arbitration provisions (and, if so, the article and paragraph number of each such provision). Where two Contracting Jurisdictions have made a notification with respect to a provision of a CTA, that provision shall be replaced by the provisions of Part VI of the MLI.

Few Snapshots of Positions[331] Taken by Countries

470. The impact of various reservations and notifications made by some jurisdictions under Part VI of the MLI is *inter alia* stated as below:

Jurisdiction	*Position Taken*	*Treaty Partner*	*Position Taken*	*Outcome under the MLI*
Australia	- Pursuant to Article 18 of the MLI, chose to apply Part VI - Reservation made under Article 19(12) - Chose to apply Article 23(5) - Reservation made under Article 23(7) - Pursuant to Article 26(1) of the MLI, notified CTAs with New Zealand & Switzerland - Reservation made under Article 28(2)(a)	India	- India has not opted in for Part VI of the MLI	Part VI would not apply

331. Refer OECD – Signatories and Parties to the MLI http://www.oecd.org/tax/treaties/beps-mli-signatories-and-parties.pdf.

Jurisdiction	*Position Taken*	*Treaty Partner*	*Position Taken*	*Outcome under the MLI*
Australia	- Pursuant to Article 18 of the MLI, chose to apply Part VI - Reservation made under Article 19(12) - Chose to apply Article 23(5) - Reservation made under Article 23(7) - Pursuant to Article 26(1) of the MLI, notified CTAs with New Zealand & Switzerland - Reservation made under Article 28(2)(a)	Canada	- Pursuant to Article 18 of the MLI, chose to apply Part VI - Reservation made under Article 19(12) - Reservation made under Article 23(3) - Chose to apply Article 23(5) - Reservation made under Article 23(7) - Pursuant to Article 26(1) of the MLI, notified CTAs with Chile, France, Greece, Iceland, Ireland, Italy, Kazakhstan, Mexico, Moldova, Mongolia, the Netherlands, Peru, South Africa - Reservation made under Article 26(4) & notified relevant provision of CTA with UK - Reservation made under Article 28(2)(a)	- Part VI would apply and supersede the provisions of the CTA to the extent of incompatibility - The rules in Article 19(12) would apply - Arbitration process in Article 23(1) would apply - Article 23(5) would apply - Article 24(2) would not apply - The reservations formulated by both jurisdictions under Article 28(2)(a) would apply

Jurisdiction	*Position Taken*	*Treaty Partner*	*Position Taken*	*Outcome under the MLI*
Australia	- Pursuant to Article 18 of the MLI, chose to apply Part VI - Reservation made under Article 19(12) - Chose to apply Article 23(5) - Reservation made under Article 23(7) - Pursuant to Article 26(1) of the MLI, notified CTAs with New Zealand & Switzerland - Reservation made under Article 28(2)(a)	Japan	- Pursuant to Article 18 of the MLI, chose to apply Part VI - Reservation made under Article 19(12) - Reservation made under Article 23(2) - Reservation made under Article 26(4) & notified relevant provision of CTA with Germany, Hong Kong, the Netherlands, New Zealand, Portugal, Sweden, United Kingdom - Reservation made under Article 28(2)(a)	- Part VI would apply and supersede the provisions of the CTA to the extent of incompatibility - The rules in Article 19(12) would apply - Arbitration process in Article 23(2) would apply - Article 23(5) would apply - Article 24(2) would not apply - The reservations formulated by both jurisdictions under Article 28(2)(a) would apply

Jurisdiction	*Position Taken*	*Treaty Partner*	*Position Taken*	*Outcome under the MLI*
Canada	- Pursuant to Article 18 of the MLI, chose to apply Part VI - Reservation made under Article 19(12) - Reservation made under Article 23(3) - Chose to apply Article 23(5) - Reservation made under Article 23(7) - Pursuant to Article 26(1) of the MLI, notified CTAs with Chile, France, Greece, Iceland, Ireland, Italy, Kazakhstan, Mexico, Moldova, Mongolia, the Netherlands, Peru, South Africa - Reservation made under Article 26(4) & notified relevant provision of CTA with UK - Reservation made under Article 28(2)(a)	France	- Pursuant to Article 18 of the MLI, chose to apply Part VI - Reservation made under Article 19(11) - Reservation made under Article 19(12) - Chose to apply Article 23(5) - Chose to apply Article 24(2) - Relevant provisions of CTA with Canada notified under Article 26(1) - Reservation made under Article 28(2)(a)	- Relevant provisions of CTA would be replaced by Part VI - The two-year period in Article 19(1)(b) would be replaced by a three-year period - The rules in Article 19(12) would apply - Arbitration process in Article 23(1) would apply - Article 23(5) would apply - Article 24(2) would not apply - The reservations formulated by both jurisdictions under Article 28(2)(a) would apply
Canada	- Pursuant to Article 18 of the MLI, chose to apply Part VI - Reservation made under Article 19(12) - Reservation made under Article 23(3) - Chose to apply Article 23(5) - Reservation made under Article 23(7) - Pursuant to Article 26(1) of the MLI, notified CTAs with Chile, France, Greece, Iceland, Ireland, Italy, Kazakhstan, Mexico, Moldova, Mongolia, the Netherlands, Peru, South Africa	Japan	- Pursuant to Article 18 of the MLI, chose to apply Part VI - Reservation made under Article 19(12) - Reservation made under Article 23(2) - Reservation made under Article 26(4) & notified relevant provision of CTA with Germany, Hong Kong, the Netherlands,	- Part VI would apply and supersede the provisions of the CTA to the extent of incompatibility - The rules in Article 19(12) would apply - Article 19 would not apply until both CAs reach agreement on the type of arbitration process - Article 23(5) would apply - Article 24(2) would not apply

Jurisdiction	*Position Taken*	*Treaty Partner*	*Position Taken*	*Outcome under the MLI*
	- Reservation made under Article 26(4) & notified relevant provision of CTA with UK - Reservation made under Article 28(2)(a)		New Zealand, Portugal, Sweden, United Kingdom - Reservation made under Article 28(2)(a)	- The reservations formulated by both jurisdictions under Article 28(2)(a) would apply
Canada	- Pursuant to Article 18 of the MLI, chose to apply Part VI - Reservation made under Article 19(12) - Reservation made under Article 23(3) - Chose to apply Article 23(5) - Reservation made under Article 23(7) - Pursuant to Article 26(1) of the MLI, notified CTAs with Chile, France, Greece, Iceland, Ireland, Italy, Kazakhstan, Mexico, Moldova, Mongolia, the Netherlands, Peru, South Africa - Reservation made under Article 26(4) & notified relevant provision of CTA with UK - Reservation made under Article 28(2)(a)	UK	- Pursuant to Article 18 of the MLI, chose to apply Part VI - Chose to apply Article 23(5) - Chose to apply Article 24(2) - Under Article 26(1), notified relevant provision of CTA with Mexico, Spain, Sweden - Reservation made under Article 26(4) & notified relevant provision of CTA with Canada	Part VI would not apply

Jurisdiction	*Position Taken*	*Treaty Partner*	*Position Taken*	*Outcome under the MLI*
Sweden	- Pursuant to Article 18 of the MLI, chose to apply Part VI - Reservation made under Article 19(11) - Reservation made under Article 23(2) - Chose to apply Article 24(2) - Under Article 26(1), notified relevant provision of CTA with UK - No reservation made under Article 26(4) in respect of CTA with UK - Reservation made under Article 28(2)(a)	UK	- Pursuant to Article 18 of the MLI, chose to apply Part VI - Chose to apply Article 23(5) - Chose to apply Article 24(2) - Under Article 26(1), notified relevant provision of CTA with Mexico, Spain, Sweden - No reservation made under Article 26(4) in respect of CTA with Sweden	- Relevant provisions of CTA would be replaced by Part VI - The two-year period in Article 19(1)(b) would be replaced by a three-year period - Arbitration process in Article 23(2) would apply - Article 23(5) would apply - Article 24(2) would apply - The reservations formulated by Sweden under Article 28(2)(a) would apply

CHAPTER 4

MLI: Procedural Provisions

The Final Provisions (Articles 27-39) contained in Part VII of the MLI deal with the procedural provisions of the MLI. These procedural provisions are relevant for the implementation of the MLI by the Parties and the Depositary and carry significant influence to impact the substance of tax treaties. Elaborate discussions have been made in respect of each procedural provision of the MLI. For the benefit of readers, meaning of the phrase 'on or after', meaning of the term 'other taxes' and various interpretational issues on EIE provisions under Article 35 of the MLI have been analysed in detail.

4.1 PART VII OF MLI: FINAL PROVISIONS

471. The Final Provisions (Articles 27-39) as contained in Part VII of the MLI deal with the procedural provisions of the MLI. These provisions are relevant for the implementation of the MLI by the Parties and the Depositary and carry significant influence to impact the substance of tax treaties.

4.1.1 Article 27: Signature and Ratification, Acceptance or Approval

472. The MLI is open for signatures as of 31 December 2016 and can be signed by:

- all States;
- non-State jurisdictions that have concluded tax agreements under the arrangements with the State responsible for their international relations, like Guernsey, the Isle of Man, and Jersey. Parties and Signatories may decide to authorise other non-State jurisdictions to become Parties to the MLI. This decision must be made by consensus, meaning that any other jurisdiction can only become a Party to the MLI if no Party or Signatory objects.

473. On 7 June 2017,[332] Ministers and high-level officials from 76 countries and jurisdictions signed or formally expressed their intention to sign the MLI that will swiftly implement a series of tax treaty measures to update the existing network of bilateral tax treaties and reduce opportunities for tax avoidance by MNEs.

474. Signature of the MLI is followed by ratification, acceptance or approval. The use of appropriate term, i.e. ratification, acceptance or approval, will depend on domestic legal requirements of the concerned jurisdiction. For example, in Albania, Austria, Barbados, Denmark, Egypt, Georgia, India, Ireland, Israel, Jordan, Kazakhstan, Korea, Latvia, New Zealand, Sweden, the term 'ratification' is used. In Finland, Iceland, Japan, the Netherlands, the term 'acceptance' is used. Once the domestic procedures have been completed, an instrument of ratification, acceptance or approval is to be deposited with the Depositary and this is the event which triggers the rule for the EIF of the MLI pursuant to Article 34 of the MLI.

475. As of now, 95 jurisdictions are Signatories to the MLI with Bahrain[333] being the latest jurisdiction to sign. The latest jurisdiction to ratify the MLI is Barbados[334] which brings the total number of jurisdictions that have ratified the MLI to 60 as on 31 December 2020.

4.1.2 Article 28: Reservations

476. Under the MLI, following the BEPS Action 15 Report, the ad hoc Group has allowed jurisdictions to make only those reservations that are listed in the substantive provisions, to help them tailor their commitment with regard to other Parties based on their tax policies. This also serves to preserve the consistent implementation of the tax treaty-related BEPS measures. Jurisdictions may only make those reservations that the ad hoc Group considered acceptable from an international tax policy perspective in the fight against BEPS. In this way, the ad hoc Group tried to balance the two opposite interests found when drafting the MLI: broad participation and integrity of the treaty.

477. As the MLI tries to ensure the consistent implementation of the treaty-related BEPS measures, it also limits the ability of the States to make reservations of their own choice. Jurisdictions are allowed to make the reservations listed in Article 28(1) of the MLI, and those specifically provided in respect of mandatory binding arbitration procedure under Article 28(2) of the MLI, while all other reservations are to be considered impermissible and lacking legal effect. Under Article 28(2), jurisdictions are

332. Refer OECD – Ground-Breaking Multilateral BEPS Convention Signed at OECD Will Close Loopholes in Thousands of Tax Treaties Worldwide https://www.oecd.org/tax/beps/ground-breaking-multilateral-beps-convention-will-close-tax-treaty-loopholes.htm accessed on 22 August 2020.
333. Refer OECD – Bahrain Signs Landmark Agreement to Strengthen Its Tax Treaties https://www.oecd.org/ctp/treaties/bahrain-signs-landmark-agreement-to-strengthen-its-tax-treaties.htm accessed on 28 November 2020.
334. Refer OECD – Barbados Deposits Its Instrument of Ratification for the Multilateral BEPS Convention https://www.oecd.org/tax/treaties/barbados-deposits-its-instrument-of-ratification-for-the-multilateral-beps-convention.htm accessed on 5 January 2021.

free to decide on the scope[335] of cases that will be eligible for arbitration to reflect their domestic policies regarding arbitration.

478. Each substantive provision of the MLI includes an exhaustive list of reservations that jurisdictions can make, which can be put under three broad categories as below:

(1) Limited reservations applicable to minimum standards under the MLI.
(2) Reservations applicable to EIE provisions under the MLI.
(3) Reservations applicable to remaining substantive provisions of the MLI.

The above-mentioned categories of reservations are discussed in detail in Tables 5.1, 5.2 and 5.3.

Table 5.1 Limited Reservations Applicable to Minimum Standards under the MLI

S.N	*Type of Reservation*	*Purpose/Intent of Reservation*	*Article of MLI Containing This Type of Reservation*
1	Not to apply an entire article or parts of an article to CTAs that already meet the respective minimum standards.	At the time of making the reservations, jurisdictions must, on their own, evaluate whether their CTAs meet the minimum standards.	6(4)
			7(15)(b), (c)
2	Not to apply an entire article or parts of the article if the Parties commit to meet the minimum standard in an alternative manner.	A State decides to meet the minimum standards for preventing treaty abuse set out in BEPS Action 6 Report through the implementation of detailed LoB rule combined with rules to address conduit financing structures.	7(15)(a)
		A Party that has chosen to apply the S-LoB rule in addition to the PPT rule can reserve the right not to apply the entire Article 7 of the MLI to its CTAs; in which case, such a Party is required to reach a mutually satisfactory solution with its treaty partners, which is in line with the minimum standards.	7(16)
		A State may reserve the right not to apply certain parts of Article 16 of the MLI if it ensures that it will adopt the	16(5)(a), (b), (c)

335. Refer Explanatory Statement to the MLI, para. 265.

S.N	*Type of Reservation*	*Purpose/Intent of Reservation*	*Article of MLI Containing This Type of Reservation*
		conduct prescribed in the referred article or that it will implement similar provisions in future bilateral amendments to the CTAs.	

Table 5.2 Reservations Applicable to EIE Provisions under the MLI

S.N	*Type of Reservation*	*Purpose/Intent of Reservation*	*Article of MLI Containing This Type of Reservation*
1	Not to apply Article 35(4) of MLI.	Article 35(4) provides for early EIE of MAP provisions under Article 16 of MLI.	35(6)
2	To replace certain dates set out in Articles 35(1), (4) & (5), 28(9), 29(6) and 36(1)-(5).	This reservation translates into the right to delay the EIE of the MLI until the jurisdiction completes its internal ratification procedure.	35(7)
3	To apply the mandatory binding arbitration procedure to proceedings that began before the MLI enters into effect for the Parties.	It applies only if the CAs of all the Parties to the CTA agree that the case should be submitted to arbitration.	36(2)

Table 5.3 Reservations Applicable to Remaining Substantive Provisions of the MLI

S.N	*Type of Reservation*	*Purpose/Intent of Reservation*	*Article of MLI Containing This Type of Reservation*
1	Not to apply the entire article of MLI or parts of the article of MLI to all the CTAs of a jurisdiction.	Most of the articles of MLI that do not set out minimum standards provide for this type of reservation, due to the high level of flexibility ensured in the MLI.	3(5)(a), (f) 4(3)(a) 8(3)(a) 9(6)(a)-(c) 10(5)(a) 11(3)(a)

S.N	*Type of Reservation*	*Purpose/Intent of Reservation*	*Article of MLI Containing This Type of Reservation*
			12(4) 13(6)(a), (c) 14(3)(a)
2	Not to apply the entire article or parts of the article to the CTAs that already address the same BEPS concern & tackle it in the same or a similar manner as the article of the MLI.	Many CTAs may already provide for the anti-BEPS measures; hence, such CTA provisions need not be updated. Thus, MLI allows Parties to preserve such anti-BEPS contained in their CTAs.	3(5)(b) 4(3)(b) 8(3)(b) 9(6)(d)-(f) 10(5)(b) 11(3)(b) 13(6)(b) 17(3)(a) 26(4)
3	To apply the entire article or parts of the article of MLI only to the CTAs that already address the same BEPS concern.	This case is antithesis of the case at Sl. No. (2) above. Jurisdictions may desire only to update the provisions of the CTAs that already deal with the same matter. The reason may be that the provisions of CTAs provide for a different solution than that of the MLI, and the jurisdictions might prefer to resolve the problem in the same fashion as the MLI.	3(5)(g) 10(5)(c)
4	Not to apply the entire article or parts of the article of MLI to the CTAs that already address the same BEPS concern, despite the fact that the CTAs tackle the BEPS practice in a different manner than the MLI.	Although the provisions of the CTAs differ from the article of the MLI, they may still achieve the purpose of avoiding BEPS practices. On the other hand, it may be the case that, due to policy reasons, the Party cannot implement the MLI article. Hence, the ad hoc Group decided to not update the provisions of the CTAs.	3(5)(c) 4(3)(c), (d)
5	Not to apply the entire article or parts of the article of MLI to the CTAs that already address the same BEPS concern and tackle it through tailor-made provisions designed for the specific needs of the Parties to the CTAs.	Since the provisions of the CTAs were specifically designed based on the tax policies, interests of the Parties and those provisions achieve the anti-BEPS measures, they do not need to be updated through the MLI.	3(5)(d), (e)

S.N	*Type of Reservation*	*Purpose/Intent of Reservation*	*Article of MLI Containing This Type of Reservation*
6	To modify the application of the provision of the MLI by replacing certain text of the provision of MLI itself.	Article 4(3)(e) of the MLI lays down that Parties may replace the last sentence of Article 4(1) of MLI with different language.	4(3)(e)*
7	Not to apply the entire article of MLI in respect of Parties which have made a reservation under that article whereby they have modified the application of a provision of the MLI by replacing certain portion of its text.	The reservation in Article 4(3)(f) of the MLI responds to the one explained in Sl. No. 6 above, where jurisdictions may reserve not to apply Article 4 of MLI to the CTAs concluded with Parties that have made a reservation to Article 4(3)(e) of MLI.	4(3)(f)
8	Not to apply the entire article of MLI to particular activities as the CTAs may already contain provisions specifically designed to address those activities.	This reservation type provides that Parties may reserve not to apply the new anti-contract splitting rule to the exploration or exploitation of natural resources, as the CTAs may already contain provisions specifically designed to address those activities.	14(3)(b)
9	Not to apply the entire article to some CTAs if the reserving Parties have chosen not to opt in to an alternative provision.	Parties that have not chosen to apply an alternative option to avoid cases of double non-taxation where the exemption method applies may reserve the right not to apply the entire article to identified CTAs.	5(8)
		Parties that do not choose to apply Option C (allows credit method) may reserve the right not to apply the entire article to identified CTAs.	5(9)
10	Not to apply the entire article of MLI to the jurisdiction's CTAs if that jurisdiction has also reserved the right not to apply other concomitant/connected provisions of the MLI.	Article 15 of MLI is only relevant if Parties to the MLI also apply the articles that modify the PE definition, as provided in Articles 12-14 of MLI. If Parties do not reserve the right not to apply Articles 12-14 of MLI, they will not be allowed to make a	15(2)

S.N	*Type of Reservation*	*Purpose/Intent of Reservation*	*Article of MLI Containing This Type of Reservation*
		reservation to the application of Article 15 of MLI, as the definition of 'a person closely related to an enterprise' is essential for the application of Articles 12-14.	
11	Not to apply the entire article of MLI to the jurisdiction's CTAs if the reserving Party commits to acting in a manner or if it commits to implementing similar provisions in future bilateral amendments to the CTAs.	This reservation deals with the application of corresponding adjustment provisions.	17(3)(b), (c)
12	To make tailor-made reservations applicable to mandatory binding arbitration procedure.	The length of time that a MAP should last before taxpayers may request the initiation of arbitration.	19(11)
		Arbitration not to apply if a decision on the impugned issue has already been rendered by a court or administrative tribunal of either Contracting Jurisdiction.	19(12)
		Pertains to the provisions relating to the type of arbitration process.	23(2), (3)
		Pertains to the non-disclosure rule.	23(6), (7)
		The possibility for CAs to resolve the case in a different fashion than the decision reached by the arbitration panel.	24(3)

* This provision could be construed as an amendment of Article 4(1) of MLI itself, instead of a reservation, as it aims to modify the text of the article and not to modify or limit its legal effect. Although the purpose of Article 4(3)(e) does not seem to be in conformity with the definition of reservations as provided for in the Vienna Convention, the ad hoc Group has labelled it as such.

479. An important characteristic of reservations is that they are not mutually exclusive[336] in all cases. A jurisdiction may simultaneously make more than one reservation listed in one of the articles of the MLI. For example, Ireland has made reservation in Article 3(5)(b), (f) to cater to the types of provisions in force in its CTAs.

480. Article 28(2)(a) provides that any Party that chooses under Article 18 to apply Part VI of the MLI may formulate one or more reservations with respect to the scope of cases that shall be eligible for arbitration under Part VI. These provisions were added to provide Parties committing to arbitration with flexibility to tailor the scope of cases that will be eligible for arbitration to reflect their domestic policies regarding arbitration. Article 28(2)(b) of the MLI provides that the free-form reservations made under Article 28(2)(a) of the MLI are subject to acceptance by the other Parties. In cases where an objection is raised to a free-form reservation pursuant to Article 28(2)(b), the entirety of Part VI is not applicable between an objecting Party and the reserving Party.

481. Article 28(3) confirms the effect of reservations made under paragraph 1 or 2 on the application of the relevant provisions of the MLI between the reserving Party and the other Parties to the MLI. Article 28(3) states that unless explicitly provided otherwise, any reservation made by a Party will modify the provisions to which it relates to the same extent for both the reserving Party and the other Party. Accordingly, unless a provision of the MLI explicitly provides otherwise, a reservation will modify the relevant provisions of the MLI as between the reserving Party and all other Parties to the MLI, i.e. for the reserving Party in its relations with the other Parties and for those other Parties in their relations with the reserving Party. In other words, reservations will apply symmetrically. Thus, the effects of reservations under Article 28(1) of the MLI are generally reciprocal and symmetrical[337] unless provided otherwise. When the effects of the reservations of the MLI are asymmetrical, they will not apply to the reserving Party, as in Article 5(8), (9) of the MLI. Technically, it may be argued that the provisions of Article 5(8), (9) are not reservations, as according to Article 2(d) of the Vienna Convention, an essential element of a reservation is that it must apply to that jurisdiction itself. However, the purpose of the provisions established in Article 5(8), (9) is to exclude the legal effect of the entirety of Article 5 or Option C, respectively, not only for the reserving Party – which, in any case, has not opted in to any option (Option C in particular) – but also for other Parties to the MLI with which it has a CTA. Such provisions, although applicable asymmetrically, pursue to rebalance the rights and obligations established in the CTAs, which could be distorted due to the unilateral decisions of one of the Parties to opt in to one of the alternative provisions of Article 5 of MLI, as Article 5 of MLI provides for the asymmetrical application of the alternative

336. *Id.*, para. 14.
337. *Id.*, para. 270.

options established therein. Thus, in a way, the provisions contained in Article 5(8), (9) do not create inequalities, but counterbalance them.[338]

482. Article 28(4) requires a Party which has included, in its list of CTAs pursuant to Article 2(1)(a) of the MLI, one or more tax agreements entered into by or on behalf of a jurisdiction or territory for whose international relations it is responsible pursuant to Article 2(1)(a) of the MLI, to deposit a separate list of reservations for that jurisdiction or territory, which may be different from the Party's own list of reservations. This separate list of reservations will apply to all agreements entered into by or on behalf of that jurisdiction or territory which are covered by the MLI. Article 28(4) is not relevant to jurisdictions which become Parties to the MLI pursuant to Article 27(1)(b) or (c) because those jurisdictions are Parties in their own right and will make their reservations as any other Party under Article 28(1), and if applicable Article 28(2) of the MLI.

483. Article 28(5) provides that reservations shall be made either at the time of signature or when depositing an instrument of ratification. This general rule is subject to the provisions of:

- Article 28(2) (the possibility for a Party which chooses to apply Part VI to formulate one or more reservations with respect to the scope of cases that shall be eligible for arbitration under the provisions of Part VI);
- Article 28(6) (the possibility to provide a definitive list of reservations at the time of signature);
- Article 28(9) (the possibility to withdraw or replace reservations); and
- Article 29(5) (the possibility to make new reservations if an agreement added to the list notified under Article 2(1)(a)(ii) is the first to fall within the scope of a reservation listed in Article 28(8) or if a newly added agreement is the first inclusion in the list of a tax agreement entered into by or on behalf of a jurisdiction or territory for whose international relations the Party is responsible).

It is possible, however, for a Party to choose to apply Part VI of the MLI after it has already become a Party. To ensure that such a Party has the opportunity to make the defined reservations related to Part VI, Article 28(5) also provides that such reservations shall be made at the time of that Party's notification to the Depositary pursuant to Article 18 that it chooses to apply Part VI.

484. Article 28(6) provides that if reservations are made at the time of signature, they shall be confirmed upon deposit of the instrument of ratification since this is the moment at which consent to be bound by the MLI is expressed following the completion of domestic procedures. At the time of the deposit of the instrument of ratification, changes may be made to the list of reservations including the addition or deletion of reservations or the modification of reservations made at the time of signature. Article 28(6) provides for an exception in a case in which a Signatory

338. Refer Nathalie Bravo's 'A Multilateral Instrument for Updating the Tax Treaty Network' IBFD Doctoral Series 52, pp. 222-224.

explicitly specifies that the list of reservations it makes at the time of signature is to be considered definitive. In such cases, no confirmation of the reservations would be required upon deposit of the instrument of ratification. The definitive nature of reservations made upon signature is, however, subject to the provisions of:

- Article 28(2) and (5) (the possibility for a Party which chooses to apply Part VI after it has become a Party to the MLI to make the reservations permitted under Part VI at the time it chooses to apply Part VI);
- Article 28(9) (the possibility to withdraw or replace reservations); and
- Article 29(5) (the possibility to make new reservations if an agreement added to the list notified under Article 2(1)(a)(ii) is the first to fall within the scope of a reservation listed in Article 28(8) or if a newly added agreement is the first inclusion in the list of a tax agreement entered into by or on behalf of a jurisdiction or territory for whose international relations the Party is responsible).

485. Article 28(7) provides that if reservations are not made at the time of signature, a provisional list of expected reservations shall be provided to the Depositary at that time. This provisional list is for transparency purposes only and is intended to give other Signatories a preliminary indication of the Signatory's intended position. This takes account of the nature of the MLI which will operate to modify existing bilateral or multilateral relationships and the reservations chosen by the other Contracting Jurisdictions will determine the way in which the existing bilateral or multilateral agreement is modified. Accordingly, provisional indications of intended positions are important to allow an understanding of the likely changes to an existing tax agreement and to facilitate domestic ratification procedures as well as to prepare for the implementation of the modifications made by the Convention. The provisional list of expected reservations under Article 28(7) does not restrict the ability of that Signatory to submit a modified list of reservations upon deposit of the instrument of ratification.

486. Article 28(8) requires that, when reservations are made under the listed provisions and based on objectively defined characteristics, an exhaustive list of the CTAs which are within the scope of the reservation as defined in the relevant provision must be provided. In the case of a reservation that applies only where a CTA contains a specific type of provision, a list of the article and paragraph number of each relevant provision must also be provided. This is intended to provide clarity as to the application of reservations which are intended to apply only to CTAs with a specific characteristic and duly notified by the reserving Party. Such reservations would not apply to any CTA which is not included in the lists required by Article 28(8).

487. In order to ensure a minimum level of coordination and enhance the consistent implementation of the tax treaty rules developed in the course of the BEPS Project, the reservations in MLI apply either to all of the CTAs of a reserving Party, as listed in Article 28(1) of the MLI, or to all of its CTAs that have certain objectively defined characteristics, as listed in Article 28(8) of the MLI. Jurisdictions making full reservations do not need to identify the provisions of the CTAs because, in principle, uncertainties derived from the application of such reservations will not arise. On the other hand, Article 28(8) lays down that for the reservations enumerated therein, the reserving Party has to provide a list of the provisions of the CTAs that are within the scope of each reservation. It also provides that the reservations enumerated therein will apply only to the provisions of CTA duly notified by the reserving Party. If a reserving Party does not notify one or several of the CTAs, the reservations based on objectively defined characteristics will not produce their intended effects. Although the obligation to list the provisions of CTAs is to provide certainty and transparency, it is, in fact, an essential requirement for the operation of many of the reservations set out in the MLI.[339] Few illustrations of notifications under Article 28(8) of the MLI are:

- Reservation by Poland under Article 8(3)(b)(i) in respect of its CTAs with Belgium, Cyprus, Denmark, Luxembourg, Malta, Norway, Portugal, Singapore, the Slovak Republic, Switzerland, UK.
- Reservation by Kenya under Article 8(3)(b)(ii) in respect of its CTAs with Canada, Denmark, Italy, Norway, Sweden.
- Reservation by India under Article 8(3)(b)(iii) in respect of its CTA with Portugal.

488. Article 28(9) provides for the possibility to withdraw a reservation made in accordance with Article 28(1) or (2) or to replace it with a reservation which is more limited in scope, by means of a notification addressed to the Depositary. The purpose of allowing the withdrawal or replacement of a reservation by another is to allow a Party to accept further modifications to be made to its CTAs by the MLI, i.e. to introduce anti-BEPS measures in CTAs to the maximum extent possible which, in the first place, is the purpose of MLI also. Accordingly, a Party can accept additional modifications of its CTAs by means of the replacement of a reservation but cannot use this mechanism to place new restrictions on the modifications of its tax agreements by the MLI.

489. Paragraph 9(a), (b) of Article 28 set out the dates on which such a withdrawal or replacement of a reservation will take effect for WHT and other taxes, subject to Article 35(7), if opted. Paragraph 9(a) applies where all Contracting Jurisdictions are States or jurisdictions which are Parties to the MLI on the date of receipt by the Depositary of the notification of withdrawal or replacement of the reservation. Under paragraph (9)(a), the event/taxable periods to apply WHT/other taxes, etc. shall come into effect on or after 1 January of the next year following a time period (of six calendar months) from the date of communication by the Depositary of the notification of withdrawal or replacement of reservation. The time period is provided so as to allow the Parties affected by the withdrawal or replacement of reservations more time to adapt their domestic laws or administrative practices. Paragraph 9(b) applies with respect to CTAs for which one or more Contracting Jurisdictions become a Party to the MLI after the date of receipt by the Depositary of the notification of withdrawal or replacement of the

339. Refer Explanatory Statement to the MLI, para. 281.

reservation. In cases under paragraph 9(b), the withdrawal or replacement shall take effect on the latest date on which the CTA enters into force for each of those Contracting Jurisdictions. This takes into account the fact that, pursuant to Articles 34 and 35, there is at least a three-month period between the date of deposit of the instrument of ratification and the EIF of the MLI (i.e., the date on which a State or jurisdiction becomes a Party) as well as an additional period before the provisions of the MLI enter into effect for the new Party. In addition, Article 35(7), if opted, provides for the possibility for a Party to further modify the rule on the EIE of the withdrawal or replacement of a reservation in order to allow for the completion of its internal procedures for this purpose.

4.1.3 Article 29: Notifications

490. Paragraph 1 of Article 29 provides that notifications made pursuant to certain provisions in the MLI shall be made either at the time of signature or when depositing the instrument of ratification. This general rule applies subject to:

- Article 29(5) (the possibility to extend the list of agreements notified under Article 2(1)(a)(ii) and to make any additional notifications that may be required in respect of the newly added agreements as well as to make new notifications if a newly added agreement is the first inclusion in the list of a tax agreement entered into by or on behalf of a jurisdiction or territory for whose international relations the Party is responsible);
- Article 29(6) (the possibility to make certain additional notifications in respect of tax agreements already included in the list notified under Article 2(1)(a)(ii)); and
- Article 35(7) (the notifications required when a Party makes a reservation to the provisions on EIE in order to allow for the completion of its internal procedures for that purpose).

491. The procedural rules of the MLI concerning the notifications set forth in Article 29(1) broadly apply under the following categories:

(a) CTAs are notified at the time of signature or ratification under Article 29(1)(a) of the MLI.
(b) Provisions of the CTAs that are within the scope of compatibility clauses are *inter alia* notified under Article 29(1)(b)-(o), (s) of the MLI.
(c) Optional provisions are *inter alia* notified under Article 29(1)(e), (f), (h), (p), (q) and (r) of MLI.
(d) Alternative provisions are *inter alia* notified under Article 29(1)(d) and (l) of the MLI.
(e) EIE notifications are made under Article 29(1)(t) of the MLI.

492. Article 29(2) requires a Party which has included, in its list of CTAs pursuant to Article 2(1)(a)(ii) of the MLI, one or more tax agreements entered into by or on behalf of a jurisdiction or territory for whose international relations it is responsible pursuant to Article 2(1)(a)(i)(B) of the MLI, to deposit a separate list of notifications for that jurisdiction or territory, which may be different from the Party's own list of notifications. This separate list of notifications will apply to all agreements entered into by or on behalf of that jurisdiction or territory which are covered by the MLI (subject to reservations applicable to CTAs that contain existing provisions with specific, objectively defined characteristics). Article 29(2) is not relevant to jurisdictions which become Parties to the MLI pursuant to Article 27(1)(b) or (c) because those jurisdictions are Parties in their own right and will make their notifications as any other Party under Article 29(1).

493. Notifications must be made at the time of signature or ratification as per Article 29(3) of the MLI. If notifications are made at the time of signature, they must be confirmed upon the deposit of the instrument of ratification. Article 29(3) provides for an exception in a case in which a Party explicitly specifies that the list of notifications it makes at the time of signature is to be considered definitive, subject to the provisions of Articles 29(5), 29(6) and 35(7). In such cases, no confirmation of the notifications would be required upon deposit of the instrument of ratification.

494. However, if the notifications are not made at the time of signature, a provisional list of expected notifications is required to be provided at that time in accordance with Article 29(4) of the MLI. This provisional list is for transparency purposes only and is intended to give other Signatories a preliminary indication of the Signatory's intended position. This takes account of the nature of the MLI which will operate to modify existing bilateral or multilateral relationships and the options chosen by the other Contracting Jurisdictions will determine the way in which the existing bilateral or multilateral agreement is modified. Accordingly, provisional indications of intended positions are important to allow an understanding of the likely changes to an existing tax agreement and to facilitate domestic ratification procedures as well as to prepare for the implementation of the modifications made by the MLI. The provisional list of expected notifications under Article 29(4) does not restrict the ability of that Signatory to submit a modified list of notifications upon deposit of the instrument of ratification.

495. Article 29(5) provides that the list of agreements notified under Article 2(1)(a)(ii) may be extended at any time by means of a notification addressed to the Depositary. If the agreement falls within the scope of any of the reservations made by the Party listed in Article 28(8), the Party must specify this in this notification. The Party must also specify any additional notifications that are required under Article 29(1)(b) through (s) to reflect the inclusion of the additional agreements. This would apply if the extension of the list resulted in the inclusion of an agreement containing existing provisions falling within the scope of the notifications required under Articles 3 through 26. In addition, Article 29(5) provides that, on the date on which a newly added agreement becomes a CTA under the MLI, the provisions on EIE in Article 35 will govern the date on which the modifications to the CTA will have effect.

496. Japan[340] was the first jurisdiction which has made a notification (communicated by the Depositary on 14 February 2020 and 22 July 2020) under Article 29(5) of the MLI. At the time of ratification of the MLI, Japan had notified 39 CTAs in its MLI position. The CTA list was extended by Japan to 41 by including Qatar and Oman as additional CTAs notified under Article 29(5) of the MLI. On 22 September 2020, the Depositary has communicated that France[341] has made a notification under Article 29(5) by extending its CTA list under the MLI and has increased the number of CTAs notified under the MLI from 91 (at the time of ratification) to 120.

497. Article 29(6) allows Parties to make additional notifications pursuant to Article 29(1)(b) through (s) after becoming a Party to the MLI by means of a notification addressed to the Depositary. Sub-paragraphs (a) and (b) of paragraph 6 of Article 29 set out when such additional notifications will take effect. This provision mirrors Article 28(9) relating to the date on which the withdrawal or replacement of a reservation will take effect. Article 35(7) provides for the possibility for a Party to modify the rule on the EIE of the additional notifications in order to allow for the completion of internal procedures for this purpose. An inadvertent omission of existing provisions can be addressed by making an additional notification pursuant to Article 29(6)[342] of MLI.

498. Article 29(6) of the MLI enables Parties to make additional notifications pursuant to Article 29(1)(b) through (s) by means of a notification to the Depositary. Thus, Parties to the MLI may, at any time, i.e. even after deposit of instrument of ratification, notify in written form to the Depositary, their decision to opt in to any of the optional provisions contained in the MLI. In this sense, a Party to the MLI that may initially be apprehensive about the application of a certain optional provision may decide to opt in to that provision in the future if, after evaluation of practical operation of that provision, it considers that the same may be suitable for its tax treaty relations. Similarly, the ad hoc Group did not expressly indicate in the MLI whether Parties can choose alternative provisions after ratification. However, based on the fact that Article 29(6) of the MLI allows Parties to make additional notifications after ratification and the fact that the notifications regarding the alternative provisions are listed among the allowed additional notifications in Article 29(1)(d), (l), it appears that Parties can notify[343] their choice of alternative options after the EIF of the MLI. The ad hoc Group had kept this window open as this will enlarge the treaty obligations of such Parties to avoid BEPS, which in effect is the main object and purpose of the MLI. However, it does not mean that Parties can 'change' the application of alternative provisions if they have already exercised such an option at the time of ratification when they submitted their final position to the Depositary.

340. Refer OECD – Signatories and Parties to the MLI http://www.oecd.org/tax/treaties/beps-mli-position-japan-consolidated.pdf.

341. *Id.*

342. Refer Explanatory Statement to the MLI, para. 18.

343. Refer Nathalie Bravo's 'A Multilateral Instrument for Updating the Tax Treaty Network' IBFD Doctoral Series 52, p. 197.

499. On 26 November 2020, the Depositary has communicated that Kazakhstan[344] has made a notification under Article 29(6) of the MLI by notifying the revised dates of EIF of its DTAAs with certain countries, correcting its notifications of treaty provisions under certain articles submitted earlier in its MLI position and has also made additional notifications under certain articles of the MLI.

4.1.4 Article 30: Subsequent Modifications of CTAs

500. On a plain reading of the provisions of Article 30, it is seen that it allows the jurisdictions to modify those provisions of the CTAs which are not modified by the MLI, as well as those provisions of CTAs which are modified by the MLI, i.e., where anti-BEPS provisions have been introduced through the MLI. The latter part is discussed in more detail hereunder.

501. The BEPS Action 15 Report[345] *inter alia* provides that in order to ensure consistency with the legal regime established by the MLI, the Parties might deem it necessary to define certain parameters for their future treaty-making activities through a forward-looking compatibility or 'obedience' clause, stipulating that Parties shall not conclude subsequent agreements which are in contradiction with the treaty. However, the MLI does not include an 'obedience' clause; therefore, it allows the conclusion of subsequent modifications without restriction, as per Article 30 of the MLI. Further, on a combined reading of paragraphs 33 and 310 of the Explanatory Statement to the MLI, it is seen that the MLI is not intended to freeze in time the underlying agreement and that Contracting Jurisdictions may decide to further amend the underlying agreement after it has been modified by the MLI. The right of the Contracting Jurisdictions to further amend their CTAs is intended to remain unaffected, irrespective of whether the further modifications relate to provisions that have been modified by the application of the MLI. As a result,[346] the Parties to the MLI seem to remain free to contract out from the provisions of this instrument, even if the agreed changes reverse their commitment to avoid creating opportunities for BEPS practices, including the abandonment of minimum standards through the PPT rule. No legal limitations can be found in the MLI that would preclude such a modification. The only possible check could come from the commitments made within the IF[347] of the OECD.

502. As a contrarian thought, in the absence of an express statement for reversal in commitments to avoid creating opportunities for BEPS practices provided in Article 30

344. Refer OECD – Signatories and Parties to the MLI http://www.oecd.org/tax/treaties/beps-mli-position-kazakhstan-consolidated.pdf.
345. Action 15: BEPS 2015 Final Report, OECD/G20 Base Erosion and Profit Shifting Project, pp. 35-36.
346. Refer Nathalie Bravo's 'A Multilateral Instrument for Updating the Tax Treaty Network' IBFD Doctoral Series 52, p. 267.
347. Refer OECD – Members of the OECD/G20 Inclusive Framework on BEPS http://www.oecd.org/tax/beps/inclusive-framework-on-beps-composition.pdf accessed on 7 September 2020 and Refer OECD – About the Inclusive Framework on BEPS https://www.oecd.org/tax/beps/beps-about.htm/#monitoring accessed on 7 September 2020.

and Explanatory Statement thereto, an alternative interpretation could be that the Parties to the MLI are required to apply the provisions in good faith and to interpret them in accordance with the ordinary meaning to be given to their terms based on their context and in light of their object and purpose (as provided for in Articles 26 and 31 of the Vienna Convention). Hence, if one were to delve into the context, object and purpose of the MLI, an inference of provisions of Article 30 can also be drawn to mean that subsequent amendments to those provisions of CTAs which are modified by the MLI, must be similar, or even more far-reaching modifications than those provided by the MLI, can be carried out in the fight against BEPS.

503. The preamble of MLI creates a multilateral context in which all Parties commit to implementing tax treaty rules that seek to prevent BEPS practices, so as to achieve a level playing field. Thus, the main object and purpose of the MLI is to eliminate BEPS practices through the implementation of coordinated and consistent tax treaty provisions. In this context, if Parties to the MLI were to conclude new agreements to adopt provisions that reduce the scope of the accepted multilateral commitment to tackle BEPS, those agreements would probably be incompatible with the object and purpose of the MLI as such, and would defeat the very purpose of joining the MLI in the first place. On following this line of thinking, it may be inferred that though Article 30 of MLI encourages Parties to modify their CTAs, it might just as well encourage Parties not to create new opportunities for BEPS practices, which is in line with the object and purpose of the MLI, monitoring process implemented within the IF and the entire BEPS Project.

504. Under the latter/contrarian interpretation of Article 30 of the MLI, Parties could conclude subsequent modifications to the CTAs, as modified by the MLI, that would even change the PPT rule, but only if the modification in this rule maintains the commitment of the Parties to preventing BEPS practices, i.e., to have a similar or a more far-reaching scope in the fight against BEPS practices.

505. In this context, in a Note[348] released by the OECD Directorate of Legal Affairs on functioning of the MLI under the public international law, it has been *inter alia* opined that:

- MLI does not freeze the underlying bilateral treaty in time;
- the mutual consent between the two jurisdictions on issues (in the context of wider multilateral consensus in the form of MLI) can continue to be modified in the future;
- the key concept is the evolution of the mutual consent between the two jurisdictions which may be expressed in different legal forms.

348. Refer Note by the OECD Directorate for Legal Affairs http://www.oecd.org/tax/treaties/legal-note-on-the-functioning-of-the-MLI-under-public-international-law.pdf (paras 17, 18) accessed on 23 August 2020.

506. To sum up, it can be inferred that Article 30 of the MLI belongs to the category of Article 41(1)(a) of the Vienna Convention which establishes the possibility of modifying multilateral treaties through *inter se* agreements between two or more Parties. Thus, Article 30 prioritises the principle of sovereignty of States, granting them flexibility to continue modifying their CTAs as modified through the MLI. In other words, the Parties to the CTAs would continue to be masters of their treaties.

4.1.5 Article 31: Conference of the Parties

507. Article 31 of the MLI provides for the possibility of convening a CoP. CoP can be convened for the purpose of achieving a uniform interpretation and application of the MLI (under Article 32(2)) or to consider an amendment to the MLI (under Article 33(2)). A CoP shall be served by the Depositary, as provided under Article 31(2) of the MLI. Following the request of the UK to the Depositary in July 2019, CoP has been convened under Article 31(3) for the purposes of taking any decisions or exercising any functions as may be required or appropriate under the provisions of the MLI. The first meeting of the MLI CoP was held on 4 October 2019[349] and the second meeting of the CoP was held on 19 November 2020. The Parties may decide to invite Signatories to participate in a CoP. The CoP could meet in person, but could also fulfil its functions by meeting remotely, for example by using videoconference or teleconference, by taking decisions through written procedure or by any other means decided upon by the Parties.

508. The MLI assigns two functions to the CoP: (i) to 'address' questions of interpretation or implementation and (ii) to 'consider' a proposed amendment to the MLI. Both functions raise crucial questions as to the procedure and effect of any decision taken by that Conference. On a reading of the MLI text, it is unclear how decisions would be reached.[350] In order to enable the CoP to discharge its functions envisaged in Articles 31, 32 and 33 of the MLI, there was a case for the CoP to devise its own 'Mandate' and 'Rules of Procedure'. Accordingly, during the second meeting of the CoP held on 19 November 2020, the following areas, *inter alia*, have been outlined:

- functions of the CoP;
- composition of the CoP;
- decision-making process of the CoP;
- role of the OECD Secretariat.

349. Refer OECD/G20 Inclusive Framework on BEPS Progress Report July 2019 – July 2020 (p. 21) https://www.oecd.org/tax/beps/oecd-g20-inclusive-framework-on-beps-progress-report-july-2019-july-2020.pdf accessed on 2 September 2020.
350. Refer Article by Werner C. Haslehner Titled 'A Multilateral Interpretation of the Multilateral Instrument (and Covered Tax Agreements)' https://research.ibfd.org/#/doc?url=/collections/bit/html/bit_2020_04_o2_2.html (s. 2.3) accessed on 2 September 2020.

4.1.6 Article 32: Interpretation and Implementation of MLI

509. The interpretation[351] of the provisions of the MLI is based not only on the text of the instrument (grammatical interpretation) but also on its context (systematic interpretation), its object and purpose (teleological interpretation) and its supplementary means of interpretation (historical interpretation).

510. As with any international agreement, the basic principle for the interpretation of the provisions of the MLI is the rule set out in Article 31(1) of the VCLT; i.e., the MLI shall be interpreted in good faith in accordance with the ordinary meaning to be given to the terms of the treaty in their context and in the light of its object and purpose.[352]

511. In accordance with Article 32(1) of the MLI, the contracting jurisdictions should use the agreement's MAP to endeavour to settle questions of interpretation and implementation of the provisions of the agreement that have been modified by the MLI.[353] This would include agreeing on how the MLI has modified that particular agreement – as long as the agreement reached between the contracting jurisdictions is consistent with the provisions of the MLI. Further, Article 32(2) of the MLI provides that questions on the interpretation or implementation of the MLI itself may be addressed by the CoP convened in accordance with the provisions of Article 31(3) of MLI. Such questions to be addressed by the CoP may include interpretation issues as to how the provisions of MLI modify the CTAs.

4.1.7 Article 33: Amendment of the MLI

512. Based on the object and purpose of the MLI, which is to strike a balance between sovereignty and international cooperation, there were ample reasons for the ad hoc Group to insert an amendment procedure of the MLI itself in the form of Article 33 of the MLI, which is applicable in conjunction with Article 31 of the MLI and Articles 39, 40 of the Vienna Convention.[354]

513. Any Party to the MLI can propose an amendment to the MLI by submitting the proposed amendment to the Depositary, following which a CoP may be convened to consider the proposed amendment in accordance with the procedure set out in Article 31(3).

4.1.8 Article 34: Entry into Force of MLI

514. The MLI has entered into force on 1 July 2018 following the expiration of period of three calendar months beginning on the date of deposit of the fifth instrument of

351. Refer Nathalie Bravo's 'A Multilateral Instrument for Updating the Tax Treaty Network' IBFD Doctoral Series 52, p. 4.
352. Refer Explanatory Statement to the MLI, para. 12.
353. *Id.*, para. 315.
354. Refer Nathalie Bravo's 'A Multilateral Instrument for Updating the Tax Treaty Network' IBFD Doctoral Series 52, pp. 278, 281, 288.

ratification. The MLI was first ratified by Austria (on 22 September 2017), followed by the Isle of Man (on 25 October 2017), Jersey (on 15 December 2017), Poland (on 23 January 2018) and Slovenia (on 22 March 2018) being the fifth jurisdiction to ratify the MLI. For all these five jurisdictions, MLI has entered into force on 1 July 2018 and they became Parties to the MLI.

515. For each Signatory ratifying the MLI post 1 July 2018, the MLI shall enter into force for that State or jurisdiction on the first day of the month following the expiration of a period of three calendar months after the date of the deposit by such State or jurisdiction of its instrument of ratification to the Depositary. Serbia, Sweden, New Zealand, UK ratified MLI in June 2018, following which the MLI entered into force for these countries on 1 October 2018. The next lot of ratifications happened in the month of September 2018 when Lithuania, Israel, the Slovak Republic, Australia, France, Japan ratified; hence, the MLI entered into force for these countries on 1 January 2019. The process of ratification of the MLI by various jurisdictions has moved forward sedately. In September 2020, another round of substantial ratifications happened when Bosnia and Herzegovina, Albania, Costa Rica, Jordan, Egypt ratified the MLI. As on 31 December 2020, a list of dates of EIF[355] of the MLI for 60 jurisdictions which have ratified it is provided in Table 6.

Table 6 EIF of MLI for Various Jurisdictions

S.N	*Jurisdiction*	*Signature*	*Ratification*	*Entry into Force*
1	Austria	07-06-2017	22-09-2017	01-07-2018
2	The Isle of Man	07-06-2017	25-10-2017	01-07-2018
3	Jersey	07-06-2017	15-12-2017	01-07-2018
4	Poland	07-06-2017	23-01-2018	01-07-2018
5	Slovenia	07-06-2017	22-03-2018	01-07-2018
6	Serbia	07-06-2017	05-06-2018	01-10-2018
7	Sweden	07-06-2017	22-06-2018	01-10-2018
8	New Zealand	07-06-2017	27-06-2018	01-10-2018
9	United Kingdom	07-06-2017	29-06-2018	01-10-2018
10	Lithuania	07-06-2017	11-09-2018	01-01-2019
11	Israel	07-06-2017	13-09-2018	01-01-2019
12	The Slovak Republic	07-06-2017	20-09-2018	01-01-2019
13	Australia	07-06-2017	26-09-2018	01-01-2019
14	France	07-06-2017	26-09-2018	01-01-2019
15	Japan	07-06-2017	26-09-2018	01-01-2019
16	Malta	07-06-2017	18-12-2018	01-04-2019
17	Singapore	07-06-2017	21-12-2018	01-04-2019

355. Refer OECD – Signatories and Parties to the MLI http://www.oecd.org/tax/treaties/beps-mli-signatories-and-parties.pdf.

S.N	*Jurisdiction*	*Signature*	*Ratification*	*Entry into Force*
18	Monaco	07-06-2017	10-01-2019	01-05-2019
19	Ireland	07-06-2017	29-01-2019	01-05-2019
20	Guernsey	07-06-2017	12-02-2019	01-06-2019
21	Finland	07-06-2017	25-02-2019	01-06-2019
22	Curaçao	07-06-2017	29-03-2019	01-07-2019
23	Georgia	07-06-2017	29-03-2019	01-07-2019
24	The Netherlands	07-06-2017	29-03-2019	01-07-2019
25	Luxembourg	07-06-2017	09-04-2019	01-08-2019
26	The United Arab Emirates	27-06-2018	29-05-2019	01-09-2019
27	Russia	07-06-2017	18-06-2019	01-10-2019
28	India	07-06-2017	25-06-2019	01-10-2019
29	Belgium	07-06-2017	27-06-2019	01-10-2019
30	Norway	07-06-2017	17-07-2019	01-11-2019
31	Ukraine	23-07-2018	08-08-2019	01-12-2019
32	Canada	07-06-2017	29-08-2019	01-12-2019
33	Switzerland	07-06-2017	29-08-2019	01-12-2019
34	Iceland	07-06-2017	26-09-2019	01-01-2020
35	Denmark	07-06-2017	30-09-2019	01-01-2020
36	Mauritius	05-07-2017	18-10-2019	01-02-2020
37	Latvia	07-06-2017	29-10-2019	01-02-2020
38	Liechtenstein	07-06-2017	19-12-2019	01-04-2020
39	Qatar	04-12-2018	23-12-2019	01-04-2020
40	Cyprus	07-06-2017	23-01-2020	01-05-2020
41	Saudi Arabia	18-09-2018	23-01-2020	01-05-2020
42	Uruguay	07-06-2017	06-02-2020	01-06-2020
43	Portugal	07-06-2017	28-02-2020	01-06-2020
44	San Marino	07-06-2017	11-03-2020	01-07-2020
45	Indonesia	07-06-2017	28-04-2020	01-08-2020
46	The Czech Republic	07-06-2017	13-05-2020	01-09-2020
47	Korea	07-06-2017	13-05-2020	01-09-2020
48	Kazakhstan	25-06-2018	24-06-2020	01-10-2020
49	Oman	26-11-2019	07-07-2020	01-11-2020
50	Bosnia and Herzegovina	30-10-2019	16-09-2020	01-01-2021
51	Albania	28-05-2019	22-09-2020	01-01-2021
52	Costa Rica	07-06-2017	22-09-2020	01-01-2021
53	Jordan	19-12-2019	29-09-2020	01-01-2021
54	Egypt	07-06-2017	30-09-2020	01-01-2021
55	Burkina Faso	07-06-2017	30-10-2020	01-02-2021

S.N	*Jurisdiction*	*Signature*	*Ratification*	*Entry into Force*
56	Panama	24-01-2018	05-11-2020	01-03-2021
57	Chile	07-06-2017	26-11-2020	01-03-2021
58	Germany	07-06-2017	18-12-2020	01-04-2021
59	Pakistan	07-06-2017	18-12-2020	01-04-2021
60	Barbados	24-01-2018	21-12-2020	01-04-2021

4.1.9 Article 35: Entry into Effect of MLI

516. The EIE of the MLI and the effect of its modifications on CTAs depend on:

- the date the MLI enters into force for the Contracting Jurisdictions involved;
- the types of tax involved;
- the choices made under Article 35(1), (2) and (3); and
- the reservations made under Article 35(6) and (7).

In view of the above, the date on which the MLI enters into effect may be different for each CTA and depending on the choices made, the date on which the MLI enters into effect for a specific CTA may be different for each Contracting Jurisdiction.

Paragraph 1

517. Paragraph 1 of Article 35 divides EIE of MLI into two categories based on the type of taxation to which they apply, i.e. 'WHTs' and 'other taxes'. Paragraph 1 (a) relates to EIE of provisions of the MLI with respect to taxes 'withheld at source' on amounts paid or credited to non-residents. In this category, the first taxes for which the provisions of the MLI will enter into effect are those for which the event giving rise to the tax occurs on or after the first day of the next calendar year that begins on or after the latest of the dates on which the MLI enters into force for each of the Contracting Jurisdictions to a CTA. Paragraph 1 (b) relates to the EIE of provisions of the MLI with respect to all 'other taxes' levied by a Contracting Jurisdiction. In this category, the first taxes for which provisions of the MLI will enter into effect are those which are levied with respect to taxable periods beginning on or after the expiration of a period of six calendar months (or a shorter period, if all Contracting Jurisdictions notify the Depositary that they intend to apply such shorter period) from the latest of the dates on which the MLI enters into force for each of the Contracting Jurisdictions to a CTA.

The notifications made by treaty partners under Article 35(1)(b) of the MLI and impact thereof on EIE of 'other taxes' provisions on respective CTAs are provided in Figure 25.

Figure 25 Article 35(1)(b): Flowchart on Notifications & Their Impact

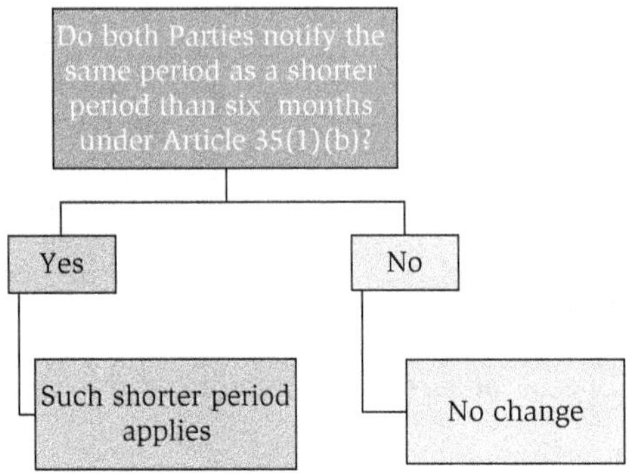

Paragraph 2

518. Paragraph 2 provides that a Party may choose to substitute 'taxable period' for 'calendar year' for the purposes of its own application of Article 35(1)(a) and 35(5)(a), and must notify the Depositary accordingly if they do so. This will permit Contracting Jurisdictions to choose to link the EIE of provisions related to WHTs to the taxable period, to address situations in which their taxable period does not follow the calendar year. In such cases, for the EIE of the provisions of the MLI with respect to a specific CTA, the Party choosing this option shall apply the rule in paragraphs 1(a) and 5(a) with reference to its taxable period but the other Contracting Jurisdiction(s) can apply that rule with reference to the calendar year (if they have not also chosen this option). Accordingly, the use of the word 'solely' at the beginning of paragraph 2 is intended to make clear that this choice would apply asymmetrically and would apply only with respect to the application of paragraphs 1(a) and 5(a) by the Contracting Jurisdiction that opted for it. Jurisdictions that have exercised this option to substitute 'taxable period'[356] for 'calendar year' are, namely, Hong Kong, India, Israel, Mauritius, Pakistan, Papua New Guinea.

The notifications made by treaty partners under Article 35(2) of the MLI and impact thereof on substitution of calendar year by taxable period for EIE of 'WHT' provisions are provided in Figure 26.

356. *Id.*

Figure 26 Article 35(2): Flowchart on Notifications & Their Impact

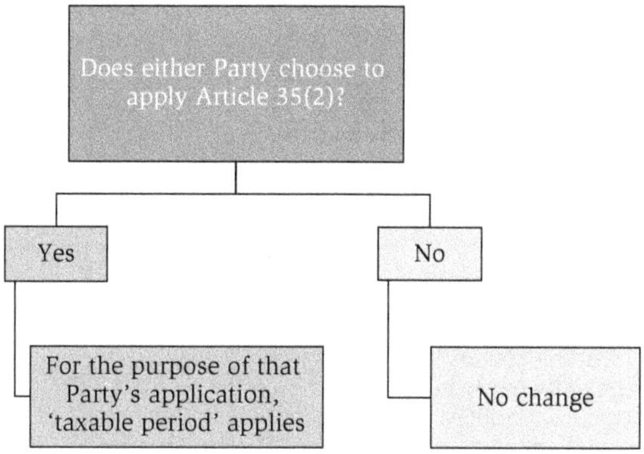

Paragraph 3

519. Paragraph 3 provides that a Party may choose to replace the reference to 'taxable periods beginning on or after the expiration of a period' with a reference to 'taxable periods beginning on or after 1 January of the next calendar year beginning on or after the expiration of a period' for the purposes of its own application of Article 35(1)(b) and 35(5)(b), and must notify the Depositary accordingly if it does so. This is to allow Contracting Jurisdictions to ensure that the EIE would take place only after the start of a calendar year. In the same manner as paragraph 2, the word 'solely' is intended to make clear that this option may lead to asymmetrical EIE of MLI's provisions between Contracting Jurisdictions. Jurisdictions that have exercised this option under paragraph 3[357] are, namely, Andorra, Argentina, Austria, Bulgaria, Chile, Costa Rica, Croatia, Denmark, Estonia, Finland, Germany, Greece, Hungary, Iceland, Indonesia, Israel, Italy, Jamaica, Jersey, Malta, Mexico, Morocco, Nigeria, North Macedonia, Peru, Romania, Russia, San Marino, Senegal, Sweden, Uruguay.

The notifications made by treaty partners under Article 35(3) of the MLI and impact thereof on EIE of 'other taxes' provisions only after the start of a calendar year are provided in Figure 27.

357. *Id.*

Figure 27 Article 35(3): Flowchart on Notifications & Their Impact

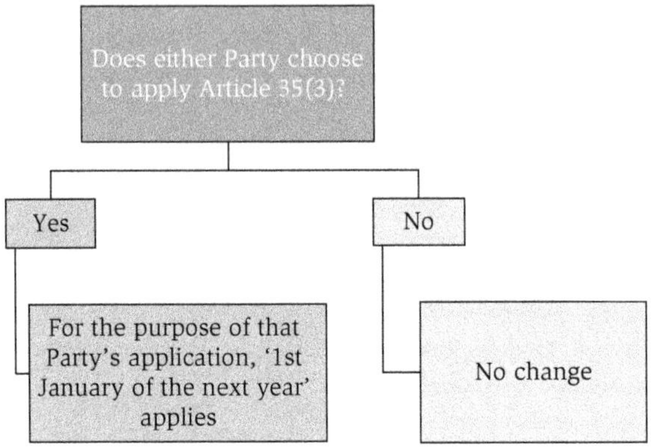

Paragraph 4

520. Paragraph 4 provides a specific rule for the EIE of Article 16 on MAP. Under this rule, Article 16 will have effect with respect to a CTA for a case presented to the CA of a Contracting Jurisdiction on or after the latest of the dates on which the MLI enters into force for each of the Contracting Jurisdictions to the CTA, except for cases that were not eligible to be presented as of that date under the CTA prior to its modification by the MLI, without regard to the taxable period to which the case relates. Paragraph 4 is intended to ensure that the provisions on MAP apply as soon as possible after the EIF of the MLI, rather than applying only after expiry of the period set out in paragraph 1, so that the provisions of Article 16 can apply to cases which are presented to the CA after the EIF of the MLI, even if they relate to taxable periods prior to the EIF of the MLI. The exception for cases which were not eligible to be presented for MAP prior to the EIF of the MLI is intended to ensure that the MLI would not 'revive' cases which had been ineligible for MAP prior to the EIF of the MLI.

Paragraph 5

521. Paragraph 5 provides for the EIE in each Contracting Jurisdiction of MLI's provisions for CTAs which result from an extension pursuant to Article 29(5) of the list of agreements notified under Article 2(1)(a)(ii). The time periods run similarly to those described above with respect to paragraph 1, except that a time period of 30 days is added in sub-paragraph (a), and the time period in sub-paragraph (b) is nine calendar months rather than six, and the time periods in both cases start running as of the date of the communication by the Depositary of the notification of the extension of the list of agreements, rather than from the latest of the dates of the EIF of the MLI for each of the Contracting Jurisdictions to the CTA. The choices set out in paragraphs 2 and 3 would also apply to the rule on EIE set out in paragraph 5(a) and (b), respectively.

The notifications made by treaty partners under Article 35(5)(b) of the MLI and impact thereof on EIE of 'other taxes' provisions on respective CTAs are provided in Figure 28.

Figure 28 Article 35(5)(b): Flowchart on Notifications & Their Impact

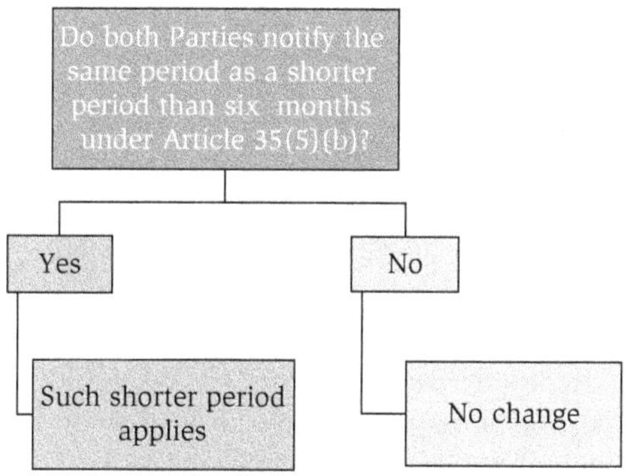

522. In accordance with notification requirement,[358] in their respective MLI positions notified to the Depositary in pursuance to Article 2(1)(a)(ii), countries have also notified Amending Protocols not yet entered into force. These Amending Protocols will not be modified by the MLI provisions, in case MLI enters into force in these tax treaties pursuant to Article 34(2) prior to such Amending Protocols entering into force. Thus, in such tax treaties, notification will have to be made by Parties to the Depositary when these Amending Protocols enter into force. These notifications in respect of such Amending Protocols shall be construed as notification of a new CTA under Article 29(5) and their EIE of MLI provisions shall be determined under Article 35(5).

Paragraph 6

523. Under paragraph 6, a Party may reserve the right for paragraph 4, which relates to the earlier EIE of Article 16 on MAP, not to apply with respect to its CTAs. In such a case, the EIE of Article 16 for a CTA concerning a Party which makes this reservation will be governed by Article 35(1) through (3). Jurisdictions that have made reservation under Article 35(6)[359] are, namely, Bulgaria, Costa Rica, Croatia, Finland, Georgia, Germany, Greece, Guernsey, Hong Kong, Hungary, Iceland, Indonesia, the Isle of Man, Israel, Jersey, Malaysia, Mauritius, Mexico, North Macedonia, Norway, Panama, Portugal, Romania, Russia, San Marino, Senegal, Seychelles, Turkey, Uruguay.

The notifications made by treaty partners under Article 35(6) of the MLI and impact thereof on EIE of MAP provisions (under Article 16 of the MLI) on respective CTAs are provided in Figure 29.

358. Refer Explanatory Statement to the MLI, para. 32.
359. Refer OECD – Signatories and Parties to the MLI http://www.oecd.org/tax/treaties/beps-mli-signatories-and-parties.pdf.

Figure 29 Article 35(6): Flowchart on Notifications & Their Impact

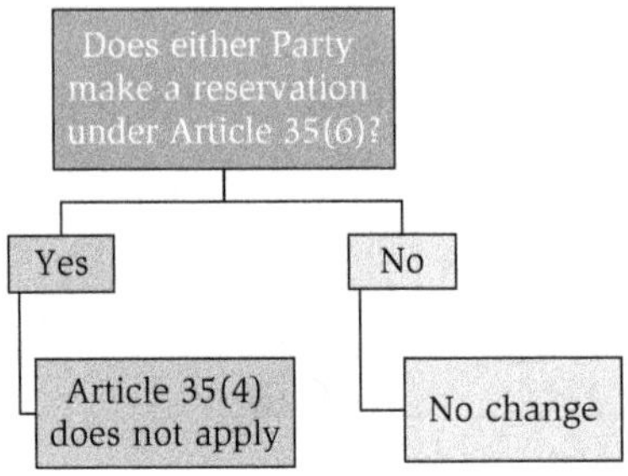

Paragraph 7

524. Paragraph 7(a) provides that a Party may reserve the right to delay the EIE of the provisions of the MLI and thus the modification of CTAs until that Party has completed its internal procedures for this purpose. In such cases, the rule on EIE set out in Article 35(1), (4) and (5) would apply as from the date that is 30 days after the Depositary has received a notification from each reserving Party (under paragraph 7) that it has completed its internal procedures with respect to a specific CTA. If more than one Contracting Jurisdiction to a CTA makes this reservation, their mutual trigger date for the rule on EIE would be 30 days after the Depositary has received a notification from the last reserving Contracting Jurisdiction that it has completed its internal procedures with respect to that CTA. The same approach would be taken to the EIE of the withdrawal or replacement of a reservation pursuant to Article 28(9), any additional notifications pursuant to Article 29(6), or the EIE of Part VI pursuant to Article 36.

525. The intention behind the reservation in paragraph 7(a) is to allow Parties which are required to amend their domestic legislation to reflect the exact changes to their tax agreements to do so before the modifications made by the MLI take effect. However, the clear understanding and expectation is that any Party which makes this reservation will complete its internal procedures as expeditiously as possible in order to fulfil its obligations under the MLI and minimise the delay in the EIE of the MLI in relation to its CTAs. An additional period of 30 days between such notification and the EIE is provided for practical reasons, to give sufficient notice for the implementation of these provisions. Jurisdictions that have made reservations under Article 35(7)(a)[360] of the MLI are, namely, Andorra, Estonia, Germany, Hong Kong, Indonesia, Italy, Kenya, Romania, Russia, Spain, Sweden, Switzerland.

The notifications made by treaty partners under Article 35(7)(a) of the MLI and impact thereof on EIE of MLI provisions on CTAs are provided in Figure 30.

360. *Id.*

Figure 30 Article 35(7)(a): Flowchart on Notifications & Their Impact

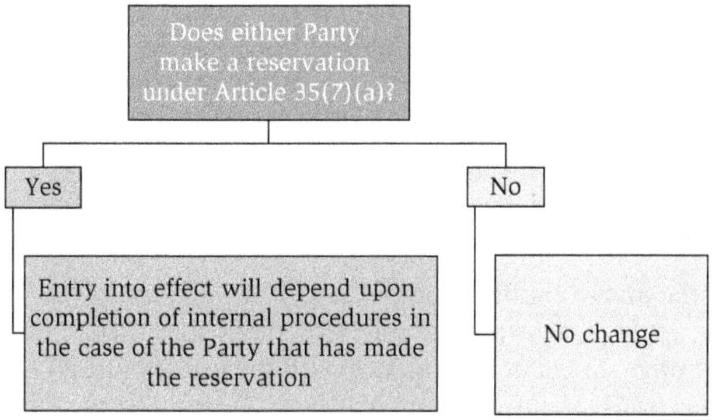

526. Paragraph 7(b) provides that the Party which made the reservation shall notify the confirmation of the completion of its internal procedures simultaneously to the Depositary and the other Contracting Jurisdiction(s) to the CTA to which the notification relates. This is important in order to provide the other Contracting Jurisdiction(s) with notice as early as possible as to when the timelines for EIE will start running with respect to the CTA. As of now, three jurisdictions have made notifications under Article 35(7)(b)[361] of the MLI, namely Indonesia (notification made on 26 November 2020), Russia (notification made on 30 April 2020 and 26 November 2020), Switzerland (notification made on 27 May 2020 and 18 December 2020).

527. Paragraph 7(c) provides that Article 35(7) shall apply symmetrically as between all Contracting Jurisdictions to a CTA. It states that where one or more Contracting Jurisdictions to a CTA make a reservation under paragraph 7, the date of EIE of the provisions of the MLI, of the withdrawal or replacement of a reservation pursuant to Article 28(9), of an additional notification pursuant to Article 29(6) with respect to that CTA, or of the EIE of Part VI pursuant to Article 36, shall be governed by Article 35(7) for all Contracting Jurisdictions to the CTA. As such, if any Contracting Jurisdiction to a CTA makes the reservation set out in paragraph 7, the modified timelines for EIE will apply to all Contracting Jurisdictions to the CTA.

Meaning of the Phrase 'on or after' Used in Article 35 of the MLI

528. In Article 35(1)(a), EIE of MLI provisions for WHT is to commence from '*on or after the first day of the next calendar year*' from the latest of the dates on which MLI enters into force for each of the Contracting Jurisdictions to the CTA. In Article 35(1)(b), EIE of MLI provisions for other taxes is to commence from '*on or after the expiration of a period of six calendar months*' from the latest of the dates on which MLI enters into force for each of the Contracting Jurisdictions to the CTA.

361. *Id.*

529. In OECD's Note[362] on EIE under Article 35(1)(a), it has been *inter alia* clarified in paragraph 6 as below:

> The logical interpretation of Article 35(1)(a) is that, in a case where the MLI enters into force for the second Contracting Jurisdiction on 1 January 2019, the provisions of the MLI should have effect for events giving rise to withholding taxes which occur on or after 1 January 2019. This follows from the use of the words 'on or after' when referring to 'the calendar year that begins on or after the latest of the dates on which this Convention enters into force for each of the Contracting Jurisdictions ...' The use of the word 'on' can only mean that the date from which the MLI can have effect can be the same as the latest of the dates of entry into force.

In view of the above clarification by the OECD in respect of 35(1)(a), the same principle can be applied in respect of 35(1)(b) provisions also. The EIE of MLI to commence '*on or after ... .*' is in consonance with the intent of BEPS Action Report 15 (which forms the basis of formulation of the MLI) envisaging implementation of anti-BEPS provisions in various treaties at the earliest possible. This consistent application of the phrase '*on or after ... .*' complies/aligns with the spirit of Articles 26 and 31 of the VCLT, 1969, providing that the treaty should be applied in good faith and is to be interpreted in the light of its object and purpose.

530. The operation of the phrase '*on or after ... .*' can be understood by analysing the following illustrations:

(a) In Australia-Denmark CTA, the respective dates of EIF of the MLI are as below:

Jurisdiction	*Entry into Force*	*Jurisdiction*	*Entry into Force*
Australia	01-01-2019	Denmark	01-01-2020

On applying Article 35(1)(a) in Australia's and Denmark's case, EIE of MLI provisions for WHT is to commence from '*on or after the first day of the calendar year*' from the latest of the dates on which MLI enters into force for each of the Contracting Jurisdictions to the CTA. Since, in the Australia-Denmark CTA, the latest of the EIF dates of MLI for both the jurisdictions involved is 01-01-2020, EIE of MLI provisions for WHT in these jurisdictions shall begin on or after 01-01-2020.

Similarly, on applying Article 35(1)(b) of MLI to Australia-Denmark CTA, since the latest EIF date is 01-01-2020 and the six-month period expires on 01-07-2020, MLI provisions for 'other taxes' in respect of Australia shall apply to taxable periods beginning on or after 01-07-2020.

For the purposes of applying Article 35(1)(b) of MLI by Denmark, it has chosen the reference to 'taxable periods beginning on or after 1 January of the next year beginning on or after the expiration of a period' under Article 35(3) of the MLI.

362. Refer Note by the OECD Secretariat on Entry into effect under Art. 35(1)(a) http://www.oecd.org/tax/treaties/beps-mli-secretariat-note-entry-into-effect-under-article-35-1-a.pdf accessed on 2 September 2020.

Accordingly, for Denmark, MLI provisions for 'other taxes' shall apply to taxable periods beginning on or after 01-01-2021.

(b) In Australia-Netherlands CTA, the respective dates of EIF of the MLI are as below:

Jurisdiction	*Entry into Force*	*Jurisdiction*	*Entry into Force*
Australia	01-01-2019	The Netherlands	01-07-2019

On applying Article 35(1)(a) in Australia's and the Netherlands' case, EIE of MLI provisions for WHT is to commence from '*on or after* the first day of the calendar year' from the latest of the dates on which MLI enters into force for each of the Contracting Jurisdictions to the CTA. Since, in the Australia-Netherlands CTA, the latest of the EIF dates for both jurisdictions involved is 01-07-2019, EIE of MLI provisions for WHT in these jurisdictions shall begin on or after 01-01-2020.

Similarly, on applying Article 35(1)(b) of MLI to Australia-Netherlands CTA, since the latest EIF date is 01-07-2019 and six-month period expires on 01-01-2020, which is the first date of the calendar year, MLI provisions for 'other taxes' in respect of these jurisdictions shall apply to taxable periods beginning on or after 01-01-2020.

531. There are jurisdictions which have exercised the option to substitute 'taxable period' for 'calendar year', namely Hong Kong, India, Israel, Mauritius, Pakistan and Papua New Guinea. The operation of the phrase '*on or after* … .' in a case where 'taxable period' is applied can be understood by analysing the Australia-India CTA as below:

Jurisdiction	*Entry into Force*	*Jurisdiction*	*Entry into Force*
Australia	01-01-2019	India	01-10-2019

On applying Article 35(1)(a) in India's case, India has opted for provisions under Article 35(2) to substitute 'taxable period' for 'calendar year' implying that EIE of MLI provisions for WHT is to commence from '*on or after the first day of the taxable period*' (instead of calendar year) from the latest of the dates on which MLI enters into force for each of the Contracting Jurisdictions to the CTA. Since, in the India-Australia CTA, the latest of the EIF dates for both jurisdictions involved is 01-10-2019, EIE of MLI provisions for WHT in the case of India is to commence when taxable period begins on or after 01-10-2019. In the case of Australia, WHT provisions shall apply where the event giving rise to taxes begins on or after 01-01-2020.

Similarly, on applying Article 35(1)(b) of MLI to Australia-India CTA, since the latest EIF date is 01-10-2019 and six-month period expires on 01-04-2020, which is the first date of taxable period for India, MLI provisions in respect of India for 'other taxes' shall apply from 01-04-2020 as per the use of the phrase '*on or after* … .' in Article 35(1)(b). In the case of Australia, 'other taxes' provisions under the MLI shall also apply where the taxable period begins on or after 01-04-2020.

532. In order to provide more illustrations on EIE of WHT and 'other taxes', such details for Denmark, India and the Netherlands and their respective treaty partners (excluding those jurisdictions ratifying MLI with which Denmark, India and the Netherlands do not have a treaty and excluding those jurisdictions ratifying MLI which have not notified Denmark, India and the Netherlands as a CTA under their respective MLI position) are provided as below:

(a) Dates of EIE of 'WHT' and 'other taxes' for Denmark and its treaty partners[363] are provided in Table 7 (date of EIF of MLI for Denmark is 01-01-2020 and it has opted in for Article 35(3)).

Table 7 EIE of 'WHT' and 'Other Taxes' for Denmark and Its Treaty Partners

EIF for Treaty Partners			*EIE for Denmark*		*EIE for Treaty Partner*	
S.N	*Jurisdiction*	*Entry into Force*	*WHT (Event Giving Rise to Taxes Begins On or After)*	*Other Taxes (Taxable Period Begins On or After)*	*WHT (Event Giving Rise to Taxes Begins On or After)*	*Other Taxes (Taxable Period Begins On or After)*
1	Australia	01-01-2019	01-01-2020	01-01-2021	01-01-2020	01-07-2020
2	Belgium	01-10-2019	01-01-2020	01-01-2021	01-01-2020	01-07-2020
3	Canada	01-12-2019	01-01-2020	01-01-2021	01-01-2020	01-07-2020
4	Chile**	01-03-2021	01-01-2022	01-01-2022	01-01-2022	01-01-2022
5	Cyprus	01-05-2020	01-01-2021	01-01-2021	01-01-2021	01-11-2020
6	The Czech Republic	01-09-2020	01-01-2021	01-01-2022	01-01-2021	01-03-2021
7	Egypt	01-01-2021	01-01-2021	01-01-2022	01-01-2021	01-07-2021
8	India*	01-10-2019	01-01-2020	01-01-2021	01-01-2020	01-07-2020
9	Indonesia***,**	01-08-2020 (26-11-2020)****	01-01-2021	01-01-2022	01-01-2021	01-01-2022
10	Ireland	01-05-2019	01-01-2020	01-01-2021	01-01-2020	01-07-2020
11	Israel**,*	01-01-2019	01-01-2020	01-01-2021	01-01-2020	01-01-2021
12	Korea	01-09-2020	01-01-2021	01-01-2022	01-01-2021	01-03-2021
13	Latvia	01-02-2020	01-01-2021	01-01-2021	01-01-2021	01-08-2020
14	Lithuania	01-01-2019	01-01-2020	01-01-2021	01-01-2020	01-07-2020
15	Luxembourg	01-08-2019	01-01-2020	01-01-2021	01-01-2020	01-07-2020
16	Malta**	01-04-2019	01-01-2020	01-01-2021	01-01-2020	01-01-2021

363. Refer OECD – Signatories and Parties to the MLI http://www.oecd.org/tax/treaties/beps-mli-signatories-and-parties.pdf.

EIF for Treaty Partners			*EIE for Denmark*		*EIE for Treaty Partner*	
S.N	*Jurisdiction*	*Entry into Force*	*WHT (Event Giving Rise to Taxes Begins On or After)*	*Other Taxes (Taxable Period Begins On or After)*	*WHT (Event Giving Rise to Taxes Begins On or After)*	*Other Taxes (Taxable Period Begins On or After)*
17	New Zealand	01-10-2018	01-01-2020	01-01-2021	01-01-2020	01-07-2020
18	Pakistan*	01-04-2021	01-01-2022	01-01-2022	01-04-2021	01-10-2021
19	Poland	01-07-2018	01-01-2020	01-01-2021	01-01-2020	01-07-2020
20	Portugal	01-06-2020	01-01-2021	01-01-2021	01-01-2021	01-12-2020
21	Russia***, **	01-10-2019 (30-04-2020)****	01-01-2021	01-01-2021	01-01-2021	01-01-2021
22	Serbia	01-10-2018	01-01-2020	01-01-2021	01-01-2020	01-07-2020
23	Singapore	01-04-2019	01-01-2020	01-01-2021	01-01-2020	01-07-2020
24	The Slovak Republic	01-01-2019	01-01-2020	01-01-2021	01-01-2020	01-07-2020
25	Slovenia	01-07-2018	01-01-2020	01-01-2021	01-01-2020	01-07-2020
26	Ukraine	01-12-2019	01-01-2020	01-01-2021	01-01-2020	01-07-2020
27	United Kingdom	01-10-2018	01-01-2020	01-01-2021	01-01-2020	01-07-2020

* Jurisdiction has opted for Article 35(2).

** Jurisdiction has opted for Article 35(3).

*** Reservation made under Article 35(7)(a).

**** Russia's and Indonesia's notification under Article 35(7)(b) received by the Depositary on 30-04-2020 and 26-11-2020, respectively.

(b) Dates of EIE of WHT and 'other taxes' for India and its treaty partners[364] are provided in Table 8 (date of EIF of MLI for India is 01-10-2019 and has opted for taxable period under Article 35(2)).

364. *Id.*

Table 8 Entry into Effect of 'WHT' and 'Other Taxes' for India and Its Treaty Partners

Entry into Force (EIF) for Treaty Partners			*Entry into Effect (EIE) for India*		*EIE for Treaty Partner*	
S.N	*Jurisdiction*	*Entry into Force*	*WHT (Taxable Period Begins On or After)*	*Other Taxes (Taxable Period Begins On or After)*	*WHT (Event Giving Rise to Taxes Begins On or After)*	*Other Taxes (Taxable Period Begins On or After)*
1	Albania	01-01-2021	01-01-2021	01-07-2021	01-01-2021	01-07-2021
2	Australia	01-01-2019	01-10-2019	01-04-2020	01-01-2020	01-04-2020
3	Austria**	01-07-2018	01-10-2019	01-04-2020	01-01-2020	01-01-2021
4	Belgium	01-10-2019	01-10-2019	01-04-2020	01-01-2020	01-04-2020
5	Canada	01-12-2019	01-12-2019	01-06-2020	01-01-2020	01-06-2020
6	Cyprus	01-05-2020	01-05-2020	01-11-2020	01-01-2021	01-11-2020
7	The Czech Republic	01-09-2020	01-09-2020	01-03-2021	01-01-2021	01-03-2021
8	Denmark**	01-01-2020	01-01-2020	01-07-2020	01-01-2020	01-01-2021
9	Egypt	01-01-2021	01-01-2021	01-07-2021	01-01-2021	01-07-2021
10	Finland**	01-06-2019	01-10-2019	01-04-2020	01-01-2020	01-01-2021
11	France	01-01-2019	01-10-2019	01-04-2020	01-01-2020	01-04-2020
12	Georgia	01-07-2019	01-10-2019	01-04-2020	01-01-2020	01-04-2020
13	Iceland**	01-01-2020	01-01-2020	01-07-2020	01-01-2020	01-01-2021
14	Indonesia***, **	01-08-2020 (26-11 -2020)****	26-12-2020	26-06-2021	01-01-2021	01-01-2022
15	Ireland	01-05-2019	01-10-2019	01-04-2020	01-01-2020	01-04-2020
16	Israel**,*	01-01-2019	01-10-2019	01-04-2020	01-10-2019	01-01-2021
17	Japan	01-01-2019	01-10-2019	01-04-2020	01-01-2020	01-04-2020
18	Jordan	01-01-2021	01-01-2021	01-07-2021	01-01-2021	01-07-2021
19	Kazakhstan	01-10-2020	01-10-2020	01-04-2021	01-01-2021	01-04-2021
20	Korea	01-09-2020	01-09-2020	01-03-2021	01-01-2021	01-03-2021
21	Latvia	01-02-2020	01-02-2020	01-08-2020	01-01-2021	01-08-2020
22	Lithuania	01-01-2019	01-10-2019	01-04-2020	01-01-2020	01-04-2020
23	Luxembourg	01-08-2019	01-10-2019	01-04-2020	01-01-2020	01-04-2020
24	Malta**	01-04-2019	01-10-2019	01-04-2020	01-01-2020	01-01-2021
25	The Netherlands	01-07-2019	01-10-2019	01-04-2020	01-01-2020	01-04-2020
26	New Zealand	01-10-2018	01-10-2019	01-04-2020	01-01-2020	01-04-2020

Entry into Force (EIF) for Treaty Partners			*Entry into Effect (EIE) for India*		*EIE for Treaty Partner*	
S.N	*Jurisdiction*	*Entry into Force*	*WHT (Taxable Period Begins On or After)*	*Other Taxes (Taxable Period Begins On or After)*	*WHT (Event Giving Rise to Taxes Begins On or After)*	*Other Taxes (Taxable Period Begins On or After)*
27	Norway	01-11-2019	01-11-2019	01-05-2020	01-01-2020	01-05-2020
28	Poland	01-07-2018	01-10-2019	01-04-2020	01-01-2020	01-04-2020
29	Portugal	01-06-2020	01-06-2020	01-12-2020	01-01-2021	01-12-2020
30	Qatar	01-04-2020	01-04-2020	01-10-2020	01-01-2021	01-10-2020
31	Russia***, **	01-10-2019 (30-04 -2020)****	30-05-2020	30-11-2020	01-01-2021	01-01-2021
32	Saudi Arabia	01-05-2020	01-05-2020	01-11-2020	01-01-2021	01-11-2020
33	Serbia	01-10-2018	01-10-2019	01-04-2020	01-01-2020	01-04-2020
34	Singapore	01-04-2019	01-10-2019	01-04-2020	01-01-2020	01-04-2020
35	The Slovak Republic	01-01-2019	01-10-2019	01-04-2020	01-01-2020	01-04-2020
36	Slovenia	01-07-2018	01-10-2019	01-04-2020	01-01-2020	01-04-2020
37	Sweden***, **	01-10-2018	Entry into effect depending on completion of internal procedures in Sweden would apply. Notification under Article 35(7)(b) by Sweden not made as yet.			
38	Ukraine	01-12-2019	01-12-2019	01-06-2020	01-01-2020	01-06-2020
39	The United Arab Emirates	01-09-2019	01-10-2019	01-04-2020	01-01-2020	01-04-2020
40	United Kingdom	01-10-2018	01-10-2019	01-04-2020	01-01-2020	01-04-2020
41	Uruguay**	01-06-2020	01-06-2020	01-12-2020	01-01-2021	01-01-2021

* Jurisdiction has opted for Article 35(2).

** Jurisdiction has opted for Article 35(3).

*** Reservation made under Article 35(7)(a).

**** Russia's and Indonesia's notification under Article 35(7)(b) received by the Depositary on 30-04-2020 and 26-11-2020, respectively.

(c) Dates of EIE of 'WHT' and 'other taxes' for the Netherlands and its treaty partners[365] are provided in Table 9 (date of EIF of MLI for the Netherlands is 01-07-2019).

365. *Id.*

Table 9 Entry into Effect of 'WHT' and 'Other Taxes' for the Netherlands and Its Treaty Partners

Entry into Force (EIF) for Treaty Partners			*Entry into Effect (EIE) for the Netherlands*		*EIE for Treaty Partner*	
S.N	*Jurisdiction*	*Entry into Force*	*WHT (Event Giving Rise to Taxes Begins On or After)*	*Other Taxes (Taxable Period Begins On or After)*	*WHT (Event Giving Rise to Taxes Begins On or After)*	*Other Taxes (Taxable Period Begins On or After)*
1	Albania	01-01-2021	01-01-2021	01-07-2021	01-01-2021	01-07-2021
2	Australia	01-01-2019	01-01-2020	01-01-2020	01-01-2020	01-01-2020
3	Austria**	01-07-2018	01-01-2020	01-01-2020	01-01-2020	01-01-2020
4	Barbados	01-04-2021	01-01-2022	01-10-2021	01-01-2022	01-10-2021
5	Bosnia & Herzegovina	01-01-2021	01-01-2021	01-07-2021	01-01-2021	01-07-2021
6	Canada	01-12-2019	01-01-2020	01-06-2020	01-01-2020	01-06-2020
7	The Czech Republic	01-09-2020	01-01-2021	01-03-2021	01-01-2021	01-03-2021
8	Egypt	01-01-2021	01-01-2021	01-07-2021	01-01-2021	01-07-2021
9	Finland**	01-06-2019	01-01-2020	01-01-2020	01-01-2020	01-01-2020
10	France	01-01-2019	01-01-2020	01-01-2020	01-01-2020	01-01-2020
11	Georgia	01-07-2019	01-01-2020	01-01-2020	01-01-2020	01-01-2020
12	Iceland**	01-01-2020	01-01-2020	01-07-2020	01-01-2020	01-01-2021
13	India*	01-10-2019	01-01-2020	01-04-2020	01-10-2019	01-04-2020
14	Indonesia***, **	01-08-2020 (26-11 -2020)****	01-01-2021	26-06-2021	01-01-2021	01-01-2022
15	Israel**,*	01-01-2019	01-01-2020	01-01-2020	01-07-2019	01-01-2020
16	Japan	01-01-2019	01-01-2020	01-01-2020	01-01-2020	01-01-2020
17	Jordan	01-01-2021	01-01-2021	01-07-2021	01-01-2021	01-07-2021
18	Kazakhstan	01-10-2020	01-01-2021	01-04-2021	01-01-2021	01-04-2021
19	Korea	01-09-2020	01-01-2021	01-03-2021	01-01-2021	01-03-2021
20	Latvia	01-02-2020	01-01-2021	01-08-2020	01-01-2021	01-08-2020
21	Lithuania	01-01-2019	01-01-2020	01-01-2020	01-01-2020	01-01-2020
22	Luxembourg	01-08-2019	01-01-2020	01-02-2020	01-01-2020	01-02-2020
23	Malta**	01-04-2019	01-01-2020	01-01-2020	01-01-2020	01-01-2020
24	New Zealand	01-10-2018	01-01-2020	01-01-2020	01-01-2020	01-01-2020
25	Norway	01-11-2019	01-01-2020	01-05-2020	01-01-2020	01-05-2020
26	Oman	01-11-2020	01-01-2021	01-05-2021	01-01-2021	01-05-2021

Entry into Force (EIF) for Treaty Partners			*Entry into Effect (EIE) for the Netherlands*		*EIE for Treaty Partner*	
S.N	*Jurisdiction*	*Entry into Force*	*WHT (Event Giving Rise to Taxes Begins On or After)*	*Other Taxes (Taxable Period Begins On or After)*	*WHT (Event Giving Rise to Taxes Begins On or After)*	*Other Taxes (Taxable Period Begins On or After)*
27	Pakistan*	01-04-2021	01-01-2022	01-10-2021	01-04-2021	01-10-2021
28	Panama	01-03-2021	01-01-2022	01-09-2021	01-01-2022	01-09-2021
29	Portugal	01-06-2020	01-01-2021	01-12-2020	01-01-2021	01-12-2020
30	Qatar	01-04-2020	01-01-2021	01-10-2020	01-01-2021	01-10-2020
31	Russia***, **	01-10-2019 (30-04-2020)****	01-01-2021	30-11-2020	01-01-2021	01-01-2021
32	Saudi Arabia	01-05-2020	01-01-2021	01-11-2020	01-01-2021	01-11-2020
33	Serbia	01-10-2018	01-01-2020	01-01-2020	01-01-2020	01-01-2020
34	Singapore	01-04-2019	01-01-2020	01-01-2020	01-01-2020	01-01-2020
35	The Slovak Republic	01-01-2019	01-01-2020	01-01-2020	01-01-2020	01-01-2020
36	Slovenia	01-07-2018	01-01-2020	01-01-2020	01-01-2020	01-01-2020
37	Sweden***, **	01-10-2018	Entry into effect depending on completion of internal procedures in Sweden would apply. Notification under Article 35(7)(b) by Sweden not made as yet.			
38	The United Arab Emirates	01-09-2019	01-01-2020	01-03-2020	01-01-2020	01-03-2020
39	United Kingdom	01-10-2018	01-01-2020	01-01-2020	01-01-2020	01-01-2020

* Jurisdiction has opted for Article 35(2).

** Jurisdiction has opted for Article 35(3).

*** Reservation made under Article 35(7)(a).

**** Russia's and Indonesia's notification under Article 35(7)(b) received by the Depositary on 30-04-2020 and 26-11-2020, respectively.

Meaning of the Term 'Other Taxes' Used in Article 35 of the MLI

533. On perusal of Article 35(1), it is seen that MLI shall have effect in the CTA, first, with respect to taxes 'withheld at source' (WHT) on amounts paid or credited to non-residents and, second, with respect to all 'other taxes' levied by the jurisdiction. Thus, the MLI has clearly outlined that at the point of levying tax by a jurisdiction, either in the form/stage of applying WHT or in the form/stage of applying 'other taxes',

MLI provisions shall be given effect through these modes only. The term 'other taxes' per se is not defined under the MLI. As per Article 2(2) of the MLI, with respect to a term not explicitly defined in the MLI, such term shall have the meaning it has under the relevant CTA. However, if the CTA does not contain a definition, but the term is nevertheless used in the CTA as an undefined term, the correct meaning should, by virtue of Article 3(2) of the OECD Model, be derived from the relevant definition in domestic law. It is seen that in domestic laws of various countries, the following are the primary modes of levying/collecting taxes:

- payment by deduction of tax at source (WHT);
- advance payment of tax;
- payment as a result of self-assessment;
- payment as a result of regular assessment.

Hence, while applying Article 35(1)(b) of MLI, 'other taxes' may comprise of the following, in accordance with domestic laws of various countries:

- advance payment of tax;
- payment as a result of self-assessment;
- payment as a result of regular assessment.

For a taxpayer complying with the provisions of MLI, 'other taxes' due shall be recovered through advance tax and self-assessment and there may not be a case to take recourse to further action by tax authorities in the form of regular assessment. However, for a taxpayer not complying with the provisions of MLI, 'other taxes' are expected to be recovered only through regular assessment. Hence, in situations where tax authorities are to levy tax, the component of 'other taxes' shall be taxes collected as a result of regular assessment.

Interpretational Issues on 'EIE' Provisions under the MLI

534. The EIE provisions concerning WHT and 'other taxes' have raised certain interpretational issues. These queries are addressed as below:

(a) Query No. 1 – How the provisions of MLI take effect under Article 35(1)(a) concerning WHT and under Article 35(1)(b) concerning 'other taxes'? Can MLI provisions enter into effect for WHT before MLI provisions enter into effect for 'other taxes'?

Reply – A plain reading of the provisions of Article 35(1) of MLI conveys that giving effect of MLI provisions through 'other taxes' lags behind the provisions of WHT. This is demonstrated by the fact that effect of Article 35(1)(a) takes place where the event giving rise to WHT occurs on or after the first day of the next calendar year, whereas effect of Article 35(1)(b) takes place after the expiration of a period of six calendar months. This implies that MLI provisions for WHT do not need to wait till MLI enters into effect for 'other taxes'. The component of 'other taxes' is payment as a result of regular assessment, which shall effectuate much later and only after the close of the taxable period. This implies that application of anti-BEPS provisions being introduced through the MLI, which in turn, enter into effect through 'other taxes' shall be applied at a much later date and that too when remittances to the non-resident during the taxable period have been made already. That is why, in order to apply anti-BEPS provisions as early as possible, MLI allows effect through WHT at the stage of amounts paid or credited to non-residents. This is also clarified in paragraph 7 of OECD's Note[366] on EIE under Article 35(1)(a) that intention is to ensure provisions of MLI move into effect as early as possible with regard to WHT on amounts paid to non-residents which follows from the use of the words 'on or after' in Article 35(1).

Further, provisions of Article 35(3) allow a jurisdiction to ensure that the EIE for 'other taxes' under Article 35(1)(b) would take place only after the start of a calendar year. This option further pushes back the EIE date for 'other taxes'.

In view of the above, MLI provides that WHT provisions can enter into effect before provisions of MLI enter into effect for 'other taxes'. Even if the option under Article 35(2) is exercised, the stated position remains the same and it is not necessary that the taxable period under Article 35(1)(a) should align with the taxable period under Article 35(1)(b). Hence, in order to apply anti-BEPS provisions as early as possible, there is always a possibility that taxable period for applicability of WHT provisions may be earlier than the taxable period for 'other taxes' (depending on the dates when the MLI enters into force for contracting jurisdictions involved).

(b) Query No. 2 – In a CTA where an event giving rise to taxes/taxable period for WHT provisions precedes taxable period for 'other taxes', as occurring at present, for instance, in Denmark's CTAs with Australia, Belgium, Canada, India, Ireland, Israel, Lithuania, etc. and in India's CTAs with Canada, Denmark, Iceland, Latvia, Norway, Qatar, Ukraine, etc. (refer Tables 7 and 8), how the application of WHT provisions under the MLI and their consequent orders by the WHT/TDS (tax deducted at source) Officer get reflected in the income tax returns of such non-resident (recipient of remittances) entities to be filed in Denmark and India, respectively? Will the concerned Assessing Officer (of such non-resident entities) in Denmark and India respectively be able to further apply the CTA provisions (as modified by the MLI) during regular assessment as withholding of taxes may have already been done at the stage of remittances to the non-resident?

Reply – First of all, as illustratively explained in Tables 7 and 8, it may be made clear that, at present, this issue of taxable period for 'other taxes' lagging behind that for WHT in Denmark's CTAs with Australia, Belgium, Canada,

366. Refer Note by the OECD Secretariat on Entry into Effect under Art. 35(1)(a) http://www.oecd.org/tax/treaties/beps-mli-secretariat-note-entry-into-effect-under-article-35-1-a.pdf accessed on 2 September 2020.

India, Ireland, Israel, Lithuania, etc. applies to the period commencing from 01-01-2020 only, as from taxable period 01-01-2021 onwards, MLI provisions shall take effect in these CTAs for both, i.e., WHT and 'other taxes'. On the other hand, this issue of taxable period for 'other taxes' lagging behind that for WHT in India's CTAs with Canada, Denmark, Iceland, Latvia, Norway, Qatar, Ukraine, etc. applies to the period commencing from 2020-2021 only, as from taxable period 2021-2022 onwards, MLI provisions shall take effect in these CTAs for both, i.e., WHT and 'other taxes'. Further, this variance in taxable periods is not present in all of Denmark's and India's CTAs; it is not a perennial issue impacting all CTAs and has relevance only for initial period in respect of few treaties, as illustratively stated above.

In order to explain this issue further in detail, in India's case, for taxable period 2020-2021, prior to remittance to a non-resident entity, applications for a certificate u/s 195/197 of the Income Tax Act, 1961 (concerning WHT) can be filed for adjudication by the WHT/TDS Officer in India. On culmination of period 2020-2021, there are two options for such non-resident (recipient of remittances) entities:

- to accept the order of withholding of taxes by applying provisions of section 115A(5) of the Income Tax Act, 1961 and not file any return u/s 139(1) of the Income Tax Act, 1961 and consequently, not be subjected to regular assessment;
- to file income tax return and be subjected to regular assessment by the Assessing Officer.

In the former situation, i.e., where order of WHT/TDS Officer is accepted and provisions of section 115A(5) of the Income Tax Act, 1961 are applied by the non-resident (recipient of remittances) entities, the matter rests and withholding of taxes at the stage of remittance remains the first and final action by tax authorities. Whereas, in the latter situation, where the return is filed by the non-resident (recipient of remittances), the Assessing Officer shall be at liberty to apply anti-BEPS measures under the MLI during regular assessment on account of the following reasons:

- The intent, object and purpose under the MLI are to apply anti-BEPS provisions as early as possible. Thus, when MLI allows WHT provisions to take effect, there can never be an intent/purpose under the MLI instrument itself to take away this taxing right while applying/giving effect to MLI under 'other taxes' (regular assessment). This would go against the spirit of Articles 26 and 31 of the VCLT, 1969, which provide that the treaty should be applied in good faith and is to be interpreted in the light of its object and purpose.
- The regular assessment will be done post taxable period 2020-2021 (for WHT) as return of income shall be filed only on culmination of taxable period 2020-2021, i.e. in the period 2021-2022. In the period 2021-2022, when regular assessment would be done, taxable period under 'other taxes' would have come into operation in respect of cases under discussion.

(c) Query No. 3 – Where taxable period for WHT provisions precedes taxable period for 'other taxes', whether taxpayers can avoid/escape the earlier application of MLI through WHT provisions by opting for a particular CTA/DTAA not to apply for such period?

> *Reply* – In accordance with the domestic laws of most jurisdictions, an incidence to apply DTAA provisions arises only after the impugned income is found taxable under the domestic law. If domestic law cannot be invoked at all, i.e. taxability does not arise in domestic law, there is no requirement to take recourse to a DTAA. Also, following the BEPS Action Plan recommendations, the anti-BEPS provisions are being incorporated/updated, from time to time, in the domestic law of various jurisdictions.

In the pre-BEPS era, despite being taxable under domestic law, the non-resident taxpayers could escape taxation on application of DTAAs (by treaty shopping due to the absence of anti-BEPS provisions in DTAAs). This escape route has been plugged by updating the DTAAs with anti-BEPS provisions through the MLI. Hence, in case a non-resident taxpayer chooses not to apply the CTA/DTAA (as updated by the MLI), its taxation shall be as per domestic law only, which now already contains anti-BEPS provisions. Thus, there shall be no escapement of income from tax and a jurisdiction's tax base shall remain protected.

535. In pursuance of ratification of the MLI by as many as 60 jurisdictions as of now, the provisions of MLI take effect in respect of their respective CTAs as per provisions prescribed in Article 35 of the MLI. The date on which MLI enters into effect may be different for each of the CTAs. Depending on the choices made, the date on which the MLI enters into effect for a specific CTA may be different for each Contracting Jurisdiction also. The WHT provisions take effect as per the provisions of Article 35(1)(a) read with Article 35(2), if opted. The 'other taxes' provisions take effect six months after trigger date as per the provisions of Article 35(1)(b) read with Article 35(3), if opted. Provisions of the MLI could take effect on different dates depending on the types of taxes involved, i.e. WHT and 'other taxes'. The MLI provides that WHT provisions can enter into effect before substantive provisions of MLI enter into effect for 'other taxes'. MLI provisions for WHT do not need to wait till MLI enters into effect for 'other taxes'. The intention is to ensure provisions of MLI move into effect as early as possible so as to prevent BEPS. Ultimately, the EIE provisions for WHT and 'other taxes' in the MLI are meant to comply and align with the spirit of Articles 26 and 31 of the VCLT, 1969, which provide that the treaty should be applied in good faith and is to be interpreted in the light of its object and purpose.

4.1.9.1 *Article 36: Entry into Effect of Part VI*

536. Article 36 of the MLI enshrines provisions in respect of EIE of Part VI of the MLI.

Paragraph 1

537. Paragraph 1 provides that notwithstanding the provisions of Article 28(9) (addressing the withdrawal of a reservation), Article 29(6) (addressing additional notifications), and Article 35 (other than paragraph 7) (addressing the EIE of the MLI), Article 36 shall govern the EIE of the provisions of Part VI of the MLI. Sub-paragraph (a) provides that Part VI will have effect with respect to cases presented to the CA of a Contracting Jurisdiction on or after the later of the dates on which the MLI enters into force for each of the Contracting Jurisdictions. Sub-paragraph (b) provides that Part VI will have effect with respect to cases presented to the CA of a Contracting Jurisdiction prior to the later of the dates on which the MLI enters into force for each of the Contracting Jurisdictions, on the date on which both Contracting Jurisdictions have notified the Depositary that they have reached mutual agreement on the application of Part VI pursuant to Article 19(10), along with information regarding the date or dates on which such cases shall be considered to have been presented to the CA of a Contracting Jurisdiction according to the terms of that mutual agreement. For this purpose, the date on which both Contracting Jurisdictions have notified the Depositary that they have reached mutual agreement on the application of Part VI pursuant to Article 19(10) is the date on which the Depositary has received the notification from the second Contracting Jurisdiction. With respect to the date on which such cases shall be considered to have been presented, the CAs of the Contracting Jurisdictions can agree on a date which applies to all cases or a specific date for each individual case. Sub-paragraph (b) is intended to allow CAs to delay the eligibility of existing cases until they have agreed the mode of application of Part VI, and to spread out the dates on which such cases become eligible for arbitration, so all existing cases do not become eligible for arbitration on the same day.

The notifications made by treaty partners under Article 36(1)(b) of the MLI and impact thereof on cases that become eligible for arbitration under Part VI of the MLI are provided in Figure 31.

Figure 31 Article 36(1)(b): Flowchart on Notifications & Their Impact

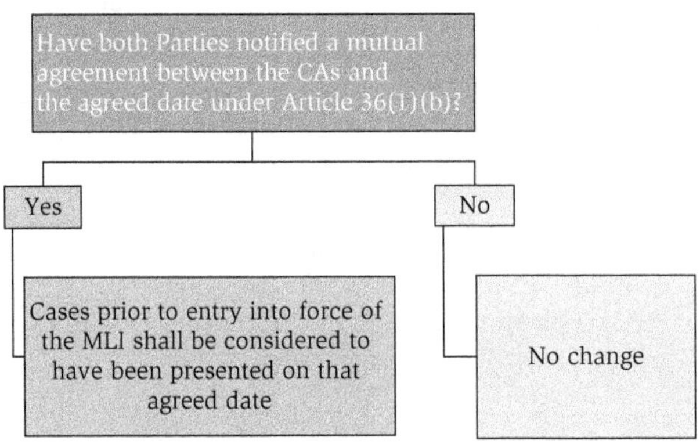

Paragraph 2

538. Paragraph 2 provides that Parties may reserve the right for Part VI to apply to a case presented to the CA of a Contracting Jurisdiction prior to the later of the dates on which the Convention enters into force for each of the Contracting Jurisdictions only to the extent that the CAs of both Contracting Jurisdictions agree that it will apply to that specific case. Where a Party has made this reservation, its existing stock of MAP cases would not be covered unless both of the CAs agree that a particular existing case may be submitted to arbitration. Among other things, this is intended to address concerns that resource constraints may make it challenging for Contracting Jurisdictions with a large backlog of cases to apply Part VI effectively to those cases, despite the ability under paragraph 1(b) to defer eligibility for arbitration. Jurisdictions that have made reservations under Article 36(2)[367] are, namely, Andorra, Austria, France, Germany, Greece, Ireland, Italy, Luxembourg, Malta, Portugal, Singapore, Slovenia, Spain.

The notifications made by treaty partners under Article 36(2) of the MLI and impact thereof on cases that become eligible for arbitration under Part VI of the MLI are provided in Figure 32.

Figure 32 Article 36(2): Flowchart on Notifications & Their Impact

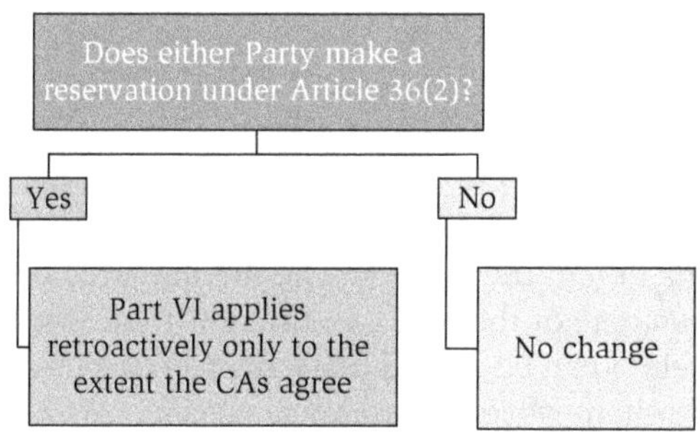

Paragraph 3

539. Paragraph 3 addresses the EIE of Part VI in the case in which a Party begins applying Part VI to a CTA only after it becomes a Party to the MLI. This may arise when a new CTA is added due to an extension by either Contracting Jurisdiction of the list of agreements notified under Article 2(1)(a)(ii). In such a case, the date of EIE is based on the date of communication by the Depositary of the relevant notification of the extension of list of agreements, rather than the date of EIF of the MLI.

367. Refer OECD – Signatories and Parties to the MLI http://www.oecd.org/tax/treaties/beps-mli-signatories-and-parties.pdf.

Paragraph 4

540. Paragraph 4 addresses the EIE of Part VI in the case in which a Party begins applying Part VI to a CTA only after it becomes a Party to the MLI. It can arise because of the withdrawal of a reservation under Article 26(4) not to apply Part VI with respect to a specific CTA, or the replacement of such a reservation with one that is more limited in scope (e.g., by replacing a reservation with respect to CTAs with one that applies only to particular CTA). In addition, it can arise where a Party that previously objected to a reservation formulated under Article 28(2) withdraws that objection. In such cases, the date of EIE is based on the date of communication by the Depositary of withdrawal or replacement of reservation, or withdrawal of objection, rather than the date of EIF of the MLI.

Paragraph 5

541. Paragraph 5 addresses the EIE of Part VI in the case in which a Party begins applying Part VI to a CTA only after it becomes a Party to the MLI. It can arise when a Party changes its policy regarding arbitration and chooses to apply Part VI to its CTAs for the first time after it becomes a Party by making an additional notification in pursuance to Article 29(1)(p) of the MLI. In such a case, the date of EIE is based on the date of communication by the Depositary of the relevant notification, rather than the date of EIF of the MLI.

4.1.10 Article 37: Withdrawal from the MLI

542. Exit clauses that allow great flexibility in withdrawing or terminating treaties encourage jurisdictions to join the treaties. The driving force being, jurisdictions get certainty that if the outcome of the treaty is different from what they expected, they may exit the treaty itself. It can be argued that exits by jurisdictions may endanger the stability of the treaty itself; however, the treaty makers have to be conscious of the fact that imposing restrictions on exits, apart from making the treaty inflexible, compromise on sovereignty of the jurisdictions also. If treaty makers wish to promote sovereignty and attain universal participation, they should facilitate exit opportunities, as has been provided for in the MLI. Therefore, provisions of MLI under Article 37 enable the Parties to withdraw from the instrument itself, at any time, thereby lending immense flexibility to the jurisdictions involved.

543. A withdrawal from the MLI will end the status of the withdrawing jurisdiction as a Party to the instrument. As a consequence, the withdrawing jurisdiction neither would be invited to participate in the CoP nor would be able to make additional notifications under the MLI.

544. The withdrawal of a Party from the MLI shall become effective on the date of receipt of the notification by the Depositary. However, in accordance with Article 39(2)(f) of the MLI, the Depositary is required to notify the withdrawal to the rest of the Parties and Signatories within one calendar month. In pursuance to Article 37 of the

MLI, the provisions of the CTAs as modified through the MLI (before the withdrawal came into effect) will remain modified even after the withdrawal becomes effective. The withdrawal will have effects only on those CTAs that have not been modified through the MLI, i.e. tax treaties listed as CTAs by one of the Parties in respect of which the MLI did not enter into force, either because the other Parties did not list that particular tax treaty (being withdrawn) as a CTA or because the other Parties did not complete ratification process of the MLI before the withdrawal became effective.

545. Article 37 of the MLI deviates from the residual rules enshrined under Articles 42, 54, 56 and 70 of the Vienna Convention. Under these provisions of the Vienna Convention, when a Party withdraws from a multilateral treaty, it is freed from its obligations to perform the treaty towards the rest of the Parties, while the rest of the Parties remain bound by the treaty in their mutual relations. On the other hand, under the MLI, the withdrawing jurisdiction will not be freed from its obligation to apply the MLI in all cases and the provisions of the CTAs as modified through the MLI (before the withdrawal came into effect) will remain modified even after the withdrawal becomes effective. In order to contract out of the obligation to apply the provisions of the MLI to such CTAs, the withdrawing Parties will have to renegotiate their tax treaties on a bilateral basis. This impediment, to some extent, restricts the sovereignty of States. Nonetheless, the right to join the MLI is already an attribute of State sovereignty and restrictions placed on exits have also been willingly agreed to by such withdrawing States at the time of adoption of the MLI text and signing the MLI. In any case, the purpose of the second sentence of Article 37(2) is to prevent a Party to the MLI from unilaterally reversing its effects and thereby producing unilateral changes to a CTA already modified through the MLI. For the purposes of withdrawal of the Parties from the MLI, the ad hoc Group, therefore, decided to replicate the approach used in amending protocols to bilateral tax treaties.[368]

546. Withdrawal would ensure that the MLI would not modify any tax agreements with States and jurisdictions that join the MLI after the date of withdrawal since they would not fall within the definition of CTAs. Article 37(2), therefore, ensures stability of treaty provisions, discourages jurisdictions to easily withdraw or terminate the commitment to combat BEPS practices. The withdrawing Parties would need to renegotiate all of their modified CTAs, which might prove difficult if their treaty partners were still Parties to the MLI and committed to tackling BEPS practices.

4.1.11 Article 38: Relation with Protocols

547. Article 38 provides that:

- the MLI may be supplemented with one or more protocols;
- to become a Party to a protocol, a State or jurisdiction must be a Party to the MLI; and

368. Refer Explanatory Statement to the MLI, para. 353.

- a Party to the MLI would not be bound by any protocol unless it becomes a Party to the protocol in accordance with its provisions.

The MLI and its Explanatory Statement are silent on the mechanism and procedures for enactment of protocols. Unlike Article 32 (Interpretation and Implementation) and Article 33 (Amendment) where CoP formed under Article 31(3) is specifically entrusted with such issues, there is no such specific provision in Article 38 authorising the CoP to perform such task. However, in accordance with the provisions of Article 31(1), if CoP decides to exercise the function of enactment of a protocol to the MLI, it may do so.

4.1.12 Article 39: Depositary

548. The Secretary General of the OECD is the Depositary of the MLI and any protocols pursuant to Article 38 of the MLI. The Depositary is required to notify the Parties and Signatories within one calendar month of the following acts, notifications or communications in relation to the MLI:

(a) any signature pursuant to Article 27 (Signature and Ratification);
(b) the deposit of any instrument of ratification pursuant to Article 27 (Signature and Ratification);
(c) any reservation or withdrawal or replacement of a reservation pursuant to Article 28 (Reservations);
(d) any notification or additional notification pursuant to Article 29 (Notifications);
(e) any proposed amendment to the MLI pursuant to Article 33 (Amendment);
(f) any withdrawal from the MLI pursuant to Article 37 (Withdrawal); and
(g) any other communication related to the MLI.

549. Another important function of the Depositary is to maintain publicly available lists of:

(a) Covered Tax Agreements;
(b) reservations made by the Parties; and
(c) notifications made by the Parties.

550. In terms of Article 31(2) of the MLI, the CoP shall also be served by the Depositary.

CHAPTER 5

MLI: Journey and Experiences

An in-depth analysis of the impact made by the MLI on the tax treaty network has been made in respect of 95 MLI Signatories as of now. Out of 95 Signatories to the MLI, all are members of the IF except Cyprus, Fiji and Kuwait. Signing of MLI by non-members of the IF is a positive signal conveying importance attached to the MLI and faith reposed in its ability to introduce anti-BEPS measures in a swift manner. MLI has opened doors for signing of more such multilateral tax treaties in future, which is why experts are positing that for implementation of proposals on tax consequences of the digitalised economy under preparation by the OECD, an instrument exactly like the MLI can be used.

5.1 THE MLI JOURNEY SO FAR: STATISTICAL DATA

551. Key facts[369] on the MLI[370] as of now are summarised as below:

- the MLI covers 95 jurisdictions, of which 60 have ratified the MLI;
- the Multilateral Convention has become effective on 1 January 2021[371] for over 600 treaties concluded among the 60 jurisdictions and will modify over 1,700 treaties once fully in effect;
- inclusion of the PPT in all of the modified agreements (Action 6);
- once all Signatories have ratified the MLI, around 65% of all agreements between OECD/G20 IF members will be modified by the MLI to include the Action 6 minimum standard (and other BEPS treaty-related provisions);

369. Refer OECD/G20 Inclusive Framework on BEPS Progress Report July 2019 – July 2020 https://www.oecd.org/tax/beps/oecd-g20-inclusive-framework-on-beps-progress-report-july-2019-july-2020.pdf (Box 1 on p. 21) accessed on 2 September 2020.

370. Refer OECD – Bahrain Signs Landmark Agreement to Strengthen Its Tax Treaties https://www.oecd.org/ctp/treaties/bahrain-signs-landmark-agreement-to-strengthen-its-tax-treaties.htm accessed on 28 November 2020.

371. Refer OECD – Barbados Deposits Its Instrument of Ratification for the Multilateral BEPS Convention https://www.oecd.org/tax/treaties/barbados-deposits-its-instrument-of-ratification-for-the-multilateral-beps-convention.htm accessed on 5 January 2021.

- 30 covered jurisdictions have opted for mandatory binding arbitration (modifying 211 CTAs to include the MLI mandatory binding arbitration provisions);
- the first meeting of the MLI CoP was held on 4 October 2019.

552. In order to further appreciate the impact made by the MLI on the tax treaty network across the world, an analysis in respect of 95 MLI Signatories[372] as on date has been carried out on the following lines and presented in a tabular form in Table 10:

- number of CTAs notified by each of the 95 Signatories;
- number of matching CTAs (where a jurisdiction has notified a particular CTA and its treaty partner (Signatory) has done likewise);
- number of One-Way CTAs (where a jurisdiction has notified a CTA but its treaty partner (Signatory) has not notified the same); and
- number of Waiting CTAs (where a jurisdiction has notified a CTA but its treaty partner has not signed the MLI till date).

372. Refer OECD – Signatories and Parties to the MLI http://www.oecd.org/tax/treaties/beps-mli-signatories-and-parties.pdf accessed on 31 December 2020.

Table 10 Impact Made by MLI on the Tax Treaty Network

S. N	Jurisdiction	Signature	Ratification	Entry into Force	CTAs Notified	Matching CTAs	One-Way CTAs	Waiting CTAs
1	Albania	28-05-2019	22-09-2020	01-01-2021	41	30	8	3
2	Andorra	07-06-2017			6	6	0	0
3	Argentina	07-06-2017			17	17	0	0
4	Armenia	07-06-2017			46	33	5	8
5	Australia	07-06-2017	26-09-2018	01-01-2019	42	33	3	6
6	Austria	07-06-2017	22-09-2017	01-07-2018	38	38	0	0
7	Bahrain	27-11-2020			44	25	3	16
8	Barbados	24-01-2018	21-12-2020	01-04-2021	31	22	5	4
9	Belgium	07-06-2017	27-06-2019	01-10-2019	99	69	2	28
10	Belize	11-01-2019			4	1	2	1
11	Bosnia and Herzegovina	30-10-2019	16-09-2020	01-01-2021	37	27	5	5
12	Bulgaria	07-06-2017			66	50	0	16
13	Burkina Faso	07-06-2017	30-10-2020	01-02-2021	3	3	0	0
14	Cameroon	11-07-2017			5	5	0	0
15	Canada	07-06-2017	29-08-2019	01-12-2019	84	68	1	15
16	Chile	07-06-2017	26-11-2020	01-03-2021	33	26	2	5
17	China	07-06-2017			101	66	3	32
18	Colombia	07-06-2017			10	9	1	0
19	Costa Rica	07-06-2017	22-09-2020	01-01-2021	2	2	0	0

S. N	*Jurisdiction*	*Signature*	*Ratification*	*Entry into Force*	*CTAs Notified*	*Matching CTAs*	*One-Way CTAs*	*Waiting CTAs*
20	Côte d'Ivoire	24-01-2018			11	9	2	0
21	Croatia	07-06-2017			62	53	3	6
22	Curaçao	07-06-2017	29-03-2019	01-07-2019	2	1	1	0
23	Cyprus	07-06-2017	23-01-2020	01-05-2020	59	46	1	12
24	The Czech Republic	07-06-2017	13-05-2020	01-09-2020	52	52	0	0
25	Denmark	07-06-2017	30-09-2019	01-01-2020	64	46	2	16
26	Egypt	07-06-2017	30-09-2020	01-01-2021	54	39	5	10
27	Estonia	29-06-2018			58	47	2	9
28	Fiji	07-06-2017			11	11	0	0
29	Finland	07-06-2017	25-02-2019	01-06-2019	70	52	1	17
30	France	07-06-2017	26-09-2018	01-01-2019	120	76	3	41
31	Gabon	07-06-2017			4	4	0	0
32	Georgia	07-06-2017	29-03-2019	01-07-2019	34	34	0	0
33	Germany	07-06-2017	18-12-2020	01-04-2021	14	14	0	0
34	Greece	07-06-2017			57	52	1	4
35	Guernsey	07-06-2017	12-02-2019	01-06-2019	9	9	0	0
36	Hong Kong	07-06-2017			36	31	1	4
37	Hungary	07-06-2017			66	58	3	5
38	Iceland	07-06-2017	26-09-2019	01-01-2020	35	33	0	2
39	India	07-06-2017	25-06-2019	01-10-2019	93	60	5	28
40	Indonesia	07-06-2017	28-04-2020	01-08-2020	47	38	3	6
41	Ireland	07-06-2017	29-01-2019	01-05-2019	71	60	0	11
42	The Isle of Man	07-06-2017	25-10-2017	01-07-2018	8	8	0	0
43	Israel	07-06-2017	13-09-2018	01-01-2019	53	40	2	11

S. N	*Jurisdiction*	*Signature*	*Ratification*	*Entry into Force*	*CTAs Notified*	*Matching CTAs*	*One-Way CTAs*	*Waiting CTAs*
44	Italy	07-06-2017			84	67	3	14
45	Jamaica	24-01-2018			14	9	3	2
46	Japan	07-06-2017	26-09-2018	01-01-2019	41	41	0	0
47	Jersey	07-06-2017	15-12-2017	01-07-2018	10	9	0	1
48	Jordan	19-12-2019	29-09-2020	01-01-2021	37	24	3	10
49	Kazakhstan	25-06-2018	24-06-2020	01-10-2020	54	36	7	11
50	Kenya	26-11-2019			14	12	2	0
51	Korea	07-06-2017	13-05-2020	01-09-2020	73	60	3	10
52	Kuwait	07-06-2017			45	39	3	3
53	Latvia	07-06-2017	29-10-2019	01-02-2020	58	47	1	10
54	Liechtenstein	07-06-2017	19-12-2019	01-04-2020	14	13	1	0
55	Lithuania	07-06-2017	11-09-2018	01-01-2019	55	47	1	7
56	Luxembourg	07-06-2017	09-04-2019	01-08-2019	81	68	0	13
57	Malaysia	24-01-2018			73	49	5	19
58	Malta	07-06-2017	18-12-2018	01-04-2019	73	64	2	7
59	Mauritius	05-07-2017	18-10-2019	01-02-2020	44	25	2	17
60	Mexico	07-06-2017			61	55	1	5
61	Monaco	07-06-2017	10-01-2019	01-05-2019	8	6	0	2
62	Morocco	25-06-2019			76	48	8	20
63	The Netherlands	07-06-2017	29-03-2019	01-07-2019	81	60	1	20
64	New Zealand	07-06-2017	27-06-2018	01-10-2018	37	30	4	3
65	Nigeria	17-08-2017			19	16	2	1
66	North Macedonia	29-01-2020			49	32	9	8
67	Norway	07-06-2017	17-07-2019	01-11-2019	28	28	0	0

S. N	*Jurisdiction*	*Signature*	*Ratification*	*Entry into Force*	*CTAs Notified*	*Matching CTAs*	*One-Way CTAs*	*Waiting CTAs*
68	Oman	26-11-2019	07-07-2020	01-11-2020	35	19	3	13
69	Pakistan	07-06-2017	18-12-2020	01-04-2021	66	43	4	19
70	Panama	24-01-2018	05-11-2020	01-03-2021	17	14	2	1
71	Papua New Guinea	23-01-2019			10	9	1	0
72	Peru	27-06-2018			7	5	1	1
73	Poland	07-06-2017	23-01-2018	01-07-2018	78	58	3	17
74	Portugal	07-06-2017	28-02-2020	01-06-2020	79	62	2	15
75	Qatar	04-12-2018	23-12-2019	01-04-2020	76	52	0	24
76	Romania	07-06-2017			91	65	3	23
77	Russia	07-06-2017	18-06-2019	01-10-2019	71	55	0	16
78	San Marino	07-06-2017	11-03-2020	01-07-2020	22	17	2	3
79	Saudi Arabia	18-09-2018	23-01-2020	01-05-2020	55	34	8	13
80	Senegal	07-06-2017			20	16	2	2
81	Serbia	07-06-2017	05-06-2018	01-10-2018	64	47	4	13
82	Seychelles	07-06-2017			28	20	0	8
83	Singapore	07-06-2017	21-12-2018	01-04-2019	86	63	6	17
84	The Slovak Republic	07-06-2017	20-09-2018	01-01-2019	64	51	2	11
85	Slovenia	07-06-2017	22-03-2018	01-07-2018	57	47	2	8
86	South Africa	07-06-2017			76	55	1	20
87	Spain	07-06-2017			86	66	1	19
88	Sweden	07-06-2017	22-06-2018	01-10-2018	64	47	0	17
89	Switzerland	07-06-2017	29-08-2019	01-12-2019	12	12	0	0
90	Tunisia	24-01-2018			28	28	0	0
91	Turkey	07-06-2017			89	62	2	25

S. N	*Jurisdiction*	*Signature*	*Ratification*	*Entry into Force*	*CTAs Notified*	*Matching CTAs*	*One-Way CTAs*	*Waiting CTAs*
92	Ukraine	23-07-2018	08-08-2019	01-12-2019	76	45	11	20
93	The United Arab Emirates	27-06-2018	29-05-2019	01-09-2019	114	60	11	43
94	United Kingdom	07-06-2017	29-06-2018	01-10-2018	121	75	2	44
95	Uruguay	07-06-2017	06-02-2020	01-06-2020	20	16	2	2

553. The pack of countries which have notified maximum number of CTAs is led by UK (121 CTAs notified), followed by France (initially, at the time of ratification 91 CTAs were notified, and this number has since increased to 120 when France made a notification under Article 29(5) of the MLI by notifying more CTAs under the MLI), UAE (114 CTAs notified), China (101 CTAs notified), Belgium (99 CTAs notified), India (93 CTAs notified), Romania (91 CTAs notified). The data set reveals that the impact of MLI will increase with more countries signing the MLI, and simultaneously, with a reduction in the number of One-Way and Waiting CTAs going forward. Out of 95 Signatories to the MLI, all are members of the IF[373] except Cyprus, Fiji and Kuwait. Signing of MLI by non-members of the IF is a positive signal conveying importance attached to the MLI and faith reposed in its ability to introduce anti-BEPS measures in a swift manner.

5.2 EXPERIENCES IN COURSE OF MLI'S IMPLEMENTATION

554. The MLI has resulted in a reasonably successful experience for the following reasons:

(a) MLI has exclusively introduced measures to eliminate instances of BEPS, as agreed in the course of BEPS Project. The ad hoc Group seems to have done a remarkable job by devising the MLI and its Explanatory Statement, where more than hundred developed and developing countries participated on an equal footing, despite their diverse economic interests and tax policies.
(b) Some of the controversial international tax laws, like, withholding rates on passive income, exemption of income subject to exclusive taxation by the State of source, etc. are not addressed in the MLI. These steps accelerated agreement between the developed and developing countries to conclude the MLI, and with it, implementation of BEPS Action Reports in a uniform manner.
(c) The MLI does not replace the existing tax treaty network, but only modifies the same.
(d) MLI preserves the tax sovereignty of its Parties and has been successful in overcoming the main barrier to the conclusion of a worldwide multilateral tax treaty until now.
(e) With the passage of time, countries are getting confident about MLI's ability to introduce anti-BEPS measures in a swift manner. This is evident from the fact that after ratifying the MLI, countries are coming forward and notifying more treaties as CTAs under the MLI. For example, France notified 91 CTAs at the time of ratification and this number has since increased to 120 when France made a notification under Article 29(5) of the

373. Refer OECD – Members of the OECD/G20 Inclusive Framework on BEPS http://www.oecd.org/tax/beps/inclusive-framework-on-beps-composition.pdf accessed on 9 September 2020.

MLI by notifying more CTAs. Similarly, Japan has also increased the notified CTAs from 39 to 41 under Article 29(5).

(f) MLI has opened doors for signing of more such multilateral tax treaties in future, which is why experts[374] are opining that for implementation of proposals on tax consequences of the digitalised economy under preparation by the OECD, an instrument exactly like the MLI can be used.

555. On the contrary, from the entire gamut of experiences had so far, it is seen that MLI's implementation has encountered the following hindrances:

(a) A number of IF member countries having a vast treaty network, like Brazil, Thailand, US and others, have not signed the MLI as of now, whereas their treaty partners have listed treaties with these jurisdictions (including treaties with countries which are non-members of the IF) as CTAs under the MLI; with the result, the Waiting CTAs are quite high. As of now, the maximum Waiting CTAs are 44 in the case of UK, followed by the United Arab Emirates having 43 Waiting CTAs and France having 41 Waiting CTAs.

(b) Similarly, there are a number of One-Way CTAs. As of now, the maximum One-Way CTAs are found to be 11 in the case of Ukraine (namely, CTAs with Austria, the Czech Republic, Georgia, Germany, Indonesia, Kuwait, Malaysia, the Netherlands, Norway, Spain, Switzerland) and the United Arab Emirates (namely, CTAs with Austria, Belize, Cameroon, Colombia, Costa Rica, the Czech Republic, Egypt, Georgia, Germany, the Slovak Republic, Switzerland). Taking Denmark's case as an example, two countries, namely, Austria and Georgia have not notified Denmark as a CTA, whereas Denmark has notified these jurisdictions as CTAs under the MLI. In India's case, five countries, namely Germany, Hong Kong, Mauritius, Oman and Switzerland have not notified India as a CTA, whereas India has notified these jurisdictions as CTAs under the MLI. In the Netherlands' case, Germany has not notified the Netherlands as a CTA, whereas the Netherlands has notified Germany as CTA under the MLI. This implies that the anti-BEPS provisions may not immediately apply in these treaties and many such One-Way CTAs; therefore, these treaties shall have to be individually negotiated.

(c) Some countries have notified very few CTAs under the MLI; for example, Switzerland has notified only 12[375] CTAs under the MLI, whereas it has

374. Refer South Centre Tax Initiative Comments on Session Paper Relating to Tax consequences of the digitalised economy – issues of relevance for developing countries https://www.un.org/development/desa/financing/sites/www.un.org.development.desa.financing/files/2020-06/CRP%2025%20_SCTI.pdf (p. 3) accessed on 10 September 2020.

375. Refer Switzerland's MLI Notification https://research.ibfd.org/#/doc?url=/linkresolver/static/tt_ch_02_fre_2017_tt__td1_a2#tt_ch_02_fre_2017_tt__td1_a2.

signed a total of 61[376] DTAAs in accordance with the international standards, out of which 55 are in force. It is also observed that at the time of ratification of the MLI, Germany has reduced the number of notified CTAs to 14,[377] whereas, at the time of signing of the MLI, it had notified 35[378] CTAs.

(d) Some Parties to the MLI have notified reservations to preclude the entire application of a number of articles of the MLI (that do not set out the minimum standard), thereby considerably reducing the implementation of BEPS measures.

(e) Similar to many other multilateral treaties, the MLI combines the use of opting-in mechanisms, alternative provisions and reservations. These mechanisms also interact with the compatibility clauses and the notification clauses under various articles of the MLI. *Inter se* operation of these mechanisms and their interaction with the CTAs make MLI's understanding and implementation a bit cumbersome.

5.3 DEVELOPMENT OF SYNTHESISED TEXTS

556. Since MLI provisions are to be read side by side with the CTA provisions, compatibility clauses determining the relationship between the MLI provisions and the CTA provisions have been incorporated in all articles of the MLI. Hence, MLI does not function[379] as an Amending Protocol to the CTA. Though, for internal purposes, a jurisdiction may develop consolidated versions of the CTA and MLI, at international level, OECD has recommended development of 'synthesised texts' and has issued Guidance[380] for their development. The Guidance has been prepared to provide suggestions to Parties for the development of documents to help various stakeholders to understand MLI's effects on CTAs it covers and modifies. The objective is to present in a single document and for each CTA: the text of a CTA, including the text of relevant amending instruments; the elements of the MLI that have an effect on the CTA as a result of the interaction of the MLI positions of its Contracting Jurisdictions; and information on the dates on which the provisions of the MLI have effect in each Contracting Jurisdiction for the CTA. The purpose of synthesised texts is primarily intended to facilitate the understanding of the MLI. For legal purposes, the provisions of the MLI must be read alongside CTAs as they remain the only legal instruments to be applied, in light of the interaction of the MLI positions of the Contracting Jurisdictions.

376. Refer 'The Swiss Tax System' 2019 Edition (s. 3.5 on p. 13) https://www.estv.admin.ch/estv/en/home/suche.html#number%20of%20DTA accessed on 24 December 2020.
377. Refer Germany's MLI Notification at the Time of Ratification of the MLI http://www.oecd.org/tax/treaties/beps-mli-position-germany-instrument-deposit.pdf.
378. Refer Germany's MLI Notification at the Time of Signing of the MLI http://www.oecd.org/tax/treaties/beps-mli-position-germany.pdf.
379. Refer Explanatory Statement to the MLI, para. 13.
380. Refer OECD – Guidance for the Development of Synthesised Texts http://www.oecd.org/tax/treaties/beps-mli-guidance-for-the-development-of-synthesised-texts.pdf.

557. Since the purpose of the synthesised text is to facilitate understanding of modification of CTA provisions by the MLI, synthesised text per se cannot be used as a tool to amend the CTA provisions themselves. This can be understood through an illustration with reference to the first sentence of paragraph 1 of Article 16 of the MLI, wherein Albania, Armenia, Austria, Bosnia and Herzegovina, Canada, Chile, China, Croatia, Curaçao, Germany, Hungary, India, Indonesia, Israel, Italy, Kenya, Latvia, Monaco, North Macedonia, Peru, Poland, Portugal, Romania, San Marino, Serbia, Singapore, the Slovak Republic, Slovenia, South Africa, Spain have made reservation under Article 16(5)(a) in respect of all CTAs so as to provide that MAP reference is to be made to CA of the 'resident' or 'national', rather than to 'either' CA. Hence, the phrase mentioning '*MAP reference to be made to CA of national in cases involving the non-discrimination provision based on nationality*' is required to be inserted in some of their CTAs so as to satisfy the minimum standard. The same can be done only through administrative measures, i.e. through an Amending Protocol and not through the synthesised text, as explained in detail hereunder:

> Para 5 of Article 16 of MLI recognises that Parties are also permitted to implement element 1.1 of the Action 14 minimum standard (requiring jurisdictions to include Article 25(1) through (3) of the OECD MTC in their tax treaties) through administrative measures, as provided under elements 3.1 and 3.3 of the Action 14 minimum standard. Hence, in respect of Article 25(1), if reservation is made under para 5(a) of Article 16 of MLI for 'either' not to be applied, minimum standard would have to be met as per element 3.1 through administrative measures, by allowing a taxpayer to present its case to the competent authority of the Contracting Jurisdiction of which it is a resident (*or a national in cases involving the non-discrimination provision based on nationality*) and that Contracting Jurisdiction will implement a bilateral notification or consultation process with the competent authority of the other Contracting Jurisdiction for cases presented by the taxpayers to its competent authority where its competent authority does not consider the taxpayer's objection to be justified (with the understanding that such notification or consultation should not be interpreted as consultation as to how to resolve the case). Such an approach is allowed under element 3.1 of the Action 14 minimum standard. Since by making a reservation, a Party has opted out of MLI provisions altogether, administrative measures as per element 3.1 are, therefore, required to be adopted to meet the minimum standards, implying that synthesised text cannot be used as a route to insert '*MAP reference to be made to CA of national in cases involving the non-discrimination provision based on nationality*' into the CTA, as synthesised text per se is meant only to explain application of MLI provisions on that CTA. Hence, provisions concerning '*MAP reference to be made to CA of national in cases involving the non-discrimination provision based on nationality*' can only be inserted through an Amending Protocol. For this reason, such provisions have not been inserted in the synthesised text of Canada-Slovenia CTA.[381] For similar results, synthesised text of India-Australia CTA[382] may be

381. Refer Canada-Slovenia Synthesised Text https://research.ibfd.org/#/doc?url=/data/treaty/docs/html/tt_ca-si_02_eng_2000_tt__td2.html accessed on 10 September 2020.
382. Refer India-Australia Synthesised Text https://research.ibfd.org/#/doc?url=/data/treaty/docs/html/tt_au-in_01_eng_1991_tt__td3.html accessed on 10 September 2020.

referred. Whereas, in the Slovak Republic-Lithuania CTA,[383] Slovak Republic-Poland CTA,[384] Slovenia-Austria CTA[385] such provisions already exist in the MAP Article (thereby not requiring introduction of MLI provisions into these CTAs), hence, in such CTAs, the issue under discussion does not have any implication at all.

558. A bird's-eye view of application of substantive provisions of the MLI in Denmark's[386] CTAs where synthesised texts have been released (status as on 31 December 2020) is summarised in a table in Annex I.

559. A bird's-eye view of application of substantive provisions of the MLI in India's[387] CTAs where synthesised texts have been released (status as on 31 December 2020) is summarised in a table in Annex II.

560. A bird's-eye view of application of substantive provisions of the MLI in the Netherlands'[388] CTAs where synthesised texts have been released (status as on 31 December 2020) is summarised in a table in Annex III.

383. Refer Slovak Republic-Lithuania Synthesised Text https://research.ibfd.org/#/doc?url = /data/treaty/docs/html/tt_lt-sk_02_eng_2001_tt__td2.html accessed on 10 September 2020.
384. Refer Slovak Republic-Poland Synthesised Text https://research.ibfd.org/#/doc?url = /linkresolver/static/tt_pl-sk_02_eng_1994_tt accessed on 10 September 2020.
385. Refer Slovenia-Austria Synthesised Text https://research.ibfd.org/#/doc?url = /data/treaty/docs/html/tt_at-si_02_eng_1997_tt__td4.html accessed on 10 September 2020.
386. Refer Synthesised Texts of Denmark's CTAs https://research.ibfd.org/#/search?N = 3 + 10 + 4294967052&Ne = 7487&Nu = global_rollup_key&Np = 2&Ntk = Text&Ntt = synthesised%20text&Nty = 1&Ntx = mode + matchallpartial accessed on 31 December 2020.
387. Refer Synthesised Texts of India's CTAs https://incometaxindia.gov.in/Pages/international-taxation/dtaa.aspx accessed on 31 December 2020.
388. Refer Synthesised Texts of the Netherlands' CTAs https://research.ibfd.org/#/search?N = 3 + 10 + 4294967221&Ne = 7487&Nu = global_rollup_key&Np = 2&Ntk = Text&Ntt = synthesised%20text&Nty = 1&Ntx = mode + matchallpartial accessed on 31 December 2020.

CHAPTER 6
Conclusion

A checklist titled 'MLI at a Glance' has been devised on MLI's features and its application on CTAs so as to encapsulate the procedural provisions of the MLI in a ready reckoner.

561. The MLI has paved way for jurisdictions to enter into more multilateral instruments, as a successful precursor is now available. The MLI happens to be the first successfully concluded multilateral tax treaty and has the distinction of universal participation, with as much as 95 jurisdictions having signed the MLI as on 31 December 2020, out of which 60 jurisdictions have ratified it.

562. A multilateral instrument of such a scale has introduced innovative mechanisms to insert anti-BEPS provisions in tax treaties across the globe. Indeed, the ad hoc Group must have faced various challenges in their pursuit of making all participating countries agree to the MLI text and its Explanatory Statement. Some of the challenges potentially faced by the ad hoc Group were:

- tax treaties invariably use different terminology and have different enumeration styles, wordings, etc.;
- although BEPS practices affect both developed and developing countries, not of all them were willing to accept the same level of commitment to counter the tax base eroding activities;
- initially, some Parties would be willing to accept few commitments under the MLI, with an intention to deepen their commitment going forward after earning trust over time in the functioning of the instrument;
- some jurisdictions would be more mindful to have clear exit options under the instrument.

In order to overcome the above-stated challenges, the ad hoc Group devised the MLI in a way that it would coexist and apply alongside the existing tax treaties so as to modify them, instead of directly amending each tax treaty. Further, the treaty makers introduced compatibility clauses, notification clauses, opting-in mechanisms, alternative provisions and opting-out mechanisms in the form of reservations in the MLI. In addition, the possibility of withdrawing reservations, further modifying the CTAs as modified through the MLI or amending the MLI without restrictions and the possibility of withdrawing from the MLI itself are the other flexible features which eventually encouraged the participating jurisdictions and members of the ad hoc Group to amicably adopt the MLI text and its Explanatory Statement on 24 November 2016.

563. The ad hoc Group has *inter alia* adopted the following measures to enhance the collective interest of the Parties to the MLI so as to preserve Parties' commitments to avoiding BEPS practices, and at the same time, balance the sovereign rights of the jurisdictions involved:

- provision of a closed list of permitted reservations;
- the impossibility to make late reservations, so as to prevent Parties from restricting their commitments to avoiding BEPS practices after ratification;
- application of permitted reservations, opt-in mechanisms and alternative provisions across a Party's entire treaty network;
- the possibility of replacing the reservations at any time, but solely on condition that the new formulation of the reservation has a more limited or restrictive scope than the original reservation, in order to expand the Parties' commitments to avoiding BEPS practices;
- the MLI has set out detailed rules dealing with withdrawal or replacement of reservations. However, no such provision has been provided under the MLI for withdrawal of opt-in provisions or the Alternative Provisions. This scheme is in complete harmony with the object and purpose of the MLI which is to implement anti-BEPS mechanisms in the CTAs in an accelerated manner. If Parties were allowed to make new reservations, withdraw their opt-ins and Alternative Provisions, they could contract out from the commitments adopted when concluding the MLI and, as a consequence, create new opportunities for BEPS practices, thereby defeating the very purpose of the MLI. Hence, in the absence of any express provision in the MLI, it can be presumed that it is impossible to withdraw opt-ins or of withdrawing or replacing Alternative Provisions;
- although Parties may withdraw from the MLI at any time, the CTAs (where MLI has entered into effect) will remain modified even after withdrawal from MLI becomes effective. Thus, for Parties, it is not possible to contract out from the commitment to combating BEPS practices solely by withdrawing from the instrument. After withdrawing from the MLI, and if they would like to contract out from their commitments to avoid BEPS practices, they would also need to renegotiate all the modified treaties.

564. In order to determine whether the MLI modifies the provisions of a CTA, one has to follow a very systematic process. As the first step, one should review whether all the Parties have notified the tax treaty as a CTA. After ascertaining that the treaty is a CTA, it should be reviewed whether one of the Parties to the CTA has made a reservation or if all the Parties to the CTA have opted in to or accepted the asymmetrical application of optional or alternative provisions. If none of the Parties to a CTA has made a reservation to the article that needs to be applied or if all the Parties have opted in to the optional provisions or the alternative provisions (or at least one of the Parties has done so and the rest have accepted its asymmetrical application), the next step is to review the compatibility clause, the notification clause and the notifications sent by the Parties. In this step, one should review whether the provision of the CTA is within the scope of the compatibility clause and, if this is the case, one has to ascertain the exact effect MLI has on the CTA (replacing, modifying, supplementing or superseding) according to the notification clause and the notifications sent by the Parties.

565. In order to consider the legal steps[389] required to give effect to the MLI, it is important to distinguish the situation in public international law and domestic law. In terms of the 'public international law', ratification of MLI by both contracting jurisdictions to the bilateral treaty is all that is needed for the MLI to modify that particular CTA. Thus, provisions of the CTA would be read as modified by the corresponding articles of MLI. In terms of 'domestic law', jurisdictions will have different methods for ensuring the implementation at the domestic level of the modifications made by the MLI to bilateral tax treaties. The method will depend on the legal framework which governs the implementation of international rights and obligations in each jurisdiction, i.e. whether the ratification of an international treaty automatically results in the integration of the rights and obligations set out in that treaty into domestic law (a 'monist system' as in India) or whether domestic legislation is required in order to transpose the rights and obligations in the treaty into domestic law (a 'dualist system' as in Ireland). In the former case, changes to the rights and obligations of taxpayers may flow directly from the ratification of the MLI, whereas, in the latter case, such changes to the rights and obligations of taxpayers will generally flow from domestic legislation.

566. Each substantive provision of the MLI implements one of the recommendations of the BEPS Action Reports 2, 6, 7 and 14 to counter BEPS. Article 3 of the MLI tackles double non-taxation of income derived by or through transparent entities or arrangements that are treated as fiscally transparent under the tax law of one of the Contracting States. Article 4 of the MLI modifies the tie-breaker rule applicable to persons other than individuals that are residents of more than one Contracting Jurisdiction. On application of Article 4 of MLI, the contracting jurisdictions will need to engage in a MAP to determine the State in which such person is deemed to be a resident. Article 5 of the MLI addresses problems arising from the inclusion of the exemption method in tax treaties with respect to items of income that are not taxed in the State of source. With the introduction of new preamble language and PPT provisions as minimum standards in tax treaties through the MLI, as contained in Articles 6 and 7 of the MLI,

389. Refer Note by the OECD Directorate for Legal Affairs http://www.oecd.org/tax/treaties/legal-note-on-the-functioning-of-the-MLI-under-public-international-law.pdf (paras 26-29) accessed on 10 September 2020.

expectations are high that incidences of treaty abuse will see a downward slide. In India, the Finance Act, 2020, has made dividends taxable in the hands of shareholders with effect from 1 April 2020, simultaneously putting an end to the dividend distribution tax regime. With this, the taxability of dividends under India's tax treaties has suddenly assumed enormous significance. Hence, modifications in all tax treaties being brought in by Article 8 of the MLI to prevent 'dividend stripping' are going to play a significant role where dividend income is taxed in the hands of the receiver. Article 9 of the MLI establishes a 365-day holding period for capital gains from the alienation of shares or comparable interests, such as interests in partnership or trust, deriving a certain part of their value from immovable property. Article 10 of the MLI establishes the anti-abuse rule for PEs situated in third jurisdictions. Article 11 of the MLI provides for the 'saving clause', whereby the Contracting States' right to tax their own residents gets confirmed, and the State of residence passes on the taxing rights to the State of source only in respect of certain specific situations. The strengthening of PE provisions in tax treaties through Articles 12-15 of the MLI are expected to result in taxation of business income in the State where economic activity is being carried out. Through Article 16 of the MLI, tax treaties will get up-to-date with the minimum standards on dispute resolution, while Article 17 of the MLI shall introduce provisions in tax treaties to relieve economic double taxation.

567. MLI has widened the scope of discussions between the CAs involved. Earlier, CA discussions were mostly confined to apply provisions of Article 7(3), 9(2) or 25 of the OECD MTC, whereas MLI has opened up more avenues for CA discussions *inter alia* under Article 4(1) of the MLI (tie-breaker rule applicable to persons other than individuals that are residents of more than one Contracting Jurisdiction), Article 7(4) of the MLI (discretionary relief on application of PPT provisions), Article 7(12) of the MLI (grant of treaty benefits on application of S-LoB provisions) and Article 10(3) of the MLI (grant of treaty benefits on application of anti-abuse rule for PEs situated in third jurisdictions).

6.1 TERMINATION OF MLI

568. The MLI does not have any rule pertaining to its own termination. This implies that it will continue to exist indefinitely. However, in accordance with Article 54 of the Vienna Convention, termination of the MLI would be possible if all of its Parties agree to it. Hence, even though the MLI does not expressly deal with this matter, if all of its Parties agree, the MLI can be terminated. According to the residual rule of Article 70 of the Vienna Convention, the termination of the MLI would release the Parties from any obligation to further perform the instrument. Again, though not expressly provided in the MLI, withdrawal from a treaty and the termination of the treaty, generally, produce the same effects. The only difference between withdrawal from a treaty and the termination of the treaty is the number of Parties involved. Applying the same effects of Article 37 of the MLI to the termination of the MLI would mean that the CTAs will remain modified after the termination becomes effective. If all Parties would like to contract out from the provisions of the MLI, they would need to further modify such CTAs, which would be a very onerous task.

6.2 WAY FORWARD

569. Since the first wave of signings on 7 June 2017 when 68 jurisdictions signed the MLI, the number of Signatories has swelled to 95 and it remains to be seen as to how soon remaining members of the IF sign the MLI. In addition to more countries signing the MLI, its impact will increase further if the number of One-Way and Waiting CTAs also gets reduced going forward. Out of 95 Signatories to the MLI, all are members of the IF except Cyprus, Fiji and Kuwait. Signing of MLI by non-members of the IF is a positive signal conveying importance attached to the MLI and immense faith reposed in its ability to introduce anti-BEPS measures in a swift manner. MLI has opened doors for signing of more such multilateral tax treaties in future, which is why experts are opining that for implementation of proposals on tax consequences of the digitalised economy under preparation by the OECD, an instrument exactly like the MLI can be used.

6.3 MLI AT A GLANCE

570. In line with the title of the book, for the benefit of readers, it is essential to encapsulate the procedural provisions of the MLI in a ready reckoner, to enable a quick understanding. Accordingly, a checklist titled 'MLI at a Glance' has been devised on MLI's features and its application on CTAs as provided in Table 11.

Table 11 MLI at a Glance

S. N.	*Query*	*Suggestive Reply*	*Basis of Reply*
1	What is BEPS?	BEPS refers to tax planning strategies used by MNEs that exploit gaps and mismatches in tax rules to avoid paying tax.	Refer http://www.oecd.org/tax/beps/about/.
2	What are BEPS Action Reports?	OECD and G20 countries adopted a 15-Point Action Plan (Reports) to address BEPS.	Refer http://www.oecd.org/tax/beps/beps-actions/.
3	Which of the BEPS Action Reports contain the minimum standards?	Four BEPS Action Reports, i.e., 5, 6, 13 and 14 contain the minimum standards.	Refer BEPS Action Reports 5, 6, 13 and 14 http://www.oecd.org/tax/beps-2015-final-reports.htm.
4	How MLI was formed?	MLI is an outcome of the BEPS Action 15 Report.	Refer BEPS Action 15 Report http://www.oecd.org/tax/beps-2015-final-reports.htm.

S. N.	*Query*	*Suggestive Reply*	*Basis of Reply*
5	Who developed the MLI?	Ad hoc Group developed the MLI. In line with the Action 15 Report, a mandate for the formation of an ad hoc Group for the development of a multilateral instrument was approved by the OECD CFA and endorsed by the G20 Finance Ministers and Central Bank Governors in February 2015.	Refer paragraph 6 of the Explanatory Statement.
6	When was the MLI text and its Explanatory Statement adopted?	On 24 November 2016.	Refer paragraph 11 of the Explanatory Statement.
7	When did the MLI enter into force?	On 1 July 2018.	Refer https://www.oecd.org/tax/milestone-in-beps-implementation-multilateral-beps-convention-will-enter-into-force-on-1-july-following-slovenia-s-ratification.htm.
8	What is the role and purpose of Explanatory Statement to the MLI?	In order to explain the MLI provisions to all concerned stakeholders, OECD has released an Explanatory Statement to the MLI, which was prepared and adopted by the ad hoc Group (including the Subgroup on Arbitration)	Refer paragraph 11 of the Explanatory Statement.
9	How many BEPS Action Reports are covered/addressed under the MLI?	The MLI covers four BEPS Action Reports, i.e., Actions 2, 6, 7 and 14; out of which, Action Reports 6 and 14 contain the minimum standards.	Refer paragraph 8 of the Explanatory Statement.
10	What is the most significant objective of the MLI?	The ad hoc Group developed the MLI to modify existing bilateral tax treaties solely in order to swiftly implement the tax treaty measures developed in the course of the OECD-G20 BEPS Project in a coordinated and consistent manner across the network of existing tax treaties without the need to bilaterally renegotiate each such treaty.	Refer paragraph 21 of the Explanatory Statement.

S. N.	*Query*	*Suggestive Reply*	*Basis of Reply*
11	What does the preamble of MLI provide?	The Preamble of the MLI *inter alia* includes the provisions of Article 6(1) of the MLI also, to make it abundantly clear at the very outset that the Parties to the MLI recognise the need to ensure that existing agreements for the avoidance of double taxation on income are interpreted to eliminate double taxation with respect to the taxes covered by those agreements without creating opportunities for non-taxation or reduced taxation through tax evasion or tax avoidance.	Refer paragraphs 22, 23 of the Explanatory Statement.
12	How does MLI operate? Does it function like an Amending Protocol?	No, MLI does not function like an Amending Protocol. The MLI modifies tax treaties without replacing them and is applied alongside existing bilateral treaties.	Refer http://www.oecd.org/tax/treaties/legal-note-on-the-functioning-of-the-MLI-under-public-international-law.pdf (paragraph 15).
13	What constitutes a jurisdiction's 'MLI position'?	A jurisdiction's list of CTAs, reservations and notifications submitted in the form of a completed template to the Depositary constitutes that jurisdiction's 'MLI position'.	Refer http://www.oecd.org/tax/treaties/legal-note-on-the-functioning-of-the-MLI-under-public-international-law.pdf (paragraph 21).
14	What are the substantive and procedural articles of the MLI?	The substantive provisions of the MLI are contained in Parts II to VI (Articles 3-26 of the MLI), whereas the procedural provisions of the MLI are contained in Part VII (Articles 27-39 of the MLI).	Refer MLI text http://www.oecd.org/tax/treaties/multilateral-convention-to-implement-tax-treaty-related-measures-to-prevent-BEPS.pdf.
15	What is the structure of each substantive provision of the MLI, i.e. Articles 3-17?	Each substantive Articles 3-17 of MLI comprises of the provisions agreed in the BEPS reports, compatibility clauses, reservations and notifications (with few exceptions suited to that article).	Refer paragraph 15 of the Explanatory Statement.

S. N.	*Query*	*Suggestive Reply*	*Basis of Reply*
16	Why does the structure of Part VI (Arbitration) differ from other substantive articles of the MLI?	The difference reflects the fact that Part VI is intended to operate as a single cohesive arbitration provision which require more details as well as more tailor-made exceptions than the tax treaty-related BEPS measures established in the other substantive provisions of the MLI.	Refer paragraph 20 of the Explanatory Statement.
17	What is a Covered Tax Agreement (CTA)?	CTA is a treaty or DTAA in force between two or more Parties to the MLI, as long as each of the Parties has notified it as a treaty covered by the MLI.	Refer Article 2(1)(a) of the MLI.
18	If one of the Parties notifies a tax treaty as a CTA and the other does not, whether MLI shall modify that tax treaty?	No.	Refer paragraph 26 of the Explanatory Statement.
19	Does a jurisdiction need to notify all its DTAAs as CTAs under the MLI or does it have a choice?	All jurisdictions have a choice not to include a specific DTAA as CTA under the MLI.	Refer paragraph 26 of the Explanatory Statement.
20	Can Parties to the MLI at any time expand the scope of application of the MLI by notifying additional tax treaties as CTAs?	Yes, it can be done as MLI does not have any time limits for producing new notifications.	Refer paragraph 303 of the Explanatory Statement.
21	Can a jurisdiction, after submitting its final MLI position on ratification of the MLI, withdraw a single CTA from its CTA list?	No. Withdrawal of a single CTA by a Party, if it was permitted, would increase uncertainty for the remaining treaty partners and disturb the stability of the instrument.	- There is no specific provision under the MLI to this effect so as to maintain integrity and consistent application of the MLI. - Only addition of a new CTA is allowed under Article 29(5).

S. N.	*Query*	*Suggestive Reply*	*Basis of Reply*
22	Can Parties to the MLI notify tax treaties which are not yet in force as CTAs under the MLI?	Yes.	Refer paragraph 32 of the Explanatory Statement.
23	While notifying a tax treaty as a CTA, are Amending Protocols or accompanying instruments thereto also required to be notified?	Yes, so as to avoid any confusion regarding the scope and content of the CTA modified through the MLI.	Refer paragraph 33 of the Explanatory Statement.
24	Does MLI change the territorial or geographical scope of the CTAs?	No.	Refer paragraph 31 of the Explanatory Statement.
25	What is the difference between a Party and a Signatory?	A Party to the MLI is a Signatory for which the MLI is in force pursuant to Article 34, whereas the term 'Signatory' refers to a State or jurisdiction which has signed the MLI but for which the MLI is not yet into force.	Refer Article 2(1)(b), (d) of the MLI.
26	What is the role of compatibility clause in a substantive article of MLI?	In order to implement BEPS measures, the MLI provides for compatibility clauses, which define the relationship of the provisions of the MLI and the provisions of the CTAs.	Refer paragraph 15 of the Explanatory Statement.
27	Is compatibility clause present in all substantive articles of MLI?	Yes, with the exception of Article 15 and Part VI.	- Refer Article 15. - Refer Part VI and paragraph 20 of the Explanatory Statement.

S. N.	*Query*	*Suggestive Reply*	*Basis of Reply*
28	What does the compatibility clause 'in place of' imply?	The compatibility clause 'in place of' implies that a provision of the MLI replaces the provisions of the CTA.	– Refer paragraph 15 of the Explanatory Statement. – Also, refer http://www.oecd.org/tax/treaties/legal-note-on-the-functioning-of-the-MLI-under-public-international-law.pdf (paragraphs 19, 20).
29	What does the compatibility clause 'applies to' or 'modifies' imply?	The compatibility clause 'applies to' or 'modifies' implies that a provision of the MLI changes the application of the provisions of the CTA without replacing them.	-do-
30	What does the compatibility clause 'in the absence of' imply?	The compatibility clause 'in the absence of' implies that a provision of the MLI supplements the provisions of the CTAs that do not contain a similar provision.	-do-
31	What does the compatibility clause 'in place of or in the absence of' imply?	The compatibility clause 'in place of or in the absence of' implies that a provision of the MLI replaces, supersedes or supplements the provisions of the CTA, depending upon certain conditions.	-do-
32	What is the role and purpose of notifications under the MLI?	Notification clauses were introduced in the MLI to ensure clarity and transparency about existing provisions of CTAs that are within the scope of the compatibility clauses.	Refer paragraph 18 of the Explanatory Statement.
33	What is the remedy for an inadvertent omission of notification of existing provisions?	Additional notification can be made pursuant to Article 29(6) of the MLI.	– Refer Article 29(6) of the MLI. – Refer paragraph 18 of the Explanatory Statement.

S. N.	*Query*	*Suggestive Reply*	*Basis of Reply*
34	What is the purpose of opting-in mechanisms under the MLI?	The purpose of opting-in mechanisms is to allow Parties which are ready to do so to commit to further action in pursuit of the objectives of the treaty and have the purpose of enlarging or increasing the obligations of the declaring State in comparison to what is generally expected from the Parties to a multilateral treaty.	- Refer paragraph 14 of the Explanatory Statement. - Also, refer BEPS Action 15 Report.
35	Opt-in provisions apply when both Parties notify likewise. Is there any exception?	Yes, provisions contained in Article 23(4). This optional provision applies to a CTA even if only one of its Parties has notified its willingness to opt in. This is a solitary case of unilateral opt-in provision.	- Refer Article 23(4). - Raison d'etre of the same lies in importance of confidentiality attached to the mandatory binding arbitration procedure.
36	Can Parties to the MLI, at any time, i.e. even after deposit of instrument of ratification, notify their decision to opt in to any of the optional provisions or alternative provisions contained in the MLI?	Yes. (however, the Parties are not allowed to change their optional or alternative provisions, if such options have already been exercised, as such replacements are not expressly allowed under the MLI).	- Article 29(6) of the MLI enables Parties to make additional notifications pursuant to Article 29(1)(b) through (s) by means of a notification to the Depositary. - In addition, Article 28(2)(a) expressly refers to the case in which a Party to the MLI decides to adopt the optional Part VI establishing the mandatory binding arbitration procedure after it has ratified the MLI. - The ad hoc Group had kept this window open as this will enlarge the treaty obligations of such Parties to avoid BEPS, which in effect is the main object and purpose of the MLI.

S. N.	*Query*	*Suggestive Reply*	*Basis of Reply*
37	What is the effect of reservations made under the MLI?	As a result of reservation made in accordance with Article 28(1) of the MLI, the provision of the MLI to which the reservation relates does not apply to all CTAs of the reserving Party or of a subset of them. The effects of reservations under Article 28(1) of the MLI are generally reciprocal and symmetrical unless provided otherwise.	- Reservations have the purpose of excluding or modifying the legal effects of treaty provisions. Therefore, reservations reduce rather than increase treaty obligations. - Also, refer paragraph 270 of the Explanatory Statement.
38	Can Parties opt out of MLI provisions containing the minimum standards?	Parties to the MLI can only opt out of the core set of rules if their CTAs already contain a provision that satisfies the minimum standards or if they intend to adopt a provision or a practice that will satisfy the minimum standards.	- Refer Article 6(4) of the MLI. - Refer Article 7(15), (16) of the MLI. - Refer Article 16(5) of the MLI. (this implies that minimum standards are to be necessarily complied with, though the ad hoc Group has provided some flexibility to the Parties).
39	Can a Party withdraw its reservations?	Withdrawal or replacement of reservations can be done at any time, with the aim that it allows Parties to further modify the CTAs through the MLI, which in turn has the larger aim to expand a Party's commitment to avoiding or countering BEPS. However, a reverse of this action is not permissible; i.e., a Party initially having made a reservation with respect to certain CTAs cannot replace it with an all-encompassing (full) reservation for the entirety of that article not to be applied to all its CTAs.	- Under Article 28(9) of the MLI, Parties which have made reservations may withdraw it or replace it with a more limited reservation by means of a notification to the Depositary. - Also, refer paragraph 282 of the Explanatory Statement.

S. N.	*Query*	*Suggestive Reply*	*Basis of Reply*
40	Post-ratification of MLI is a Party permitted to make new reservations?	Post-ratification of MLI, a Party is not permitted to make new reservations, so as to maintain integrity and consistent application of the MLI, except under following circumstances: - Opting for a new CTA under Article 29(5) of MLI, or - A Party subsequently opts in for Part VI of MLI and is then allowed to make reservations pertaining to Part VI only.	- Refer Article 28(5) of the MLI which permits reservations under Article 28(1)(p), (q), (r), (s). - Refer Article 29(5) of the MLI, which permits reservations under Article 28(8). - Refer Article 28(2)(a) of the MLI which permits reservations with respect to scope of cases eligible for arbitration.
41	Are treaty-by-treaty reservations permitted under the MLI?	Treaty-by-treaty reservations are generally not permitted under the MLI. However, to avoid that provisions of CTAs that already counter BEPS practices are modified through the MLI, the ad hoc Group created categories of reservations based on objectively defined characteristics. The effects of reservations based on objectively defined characteristics are subject to the notifications provided for in Article 28(8) of the MLI, which provides that reservations enumerated therein will apply only to the provisions of the CTAs duly notified by the reserving Party. Such reservations would not apply to any CTA which is not included in the lists required by Article 28(8) of the MLI.	- Refer Article 28(8) of the MLI. - Refer paragraph 281 of the Explanatory Statement.
42	Can CTAs modified by the MLI be further amended as agreed by the contracting jurisdictions involved?	Yes, MLI does not freeze the underlying bilateral treaty in time.	- Refer Article 30 of the MLI. - Also refer http://www.oecd.org/tax/treaties/legal-note-on-the-functioning-of-the-MLI-under-public-international-law.pdf (paragraphs 17, 18).
43	Can MLI itself be amended?	Yes.	- Refer Article 33 of the MLI.

S. N.	*Query*	*Suggestive Reply*	*Basis of Reply*
44	Can a Party withdraw from the MLI?	Yes. However, provisions of the CTAs as modified through the MLI (before the withdrawal came into effect) will remain modified even after the withdrawal becomes effective.	– Refer Article 37 of the MLI.
45	What are synthesised texts?	OECD has recommended development of 'synthesised texts' and has issued Guidance for their development. The Guidance has been prepared to provide suggestions to Parties to the MLI for the development of documents they could produce to help users of the MLI to understand its effects on CTAs it covers and modifies. The purpose of synthesised texts is primarily intended to facilitate the understanding of the MLI.	Refer http://www.oecd.org/tax/treaties/beps-mli-guidance-for-the-development-of-synthesised-texts.pdf.

571. The interplay between substantive provisions (Articles 3-17) of the MLI, BEPS Action Reports and the resulting provisions of the OECD MTC 2017 is summarised in a table in Annex IV.

572. The structure of substantive provisions (Articles 3-17) of the MLI is summarised in a table in Annex V.

Annexes

Annex I

Bird's-Eye View of Application of MLI Provisions in Denmark's DTAAs Where Synthesised Texts Released (Status as on 31-12-2020)

S. No.	Denmark's CTA with Treaty Partner	Articles of MLI																							
		3	4	5(6)	6(1)	7(1)	7(8-13)	8	9(1)	9(4)	10	11	12(1)	12(2)	13(2)	13(4)	14	15	16(1)(1st)	16(1)(2nd)	16(2)(1st)	16(2)(2nd)	16(3)(1st)	16(3)(2nd)	17	Part VI
1	Poland	√	√	√	√	√				√		√														
2	Serbia		√		√	√		√		√			√	√	√	√	√	√								
3	Slovenia		√		√	√		√		√	√		√	√	√	√		√								√
4	United Kingdom	√	√		√	√						√				√		√	√	√		√		√	√	√

Annex II

Bird's-Eye View of Application of MLI Provisions in India's DTAAs Where Synthesised Texts Released (Status as on 31-12-2020)

S. No.	India's CTA with Treaty Partner	Articles of MLI																								
		3	4	5(6)	6(1)	7(1)	7(8-13)	8	9(1)	9(4)	10	11	12(1)	12(2)	13(2)	13(4)	14	15	16(1)(1st)	16(1)(2nd)	16(2)(1st)	16(2)(2nd)	16(3)(1st)	16(3)(2nd)	17	Part VI
1	Australia		√		√	√			√			√			√	√	√	√					√	√		
2	Austria				√	√					√				√											
3	Belgium				√	√			√*			√	√	√		√		√		√				√	√	
4	Canada		√		√	√		√		√										√						
5	Cyprus				√	√																				
6	The Czech Republic				√	√																				
7	Finland				√	√																				
8	Georgia				√	√																				
9	Ireland		√		√	√				√						√	√	√								
10	Japan		√		√	√				√	√		√	√	√	√		√							√	
11	Latvia				√	√																				
12	Lithuania				√	√							√	√		√	√	√							√	
13	Luxembourg				√	√																				
14	Malta				√	√				√																
15	The Netherlands		√	√**	√	√			√		√				√	√	√	√								
16	Poland		√		√	√				√		√														
17	Portugal				√	√				√		√				√		√								
18	Russia		√		√	√	√			√	√	√	√	√	√	√	√	√							√	
19	Serbia		√		√	√		√		√			√	√	√	√	√	√								
20	Singapore				√	√																				
21	The Slovak Republic		√	√	√	√	√	√		√	√	√	√	√	√	√	√	√							√	
22	Slovenia		√		√	√		√		√	√		√	√	√	√		√								
23	UAE				√	√														√					√	

S. No.	India's CTA with Treaty Partner	Articles of MLI																							
		3	4	5(6)	6(1)	7(1)	7(8-13)	8	9(1)	9(4)	10	11	12(1)	12(2)	13(2)	13(4)	14	15	16(1)(1st)	16(1)(2nd)	16(2)(1st)	16(2)(2nd)	16(3)(1st)	16(3)(2nd)	17	Part VI
24	Ukraine				√	√				√	√		√	√	√	√	√	√								
25	United Kingdom		√		√	√						√				√		√		√		√		√		

* Only sub-paragraph (b) of paragraph 1 of Article 9 of MLI to apply, as Belgium has made a reservation for sub-paragraph (a) of paragraph 1 not to apply to India-Belgium CTA.

** Option A of Article 5 applies with respect to residents of the Netherlands.

ANNEX III

Bird's-Eye View of Application of MLI Provisions in the Netherlands' DTAAs Where Synthesised Texts Released (Status as on 31-12-2020)

S. No.	The Netherlands' CTA with Treaty Partner	Articles of MLI																								Part VI
		3	4	5(2)	6(1), (3)	7(1)	7(8-13)	8	9(1)	9(4)	10	11	12(1)	12(2)	13(2)	13(4)	14	15	16(1)(1st)	16(1)(2nd)	16(2)(1st)	16(2)(2nd)	16(3)(1st)	16(3)(2nd)	17	
1	Australia	√	√	√*	√	√**			√						√	√	√	√	√					√		√
2	Austria			√	√***	√					√				√					√		√			√	√
3	India		√	√*	√***	√			√		√				√	√	√	√								
4	Japan		√	√*	√	√			√		√				√	√		√	√						√	
5	Serbia		√		√	√		√							√	√	√	√				√			√	
6	Slovenia		√	√	√	√		√	√		√				√	√		√								√
7	United Kingdom		√	√*	√	√**										√		√	√			√			√	

* Option A of Article 5 applies with respect to residents of the Netherlands.

** Paragraph 4 of Article 7 of the MLI also applies.

*** Only paragraph 1 of Article 6 applies.

Annex IV

Interplay Between MLI, BEPS Final Reports and OECD MTC 2017

S. No.	MLI		BEPS Final Report		OECD MTC 2017	
	Article	*Title of Article*	*BEPS Action Plan*	*Title of BEPS Action Plan*	*Article*	*Title of Article*
1	3	Transparent Entities	Action 2	Neutralising the Effects of Hybrid Mismatch Arrangements	1(2)	Persons Covered
			Action 6	Preventing the Granting of Treaty Benefits in Inappropriate Circumstances	23A, 23B	Methods for Elimination of Double Taxation
2	4	Dual Resident Entities	Action 6	Preventing the Granting of Treaty Benefits in Inappropriate Circumstances	4(3)	Resident
3	5	Application of Methods for Elimination of Double Taxation	Action 2	Neutralising the Effects of Hybrid Mismatch Arrangements	23A(4), 23B	Methods for Elimination of Double Taxation
4	6	Purpose of a Covered Tax Agreement**	Action 6	Preventing the Granting of Treaty Benefits in Inappropriate Circumstances	Preamble	
5	7	Prevention of Treaty Abuse**	Action 6	Preventing the Granting of Treaty Benefits in Inappropriate Circumstances	29(1)-(7), (9)	Entitlement to Benefits
6	8	Dividend Transfer Transactions	Action 6	Preventing the Granting of Treaty Benefits in Inappropriate Circumstances	10(2)(a)	Dividends
7	9	Capital Gains from Alienation of Shares or Interests of Entities Deriving Their Value Principally from Immovable Property	Action 6	Preventing the Granting of Treaty Benefits in Inappropriate Circumstances	13(4)	Capital Gains

S. No.	*MLI*		*BEPS Final Report*		*OECD MTC 2017*	
	Article	*Title of Article*	*BEPS Action Plan*	*Title of BEPS Action Plan*	*Article*	*Title of Article*
8	10	Anti-abuse Rule for Permanent Establishments Situated in Third Jurisdictions	Action 6	Preventing the Granting of Treaty Benefits in Inappropriate Circumstances	29(8)	Entitlement to Benefits
9	11	Application of Tax Agreements to Restrict a Party's Right to Tax Its Own Residents	Action 6	Preventing the Granting of Treaty Benefits in Inappropriate Circumstances	1(3)	Persons Covered
10	12	Artificial Avoidance of Permanent Establishment Status Through Commissionaire Arrangements and Similar Strategies	Action 7	Preventing the Artificial Avoidance of Permanent Establishment Status	5(5), 5(6)	Permanent Establishment
11	13	Artificial Avoidance of Permanent Establishment Status Through the Specific Activity Exemptions	Action 7	Preventing the Artificial Avoidance of Permanent Establishment Status	5(4)*, 5(4.1)	Permanent Establishment
12	14	Splitting-Up of Contracts	Action 7	Preventing the Artificial Avoidance of Permanent Establishment Status	5(3)****	Permanent Establishment
13	15	Definition of a Person Closely Related to an Enterprise	Action 7	Preventing the Artificial Avoidance of Permanent Establishment Status	5(8)	Permanent Establishment
14	16	Mutual Agreement Procedure**	Action 14	Making Dispute Resolution Mechanisms More Effective	25(1)-(3)	Mutual Agreement Procedure
15	17	Corresponding Adjustments***	Action 14	Making Dispute Resolution Mechanisms More Effective	9(2)	Associated Enterprises

* Also, refer to paragraph 78 of the Commentary on Article 5(4) of OECD MTC 2017.

** Articles 6, 7, 16 of the MLI *inter alia* implement a BEPS Minimum Standard.

*** Article 17 implements a Best Practice.

**** Also, refer to paragraph 52 of the Commentary on Article 5(3) of OECD MTC 2017.

ANNEX V

Structure of Substantive Provisions of MLI – At a Glance

Article of MLI	*Substantive (BEPS) Provisions under Paragraph(s)*	*Opt-In Provisions under Paragraph*	*Alternative Provisions under Paragraph*	*Compatibility Clause*		*Reservations under Paragraph*	*Notifications under Paragraph*
				Paragraph	*Type*		
3	1-3	None	None	4	'in place of or in the absence of'	5	5, 6
4	1	None	None	2	'in place of or in the absence of'	3	3, 4
5	1, 2, 4, 6	None	2, 4, 6	3, 5, 7	'applies to' and 'in place of'	8, 9	8, 9, 10
6	1, 3	3	None	2	'in place of or in the absence of'	4	4, 5, 6
7	1, 4, 8-13	3-5, 6-14, Statement in paragraph (17)(a)	None	2, 5, 14	'in place of or in the absence of' and 'applies to'	15, 16	15, 16, 17
8	1	None	None	2	'in place of or in the absence of'	3	3, 4
9	1, 4	3-5	None	2*,5	'in place of or in the absence of'	6	6, 7, 8
10	1-3	None	None	4	'in place of or in the absence of'	5	5, 6
11	1	None	None	2	'in place of or in the absence of'	3	3, 4
12	1, 2	None	None	3(a),(b)	'in place of'	4	4, 5, 6
13	1-4	None	2, 3	5(a),(b)	'in place of' and 'applies to'	6	6, 7, 8
14	1	None	None	2	'in place of or in the absence of'	3	3, 4
15	1	None	None	None	–	2	2
16	1-3	None	None	4	'in place of or in the absence of', 'in place of' and 'in the absence of'	5	5, 6
17	1	None	None	2	'in place of or in the absence of'	3	3, 4

* Paragraph 2 is the compatibility clause of paragraph 1(a) of Article 9 as paragraph 1(b) of Article 9 already describes the relationship with shares or rights covered by existing provisions.

Bibliography

Action 1: BEPS 2015 Final Report, OECD/G20 Base Erosion and Profit Shifting Project http://www.oecd.org/tax/beps-2015-final-reports.htm.

Action 2: BEPS 2015 Final Report, OECD/G20 Base Erosion and Profit Shifting Project http://www.oecd.org/tax/beps-2015-final-reports.htm.

Action 3: BEPS 2015 Final Report, OECD/G20 Base Erosion and Profit Shifting Project http://www.oecd.org/tax/beps-2015-final-reports.htm.

Action 4: BEPS 2015 Final Report, OECD/G20 Base Erosion and Profit Shifting Project http://www.oecd.org/tax/beps-2015-final-reports.htm.

Action 5: BEPS 2015 Final Report, OECD/G20 Base Erosion and Profit Shifting Project http://www.oecd.org/tax/beps-2015-final-reports.htm.

Action 6: BEPS 2015 Final Report, OECD/G20 Base Erosion and Profit Shifting Project http://www.oecd.org/tax/beps-2015-final-reports.htm.

Action 7: BEPS 2015 Final Report, OECD/G20 Base Erosion and Profit Shifting Project http://www.oecd.org/tax/beps-2015-final-reports.htm.

Actions 8-10: BEPS 2015 Final Report, OECD/G20 Base Erosion and Profit Shifting Project http://www.oecd.org/tax/beps-2015-final-reports.htm.

Action 11: BEPS 2015 Final Report, OECD/G20 Base Erosion and Profit Shifting Project http://www.oecd.org/tax/beps-2015-final-reports.htm.

Action 12: BEPS 2015 Final Report, OECD/G20 Base Erosion and Profit Shifting Project http://www.oecd.org/tax/beps-2015-final-reports.htm.

Action 13: BEPS 2015 Final Report, OECD/G20 Base Erosion and Profit Shifting Project http://www.oecd.org/tax/beps-2015-final-reports.htm.

Action 14: BEPS 2015 Final Report, OECD/G20 Base Erosion and Profit Shifting Project http://www.oecd.org/tax/beps-2015-final-reports.htm.

Action 15: BEPS 2015 Final Report, OECD/G20 Base Erosion and Profit Shifting Project http://www.oecd.org/tax/beps-2015-final-reports.htm.

Amending Protocol of India-China DTAA notified on 17-07-2019 https://www.incometaxindia.gov.in/Pages/international-taxation/dtaa.aspx accessed on 26 July 2020.

Argentina-Chile CTA https://research.ibfd.org/#/doc?url = /linkresolver/static/tt_ar-cl_02_eng_2015_tt#tt_ar-cl_02_eng_2015_tt__td1_a24.

Armenia-Spain CTA https://research.ibfd.org/#/doc?url = /linkresolver/static/tt_am-es_02_eng_2010_tt accessed on 3 September 2020.

Article by Ameya Mithe Titled 'Critical Analysis of the Principal Purpose Test and the Limitation on Benefits Rule: A World Divided but It Takes Two to Tango' https://research.ibfd.org/#/doc?url = /collections/wtj/html/wtj_2020_01_in_1.html accessed on 3 August 2020.

Article by Jonathan Schwarz Titled 'The Impact of the New Preamble on the Interpretation of Old and New Treaties and on the Policy of Abuse Prevention' https://research.ibfd.org/#/doc?url = /collections/bit/html/bit_2020_04_o2_1.html accessed on 3 August 2020.

Article by Michael Lang Titled 'The Signalling Function of Article 29(9) of the OECD Model: The Principal Purpose Test' https://research.ibfd.org/#/doc?url = /collections/bit/html/bit_2020_04_o2_5.html accessed on 4 August 2020.

Article by Robert J. Danon Titled 'The PPT in Post-BEPS Tax Treaty Law: It Is a GAAR but Just a GAAR!' https://research.ibfd.org/#/doc?url = /collections/bit/html/bit_2020_04_o2_9.html (sections 3.3, 4) accessed on 4 August 2020.

Article by Werner C. Haslehner Titled 'A Multilateral Interpretation of the Multilateral Instrument (and Covered Tax Agreements)' https://research.ibfd.org/#/doc?url = /collections/bit/html/bit_2020_04_o2_2.html accessed on 2 September 2020.

ATO's PSLA 2020/2 https://www.ato.gov.au/law/view/view.htm?docid = %22PSR%2FPS20202%2FNAT%2FATO%2F00001%22 accessed on 20 November 2020.

Australia's Objection under Article 28(2)(b) of the MLI http://www.oecd.org/tax/treaties/beps-mli-objection-australia-to-denmark.pdf.

Australia's Position under the MLI http://www.oecd.org/tax/treaties/beps-mli-position-australia-instrument-deposit.pdf.

Australia-New Zealand Synthesised Text https://research.ibfd.org/#/doc?url = /data/treaty/docs/html/tt_au-nz_01_eng_2009_tt__td2.html.

Australia-Norway CTA https://research.ibfd.org/#/doc?url = /linkresolver/static/tt_au-no_01_eng_2006_tt accessed on 5 September 2020.

Austria's Position under the MLI http://www.oecd.org/tax/treaties/beps-mli-position-austria-instrument-deposit.pdf.

Barbados' Position under the MLI http://www.oecd.org/tax/treaties/beps-mli-position-barbados.pdf and http://www.oecd.org/tax/treaties/beps-mli-position-barbados-instrument-deposit.pdf.

Belize's Position under the MLI https://research.ibfd.org/#/doc?url = /linkresolver/static/tt_bz_02_eng_2019_tt__td1_a2#tt_bz_02_eng_2019_tt__td1_a2 and http://www.oecd.org/tax/treaties/beps-mli-position-belize.pdf.

Bulgaria's Position under the MLI http://www.oecd.org/tax/treaties/beps-mli-position-bulgaria.pdf.

Canada's Objection under Article 28(2)(b) of the MLI http://www.oecd.org/tax/treaties/beps-mli-objection-canada-to-denmark.pdf.

Canada-Slovenia Synthesised Text https://research.ibfd.org/#/doc?url = /data/treaty/docs/html/tt_ca-si_02_eng_2000_tt__td2.html accessed on 10 September 2020.

CBDT's Circular No. 7 of 2017 Providing Clarification on Implementation of GAAR https://www.incometaxindia.gov.in/communications/circular/circular7_2017.pdf (Question No. 2) accessed on 3 September 2020.

China's Position under the MLI http://www.oecd.org/tax/treaties/beps-mli-position-china.pdf.

Convention Between France and Kuwait https://research.ibfd.org/#/compare/side-by-side?url = tt_fr-kw_04_eng_1982_tt__ad4,tt_fr-kw_04_eng_1982_tt__td3 accessed on 5 July 2020.

Convention Between Germany and Denmark https://research.ibfd.org/#/compare/side-by-side?url = tt_dk-de_06_eng_1995_tt__ad2,tt_dk-de_06_eng_1995_tt__td1 accessed on 5 July 2020.

Denmark's Position under the MLI http://www.oecd.org/tax/treaties/beps-mli-position-denmark-instrument-deposit.pdf.

Denmark-US DTAA https://research.ibfd.org/#/doc?url = /data/treaty/docs/html/tt_dk-us_01_eng_1999_tt__td2.html.

Denmark-Poland Synthesised Text https://research.ibfd.org/#/doc?url = /data/treaty/docs/html/tt_dk-pl_02_eng_2001_tt__td3.html.

Egypt's Position under the MLI http://www.oecd.org/tax/treaties/beps-mli-position-egypt.pdf.

Explanatory Statement to the MLI http://www.oecd.org/tax/treaties/explanatory-statement-multilateral-convention-to-implement-tax-treaty-related-measures-to-prevent-BEPS.pdf.

France – Information on Residency for Tax Purposes, section II(2) https://www.oecd.org/tax/automatic-exchange/crs-implementation-and-assistance/tax-residency/France-Tax-Residency.pdf accessed on 25 December 2020.

Germany's MLI Notification at the Time of Ratification of the MLI http://www.oecd.org/tax/treaties/beps-mli-position-germany-instrument-deposit.pdf and Germany's MLI Notification at the Time of Signing of the MLI http://www.oecd.org/tax/treaties/beps-mli-position-germany.pdf.

Global Tax Guide to Doing Business in Argentina https://www.dentons.com/en/issues-and-opportunities/global-tax-guide-to-doing-business-in/argentina accessed on 25 December 2020.

Greece's Position under the MLI http://www.oecd.org/tax/treaties/beps-mli-position-greece.pdf.

India's Position under the MLI http://www.oecd.org/tax/treaties/beps-mli-position-india-instrument-deposit.pdf.

India-Australia Synthesised Text https://research.ibfd.org/#/doc?url = /data/treaty/docs/html/tt_au-in_01_eng_1991_tt__td3.html accessed on 10 September 2020.

India-Canada Synthesised Text https://research.ibfd.org/#/doc?url = /data/treaty/docs/html/tt_ca-in_02_eng_1996_tt__td2.html#tt_ca-in_02_eng_1996_tt__td2_a9.

India-China DTAA https://www.incometaxindia.gov.in/Pages/international-taxation/dtaa.aspx accessed on 27 July 2020.

India-UK Synthesised Text https://www.incometaxindia.gov.in/Pages/international-taxation/dtaa.aspx accessed on 1 September 2020.

Ireland's Position under the MLI http://www.oecd.org/tax/treaties/beps-mli-position-ireland-instrument-deposit.pdf.

Jamaica's Position under the MLI https://research.ibfd.org/#/doc?url=/linkresolver/static/tt_jm_02_eng_2018_tt__td1_a2#tt_jm_02_eng_2018_tt__td1_a2 and http://www.oecd.org/tax/treaties/beps-mli-position-jamaica.pdf.

Japan's Position under the MLI http://www.oecd.org/tax/treaties/beps-mli-position-japan-instrument-deposit.pdf.

Japan-New Zealand Synthesised Text https://research.ibfd.org/#/doc?url=/data/treaty/docs/html/tt_jp-nz_01_eng_2012_tt__td2.html accessed on 28 July 2020.

Jean-Philippe Van West's 'The Anti-abuse Rule for Permanent Establishments Situated in Third States – A Legal Analysis of Article 29(8) OECD Model' – WU Institute for Austrian and International Tax Law – Tax Law and Policy Series 16, IBFD.

Kenya-Canada CTA https://research.ibfd.org/#/doc?url=/linkresolver/static/tt_ca-ke_02_eng_1983_tt accessed on 3 September 2020.

Members of the OECD/G20 Inclusive Framework on BEPS https://www.oecd.org/tax/beps/inclusive-framework-on-beps-composition.pdf.

MLI Text http://www.oecd.org/tax/treaties/multilateral-convention-to-implement-tax-treaty-related-measures-to-prevent-BEPS.pdf.

Moritz Scherleitner's 'Addressing Tax Arbitrage with Hybrid Financial Instruments – A Multidisciplinary Study and Proposal for Developed and Developing Countries' IBFD Doctoral Series 54.

Nathalie Bravo's 'A Multilateral Instrument for Updating the Tax Treaty Network' IBFD Doctoral Series 52.

Norway's Position under the MLI http://www.oecd.org/tax/treaties/beps-mli-position-norway-instrument-deposit.pdf.

Note by the OECD Directorate for Legal Affairs http://www.oecd.org/tax/treaties/legal-note-on-the-functioning-of-the-MLI-under-public-international-law.pdf.

Note by the OECD Secretariat on Entry into Effect under Article 35(1)(a) http://www.oecd.org/tax/treaties/beps-mli-secretariat-note-entry-into-effect-under-article-35-1-a.pdf.

OECD – About the Inclusive Framework on BEPS https://www.oecd.org/tax/beps/beps-about.htm/#monitoring accessed on 7 September 2020.

OECD – Bahrain Signs Landmark Agreement to Strengthen Its Tax Treaties https://www.oecd.org/ctp/treaties/bahrain-signs-landmark-agreement-to-strengthen-its-tax-treaties.htm accessed on 28 November 2020.

OECD – Barbados Deposits Its Instrument of Ratification for the Multilateral BEPS Convention https://www.oecd.org/tax/treaties/barbados-deposits-its-instrument-of-ratification-for-the-multilateral-beps-convention.htm accessed on 5 January 2021.

OECD – BEPS Action 5, Harmful Tax Practices – Minimum Standard http://www.oecd.org/tax/beps/beps-actions/action5/ accessed on 1 July 2020.

OECD – BEPS Action 6, Prevention of Tax Treaty Abuse – Minimum Standard http://www.oecd.org/tax/beps/beps-actions/action6/ accessed on 1 July 2020.

OECD – BEPS Actions http://www.oecd.org/tax/beps/beps-actions/ accessed on 1 July 2020.

OECD, Double Taxation Conventions and the Use of Conduit Companies, in OECD, Model Tax Convention on Income and on Capital: Full Version, R (6), Vol. I and II, paragraph 7 (OECD 2010) https://read.oecd-ilibrary.org/taxation/model-tax-convention-on-income-and-on-capital-2014-full-version/r-6-double-taxation-conventions-and-the-use-of-conduit-companies_9789264239081-99-en#page4.

OECD – Ground-Breaking Multilateral BEPS Convention Signed at OECD Will Close Loopholes in Thousands of Tax Treaties Worldwide http://www.oecd.org/tax/ground-breaking-multilateral-beps-convention-will-close-tax-treaty-loopholes.htm accessed on 4 July 2020.

OECD – Guidance for the Development of Synthesised Texts http://www.oecd.org/tax/treaties/beps-mli-guidance-for-the-development-of-synthesised-texts.pdf.

OECD – Signatories and Parties to the MLI; Position Taken by Signatories and Parties under the MLI http://www.oecd.org/tax/treaties/beps-mli-signatories-and-parties.pdf.

OECD – Tax Sparing – A Reconsideration https://read.oecd-ilibrary.org/taxation/tax-sparing_9789264162433-en#page1 accessed on 29 July 2020.

OECD – Toolkit for Application of the Multilateral Instrument for BEPS Tax Treaty Related Measures https://www.oecd.org/tax/treaties/application-toolkit-multilateral-instrument-for-beps-tax-treaty-measures.htm.

OECD – What Is BEPS? http://www.oecd.org/tax/beps/about/ accessed on 1 July 2020.

OECD (1999), The Application of the OECD Model Tax Convention to Partnerships, Issues in International Taxation, No. 6, OECD Publishing, Paris.

OECD MTC 2017 – Commentary.

OECD Work on Taxation (2018-19) (p. 15) http://www.oecd.org/tax/centre-for-tax-policy-and-administration-brochure.pdf accessed on 1 July 2020.

OECD/G20 Inclusive Framework on BEPS Progress Report July 2019 – July 2020 (p. 21) https://www.oecd.org/tax/beps/oecd-g20-inclusive-framework-on-beps-progress-report-july-2019-july-2020.pdf accessed on 2 September 2020.

OECD's FAQs on MLI https://community.oecd.org/docs/DOC-113848.

Poland's Position under the MLI http://www.oecd.org/tax/treaties/beps-mli-position-poland-instrument-deposit.pdf.

Russia's Position under the MLI http://www.oecd.org/tax/treaties/beps-mli-position-russian-federation-instrument-deposit.pdf.

Russia-Portugal CTA https://research.ibfd.org/#/doc?url=/linkresolver/static/tt_pt-ru_01_eng_2000_tt accessed on 3 September 2020.

Serbia's Position under the MLI http://www.oecd.org/tax/treaties/beps-mli-position-serbia-instrument-deposit.pdf.

Singapore's Position under the MLI http://www.oecd.org/tax/treaties/beps-mli-position-singapore-instrument-deposit.pdf.

Slovak Republic's Position under the MLI http://www.oecd.org/tax/treaties/beps-mli-position-slovak-republic-instrument-deposit.pdf.

Slovak Republic-Lithuania Synthesised Text https://research.ibfd.org/#/doc?url=/data/treaty/docs/html/tt_lt-sk_02_eng_2001_tt__td2.html accessed on 10 September 2020.

Slovak Republic-Poland Synthesised Text https://research.ibfd.org/#/doc?url=/linkresolver/static/tt_pl-sk_02_eng_1994_tt accessed on 10 September 2020.

Slovenia's Position under the MLI http://www.oecd.org/tax/treaties/beps-mli-position-slovenia-instrument-deposit.pdf.

Slovenia-Austria Synthesised Text https://research.ibfd.org/#/doc?url=/data/treaty/docs/html/tt_at-si_02_eng_1997_tt__td4.html accessed on 10 September 2020.

South Centre Tax Initiative Comments on Session Paper Relating to Tax Consequences of the Digitalized Economy – Issues of Relevance for Developing Countries https://www.un.org/development/desa/financing/sites/www.un.org.development.desa.financing/files/2020-06/CRP%2025%20_SCTI.pdf (p. 3) accessed on 10 September 2020.

Sustainable Development Goals https://www.un.org/sustainabledevelopment/sustainable-development-goals/ accessed on 1 July 2020.

Switzerland's MLI Notifications https://research.ibfd.org/#/doc?url=/linkresolver/static/tt_ch_02_fre_2017_tt__td1_a2#tt_ch_02_fre_2017_tt__td1_a2.

Synthesised Texts of Denmark's CTAs https://research.ibfd.org/#/search?N=3+10+4294967052&Ne=7487&Nu=global_rollup_key&Np=2&Ntk=Text&Ntt=synthesised%20text&Nty=1&Ntx=mode+matchallpartial accessed on 31 December 2020.

Synthesised Texts of India's CTAs https://incometaxindia.gov.in/Pages/international-taxation/dtaa.aspx accessed on 31 December 2020.

Synthesised Texts of Netherlands' CTAs https://research.ibfd.org/#/search?N=3+10+4294967221&Ne=7487&Nu=global_rollup_key&Np=2&Ntk=Text&Ntt=synthesised%20text&Nty=1&Ntx=mode+matchallpartial accessed on 31 December 2020.

The Netherlands – Information on Residency for Tax Purposes https://www.oecd.org/tax/automatic-exchange/crs-implementation-and-assistance/tax-residency/Netherlands-Tax-Residency.pdf accessed on 28 July 2020.

The Netherlands' Position under the MLI http://www.oecd.org/tax/treaties/beps-mli-position-netherlands-instrument-deposit.pdf.

The Netherlands-Japan Synthesised Text https://research.ibfd.org/#/doc?url=/data/treaty/docs/html/tt_jp-nl_01_eng_2010_tt__td3.html.

The Netherlands-Serbia Synthesised Text https://research.ibfd.org/#/doc?url=/data/treaty/docs/html/tt_nl-rs_02_eng_1982_tt__td2.html#tt_nl-rs_02_eng_1982_tt__td2_a23.

The Netherlands-Slovenia Synthesised Text https://research.ibfd.org/#/doc?url=/data/treaty/docs/html/tt_nl-si_01_eng_2004_tt__td2.html#tt_nl-si_01_eng_2004_tt__td2_a22.

'The Swiss Tax System' 2019 Edition (section 3.5 on p. 13) https://www.estv.admin.ch/estv/en/home/suche.html#number%20of%20DTA accessed on 24 December 2020.

UN Model Double Taxation Convention 2017 – Commentary.

UN Economic and Social Council, Report of Secretary General (paragraph 38, under the head 'Finance') https://undocs.org/E/2019/68 accessed on 1 July 2020.

UN Ad Hoc Group of Experts, Contributions to International Co-operation in Tax Matters: Treaty Shopping, Thin Capitalization, Co-operation Between Tax Authorities, Resolving International Tax Disputes, paragraph 8 (1988).

Vienna Convention on the Law of Treaties https://treaties.un.org/doc/publication/unts/volume%201155/volume-1155-i-18232-english.pdf.

Index

F

G

H

I

J

L

M

N

O

P

U

V

W